"For those of us who have sometimes felt let down after encounters with lackluster approaches to the question of evil and suffering, this remarkable collection of essays provides clarity, hope, and inspiration. The authors take fresh and invigorating dives into oceans of philosophical, theological, and literary material; we are the fortunate beneficiaries of their rich findings and reflections. Their energetic and synergistic efforts combine to provide us with multiple approaches and paths of wisdom that highlight the creative and transformative possibilities for human beings facing the inevitable trials of this world."

Kristin Zahra Sands, *Frieda Wildy Riggs Chair in Religious Studies, Sarah Lawrence College*

"The product of an innovative and collaborative conference on evil, suffering, and the COVID-19 pandemic, *From the Divine to the Human* makes a distinctive contribution to the globalization of philosophy of religion, advancing a unique array of Islamic perspectives on the classic problem of evil, many of which relocate the 'problem' to the human sphere, where 'evil' serves as a catalyst of spiritual and ethical development."

Timothy D. Knepper, *Professor of Philosophy, Director of The Comparison Project, Drake University*

"This incredibly rich volume brings together a series of eloquent and inspiring studies that mine the spiritual and intellectual contributions of a wide range of Muslim luminary thinkers, past and present, for wisdom and understanding in the face of suffering, including the extraordinary global suffering brought about by the COVID-19 pandemic. Few books demonstrate as broadly and powerfully as this one the continuing relevance, vibrancy, and practical applications of Muslim philosophical, theological, ethical, and mystical thought to our contemporary human struggle."

Maria Massi Dakake, *Associate Professor of Religious Studies, George Mason University*

"Muhammad Faruque and Mohammed Rustom are to be congratulated for this scholarly tour de force that brings some of the best minds in contemporary Islamic thought to weigh in on one of the most vexing problems in the history of human thought. The so-called problem of evil is here cast in an entirely new light that will be as instructive for Islamic Studies as it will for a variety of other disciplines across the humanities and the social sciences."

Yousef Casewit, *Associate Professor of Quranic Studies, University of Chicago Divinity School*

"At a time when indigenous Muslim perspectives on issues related to human suffering are often overlooked, this volume amplifies the voices of premodern and contemporary Islamic philosophers and theologians. It speaks to the most pressing questions that pull at the strings of our conscience in a way that is academically rigorous and publicly accessible, shifting the current focus in the discipline of the philosophy of religion from the divine to the human experience. As such, *From the Divine to the Human* offers compelling insights on global challenges ranging from climate change and mental health to the pandemic and post-traumatic healing."

Hadia Mubarak, *Assistant Professor of Religion, Queens University of Charlotte*

"Resplendent with insights, this volume presents a range of vibrant voices that collectively construct a philosophy of religion based on Islamic sources. The original thinking assembled here demonstrates the plurality of perspectives and practices internal to the Islamic tradition. The contributors also highlight several critical concepts from Sufi virtue ethics for thinking creatively and compassionately about the tribulations facing our planet today, from COVID-19 to climate change."

Ali Altaf Mian, *Assistant Professor of Religion and Izzat Hasan Sheikh Fellow in Islamic Studies, University of Florida*

FROM THE DIVINE TO THE HUMAN

Featuring the work of leading contemporary Muslim philosophers and theologians, this book grapples with various forms of evil and suffering in the world today, from COVID-19 and issues in climate change to problems in palliative care and human vulnerability.

Rather than walking down well-trodden paths in philosophy of religion which often address questions of evil and suffering by focusing on divine attributes and the God-world relationship, this volume offers another path of inquiry by focusing on human vulnerability, potential, and resilience. Addressing both the theoretical and practical dimensions of the question of evil, topics range from the transformative power of love, virtue ethics in Sufism, and the necessity of suffering, to the spiritual significance of the body and Islamic perspectives on embodiment. In doing so, the contributors propose new perspectives based on various pre-modern and contemporary materials that can enrich the emerging field of the global philosophy of religion, thereby radically transforming contemporary debates on the nature of evil and suffering.

The book will appeal to researchers in a variety of disciplines, including Islamic philosophy, religious studies, Sufism, and theology.

Muhammad U. Faruque is Inayat Malik Assistant Professor of Islamic and Cross-Cultural Philosophy at the University of Cincinnati.

Mohammed Rustom is Professor of Islamic Thought and Director of the Carleton Centre for the Study of Islam at Carleton University.

Routledge Studies in Islamic Philosophy
Series Editor
Oliver Leaman
University of Kentucky

The Routledge Studies in Islamic Philosophy Series is devoted to the publication of scholarly books in all areas of Islamic philosophy. We regard the discipline as part of the general philosophical environment and seek to include books on a wide variety of different approaches to Islamic philosophy.

Philosophical Sufism
An Introduction to the School of Ibn al-ʿArabī
Mukhtar H. Ali

The Crisis of Muslim Religious Discourse
The Necessary Shift from Plato to Kant
Lahouari Addi

Miskawayh's *Tahḏīb al-aḫlāq*
Happiness, Justice and Friendship
Ufuk Topkara

The Covenants of the Prophet Muḥammad
From Shared Historical Memory to Peaceful Co-existence
Ibrahim Mohamed Zain and Ahmed El-Wakil

Vicegerency in Islamic Thought and Scripture
Towards a Qur'anic Theory of Human Existential Function
Chauki Lazhar

From the Divine to the Human
Contemporary Islamic Thinkers on Evil, Suffering, and the Global Pandemic
Edited by Muhammad U. Faruque and Mohammed Rustom

For more information about this series, please visit: www.routledge.com/middleeaststudies/series/RSINIP

From the Divine to the Human

Contemporary Islamic Thinkers on Evil, Suffering, and the Global Pandemic

Edited by Muhammad U. Faruque and Mohammed Rustom

Routledge
Taylor & Francis Group
LONDON AND NEW YORK

First published 2023
by Routledge
4 Park Square, Milton Park, Abingdon, Oxon OX14 4RN

and by Routledge
605 Third Avenue, New York, NY 10158

Routledge is an imprint of the Taylor & Francis Group, an informa business

British Library Cataloguing-in-Publication Data
A catalogue record for this book is available from the British Library

Library of Congress Cataloging-in-Publication Data
Names: Faruque, Muhammad U., editor. | Rustom, Mohammed, editor.
Title: From the divine to the human : contemporary Islamic thinkers on evil, suffering, and the global pandemic / edited by Muhammad U. Faruque and Mohammed Rustom.
Description: First. | New York : Routledge, 2023. | Series: Routledge studies in Islamic philosophy | Includes bibliographical references and index.
Identifiers: LCCN 2022059852 (print) | LCCN 2022059853 (ebook) | ISBN 9781032443409 (hardback) | ISBN 9781032443423 (paperback) | ISBN 9781003371670 (ebook)
Subjects: LCSH: Good and evil—Religious aspects—Islam. | Suffering—Religious aspects—Islam. | Islamic ethics. | Theodicy.
Classification: LCC BP188 .F76 2023 (print) | LCC BP188 (ebook) | DDC 297.5—dc23/eng/20230206
LC record available at https://lccn.loc.gov/2022059852
LC ebook record available at https://lccn.loc.gov/2022059853

ISBN: 978-1-032-44340-9 (hbk)
ISBN: 978-1-032-44342-3 (pbk)
ISBN: 978-1-003-37167-0 (ebk)

DOI: 10.4324/9781003371670

Typeset in Times New Roman
by Apex CoVantage, LLC

For the grief-stricken and the broken-hearted

Contents

Acknowledgements *xi*
About the Contributors *xii*

An Anthropocentric Approach to Evil 1
MUHAMMAD U. FARUQUE AND MOHAMMED RUSTOM

1 **Remarks on Evil, Suffering, and the Global Pandemic** 7
SEYYED HOSSEIN NASR

2 **The Existential Threat of Climate Change: A Practical Application of Avicenna's Theory of Evil** 14
ROSABEL ANSARI

3 **On Self-Knowledge, Divine Trial, and Discipleship** 29
MUKHTAR H. ALI

4 **Necessitated Evil: An Islamic Neoplatonic Theodicy From the Ismaili Tradition** 44
KHALIL ANDANI

5 **Seyyed Hossein Nasr's Metaphysical Theodicy** 67
JUSTIN CANCELLIERE

6 **Hume on Trial: Can Evil and Suffering Be Justified?** 89
MUHAMMAD U. FARUQUE

7 **Cultivating Prayerful Presence at the Bedside: From Mastery Towards Mystery** 111
HINA KHALID

8 **The Gifts of Suffering and the Virtues of the Heart** 143
ATIF KHALIL

9 **Cain, Systemic Evil, and Our Inhumanity** 158
MARTIN NGUYEN

10 **Practical Muslim Theodicy: A Ghazalian Perspective on Emotional Pain** 164
JOEL RICHMOND

11 **The Student and the Sage** 178
MOHAMMED RUSTOM

12 **Trials as Transformation in Islamic Chaplaincy** 187
AILYA VAJID

13 **Transformative Love Amid Suffering in Hilmi Ziya Ülken** 201
TARANEH WILKINSON

14 **Suffering as Metaphysical Narrative: Exploring an Islamic Theodicy of Authorship** 214
CYRUS ALI ZARGAR

Index 227

Acknowledgements

We would like to thank the Templeton Foundation Global Philosophy of Religion Project/University of Birmingham, the University of Cincinnati, and the Carleton Centre for the Study of Islam for sponsoring the conference out of which this volume grew. We are also grateful to Yujin Nagasawa, Thérèse Migraine-George, Nosheen Mian, Noah Taj, Luis Barreto, Aly Ibrahim, Nicole Dutil, Syed A. H. Zaidi, and Cyrus Ali Zargar for their help along the way.

About the Contributors

Mukhtar H. Ali is Assistant Professor of Islamic Studies at the University of Illinois Urbana-Champaign.

Khalil Andani is Assistant Professor of Religion at Augustana College.

Rosabel Ansari is Assistant Professor of Philosophy at Stony Brook University.

Justin Cancelliere is an independent scholar who specializes in Islamic philosophy, Sufism, and the Platonic-Aristotelian tradition.

Muhammad U. Faruque is Inayat Malik Assistant Professor of Islamic and Cross-Cultural Philosophy at the University of Cincinnati.

Hina Khalid is a doctoral candidate in comparative theology at the University of Cambridge.

Atif Khalil is Associate Professor of Religious Studies at the University of Lethbridge.

Seyyed Hossein Nasr is University Professor of Islamic Studies at The George Washington University.

Martin Nguyen is Professor of Islamic Studies and Chair of the Religious Studies Department at Fairfield University.

Joel Richmond is Lecturer in Islamic Studies at Toronto Metropolitan University.

Mohammed Rustom is Professor of Islamic Thought and Director of the Carleton Centre for the Study of Islam at Carleton University.

Ailya Vajid is a student of Unani Tibb at the College of Medicine and Healing Arts.

Taraneh Wilkinson is currently pursuing her second doctorate in the Philosophy of Science at the University of Cincinnati.

Cyrus Ali Zargar is Al-Ghazali Distinguished Professor of Islamic Studies at the University of Central Florida.

An Anthropocentric Approach to Evil

Muhammad U. Faruque and Mohammed Rustom

With the pandemic of COVID-19 unleashing the deadly effects of its virus that has claimed millions of casualties all over the globe, the question of evil and suffering cannot be more relevant today. Given the complexities of the pandemic, one should look at it from multiple standpoints, beginning with the science of the virus in question. So, questions such as "Where did the virus come from?," "How is it transmitted?," or "What can be done to stop its spread?" should be investigated and examined using our best scientific models and evidence, especially because conflicting messages from the media and officials across different countries and organizations and unfounded conspiracy theories on the origins of the virus have only served to increase the level of anxiety among people.[1] It is also important to make ourselves aware of the failed economic and government policies that could have curtailed the impact of the pandemic. For instance, Debora MacKenzie outlines the lessons we failed to learn from such previous outbreaks as SARS, H1N1, Zika, and Ebola. She details the arrival and spread of COVID-19, offering a critique of the steps that governments could have taken to prevent or at least prepare for it.[2]

The pandemic has also elicited a variety of "how to" responses from physicians, sociologists, and psychologists. The neurosurgeon and CNN medical reporter Sanjay Gupta argues that we need to prepare for a new era where pandemics will be more frequent, and possibly even more deadly. Offering practical tools to ready ourselves for the future, he addresses critical questions such as, "Can we eradicate the virus for good, and if not, how do we live with it?", and "Does it make sense to spend more on health insurance to deal with any long-term effects?"[3] Others like Nicholas Christakis and Steven Taylor discuss what it means to live in a time

1 See Raul Rabadan, *Understanding Coronavirus* (Cambridge: Cambridge University Press, 2020).

2 Debora Mackenzie, *COVID-19: The Pandemic That Never Should Have Happened and How to Stop the Next One* (New York: Hachette, 2020), 1–36. One thing the Western scientific community failed to do at the outbreak of the pandemic was to engage more seriously with the findings of its non-Western counterpart. See the inquiry in Alexus McLeod, "Editor's Note: On Philosophy, a Pandemic, and Our International Future," *Philosophical Forum* 53, no. 1 (2022): 3–9.

3 Sanjay Gupta and Kristin Loberg, *World War C: Lessons from the COVID-19 Pandemic and How to Prepare for the Next One* (New York: Simon & Schuster, 2021).

DOI: 10.4324/9781003371670-1

of pandemic. These authors shed light on the social and psychological factors that are important for understanding and managing issues associated with pandemics, including the spreading of excessive fear, stigmatization, and xenophobia which occur when people are threatened with infection.[4]

There is little doubt that much can be learned about the nature of COVID-19 from all these approaches and domains. However, it would be premature to think that they somehow exhaust all the possible inquiries regarding the pandemic, especially inquiries which pertain to the philosophical, ethical, and spiritual spheres. This is where *From the Divine to the Human* intervenes in the field of the global philosophy of religion by utilizing the rich and unique resources of the Islamic intellectual tradition as well as contemporary Muslim philosophers' creative engagements with these materials. Even though evil and the cause of human suffering is perhaps one of the most debated questions in philosophy of religion, the coronavirus pandemic forces us to look at this issue with renewed fervor, not least because it challenges us to rethink the role of a powerful and merciful God in the face of human suffering. Considering the wide-scale afflictions of the pandemic thus far, we face the challenge of explaining whether it is possible to think of this world as the work of an omnipotent Creator who is motivated by and/or defined as limitless love and compassion.

Rather than taking up the question of evil and suffering by walking down well-trodden paths in philosophy of religion which often address the problematic by focusing on divine attributes and the God-world relationship, this volume offers another path of inquiry by focusing on human vulnerability, potential, and resilience. Numerous Islamic philosophical texts, and therefore the work of contemporary Muslim thinkers who draw inspiration from and develop them in their own intellectual projects, view the question of evil and suffering with reference to what they mean for the becoming of human personhood, the actualization of latent spiritual possibilities, and the realization of human felicity and fulfilment.

By shifting focus from the divine to the human vis-à-vis the question of suffering, new insights and questions which are amenable to philosophical attention come to the fore: How do human presence and remoteness contribute to a wider, truly global understanding of the problem of evil? Can human suffering be a meaningful event, both on individual and collective scales? Can virtues be cultivated and character traits refined through a more robust understanding of human becoming in the face of suffering? Can traditions such as Islamic philosophy and Sufism—both of which place the human being and therefore the lived human experience at the center of their inquiries—help sharpen our analysis of evil and

4 See Steven Taylor, *The Psychology of Pandemics: Preparing for the Next Global Outbreak of Infectious Disease* (Cambridge: Cambridge Scholars Publishing, 2020), chapter 3; Nicholas A. Christakis, *Apollo's Arrow: The Profound and Enduring Impact of Coronavirus on the Way We Live* (Boston: Little, Brown Spark, 2020), chapter 4.

suffering in ways heretofore unimagined by ordinary theological expositions which veer more towards the abstract?

More often than not, existing philosophical and theological responses confine themselves to purely theoretical discussions concerning evil and the existence/non-existence of God, thereby failing to address how people can respond to suffering and what difference it can make for their personhood. For instance, the so-called logical problem of evil states that God is good, just, and all-powerful. However, there is also "evil" in the world, which leads to the following dilemmas with respect to God's essential attributes:

1. God wishes to eradicate evil because He is good. So why is there evil?
2. God wishes to remove evil but cannot do so. Does He therefore lack power?
3. God can exterminate evil because He is all-powerful but will not do so. How then is He good?

The logical problem of evil therefore discounts the existence of God by arguing how evil is incompatible with a good, all-powerful God. Similarly, the evidential problem of evil explains to what extent certain instances, kinds, quantities, or distributions of evil constitute evidence against the existence of God. More particularly, atheist philosophers point to the cases of what Marilyn Adams calls "horrendous evils," i.e., "evils the participation in which (that is, the doing or suffering of which) constitutes prima facie reason to doubt whether the participant's life could (given their inclusion in it) be a great good to him/her on the whole."[5] They attempt to disprove God's existence by recounting stories of horrendous suffering in the world, such as the Holocaust and the Boxing Day Tsunami of 2004.

In light of these critiques, many contemporary theistic responses attempt to redefine evil and suffering through some kind of freewill defense that points to God's provision of free will and humanity's misuse of it.[6] The basic idea is that a world created with free agents who are free to perform good and evil, and who tend towards performing more good than evil, is better than a world containing no free creatures at all.

This perspective has a parallel in the Ashʿarī-Muʿtazilī debate on the question of evil in relation to divine justice. Muʿtazilī theodicy begins with the premise that it is impossible for God to perform a bad act. According to the Muʿtazilīs, human actions are the result of autonomous will and power. If human actions are determined by God, it would be unjust of Him to either reward or punish His creatures based on their actions.[7] This is so because if God is the sole agent of every good and

5 Marilyn Adams, *Horrendous Evils and the Goodness of God* (Melbourne: Melbourne University Press, 1999), 26.

6 See, in particular, Alvin Plantinga, *God, Freedom, and Evil* (Grand Rapids: Eerdmans, 1977).

7 The Ashʿarīs believe humans "acquire" their acts, while God creates them—a theory known as *kasb* or "acquisition." For more on this doctrine, see Jan Thiele, "Conceptions of Self-Determination in Fourth/Tenth-Century Muslim Theology: Al-Bāqillānī's Theory of Human Acts in Its Historical Context," *Arabic Science and Philosophy* 26 (2016): 245–269. We are grateful to Ayman Shihadeh for this reference.

bad action, He would end up punishing the bad person for a crime that He Himself has implanted in that person in the first place. Thus, God's justice requires humans to have free choice and control over their actions. The Muʿtazilīs also believe that, despite any suffering that may exist in it, the world is ultimately beneficial for people because it gives them an opportunity to attain rewards and blessings that far exceed the suffering. Furthermore, the Muʿtazilīs affirm that the moral value of an act is objective and within the reach of reason. In other words, ethical terms such as "good" or "bad" refer to real and objective properties of acts. The Ashʿarīs, who reject ethical realism, affirm God's unlimited omnipotence and will. In their view, God's actions are not restricted by ethical considerations. The Ashʿarīs embrace the doctrine of divine voluntarism that places God above the constraints of human reason. Unlike the Muʿtazilīs, they reject belief in free will and argue that all things are determined by divine decree.[8]

Other prominent responses to the problem of evil include "open theism," "skeptical theism," and "Neoplatonic-Avicennan theodicy."[9] Open theism describes a position in which God's omniscience is interpreted in such a way that it does not allow God to either have foreknowledge (knowledge of what His creatures will do) or middle knowledge (knowledge of what free agents would freely choose to do in any possible situation). Hence, the occurrence of evil in the world is justified at the expense of diminishing confidence in such traditional attributes of God as omniscience or omnipotence.[10] Similarly, skeptical theism capitalizes on the idea of the inscrutability of God's ways and the epistemic distance that separates the divine from the human. It emphasizes the limitations of human cognition and its failure to judge as improbable the statement that God can serve a meaningful purpose through the existence of evil.[11] Regardless, both open and skeptical theism face serious criticism as they compromise traditional conceptions of God and His attributes. As for Neoplatonic-Avicennan theodicy, it affirms a cosmic order which represents overall goodness rather than evil. For Avicenna, who denies that there is absolute evil, evil is found only in the sublunar sphere and always exists in a

8 See Muhammad U. Faruque, "Does God Create Evil? A Study of Fakhr al-Dīn Rāzī's Exegesis of *Sūrat al-falaq*," *Islam and Christian-Muslim Relations* 28, no. 3 (2017): 271–291.

9 One can also mention the theological inquiries of Sherman Jackson and Safaruk Chowdhury. The former creatively seeks to understanding suffering, particularly black suffering and its relation to divine providence, through the lens of Sunni (i.e., Ashʿarī, Muʿtazilī, and Māturīdī) theology. The latter uses the tools of analytic theology to address issues pertaining to human disability, the existence of Hell, natural selection, and the suffering of animals. See, respectively, Sherman Jackson, *Islam and the Problem of Black Suffering* (New York: Oxford University Press, 2009); Safaruk Chowdhury, *Islamic Theology and the Problem of Evil* (Cairo: AUC Press, 2021).

10 See the inquiry in Clark Pinnock et al., *The Openness of God: A Biblical Challenge to the Traditional Understanding of God* (Downers Grove: InterVarsity Press, 1994).

11 William Alston, "The Inductive Argument from Evil and the Human Cognitive Condition," *Philosophical Perspectives* 5 (1991): 29–67.

relative way to sustain and perfect the natural order.[12] From a slightly different perspective, the great Islamic philosopher Mullā Ṣadrā makes sense of evil through his gradational ontology, distinguishing between the cosmos and the contingent effects of God in their totality from the differentiated details of the hierarchy of the cosmos.[13]

While engaging some of these views, the thinkers in this volume attempt to address both the theoretical and practical dimensions of the question of evil. They do not overlook the metaphysical origin of evil and suffering but tend to focus on anthropocentric conceptions of them without, however, denying God as the transcendent principle of human existence. That is to say, the focus in this volume is largely (although not exclusively) on the human subject and its ethical formation in the face of widescale evil and suffering.

Some of our authors explore virtue ethics in Sufism. By looking at how such virtues as patience, gratitude, and reliance upon God are utilized to overcome emotional pain and the internal reactions to outward suffering, these philosophers show that the problem of theodicy can be extended well beyond theoretical understandings of evil in relation to God's providence and the world. Several essays draw attention to the necessity of suffering in our experience of the world and the spiritually transformative power of pain. Sometimes it is through life's greatest hardships and suffering that we experience the deepest transformations. Seen in this way, suffering can become a means towards cultivating higher modes of selfhood and can be experienced not only as hardship, but also as a form of sacred instruction and a divine gift and blessing.

Apart from the importance of cultivating virtues in the face of trials and suffering, some of our philosophers draw on the spiritual significance of the body to set forth accounts of what it means to be present, as an embodied mode of love and attentive care, with those who are experiencing trauma or are dying. Such a presence, which is now enacted through our bodies, is not about "controlling" or "curing" suffering but about meditatively bearing witness to it. Islamic perspectives on embodiment as a locus of sacral significance therefore offer us resources to conceive of human fragility and vulnerability not as encumbrances to be stoically surpassed or abstractly theorized about, but as experiential realities that lie at the core of our human condition. Still other contributions in this volume emphasize love and its transformative power both as a response to the human condition of suffering and as an intentional route to address the suffering and isolation caused by human injustice.

From the Divine to the Human thus intends to bring new options to the table by drawing our focus away from traditional philosophy of religion—which tends to

12 Mohammed Rustom, "Devil's Advocate: ʿAyn al-Quḍāt's Defence of Iblis in Context," *Studia Islamica* 115, no. 1 (2020): 65–100; Ayman Shihadeh, "Avicenna's Theodicy and al-Rāzī's Anti-Theodicy," *Intellectual History of the Islamicate World* 7, no. 1 (2019): 61–84.

13 Ibrahim Kalin, "Mullā Ṣadrā and the Best of All Possible Worlds," *Oxford Journal of Islamic Studies* 18, no. 2 (2007): 183–201; Sajjad Rizvi, "Considering Divine Providence in Mullā Ṣadrā Šīrāzī (d. 1045/1636): The Problem of Evil, Theodicy, and the Divine Eros," *Oriens* 49, no. 3–4 (2021): 318–369.

zero in on God and divine attributes—and redirecting it to human beings and their ethical and spiritual growth. In doing so, the contributors propose new perspectives based on various pre-modern and contemporary materials that can enrich the emerging field of the global philosophy of religion, thereby radically transforming contemporary debates on the nature of evil and suffering.

References

Adams, Marilyn. *Horrendous Evils and the Goodness of God*. Melbourne: Melbourne University Press, 1999.

Alston, William. "The Inductive Argument from Evil and the Human Cognitive Condition." *Philosophical Perspectives* 5 (1991): 29–67.

Chowdhury, Safaruk. *Islamic Theology and the Problem of Evil*. Cairo: AUC Press, 2021.

Christakis, Nicholas A. *Apollo's Arrow: The Profound and Enduring Impact of Coronavirus on the Way We Live*. Boston: Little, Brown Spark, 2020.

Faruque, Muhammad. "Does God Create Evil? A Study of Fakhr al-Dīn Rāzī's Exegesis of *Sūrat al-falaq*." *Islam and Christian-Muslim Relations* 28, no. 3 (2017): 271–291.

Gupta, Sanjay, and Kristin Loberg. *World War C: Lessons from the Covid-19 Pandemic and How to Prepare for the Next One*. New York: Simon & Schuster, 2021.

Jackson, Sherman. *Islam and the Problem of Black Suffering*. New York: Oxford University Press, 2009.

Kalin, Ibrahim. "Mullā Ṣadrā and the Best of All Possible Worlds." *Oxford Journal of Islamic Studies* 18, no. 2 (2007): 183–201.

Mackenzie, Debora. *COVID-19: The Pandemic That Never Should Have Happened and How to Stop the Next One*. New York: Hachette, 2020.

McLeod, Alexus. "Editor's Note: On Philosophy, a Pandemic, and Our International Future." *Philosophical Forum* 53, no. 1 (2022): 3–9.

Pinnock, Clark, Richard Rice, John Sanders, William Hasker, and David Basinger. *The Openness of God: A Biblical Challenge to the Traditional Understanding of God*. Downers Grove: InterVarsity Press, 1994.

Plantinga, Alvin. *God, Freedom, and Evil*. Grand Rapids: Eerdmans, 1977.

Rabadan, Raul. *Understanding Coronavirus*. Cambridge: Cambridge University Press, 2020.

Rizvi, Sajjad. "Considering Divine Providence in Mullā Ṣadrā Šīrāzī (d. 1045/1636): The Problem of Evil, Theodicy, and the Divine Eros." *Oriens* 49, no. 3–4 (2021): 318–369.

Rustom, Mohammed. "Devil's Advocate: ʿAyn al-Quḍāt's Defence of Iblis in Context." *Studia Islamica* 115, no. 1 (2020): 65–100.

Shihadeh, Ayman. "Avicenna's Theodicy and al-Rāzī's Anti-Theodicy." *Intellectual History of the Islamicate World* 7, no. 1 (2019): 61–84.

Taylor, Steven. *The Psychology of Pandemics: Preparing for the Next Global Outbreak of Infectious Disease*. Cambridge, MA: Cambridge Scholars Publishing, 2020.

Thiele, Jan. "Conceptions of Self-Determination in Fourth/Tenth-Century Muslim Theology: Al-Bāqillānī's Theory of Human Acts in Its Historical Context." *Arabic Science and Philosophy* 26 (2016): 245–269.

1 Remarks on Evil, Suffering, and the Global Pandemic*

Seyyed Hossein Nasr

The general problem of evil is a subject about which many books have been written for thousands of years and much of great depth has been said already. It also became very critical with the rise of modernism in the sense that a lot of people in the West and even in Western Christianity in general have left religion because they could not answer the question, "If God is good, why is there evil in the world which is created by Him?" Many variations of this question thus permeate both Western philosophy and Western literature, not to speak of Christian theology.

The Islamic perspective on the problem of evil is in general very different from what one finds in the mainstream in the West. You cannot find Muslims who turn against God because of the presence of evil in the world; and the few who do are Westernized Muslims who think that to be fully modernized and Westernized, one should also have the same "pains" in facing the world from which many Westerners suffer. Such Muslims do not turn to their own tradition's intellectual and spiritual resources to deal with this issue, such as the remarkable and also diversified discussions in the writings of al-Ghazālī, Fakhr al-Dīn al-Rāzī, Ibn Sīnā, Ibn ʿArabī, and others. These authors always deal with the problem of evil on the basis of their complete acceptance that God is real and that He is good. Thus, their attempts to solve the problem of the existence of evil did not affect their belief in the reality of God. With these words in mind, allow me to now delve into this very contentious and difficult issue.

First of all, let us ask the question, "What is evil?" Let me point out that in the Islamic tradition, a common word for "evil" is the Arabic term *qubḥ*; the word that is opposed to it is *ḥusn* or "goodness." But these terms, moreover, also mean "ugliness" and "beauty," respectively. Thus, from the Islamic point of view, you could say that goodness is that which is beautiful and evil is that which is ugly.

The dualism of pre-Islamic Iranian religions such as Zoroastrianism, that is, dualism between good and evil as two independent realities, between Ahura Mazda and Ahriman, works perfectly well on the ethical and practical level, but not so on

* This piece is an edited transcription of Professor Nasr's keynote address delivered at the conference upon which the present volume is based—Eds.

DOI: 10.4324/9781003371670-2

the metaphysical level, for there cannot be two Divine Principles. This explains why there have been certain metaphysicians and Sufis in the Islamic world who have gone so far as to say that there is no evil in the ontological sense. Rūmī, for example, speaks about this issue and defends it; but one must understand what he means. Since the Divine, the Absolute (*al-muṭlaq*), who is also the All-Good, is ultimately all that there is and there is no evil in It, evil as such does not exist. This is what Rūmī and others mean when they say there is no evil. In the Absolute, there is only the Absolute; there is nothing else. A famous Hadith tells us that "God was and there was nothing with Him" (*kāna Allāh wa-mā kāna maʿahu shayʾun*). And to this saying the Islamic metaphysicians add, "And it is now as it was" (*wa'l-ān kamā kān*).[1] So evil does not have the same ontological basis as does goodness. From the metaphysical point of view, there is therefore no equivalent ontological juxtaposition between good and evil.

Nevertheless, if there is no evil per se in the absolute sense, that does not negate the fact that evil is real on the level of relative existence, which is that of this world. Otherwise, the Quran would not affirm the reality of some form of evil on practically every other page, such as when it warns man not to perform evil acts. Evil is as real as the shadow under a tree beneath which a person sits in order to protect himself from the sun. This shadow does have an ontological reality, but it is essentially the absence of light. On the plane of the relative, evil is as real as we are as fallen human beings; but on the level of the Absolute, it is as unreal as we are.

Now, there is also this point to add about which the Sufis have always spoken, and which is the most important way to understand why there is evil. If we conceive of God as Light—after all He Himself says that He is the "Light of the heavens and the earth" (Q 24:35)[2]—and we conceive of Him as the Light of lights (*nūr al-anwār*), as we move away from It, the illumination of this Light becomes less and less, and darkness becomes more and more pervading until we get so far from the source of Light that there is only darkness. But darkness is not a substance, as is light. Darkness is simply the absence of light. Evil is seen in Islamic inner teachings in this way. Only God is Good, but He also creates. Creation implies separation—separation from the Source—and that separation means the gradual weakening of the Light of the Divine Sun. The crystallization of this separation is what we call "evil." To understand in depth this one principle is to understand everything about the root of the existence of evil in this world of separative existence.

Ultimately, evil is the result of separation from the good: Dante said so beautifully in the *Divine Comedy* that evil is separation from God. On the human plane, being the ordinary human beings that we are, we live in separation from God,

1 For an exposition of this saying, see ʿAyn al-Quḍāt, *The Essence of Reality: A Defense of Philosophical Sufism*, ed. and trans. Mohammed Rustom (New York: New York University Press, 2022), 111–113.

2 See the commentary upon this verse in Seyyed Hossein Nasr, Caner Dagli, Maria Dakake, Joseph Lumbard, and Mohammed Rustom (eds.), *The Study Quran: A New Translation and Commentary* (New York: HarperOne, 2015), 878–880.

which is why evil is as real as we are. If there were no separation from God, there would be no creation and no evil. Creation implies limitation—limitation because of separation from that which is Absolute and Infinite, hence limitless. From this separation there arises evil in various forms.

We must at the same time be careful not to trivialize evil, which is one of the great errors of modernism. It not only relativizes both good and evil in denying the Absolute as well as the relatively absolute, but often denies the ultimate significance of both by relating them simply to social norms and the like; that is, rather than denying evil on the level of the Absolute, this tendency in question seeks to deny it on the level of the relative. Yet denying evil on the level of relativity is like absolutizing the relative, which is of course the cardinal sin of modern atheism from a theological point of view and an error from the metaphysical point of view. I have in mind here those people who say that everything is relative, except of course their statement that everything is relative.

How remarkable it is that Islamic thought, even before modern times, was fully aware of the problem of relativizing the relative which derives its reality from the One who alone is Real, and also the problem of confusing the relative with the Absolute. This view is totally different from what some sages such as Frithjof Schuon have called, as just mentioned, the "relatively absolute," namely the manifestation of the Absolute in a relative way that retains something of that absoluteness in it. An example of this reality would be the Quran itself. There is something absolute about it as revelation coming from God, the Absolute. There are no other books that compare to it; yet the Quran is not the Absolute as such, but a reality that reflects the Divine Reality and the Will of God. Only God is the Absolute.

Allow me to come back to the question of beauty and ugliness, for it is not a superficial matter. One of the most remarkable features of traditional civilizations is the presence of so much beauty and so little ugliness. The stable in which Christ was born was much more beautiful than any one of these modern churches built on M street in Washington, DC; there is no doubt about it. That is why we go and visit those old sites which were simple, even stables where horses or animals were kept. This idea of the centrality of beauty was especially strong in Islam, where you have the famous Hadith, "God is beautiful, and He loves beauty."[3] So our whole attachment to God involves God's beauty and also love. If you love God, you must love what God loves, and thus you must love beauty. Islamic civilization was remarkably successful in creating things of beauty, from the carpets on which people sat to the minarets from which the call to prayer was made, and nearly all the objects, buildings, and surfaces in between.

From the Islamic point of view aesthetics and ethics are not separated from each other; although evil has to do with ethics, whereas ugliness has to do with aesthetics, the two are closely related. This is totally different from the view that

3 Aḥmad b. Ḥanbal, *Musnad,* in *Jamʿ jawāmiʿ al-aḥādīth wa'l-asānīd wa-maknaz al-ṣiḥāḥ wa'l-sunan wa'l-masānīd*, vol. 12 (Vaduz: Jamʿiyyat al-Maknaz al-Islāmī, 2000), # 386.

is now prevalent in many religious circles in the West and even to some extent in some parts of the Islamic world where Muslims have done a good job in matching Westerners in building ugly mosques, not to speak of other elements from interior design to everyday utensils. Traditionally, goodness was also associated with the beauty of the soul and evil with its ugliness. Even in English when one says, "I did something ugly" or "This was an ugly act," it refers to an evil act and not a good one.

A comment is also in order concerning our responsibility before evil. In Islam, we are always responsible for our actions. If something happens for which we are not responsible, we will not be judged by God for its consequences. The question of responsibility involves not only the act itself but also the conditions in which the act is performed. What is evil? It is what we know to be evil and nevertheless commit with our free will. If we had no free will, we could not commit evil. So the question of responsibility in relation to evil is very important, and this fact necessitates saying something about knowledge. Without knowledge, there cannot really be evil; we have to know what is good and bad before being responsible for our actions, which is why all sacred scriptures emphasize this point so much. We have to know what God wants of us. Without this knowledge, one would be innocent; ignorance is innocence in this sense. However, we are also required to try to not be ignorant, which takes us back to responsibility.

I now turn to the question of suffering. One might say that suffering comes ultimately from separation from God. When we were in Paradise, close to God, we did not suffer; suffering comes from separation from who we really are, from our *fiṭra* or primordial nature. We have fallen on earth and have fallen away from who we are really, but nevertheless we carry something of that reality within us. The whole of the religious life is based on us seeking to return to the real us, to how God created us. Suffering thus has to do with a loss of identity in a sense, more than anything else. That is the height of it. With it comes all other forms of suffering human beings experience: physical pain, psychological pain, economic suffering, wars, pestilence, etc. There is, however, a very important difference in the use and interpretation of this universal human experience in the religious life, and this reality is important to mention these days because, despite the prevalence of secularism for many Westerners, Christianity is still the dominant religion and Christian ethics and ideals are still prevalent even among secularists.

Christ suffered in a way that the Prophet of Islam did not. The Prophet also suffered, but Christ suffered on the cross. He suffered excruciating pain, and the image of Christ in the Christian mind—the cross being the sacred symbol of Christianity—is that of Christ suffering. Has one ever seen a picture of Christ laughing on the cross? The famous paintings of Velazquez, Michelangelo, or even Giotto are scenes of Christ's life where Christ is smiling. But on the cross He is suffering; He is in pain, sometimes with His head down. And so, suffering plays a special religious role in Christianity that it does not in Islam. Moreover, Buddhism shares this perspective to some extent with Christianity, paying specific attention to the fact that this world is characterized by suffering, although images of the Buddha himself are characterized by the state of bliss rather than pain. For Muslims, therefore, suffering does not pose the same theological significance as it does for Christians, although it is considered to be a part of human life.

Some people suffer more, some less; some people know why they suffer, some do not; and so on. In any case, we must remember that ordinary human beings only know so much of the trajectory of their lives—they do not really know what came before and they do not know what is going to come after. We cannot judge our relationship with God and His Presence or the lack thereof in our lives only in relation to what we remember of the acts that we have performed or not performed, since this type of awareness concerns only a small part of the trajectory of our lives that extends to before our coming into this world and after our departing from it. When Muslims think of the Prophet, they think of all the difficulties he had, all the problems that he and his Companions faced. But they do not identify his life essentially with suffering. The Prophet came to bring knowledge of the One (*lā ilāh*[a] *illā 'Llāh*), as he said, "Say, 'There is no god but God,' and be saved."[4] That is it. That was his message. He came to the world to reveal that basic truth. Everything else in Islam comes from this one teaching concerning the reality of God and our relation to Him.

Spiritually speaking, suffering should always be an occasion for us to draw closer to God. The word *dard* in Persian, which can mean "pain" or "suffering," was often used by Sufis in a positive sense. There are many Sufi texts about this matter, and there is even a famous Sufi poet of India whose *takhalluṣ* or penname was Dard. Suffering should always have a spiritual element connected to it. We should accept pain and suffering as part of our destiny and should not rebel against Heaven because we suffer and question God by asking why if one is good do bad things happen to him or her, and the like. This type of attitude is prevalent in the modern world, but it is an error from the Islamic point of view. God knows best—He has created us. Suffering should bring us closer to Him.

This brings me to the final issue, namely the pandemic. The pandemic is a very concrete lesson about what I have already discussed. From the human point of view, yes the pandemic is evil. But from the point of view of the viruses that created the pandemic, it is not evil at all because it is the expansion of their kingdom. And I hate to say this, but with respect to the preservation of the natural environment, the pandemic has not been negative. Yes, we are sad that several million people have died. Yet we should also look at how much waste several million people can create over a period of two years. It is very tragic to say it, but we human beings are living in such a way that our very existence is a danger to the continuation of life on earth, and the pandemic should first and foremost be a reminder to us that we are not the lords of nature. Nature can play the same game, and little viruses that mean nothing to you can outwit you and rob you years of a healthy life, leaving even the best scientists unable to do something about them. In helping us to realize our limited power over nature, the experience of the pandemic

4 Aḥmad b. Ḥanbal, *Musnad,* # 16,871.

should also remove some of the hubris of the modern natural sciences which has percolated into the whole of modern society. It should bring about a sense of humility. This triumphalism which has been wed to modern science since before the time of Galileo in the early 17th century needs to be changed, as it is very dangerous for human life and the future of the earth.

With this humility should come an awareness of how precious life is, of how we usually take everything for granted. Three years ago, when we walked in the street we did not constantly think about viruses, wear masks, wash our hands, wipe down surfaces, etc. The suddenness of the pandemic alone should make us more humble and should make us realize that life is not to be taken for granted. It is one of the great sins of modern man that he takes existence itself and all the blessings that God has given to him for granted, thinking that it is his right to exist and have blessings, and always wanting more. He should rather ask himself these questions: "Did I create myself?" No. "Can I make my own liver?" No. "What did I do that makes me who I am?" Nothing. Yes, he eats to make his body grow; but even when he eats, he does not know how his body grows. The cells in his body that are absorbing the food, applying the oxygen, and so forth are not under his control; they are performing their own functions according to their nature. These observations are important to keep in mind in order to bring about within us an appreciation of the preciousness of life and along with it a sense of inwardness. You cannot have happiness by relying only on outward factors, as the outward world around you might crumble at any moment. We have to find our joy within ourselves. "The Kingdom of God is within you," Christ said, and the Prophet said, *qalb al-muʾmin ʿarsh al-Raḥmān*, "The heart of the faithful is the Throne of the All-Merciful."[5]

Finally, the experience of the pandemic should bring about in us greater *tawakkul*, greater reliance upon God and less reliance upon the absoluteness of human will and capability. This is not to say that we should not rely on the gifts which God has given to us, because the fact that we can do something itself comes from God. I use the Arabic term *tawakkul*, the idea of total reliance upon God, because it is so important in Islam. What is negative, what belongs to the shadows, namely the evils of the pandemic, can also bring about some good. There is nothing in life that happens from which one cannot draw a positive lesson, and happy are those whom God allows to do so.

References

Aḥmad b. Ḥanbal. *Musnad.* In *Jamʿ jawāmiʿ al-aḥādīth wa'l-asānīd wa-maknaz al-ṣiḥāḥ wa'l-sunan wa'l-masānīd*, vol. 12. Vaduz: Jamʿiyyat al-Maknāz al-Islāmī, 2000.

ʿAyn al-Quḍāt. *The Essence of Reality: A Defense of Philosophical Sufism*. Edited and translated by Mohammed Rustom. New York: New York University Press, 2022.

5 For an exposition of this Hadith, see Seyyed Hossein Nasr, "The Heart of the Faithful Is the Throne of the All-Merciful," in *Paths to the Heart: Sufism and the Christian East*, ed. James Cutsinger (Bloomington: World Wisdom, 2004), 32–45.

Nasr, Seyyed Hossein. "The Heart of the Faithful Is the Throne of the All-Merciful." In *Paths to the Heart: Sufism and the Christian East*, edited by James Cutsinger, 32–45. Bloomington: World Wisdom, 2004.

Nasr, Seyyed Hossein, Caner Dagli, Maria Dakake, Joseph Lumbard, and Mohammed Rustom (eds.). *The Study Quran: A New Translation and Commentary*. New York: HarperOne, 2015.

2 The Existential Threat of Climate Change

A Practical Application of Avicenna's Theory of Evil

Rosabel Ansari

Introduction

Undeniably, human health is inseparable from our larger environment. Likewise, human beings are as much a part of the natural world as the natural world is a part of us. The deeply interconnected relationship between human health and the environment means that our relationship to the natural world must always figure into any discussions concerning health and disease. Instead of an object of human action, whether consumption, protection, or study, the world around us ought to be conceived as constitutive of the human fabric.

This is true not only for the environment of the individual inasmuch as it concerns individual health. It is also true for global human health within the larger global environment. As medical researchers have signaled, there is a connection between global climate change and an increased risk of disease. The immediate cause of the COVID-19 pandemic still undetermined, researchers have pointed to climate change as part of the larger story and context in which the pandemic emerged, and from which we might expect future pandemics.[1] For example, pathogenic spillover from animals to humans becomes all the more likely as animal habitats are lost, species migrate, and agricultural practices bring millions of animals into close proximity. The impact of climate change on temperature and rainfall patterns can also create more favorable conditions for a number of waterborne and mosquito-borne diseases. Similarly, air pollution can worsen respiratory diseases.

Such factors have led Aaron Bernstein, the Director of the Center for Climate, Health, and the Global Environment at Harvard University, to refer to the separation of health and environmental policy as "a dangerous delusion." Bernstein warns that while human beings have historically grown in partnership with the plants and

1 See Saloni Gupta, Barry T. Rouse, and Pranita P. Sarangi, "Did Climate Change Influence the Emergence, Transmission, and Expression of the COVID-19 Pandemic?" *Frontiers in Medicine* 8 (2021): 769208; Xavier Rodó et al. "Changing Climate and the COVID-19 Pandemic: More Than Just Heads or Tails," *Nature Medicine* 27 (2021): 576–579. Such discussions arose as early as 2010: Emily K. Shuman, "Global Climate Change and Infectious Diseases," *New England Journal of Medicine* 362 (2010): 1061–1063.

DOI: 10.4324/9781003371670-3

animals we live with, we have now changed the rules of the game. Consequently, we have to expect that it will affect our health.[2]

Yet, more than just looming pandemics, climate change endangers human life with many more cataclysmic changes to our habitat. These alarming changes to our world, associated with human behaviors, are increasingly discussed and framed as an existential threat to human life. While pandemic is part and parcel of the framed climate emergency for the reasons just outlined, this chapter focusses on the larger issue of the climate emergency alongside the many dangers (including pandemic) with which it threatens human life. More specifically, this chapter discusses the significant shift in discourse since 2018 that describes climate change as an "existential threat" and how we might make sense of this within the framework of Avicennan philosophy.

The famed Islamic philosopher and physician Avicenna (d. 1037), or Ibn Sīnā in Arabic, lived over a thousand years ago. His philosophy shaped centuries of philosophical thinking across vast traditions, languages, and geographies, and it continues to inform Islamic thought to this day. An important aspect of Avicenna's philosophical system is the theory of providence, according to which the world is governed by the Order of the Good (*niẓām al-khayr*). Although Avicenna considered the existence of some evil to be necessary for the functioning of the world, he argued that evil could only ever be accidental and partial. He thought that it could not afflict a species as such, but only individual members of a species at certain times. The question arises, therefore, as to how Avicennan philosophy might understand the existence of an evil such as climate change that could wipe out the human race. This chapter investigates how, and if, Avicennan philosophy can account for such a possibility. The question bears light on the themes of evil, suffering, and pandemic in Islamic philosophy through investigating (1) the possibility of human activity as the cause for human extinction, and (2) how this could make sense within the Order of the Good and the relationship between God and human beings.

Climate Change as Existential Threat

Language about climate change as an existential threat took off with the issuing of the blockbuster report "Global Warming of 1.5°C" in 2018 by the UN's Intergovernmental Panel on Climate Change (IPCC).[3] Long acknowledged by scientists, this report stressed that human activity and carbon dioxide emissions are responsible for warming the planet. Yet the 2018 IPCC report brought new

2 Harvard University, "Coronavirus, Climate Change, and the Environment: A Conversation on COVID-19 with Dr. Aaron Bernstein, Director of Harvard Chan C-Change," www.hsph.harvard.edu/c-change/subtopics/coronavirus-and-climate-change/ (last accessed 20 July 2022).

3 IPCC, *Global Warming of 1.5°C: IPCC Special Report on Impacts of Global Warming of 1.5°C Above Pre-Industrial Levels in Context of Strengthening Response to Climate Change, Sustainable Development, and Efforts to Eradicate Poverty* (Cambridge: Cambridge University Press, 2018).

striking data and modelling. It emphatically warned that global warming must be kept to 1.5°C from pre-industrial temperatures to reduce the odds of the worst consequences of climate change. In order to achieve this goal, however, global carbon dioxide emissions would need to be cut in half by 2030 from 2010 emissions. The report argues, however, this would still only give a 67% chance of staying within 1.5°C global warming. On the other hand, if we do nothing and continue with "business-as-usual," global temperatures could rise by 4°C, making our planet potentially incompatible with human life. The report has given rise to widespread countdowns of how many years left we have to act in order to avert catastrophe.[4]

Since the issuing of the 2018 IPCC report, global climate change has captured the world's attention more than ever before. From politics and activism to media and popular culture to business investment, growing currents among human societies are recognizing the threat of climate change as a looming emergency. For the first time, these currents stretch beyond the confines of scientists and focused environmentalist groups. In addition to this damning report, there is an ever-growing body of research pointing to the disastrous consequences of climate change for life on earth. Human habitats, sometimes including entire countries, are slated to become unlivable (or, in the case of rising sea levels, non-existent) in our own lifetimes.[5] Increased temperatures are linked to the melting of the polar icecaps, permafrost, and the release of more carbon dioxide that will further increase temperatures, leading to more extreme weather events that demolish human lives in a cycle that is only slated to get worse.[6] In fact, increased temperatures are now also linked to decreased fertility, through the toxicity of wildfire fumes, or even due to the sheer burden that heat exhaustion takes on expectant mothers.[7] What we see unfolding in the climate crisis has prompted the current discourse surrounding global climate change as an existential threat to the human species.

4 For example: United Nations: Meetings Coverage and Press Releases, "Only 11 Years Left to Prevent Irreversible Damage from Climate Change, Speakers Warn During General Assembly High-Level Meeting," https://press.un.org/en/2019/ga12131.doc.htm (last access 29 July 2022); Mark Fischetti, "There's Still Time to Fix Climate—About 11 Years," *Scientific American*, October 27, 2021, www.scientificamerican.com/article/theres-still-time-to-fix-climate-about-11-years/ (last accessed 29 July 2022); Matt McGrath, "Climate Change: 12 Years to Save the Planet? Make That 18 Months," *BBC News*, July 24, 2019, www.bbc.com/news/science-environment-48964736 (last accessed 29 July 2022).

5 Jeremy S. Pal and Elfatih A. B. Eltahir, "Future Temperature in Southwest Asia Projected to Exceed a Threshold for Human Adaptability," *Nature Climate Change* 6 (2016): 197–200; J. Lelieveld et al., "Strongly Increasing Heat Extremes in the Middle East and North Africa (MENA) in the 21st Century," *Climatic Change* 137 (2016): 245–260.

6 A. Vaks et al., "Speleothems Reveal 500,000-Year History of Siberian Permafrost," *Science* 340.6129 (2013): 183–186.

7 Amelia K. Wesselink and Gregory A. Wellenius (eds.), "Pediatric and Perinatal Epidemiology," *A Special Issue of Climate Change and Reproductive, Perinatal, and Paediatric Health* 36, no. 1 (2022): i–iv, 1–168.

This discourse is growing among general populations, including local and indigenous communities.[8] It is spearheaded by youth movements, epitomized by Greta Thunberg, who told the UN General Assembly in 2019 that we face "the beginning of a mass extinction."[9] It is embodied by groups such as Extinction Rebellion who have shown that they are willing to risk imprisonment, promoting tactics that are described by others as promoting lawlessness, because it is not the time to worry about the legality of disruptive behavior when human life is threatened with extinction due to our own making.[10] In fact, according to such movements, rebellion becomes the sole mechanism for human salvation as we move towards the point of no return.

Moreover, the discourse of an existential threat is now echoed by politicians and world leaders. On November 1, 2021, at the United Nations' 26th annual Climate Change Conference of the Parties (COP26) held in Glasgow, US President Joe Biden declared climate change an "existential threat to human existence as we know it,"[11] echoing a similar statement made by UN Secretary-General António Guterres in 2018.[12] More recently, on July 18, 2022, Guterres declared regarding the climate crisis that humanity either has the choice of collective action or "collective suicide."[13]

The notion of climate change as an existential threat stretches the terrain of human discourse and communication. In the scholarly realm, the substantial academic volume *Global Climate Change* that encompasses the vast array of up-to-date scientific research dedicates its first chapter to "Climate change and existential threats."[14] On the other end of the spectrum, the notion is symbolized and enacted in popular culture, such as the recent Netflix film *Don't Look Up* in which a large comet hurtles towards the planet, eventually colliding and putting an end to life on earth.

8 See, for example, the United Nations' Office of the Secretary-General's Envoy on Youth: "Meet 13 Indigenous Young Indigenous Rights Activists," www.un.org/youthenvoy/2021/08/meet-13-indigenous-young-indigenous-rights-activists/ (last accessed 22 July 2022).

9 Greta Thunberg, *The World Is Waking Up* (New York: UN General Assembly, 23 September 2019). See also Greta Thunberg, *No One Is Too Small to Make a Difference* (New York: Penguin Books, 2019), 96–99.

10 Extinction Rebellion, "About Us," https://rebellion.global/about-us/ (last accessed 22 July 2022); BBC, "Extinction Rebellion Disrupts London's West End," www.bbc.com/news/uk-england-london-61050643 (last accessed 22 July 2022).

11 Joe Biden, "Remarks by President Biden at the COP26 Leaders Statement," www.whitehouse.gov/briefing-room/speeches-remarks/2021/11/01/remarks-by-president-biden-at-the-cop26-leaders-statement/(last accessed 22 July 2022).

12 United Nations: UN News, "Climate Change: An 'Existential Threat' to Humanity, UN Chief Warns Global Summit," https://news.un.org/en/story/2018/05/1009782 (last accessed 22 July 2022).

13 United Nations: Meetings Coverage and Press Releases, "Multilateral Efforts Needed to Reverse Climate Crisis, Secretary-General Says, Stressing Choice Between 'Collective Action or Collective Suicide'," https://press.un.org/en/2022/sgsm21376.doc.htm (last accessed 22 July 2022).

14 Abhishek Kumar, Shilpi Nagar, and Shalini Anand, "Climate Change and Existential Threats," in *Global Climate Change*, edited by Suruchi Singh (Amsterdam: Elsevier, 2021), 1–31.

The existential threat discourse goes beyond words and talk. It is also tied to important changes in human behavior. For example, consequent to the threat of climate change induced by overconsumption, the sustainability industry has emerged as increasingly profitable. The global green technology and sustainability market size was valued at $10.31 billion in 2020 and is projected to reach $74.64 billion by 2030.[15] Beyond consumer products and lifestyle choices, the existential threat of climate change looms large in the lives of young people. The seeming inevitability and even apocalyptic nature of the climate disaster has increased anxiety among the young.[16] In addition, if the decreased fertility caused by the biological impacts of climate change is not enough, there is a growing tide of environmentalist antinatalism among certain segments of society.[17]

This short survey of research, discourse, and behavior gives a brief overview of how climate change is understood to pose an existential threat to human life. It also indicates the exponentially growing importance of this topic within public discourse and behavior. Consequently, not only does it deserve our attention, but it also deserves to be thought about philosophically. Moreover, this survey reveals how the significant changes in discourse surrounding climate change is intimately tied to the understanding that human action is the cause for the climate emergency. As a result, the emergency is seen as a creation of our own making that may jeopardize our own existence.

Enter Avicenna

I will now explore what the previous discussion means philosophically, within an Avicennan framework. As Avicenna defines evil as "privation," the privation or loss of a species would be considered an evil for Avicenna. I argue that potential

15 Shadaab Khan, Vaibhav Modi, and Vineet Kumar, "Green Technology and Sustainability Market by Technology (Internet of Things (IoT), Cloud Computing, Artificial Intelligence & Analytics, Digital Twin, Cybersecurity, and Blockchain) and Application (Green Building, Carbon Footprint Management, Weather Monitoring & Forecasting, Air & Water Pollution Monitoring, Forest Monitoring, Crop Monitoring, Soil Condition/Moisture Monitoring, Water Purification, and Others): Global Opportunity Analysis and Industry Forecast, 2021–2030," *Allied Market Research*, October 2021, www.alliedmarketresearch.com/green-technology-and-sustainability-market-A06033 (last accessed July 22, 2022).

16 Caroline Hickman et al., "Climate Anxiety in Children and Young People and Their Beliefs About Government Responses to Climate Change: A Global Survey," *The Lancet Planetary Health* 5, no. 12 (2021): E863–E873. Organizations such as Force of Nature specifically offer climate activist mobilization for young people. See www.forceofnature.xyz (last accessed July 22, 2022).

17 Matthew Schneider-Mayerson and Leong Kit Ling, "Eco-Reproductive Concerns in the Age of Climate Change," *Climatic Change* 163 (2020): 1007–1023. In the media there has been anecdotal reporting of a growing antinatalism: Simon Usborne, "'More People Is the Last Thing This Planet Needs': The Men Getting Vasectomies to Save the World," *The Guardian*, January 12, 2022, www.theguardian.com/lifeandstyle/2022/jan/12/more-people-is-the-last-thing-this-planet-needs-the-men-getting-vasectomies-to-save-the-world (last accessed July 23, 2022); Amy Fleming, "Would You Give Up Having Children to Save the Planet? Meet the Couples Who Have," *The Guardian*, June 20, 2018, www.theguardian.com/world/2018/jun/20/give-up-having-children-couples-save-planet-climate-crisis (last accessed July 23, 2022).

loss of humankind would indeed be an insurmountable challenge to Avicennan philosophy unless we accept that human beings do not have a special function in knowing God.

In classical Islamic philosophy, the theory of evil is discussed within chapters on providence (*ʿināya*) and not as a standalone topic or theodicy. The difference is significant in as far as philosophers within the Avicennan tradition, and Islamic philosophers more broadly, do not consider that "the problem of evil" must be addressed in order to prove the existence of God. While traditional philosophy of religion postulates that the presence of evil in the world needs to be explained in order to prove or justify the existence of God,[18] Avicenna and other Islamic philosophers do not hypostasize evil as an issue that has bearing on whether God exists. Instead, the presence of evil in the world is considered a fact of how the world works. It is discussed and explained within discussions of the Order of the Good that governs the world. On this account, proving the existence of God is separate from investigating the presence of evil in the world and its causes. This discussion can be found in Avicenna's chapter on providence in the *Metaphysics of the Healing* 9.6.[19]

Avicenna's theory of providence explains the manner with which the universe is governed. At the beginning of *Met.* 9.6 he tells us that providence is for being (*al-wujūd*) to be in accordance with the Order of the Good and for it to emanate from God in the manner most complete and most conducive to order.[20] Originating in Greek philosophy, providence and emanation are two theories that were adapted into Arabic and that reflect a certain necessitarianism in the way the world functions.[21] According to the theory of emanation, the world is a coeternal and

18 On the problem of evil from the perspective of contemporary philosophy of religion, see Michael Tooley, "The Problem of Evil," in *Stanford Encyclopedia of Philosophy*, ed. Edward N. Zalta, https://plato.stanford.edu/archives/win2021/entries/evil/ (last accessed July 23, 2022). As stated in the introduction, the question posed is whether evil in the world provides "the basis for an argument that makes it unreasonable to believe in the existence of God." See also Hugh J. McCann and Daniel M. Johnson, "Divine Providence," in *Stanford Encyclopedia of Philosophy*, ed. Edward N. Zalta, https://plato.stanford.edu/archives/spr2017/entries/providence-divine/ (last accessed July 24, 2022), which surveys the arguments for harmonizing God's omnibenevolence with the presence of evil in the world.

19 Avicenna, *The Metaphysics of the Healing*, ed. and trans. Michael E. Marmura (Provo: Brigham Young University Press, 2005), 339–347.

20 Avicenna, *Metaphysics*, 339.4–12.

21 The theory of emanation entered into Arabic through the Neoplatonica Arabica and is often contrasted with the doctrine of creation. While creation posits that God freely created the world out of nothing according to His will, emanation holds that the world is an eternal, necessary effect of God's being. On emanation and its development from Greek into Arabic, see Cristina d'Ancona, "Emanation," in *Enyclopaedia of Islam 3*, ed. Kate Fleet et al. (Leiden: Brill, 2007-), http://dx.doi.org/10.1163/1573-3912_ei3_COM_26173 (last accessed July 22, 2022). The theory of providence entered Arabic through the translation of Alexander of Aphrodisias' (fl. 200) treatise on the topic. See Alexander of Aphrodisias, *Traité de la Providence*, ed. and trans. Pierre Thillet (Paris: Verdier, 2003). In Alexander, the theory of providence refers to the causality of the First Principle that reaches the sublunar world through the movement of the heavenly bodies. While providence does

necessary effect of God's being. The theory of providence builds on this by further stipulating that the being of the world is according to the Order of the Good. Rather than contesting the place of evil in the world, it is incorporated into the theory of providence as a necessary aspect of the world's functioning. After introducing providence, Avicenna defines evil as the privation of what is necessary or manifestly beneficial for a species' primary perfections.[22]

In this system, as the First Cause of the world, God's being is perfect. Consequently, the being of the world emanates from God according to the Order of the Good. This leads Avicenna to argue that evil only afflicts individual members of a species at certain moments, while the species as a whole is preserved.[23] This theory goes at least as far back as Alexander of Aphrodisias who, in order to explain the presence of evil in our world, argued that providence extends to the preservation of the species but not individuals.[24] Towards the end of *Met.* 9.6 Avicenna concludes that the presence of evil in the world is necessary for what the world is. He tells us that it would be impossible to prevent the presence of evil in the world because then things would not be what they are. In other words, the being of the world is such that evil cannot be prevented from it.[25] Moreover, due to the states of the world, some evil necessarily occurs to individuals as a result of the universal order.[26] By this, Avicenna explains that the interplay of causes in the world, which form what the world is, necessarily lead to instances of evil. Nevertheless, evil is only required accidentally, while the good is required essentially.[27] Through the theory of providence, Avicenna, therefore, sees the world as governed by the Order of the Good and the existence of evil as necessary for how the world functions, but only accidentally so. In the grand scheme of the world, evil, Avicenna tells us, is little (*qalīl*).[28]

---

not extend to individuals, the motion of the heavenly bodies is said to preserve the continuity of the species. Abū Naṣr al-Fārābī (d. 950) develops the theory from a question of celestial motion to one of ontological justice, on which see Badr El Fekkak, "Alexander's *ʿInāya* Transformed: Justice as Divine Providence in Al-Fārābī," *Documenti e studi sulla tradizione filosofica medievale* 21 (2010): 1–17.

22 Avicenna, *Metaphysics*, 340.11–12.

23 Avicenna, *Metaphysics*, 341.9–10.

24 Alexander presents his theory of providence as a middle ground between (1) those who reject providence all together, arguing that there is no order to the world, and (2) those who consider providence to extend to every individual thing (*Traité de la Providence*, 10.15–23). The latter position, Alexander argues, does not account for evil in the world that should not be attributed to God's providence. Consequently, Alexander takes the position that providence only extends to our world through the eternal preservation of essence that is found in the species (10.24–25 and 20.21–21.9). Interestingly, Alexander gives as evidence of providence the example of the earth's climate which is suitable for life (10.25–11.10).

25 Avicenna, *Metaphysics*, 346.7–10.

26 Avicenna, *Metaphysics*, 346.18–19.

27 Avicenna, *Metaphysics*, 345.12.

28 Avicenna, *Metaphysics*, 342.4.

Given this theory, we might ask whether there is any space in Avicenna's philosophy for the possibility of an existential threat to the human species or whether his philosophical system simply cannot address this issue. This question could be expanded to address the possible (and actual) extinction of all species. Of course, unbeknownst to Avicenna, the extinction of species has occurred naturally over millennia. A potential solution to the problem of the historical extinction of species could therefore be to incorporate the natural extinction of species into the Order of the Good. On this basis, whenever a species, for whatever reason, cannot survive on earth, the evil of its extinction is nevertheless part of the universal good, as life on earth adapts to the changing environment.

Yet, the notion of modern-day climate change as an existential threat to human life has important distinguishing factors from the historical extinction of species that require more philosophical attention. In today's case, climate change is considered anthropogenic, meaning it is caused, at least in part, by human activities. Moreover, the existential threat to human life poses a particular philosophical problem because Avicennan philosophy places a special importance on human life and human knowledge in the universe. In order to explore how Avicennan philosophy might address the issue, then, we need to turn to Avicenna's theory of evil acts discussed in *Met*. 9.6. Understood within Avicenna's theory of evil acts, we can reflect on how the possible extinction of the human race due to human induced climate change could make sense within Avicenna's philosophy.

In *Met*. 9.6 Avicenna tells us that evil acts are those that cause an individual or polity to lose its perfection. That is to say, an evil act is one that hinders a person or a polity from achieving its ultimate goal. Avicenna gives the example of injustice and adultery.[29] Despite the evil such acts entail, Avicenna explains that all evil acts are still perfections for the causes enacting them, as the evil proceeds from the effects, not the causes. In this vein, injustice is evil with respect to the person who suffers it due to the privation of what is due to such an individual. Yet, the act is both a perfection and an evil with respect to the person committing injustice. It is a perfection for the person's irascible power that seeks subjugation. At the same time, it is an evil for the person's rational soul whose perfection lies in subduing the irascible power. Like the sufferer of injustice, in this way an evil act also causes the rational soul of the person committing injustice to suffer the privation of what is due to it.[30] This effect of privation is what makes such acts evil, even if they are perfections for their causes. Similarly, as burning is a perfection with respect to fire, its cause, but it is an evil in relation to the person it burns, who suffers the privation of health.[31]

While Avicenna seems to admit that evil acts inflict harm, he nevertheless considers the existence of evil acts to be a necessary part of the world due to the confluence of celestial, terrestrial, natural, and psychological powers. Although the world

29 Avicenna, *Metaphysics*, 343.17–344.1.
30 Avicenna, *Metaphysics*, 344.3–18.
31 Avicenna, *Metaphysics*, 344.18–21.

is governed by the Order of the Good, and these various powers are organized in such a way to preserve this universal order, sometimes it happens that the causal relations necessitate evil acts. Following a form of determinism, Avicenna considers that such acts could not be otherwise, as they are the result of causes that could not be otherwise. He gives the example of burning a poor man's garment. While this would be an evil act, he argues that it could not be any other way when the confluence of active and passive powers, celestial and terrestrial, natural and psychological are found in such a way that this act takes place.[32] Individual instances of evil are therefore necessary for the preservation of the universal order of causes, and it is impossible for it to be otherwise. Consequently, in Avicenna's view, even acts of injustice must in some way contribute to the universal Order of the Good, at least in preserving the laws of causality. Avicenna's discussion of evil, as embedded within the theory of providence, entails a degree of determinism in as much as the Order of the Good is defined by the laws of causality (be they celestial, terrestrial, natural, or psychological) which is what necessitates the existence of some evil.

Avicenna's theory of evil acts gives us some basis to apply his thought to the notion of human-induced climate change and the existential threat it poses to human life. In applying this thinking to the notion of climate change caused by human activity we must consider what causes lead to the human activity that induces climate change. Just as the soul's irascible power is a cause for injustice, we can identify the soul's appetitive power to be what fuels the overwhelming human desire for consumption that is understood to be the root cause of anthropogenic climate change. As we will see, the appetitive power can be identified with a dual function that is both life-sustaining on the individual level and life-destroying on the universal level.

According to Avicenna, the most basic perfection of the human species, shared among all species of life, is the perpetuation of existence through nutrition and reproduction. In animals and humans, the appetitive power drives us towards those goals and thereby sustains life. In this way, consumption fulfills a perfection of the appetitive power. Yet, at the same time, it is this appetitive power, left unchecked, that has led to the overwhelming consumption of the earth's resources among certain segments of the human population. Moreover, this human activity—consumption of resources and the associated carbon dioxide emissions—is what is understood to induce the climate change that is now considered an existential threat.

Through applying this thinking to our contemporary situation of human-induced climate change, what emerges is an appetitive power that is so strong it leads to a consumption that ultimately threatens the human habitat. In Avicennan terms, such a situation would be the privation of human life by the very power in the soul that ought to produce and sustain it. As such, we can consider the perfection of the appetitive power in certain individuals to cumulatively lead to evil in the privation

32 Avicenna, *Metaphysics*, 346.19–347.1.

of habitat for the species. This privation of habitat poses an existential threat to all of humankind. Is it possible to see this within the Order of the Good that Avicenna's theory of providence calls for?

Avicenna thought that the species must always be preserved, limiting evil to the affliction of individuals. Yet, as his example of burning the poor man's garment illustrated, all evil in the world, including volitional evil acts, can be attributed to a series of causes that could not be any other way. Given this degree of determinism, the only way to account for extinction (regardless of what causes that extinction) is to subsume it within the Order of the Good. In what way, however, could the extinction of the human species fall within the Order of the Good? Avicenna may not have endorsed the notion that the end of human life could fall within the Order of the Good, but his theory of evil acts gives us the tools to think about the notion of an existential threat to human life precisely within that context.

Avicenna taught that of all life on earth human beings are uniquely endowed with the rational soul. In fact, of terrestrial life, Avicenna considered humankind to be the most excellent.[33] This is because, on account of the rational soul, human beings can both attain true knowledge of reality and live virtuously. Furthermore, through perfecting the rational soul we can attain salvation and eternal happiness. The perfection of the rational soul, however, requires not only intellectual and theoretical training, but also a practical power for moderation in appetites, passions, and governance.[34] Therefore, just as performing an unjust act is both a perfection to the irascible power and an evil to the rational soul, an overwhelming consumption is both a perfection to the appetitive power and an evil to the rational soul. In order to fulfill our human function, telos, and perfection, we must use our rational soul to subdue and moderate the appetitive power within us.

From this Avicennan perspective, in today's world of rampant consumption of resources that is associated with the climate emergency, the rational soul must emerge on the collective level. The collective rational soul must fulfill its own perfection by subduing the appetitive power in human individuals, either through education or through the force of regulation, in order to ward off the evil created by the unchecked appetitive power. Although the appetitive power and overwhelming consumption is left unchecked in only a segment of humankind, it leads to the destruction suffered by all. If the subduing of this segment's consumption does not take place, in an Avicennan framework, not only has the life-sustaining appetitive power within us led to the destruction of our own habitat, but the telos of the human being is unfulfilled. Consequently, if we cannot reform ourselves through actualizing the rational soul, the threat to human existence may become inevitable. Given the framework of human-induced climate change and privation of habitat, it is hard to see any alternative unless the appetitive powers of individuals can be subdued before overconsumption destroys human habitat.

33 Avicenna, *Metaphysics*, 10.1, 358.14.
34 Avicenna, *Metaphysics*, 10.5, 378.10–13.

In this case, Avicennan philosophy would face a deadlock unless we accept that human self-destruction is a part of the Order of the Good. Perhaps the way to understand this position within an Avicennan framework, even if it is ultimately incompatible with Avicennan philosophy, would be to consider it the winning of the appetitive power and failing of the rational soul. In the context of human-induced climate change, if the rational soul is what defines humankind and distinguishes us from other species, the failure to regulate our appetitive power represents the obstruction of our capacity to fulfill our own telos. Once, as a result of the loss of habitat, there is no capacity to fulfill our own telos, perhaps we would have to consider the end of human life to be within the Order of the Good. Such a position would understandably be heterodox by Avicennan standards. Yet, the situation of an existential threat to all human life as the result of human activity would also be novel to Avicenna's philosophy.

The extinction of human life would be heterodox in Avicennan philosophy on another count. The obstruction to fulfilling the human telos is not only a loss of our perfection, but it also pertains to the cosmic function of human life. Through the attainment of true knowledge, human beings connect the terrestrial and celestial spheres, serving as a juncture between the material world and the intelligible world beyond. In attaining true knowledge and perfecting the rational soul, human beings love and yearn for God. This much is uncontroversial. From a different perspective, however, human beings serve a further cosmic function. While human beings love to become God-like, in the *Treatise on Love* Avicenna also tells us that God loves for His self-disclosure to be attained by God-like souls.[35] The implications of human extinction need to be explored in light of this relationship. For if human beings have a particular role as objects of God's love, an existential threat to human life poses a problem for Avicenna's philosophical system.

It remains debated to what extent Avicenna's God can be said to love the world. Certainly, love and yearning for God is an impulse that pervades the universe and propels beings towards actualization and perfection.[36] Avicenna tells us that it is "due to His essence (*li-dhātihi*)" that God loves Himself and is loved by others.[37] In other words, love of God is essential and follows from who God is. While love of God among beings in the world is an integral part of Avicenna's philosophy, it is not immediately clear that God has the same relation to the world. Avicenna often discusses love within a framework of attainment, such that the lover attains (*nāʾil*)

35 Ibn Sīnā, *Risāla fī'l-ʿIshq*, in *Traités mystiques d'Aboū Alī al-Hosain b. Abdallāh b. Sīnā, ou d'Avicenne*, ed. August F. Mehren, vol. 3 (Leiden: Brill, 1899), 36.11; partial English translation in William Chittick, *Divine Love: Islamic Literature and the Path to God* (New Haven: Yale University Press, 2013), 284–287.

36 Ibn Sīnā, *al-Ishārāt wa'l-tanbīhāt*, ed. Mujtabā al-Zāriʿī (Qum: Būstān-i Kitāb, 2008), II 8.18–19, 350–352; English translation in *Ibn Sīnā on Mysticism: Remarks and Admonitions, Part Four*, trans. Shams Inati (London: Kegan Paul, 1996).

37 Ibn Sīnā, *Ishārāt*, II 8.18, 351.4–5.

joy in the presence of God.[38] Yet the notion of attainment is significant because it points to the lover's objectification of the beloved. It is not clear that the world fulfills that role in Avicenna's philosophy.

Avicenna accepts the existence of sincere and holy saints that attain love of God in the afterlife.[39] It thus remains to be seen, however, to what extent human beings might be an object of God's love. In the *Treatise on Love* Avicenna tells us that there would be nothing in existence if God did not disclose Himself and if there were nothing attained of Him. God loves the being of the things for which He is a cause (*wujūd maʿlūlātihi*). The object of His love, Avicenna clarifies, is for His self-disclosure to be attained, which is the attainment of the God-like souls.[40] In this short passage Avicenna suggests that as a function of God's self-love, God loves for His self-disclosure to be attained. The object of God's love is not strictly speaking something other than God, but it is the fulfillment of His own self-disclosure being attained. The attainment of God's self-disclosure by God-like souls nevertheless involves the function and telos of human life. The cosmic function of human beings is therefore not only our own perfection and love of God, but also our attainment of God's self-disclosure that is the object of divine love. On this basis, God's love of Himself is not devoid of a relation to human beings and the world. Rather, God's love of Himself involves our love and attainment of Him.

Divine Love

The question of God's love of the world speaks to the crux of the issue concerning the broader question of God's relation to the world, the theory of emanation, and the status of the world as a co-eternal necessary effect of God. The eternal, necessary relationship between God and the world has been understood to mean that Avicenna's God is empty of love and care for the world. This short reflection on Avicenna's philosophy of love pulls that into question, even if it problematizes the notion that Avicenna's God loves the world. It also speaks to the question at hand in this chapter: if God loves for His self-disclosure to be attained, the extinction of human life would pose a problem for the Order of the Good. It is true that Avicenna's cosmology involves other celestial beings of higher stations that attain higher degrees of love of God and His self-disclosure. Yet, human beings are still among those who yearn for God and the attainment of His self-disclosure. Within this context, it would not seem possible for the extinction of human beings to be within the Order of the Good.

If God loves the attainment of His self-disclosure, the framing of climate change as an existential threat might indeed pose an insurmountable problem to Avicennan philosophy. The possible end of human life would close an opportunity to attain divine self-disclosure. This might be less problematic for Avicenna if we accept

38 Ibn Sīnā, *Ishārāt*, II 8.18, 350.13–351.10.
39 Ibn Sīnā, *Ishārāt*, II 8.18, 351.7–8, 352.1.
40 Ibn Sīnā, *Risāla fī'l-ʿIshq*, 36.7–11.

that, given the place of celestial beings, it need not be human beings who attain God's self-disclosure. In other words, God loves the attainment of His self-disclosure, with no special regard for human beings fulfilling that attainment. In this vein, we might say that the loss of humankind could be within the Order of the Good in the situation where we are incapable of fulfilling our human telos. The situation in which our rational soul is unable to subdue the appetitive power, leading to our collective destruction through loss of habitat could mean that it is within the Order of the Good for human life to come to an end. This position would nevertheless be heterodox within Avicenna's philosophy traditionally articulated. Within this system, providence ensures the eternity of the species and evil is limited to the affliction of individuals. In addition to the historical extinction of species, the novel situation of climate change induced by human activity, however, and its framing as an existential threat, lead us to think about new ways to apply Avicenna's thought.

References

Alexander of Aphrodisias. *Traité de la Providence*. Edited and translated by Pierre Thillet. Paris: Verdier, 2003.

Avicenna [Ibn Sīnā]. *Risāla fī'l-'Ishq*. In *Traités mystiques d'Aboū Alī al-Hosain b. Abdallāh b. Sīnā, ou d'Avicenne*, edited by August F. Mehren, vol. 3, 1–37. Leiden: Brill, 1899.

Avicenna [Ibn Sīnā]. *Ibn Sīnā on Mysticism: Remarks and Admonitions, Part Four*. Translated by Shams Inati. London: Kegan Paul, 1996.

Avicenna [Ibn Sīnā]. *The Metaphysics of the Healing*. Edited and translated by Michael E. Marmura. Provo: Brigham Young University Press, 2005.

Avicenna [Ibn Sīnā]. *al-Ishārāt wa'l-tanbīhāt*. Edited by Mujtabā al-Zāri'ī. Qum: Būstān-i Kitāb, 2008.

BBC. "Extinction Rebellion Disrupts London's West End." www.bbc.com/news/uk-england-london-61050643 (last accessed July 22, 2022).

Biden, Joe. "Remarks by President Biden at the COP26 Leaders Statement." www.whitehouse.gov/briefing-room/speeches remarks/2021/11/01/remarks-by-president-biden-at-the-cop26-leaders-statement/ (last accessed July 22, 2022).

Chittick, William. *Divine Love: Islamic Literature and the Path to God*. New Haven: Yale University Press, 2013.

d'Ancona, Cristina. "Emanation." In *Enyclopaedia of Islam 3*, edited by Kate Fleet et al. Leiden: Brill, 2007-. http://dx.doi.org/10.1163/1573-3912_ei3_COM_26173 (last accessed July 22, 2022).

El Fekkak, Badr. "Alexander's *'Ināya* Transformed: Justice as Divine Providence in Al-Fārābī." *Documenti e Studi Sulla Tradizione Filosofica Medievale* 21 (2010): 1–17.

Extinction Rebellion. "About Us." https://rebellion.global/about-us/ (last accessed July 22, 2022).

Fischetti, Mark. "There's Still Time to Fix Climate—About 11 Years." *Scientific American*, October 27, 2021. www.scientificamerican.com/article/theres-still-time-to-fix-climate-about-11-years/ (last accessed July 29, 2022).

Fleming, Amy. "Would You Give Up Having Children to Save the Planet? Meet the Couples Who Have." *The Guardian*, June 20, 2018. www.theguardian.com/world/2018/jun/20/give-up-having-children-couples-save-planet-climate-crisis (last accessed July 22, 2022).

Force of Nature. www.forceofnature.xyz (last accessed July 22, 2022).

Gupta, Saloni, Barry T. Rouse, and Pranita P. Sarangi. "Did Climate Change Influence the Emergence, Transmission, and Expression of the COVID-19 Pandemic?" *Frontiers in Medicine* 8 (2021): 769208.

Harvard University. "Coronavirus, Climate Change, and the Environment: A Conversation on COVID-19 with Dr. Aaron Bernstein, Director of Harvard Chan C- Change." www.hsph.harvard.edu/c-change/subtopics/coronavirus-and-climate- change/ (last accessed July 20, 2022).

Hickman, Caroline et al. "Climate Anxiety in Children and Young People and Their Beliefs About Government Responses to Climate Change: A Global Survey." *The Lancet Planetary Health* 5, no. 12 (2021): E863–E873.

IPCC. *Global Warming of 1.5°C: IPCC Special Report on Impacts of Global Warming of 1.5°C Above Pre-Industrial Levels in Context of Strengthening Response to Climate Change, Sustainable Development, and Efforts to Eradicate Poverty*. Cambridge: Cambridge University Press, 2018.

Khan, Shadaab, Vaibhav Modi, and Vineet Kumar. "Green Technology and Sustainability Market by Technology (Internet of Things (IoT), Cloud Computing, Artificial Intelligence & Analytics, Digital Twin, Cybersecurity, and Blockchain) and Application (Green Building, Carbon Footprint Management, Weather Monitoring & Forecasting, Air & Water Pollution Monitoring, Forest Monitoring, Crop Monitoring, Soil Condition/Moisture Monitoring, Water Purification, and Others): Global Opportunity Analysis and Industry Forecast, 2021–2030." *Allied Market Research*, October 2021. www.alliedmarketresearch.com/green-technology-and-sustainability-market-A06033 (last accessed July 22, 2022).

Kumar, Abhishek, Shilpi Nagar, and Shalini Anand. "Climate Change and Existential Threats." In *Global Climate Change*, edited by Suruchi Singh et al., 1–31. Amsterdam: Elsevier, 2021.

Lelieveld, J. et al. "Strongly Increasing Heat Extremes in the Middle East and North Africa (MENA) in the 21st Century." *Climatic Change* 137 (2016): 245–260.

McCann, Hugh J., and Daniel M. Johnson. "Divine Providence." In *Stanford Encyclopedia of Philosophy*, edited by Edward N. Zalta. https://plato.stanford.edu/archives/spr2017/entries/providence-divine/ (last accessed July 23, 2022).

McGrath, Matt. "Climate Change: 12 Years to Save the Planet? Make That 18 Months." *BBC News*, July 24, 2019. www.bbc.com/news/science-environment-48964736 (last accessed July 29, 2022).

Pal, Jeremy S., and Elfatih A. B. Eltahir. "Future Temperature in Southwest Asia Projected to Exceed a Threshold for Human Adaptability." *Nature Climate Change* 6 (2016): 197–200.

Rodó, Xavier et al. "Changing Climate and the COVID-19 Pandemic: More Than Just Heads or Tails." *Nature Medicine* 27 (2021): 576–579.

Schneider-Mayerson, Matthew, and Leong Kit Ling. "Eco-Reproductive Concerns in the Age of Climate Change." *Climatic Change* 163 (2020): 1007–1023.

Shuman, Emily K. "Global Climate Change and Infectious Diseases." *New England Journal of Medicine* 362 (2010): 1061–1063.

Thunberg, Greta. *No One Is Too Small to Make a Difference*. New York: Penguin Books, 2019.

Thunberg, Greta. *The World Is Waking Up*. New York: UN General Assembly, September 23, 2019.

Tooley, Michael. "The Problem of Evil." In *Stanford Encyclopedia of Philosophy*, edited by Edward N. Zalta. https://plato.stanford.edu/archives/win2021/entries/evil/ (last accessed July 24, 2022).

United Nations: Meetings Coverage and Press Releases. "Multilateral Efforts Needed to Reverse Climate Crisis, Secretary-General Says, Stressing Choice Between 'Collective Action or Collective Suicide'." https://press.un.org/en/2022/sgsm21376.doc.htm (last accessed July 22, 2022).

United Nations: Meetings Coverage and Press Releases. "Only 11 Years Left to Prevent Irreversible Damage from Climate Change, Speakers Warn During General Assembly High-Level Meeting." https://press.un.org/en/2019/ga12131.doc.htm (last accessed July 29, 2022).

United Nations: Office of the Secretary-General's Envoy on Youth. "Meet 13 Indigenous Young Indigenous Rights Activists." www.un.org/youthenvoy/2021/08/meet-13-indigenous-young-indigenous-rights-activists/ (last accessed July 22, 2022).

United Nations: UN News. "Climate Change: An 'Existential Threat' to Humanity, UN Chief Warns Global Summit." https://news.un.org/en/story/2018/05/1009782 (last accessed July 22, 2022).

Usborne, Simon. "'More People Is the Last Thing This Planet Needs': The Men Getting Vasectomies to Save the World/." *The Guardian*, January 12, 2022. www.theguardian.com/lifeandstyle/2022/jan/12/more-people-is-the-last- thing-this-planet-needs-the-men-getting-vasectomies-to-save-the-world (last accessed July 22, 2022).

Vaks, A. et al. "Speleothems Reveal 500,000-Year History of Siberian Permafrost." *Science* 340, no. 6129 (2013): 183–186.

Wesselink, Amelia K., and Gregory A. Wellenius (eds.). "Pediatric and Perinatal Epidemiology." *A Special Issue of Climate Change and Reproductive, Perinatal, and Paediatric Health* 36, no. 1 (2022): i–iv, 1–168.

3 On Self-Knowledge, Divine Trial, and Discipleship

Mukhtar H. Ali

The Imperative of Self-knowledge

Islamic spirituality is rooted in self-knowledge (*ma ʿrifat al-nafs*). It is through the self that one fathoms reality, recognizes truth, and attains various degrees of human perfection. Islamic discourse on spiritual psychology employs various terms for the self, such as *soul* (*nafs*), *heart* (*qalb*), *intellect* (*ʿaql*), and *spirit* (*rūḥ*). The emphasis throughout this study is the *nafs* (soul), even though the *nafs* is always conceived within the context of the heart and intellect. In the language of revelation, the soul's innate ability to recognize truth is called *fiṭra*. The Quran describes *fiṭra* as a God-given innate human nature, "Turn your face towards the religion in pure faith—with the divine innate nature upon which God originated mankind. There is no altering God's creation. That is the upright religion, but most men know not" (30:30). The Quran also reveals that human nature is the manifestation of the inviolable divine spirit, "When I have fashioned him and breathed into him from My spirit, bow down before him" (Q 15:29). It is the origin of man and his very path and return to God, expressed as the "upright religion." The Prophet affirmed that the gnosis of God is through the door of self-knowledge, "He who knows himself has come to know his Lord."[1]

Just as the soul is the path to God, it is also the means of knowing creation, as Imam ʿAlī b. Abī Ṭālib (d. 661) said, "Do not be ignorant of yourself, for he who is ignorant of himself is ignorant of all things."[2] True knowledge of things corresponds to the degree of one's self-knowledge, because one contemplates existence in the mirror of the soul through the light of intelligence. God reveals Himself in outward existence as He does in the heart of man. These are the divine signs and the places of contemplation as the Quran describes, "We will show them our signs on the horizons and in themselves until they know that it is the truth" (Q 41:53) and "Have they not reflected in themselves? God has not created the heavens and the earth, and all that is in between, except in truth and a specified term. Most men

1 ʿAbd al-Wāḥid Āmidī, *Ghurar al-ḥikam wa-durar al-kalim* (Tehran: Daftar-i Nashr-i Farhang-i Islāmī, 2000), no. 7946.
2 Āmidī, *Ghurar al-ḥikam*, 9965.

DOI: 10.4324/9781003371670-4

disbelieve in the meeting with their Lord" (Q 30:8). Both verses indicate that the divine signs are fathomed through self-reflection so that the real trove of knowledge, which is the human soul, will not reveal its secrets until it is mined. Muslim sources cite Jesus saying:

> Do not say, "Knowledge is in the heavens so who will ascend and bring it back?," or "Knowledge is in the earth, so who will go down and mine it?," or "Knowledge is across the ocean, so who will cross it and return with it?" Knowledge is forged into your hearts! Refine yourself before God through the conduct of the spiritual and adorn yourself with the character of the truthful, and knowledge will manifest from your hearts until it immerses you and overflows from you.[3]

Since human potential is mined through perfection of character, self-knowledge constitutes knowing how to discipline and transform the soul, from its base substance to its brilliant essence. Imam ʿAlī said, "The soul is a precious gem; he who guards it elevates it, and he who squanders it debases it"[4] and "The more a person increases in knowledge, the more he pays attention to his own soul and the more he strives to discipline and rectify it."[5]

The Path to God

The path to God in the Islamic mystical tradition is called wayfaring or *sayr wa sulūk*. *Sayr* means traversing a path, and *sulūk* means advancing in stages of proximity to the divine presence, in action and in state. *Sulūk* also means the transference from one state of worship to another, one action to another, one abstention to another, from action to abstention, one theophany to another, or one level of the soul to another. It is also said that *sulūk* is purifying the heart from blameworthy character traits and inculcating it with praiseworthy ones. However, not all who tread the path arrive. Some do not complete the journey, or they perish along the way. Some flee (*al-sālik al-hārib*), and some stop midway (*al-sālik al-wāqif*), but if they repent, they return as wayfarers, otherwise they remain stagnant or regress. Those who attain the divine presence are the realized wayfarers (*al-sālik al-wāṣil*).

Whether one is a wayfarer or not in the technical sense, there is no escape from striving because Islam regards this temporal world as illusory and the hereafter as real: "The life of this world is merely a diversion and amusement; the true life is in the Hereafter, if only they knew" (Q 29:64). Furthermore, God asks rhetorically in the Quran, "So where are you going?" then He answers, "To your Lord is your return" (Q 81:26). "O mankind, you are ever toiling towards your Lord and will

3 Ḥaydar Āmulī, *Jāmiʿ al-asrār wa-manbaʿ al-anwār*, ed. Henry Corbin and Osman Yahia (Beirut: Muʾassasat al-Taʾrīkh al-ʿArabī, 1969), 513.

4 Āmidī, *Ghurar al-ḥikam*, 3494.

5 Āmidī, *Ghurar al-ḥikam*, 7204.

meet Him" (Q 84:6). God has therefore guided everyone on a particular trajectory, some of whom He predisposed to matters of truth and knowledge. Among them, those "who purify [the soul] succeed and those who corrupt it fail" (Q 91:9–10). Experts have identified seven stages of the soul's ruin: (1) those who turn away from the truth, reject divine signs; (2) those who reject divine signs become veiled; (3) the veiled are separated from the truth and become preoccupied with falsehood and illusion; (4) divine blessings are withdrawn (*salb al-mazīd*), (5) then God strikes out past deeds (*salb al-qadīm*); (6) one dismisses all matters of spirituality, (7) then ultimately, harbors enmity towards God, the saints, and the people of truth.

Success on the path to God entails self-discipline and purification of the soul. According to the famous Hadith, "The Prophet of God dispatched a contingent of the army (to the battlefront). Upon their return, he said: 'Blessed are those who have performed the minor *jihād* and have yet to perform the major *jihād*.' When asked, 'What is the major *jihād*?' The Prophet replied: 'The *jihād* of the self.'"[6] *Jihād* lexically means to strive and struggle, but in the context of the Hadith, it means to engage in warfare with the self because the soul is the origin of conflict and contrary properties; it is the battlefield of the angels, satans, and beasts. At inception, human souls are devoid of inscription, image, vice, or virtue, as traits are established within it through repetitive actions and attitudes. However, Muslim metaphysicians generally view the soul in a negative light. Al-Qushayrī (d. 1074) writes that the soul (*nafs*) refers to "those qualities of the servant that are defective and character traits and acts that are blameworthy."[7] The Quran affirms that "the soul, indeed, commands to evil" (Q 12:53) and the Prophet said, "Your greatest enemy is the soul between your two sides."[8] True humanity, however, lies in conquering the soul through the light of the intellect, as Imam ʿAlī said, "God Almighty composed the angels of intellect but without desire and composed the animals of desire but without intellect yet composed man of both. Thus, he whose intellect conquers his desire is superior to the angels and he whose desire dominates his intellect is worse than the animals."[9] He also said, "Struggle against your soul in obeying God, just as one fights an enemy and overcomes it. The strongest of people is one who has triumphed over his soul."[10] He also said, "Take command of your souls by continuously struggling with them."[11] "O people take charge of the disciplining of yourselves and redress them from the wildness of their habits."[12]

With respect to the various effects arising from the soul's angelic, satanic, and bestial nature, Abū Ṭālib al-Makkī (d. 996) says, "The soul is afflicted with four diverse qualities: The first is the meanings derived from the attributes of Lordship

6 Ibn Babawayh, *Maʿānī al-akhbār* (Beirut: Muʾassasat al-Tārīkh al-ʿArabī, 2009), 160.
7 Al-Qushayrī, *al-Risāla al-Qushayriyya* (Cairo: Dār al-Kutub al-Ḥadītha, 2001), 305.
8 Muḥammad Rayshahrī, *Mīzān al-ḥikma*, vol. 6 (Beirut: Dār Iḥyāʾ al-Turāth al-ʿArabī, 2001), 2439.
9 Ibn Bābawayh, *ʿIlal al-sharāʾiʿ* (Beirut: Dār al-Murtaḍā, 2006), 1:4, chapter 6, no. 1.
10 Āmidī, *Ghurar al-ḥikam*, no. 4761.
11 Āmidī, *Ghurar al-ḥīkam*, no. 2489.
12 al-Sharīf al Raḍī, *Nahj al-balāgha*, ed. Subḥī al-Ṣāliḥ (Beirut: Dār Kutub al-Lubnānī), saying no. 359.

such as arrogance, invincibility, love of praise, mightiness, and autonomy. It is also afflicted with the character traits of the satans, such as deception, cunning, envy, and suspicion. It is afflicted with the nature of beasts, that is, the love of food, drink, and copulation. Despite all this, it is held responsible for the qualities of servanthood, such as fear, humility and lowliness."[13]

Sufi authors describe the interrelationships between the soul, body, and spirit in the following way: the soul acts as an intermediary between the immaterial spirit and the material body, the nexus through which the divergent properties of each interact. The spirit is active and the soul is passive; the spirit possesses life, knowledge, power, speech, hearing, and sight, and through its receptivity, the soul actualizes these powers through the body. When the spirit fertilizes the soul, it gives birth to bodily functions in the external world. Alternatively, the spirit like the father and the body like the mother give birth to the soul, a child that is born from the marriage between spirit and body. The bodily powers, however, are not intrinsic to the soul as they are for the spirit. It is only through the relationship between the spirit and the soul do these powers arise in the body.

The ancient philosophers maintained that there are three souls: the vegetal, animal, and rational. Dawūd al-Qayṣarī (d. 1350) says that it is called the soul "because of its attachment and governance of the body. When vegetal activity arises through its attendants, it is called the 'vegetal soul' (*al-nafs al-nabātiyya*), and when animal activity arises, it is called the 'animal soul' (*al-nafs al-ḥaywāniyya*)."[14] When referring to the vital substance of the vegetal realm, it is called the vegetal soul; when referring to the life-giving force of animality, it is called the animal soul; when referring to the power of reason, it is called the rational soul. According to Imām ʿAlī, there is a fourth type of soul, which he calls the universal divine soul:

> There are four souls: the growing vegetal, the sensory animal, the sacred rational, and the universal divine. The growing vegetal soul is a power originating from the four elements that begins at conception; it resides in the liver; its substance is derived from the rarified aspects of food; its activity is growth and increase. When it separates, it reintegrates with its origin and does not have independent existence.
>
> The sensory animal soul is a celestial power and instinctual fire whose origin is the celestial spheres; its genesis occurs at physical birth; its activity is life, movement, domination, worldliness, and desire; it resides in the heart and separates upon deterioration.
>
> The sacred rational soul is a divine power that originates at the time of birth in this world. Its seat is true metaphysical knowledge; its substance is the intellect's affirmations; its activity is gnosis of the divine. The reason for its separation is the dissolution of the physical apparatus. When it returns to its origin it remains autonomous.

13 Abū Ṭālib al-Makkī, *Qūt al-qulūb* (Beirut: Dār Kutub ʿIlmiyya, 1997), 159.

14 Dāwūd al-Qayṣarī, *Sharḥ Fuṣūṣ al-ḥikam*, ed. Ḥasanzada Āmulī (Qum: Bustān-i Kitāb, 2002), 209.

> The universal divine soul is a divine power, a self-subsisting simple essence; its origin is the Intellect to which it orients and returns when it becomes complete, resembling it. . . . It is the lofty Essence of God. He who knows it will not be wretched and he who is ignorant of it is lost and astray.[15]

The universal divine soul originates in the intellect which is the first and highest creation of God. It is the foundation of the path to God and much has been written on the nature of the intellect and heart. It suffices to quote a Hadith attributed to the Prophet who describes the primordial supremacy of the Intellect and its attending characteristics:

> God created the Intellect from a hidden, treasured[16] light in His ancient knowledge, of which neither a sent messenger nor a proximate angel had any awareness. He made knowledge its soul, understanding its spirit, abstinence its head, modesty its eyes, wisdom its tongue, compassion its concern, and mercy its heart. Then He adorned it and strengthened it with ten things: certainty, faith, truthfulness, serenity, sincerity, companionship, generosity, contentment, submission, and gratitude. Then He commanded it to go back so the Intellect went back. Then God commanded it to draw near, so it drew near. Then He said, "Speak!" It said, "Praise be to God who does not have an opposite, nor equal, nor similar, nor equal, nor substitute, nor equivalent, before whom all things are humble and abased."
>
> God, the Almighty said, "By My Might and Majesty, I have not created anything better than you, nor more obedient to me, nor loftier, nor nobler, nor more honorable than you. By you I impose, I bestow, I am acknowledged as One, worshipped, called upon, hoped for, yearned for, feared, and warned against. Reward is through you and punishment is through you."[17]

The Degrees of the Soul's Perfection

The goal of every wayfarer is the soul's perfection, the degrees of which Sufi authors have identified in manuals of spiritual wayfaring. Adhering to the Quranic typology, Qayṣarī defines the three levels of the soul:

> When the animal powers dominate the spiritual powers, the soul is called "commanding" [*ammāra*] soul. However, when there is a glimmer of the heart's light from the Unseen, revealing its perfection, the rational soul's

15 Muḥsin Fayḍ Kāshānī, *al-Ḥaqā'iq fī maḥāsin al-akhlāq* (Qum: Dār al-Kitāb al-Islāmī, 2002), 363.

16 "Treasured" may refer to the famous Hadith of the Hidden Treasure: "I was a Hidden Treasure and I loved to be known, so I created the world that I may be known."

17 Muḥammad Bāqir Majlisī, *Biḥār al-anwār* (Beirut: Dār Iḥyā' al-Turāth al-'Arabī, 1983), 3:94, chapter 4.

> awareness of its iniquitous end and the corruption of its states, the soul is called the "reproaching" [*lawwāma*], since it reproaches its actions.
>
> This degree is a preliminary for the manifestation of the degree of the heart, because if the heart's light prevails and its dominion appears over the powers of the animal soul, the soul attains peace and is called "tranquil" [*muṭma'inna*].[18]

Though the stations of wayfaring are numerous, there are seven key stations of the soul's development before reaching perfection.[19] Upon commencing the spiritual journey, the first station is called the commanding soul (*al-nafs al-ammāra*), which is the carnal, animal soul, mentioned in the verse, "I do not absolve my own soul, for the [carnal] soul indeed commands to evil" (Q 12:53). The Prophet said, "My Lord, do not entrust me to my soul even for the blink of an eye."[20] A soul that is immersed in animal desires is figuratively human although it exhibits some human attributes, as Imām ʿAlī states, "His form is that of a human, but his heart is that of an animal."[21] Imām Zayn al-ʿĀbidīn (d. 713) says in one of his supplications:

> My God, to You I complain of a soul commanding to evil, rushing to offenses, eager to disobey You, and exposing itself to Your anger. It takes me on the roads of disasters, it makes me the easiest of perishers before You; many its pretexts, drawn out its expectations; when evil touches it, it is anxious, when good touches it, inclining to sport and diversion,[22] full of heedlessness and inattention.[23]

The commanding soul is engulfed in veils of darkness and is thus not concerned with divine commandments or prohibitions; it follows only the impulses of innate carnal desire. By recognizing the patterns and characteristics of this soul, one can apply a suitable spiritual formula or invocation (*dhikr*) to break its fetters and allow progress to the next stage. As it is immersed in carnal nature, the abode of this soul is the material world, which is the furthest realm from divinity. The only recourse to resist the commanding soul is to firmly stand up against it, as the Quran advises, "Say: 'I advise you to one thing and that is to rise up for God, singly or in pairs, then contemplate." The appropriate invocation here is to declare, "There is no god but God!"

18 Qayṣarī, *The Horizons of Being: The Metaphysics of Ibn al-ʿArabī in the Muqaddimat al-Qayṣarī*, trans. Mukhtar H. Ali (Leiden: Brill, 2020), 209.

19 The remainder of this section of the article is based on Professor Akram Almajid's oral commentary upon Baḥr al-ʿUlūm's (d. 1797) treatise, *Tuḥfat al-mulūk fī sayr wa-sulūk*.

20 al-Nasāʾī, *Sunan* (Beirut: Dār al-Ḥaḍāra, 2015), 6:147.

21 Raḍī, *Nahj al-balāgha*, 119.

22 Allusion to the Q 70:19–21, "Surely man was created fretful—when evil touches him, he is anxious; when good visits him, he is grudging."

23 ʿAlī b. Husayn (Zayn al-ʿĀbidīn), *The Psalms of Islam*, trans. William Chittick (London: Muhammadi Trust, 1988), 235.

When the light of faith flickers within the soul, it begins to discern truth from falsehood and enters the second station called the reproaching soul (*al-nafs al-lawwāma*), according to the Quranic verse, "I swear by the self-reproaching soul" (Q 75:2). It begins to reproach its vile attributes and loathsome actions, regretting its previous states of animality. Thus, it begins to adhere to the divine commandments, admits wrongdoing, holds itself accountable, and regrets past deeds. Characteristic of the reproachful soul is that it faces veils of light rather than darkness, so it differentiates between truth and falsehood and engages in good works. However, because it is governed by reproach, it blames itself and becomes hypercritical of others. This soul has not reached the level of sincerity, so it is afflicted with ostentation, vanity, and love of leadership. Because of these fatal vices and its proximity to the commanding soul, it is in grave danger, as the Prophet indicates, "Mankind is doomed, except the knowers. The knowers are doomed except the doers, the doers are doomed except the sincere and the sincere are in grave danger."[24] The highest station of the reproachful soul is the station of sincerity. It is the last stage of the pious (*abrār*) before they enter the stations of those drawn near to God (*muqarrabīn*), that is, those who dwell in the third station and beyond. The proximate consider the reproachful soul as a vice, as the famous dictum expresses, "The good deeds of the virtuous are the vices of the proximate."[25] The soul is not safe in the station of sincerity until one transcends even the awareness of sincerity. This is accomplished by realizing that every good deed originates and belongs to God. Transcending self-awareness—experientially, not intellectually—is the effacement of witnessing one's deeds. This is the state of those drawn proximate to God. They have set their eyes solely on God, and thus attribute no deeds to themselves.

If the soul persists in abstaining from vices and whims of the desirous carnal soul, it begins to receive inspiration (*ilhām*), and enters the third station. It is called the inspired soul (*al-nafs al-mulhama*) according to the Quranic verse, "By the soul and He who fashioned it and inspired it with its vices and virtues" (Q 91:8). The inspired soul is a lofty station in which it encounters veils of light, not darkness; those who reach this station are considered gnostics (*ʿārif*). Entering the unseen, the wayfarer "hears" the angels and satans without instrument, whereas in the previous stations, which are closer to animality, he hears nothing. The experts consider this to be the most dangerous place for the wayfarer due to the difficulty in distinguishing the majestic from the beatific and the angelic from the satanic. The danger lies in the fact that the soul still contains remnants of nature and humanness (*bashariyya*). So, it is possible for the wayfarer to plummet to the station of the commanding soul, "the lowest of the low," or transform into a devil and an enemy of the spiritual master (*shaykh*), the path and the brethren.

24 Abū Ḥāmid al-Ghazālī, *Iḥyā ʾulūm al-dīn* (Beirut: Dār al-Kutub al-ʿIlmiyya, 1986), 4:156.

25 al-ʿAjlūnī, *Kashf al-khafāʾ* (Beirut: Dār Iḥyāʾ al-Turāth al-ʿArabī, 1968), 1:357. This statement is attributed to the early Sufi master al-Kharrāz (d. 899).

At this stage, adhering to the *shaykh* is paramount because the inexperienced wayfarer travels through uncharted realms of the soul and worlds he has never experienced. Upon receiving inspiration, the wayfarer may feel that he has reached the highest station and may even make claims to divinity. To safeguard from these perils, the wayfarer must adhere to the *sharīʿa* (law) outwardly and inwardly, or the *sharīʿa* and *ṭarīqa* (way), from the very beginning of *sulūk* until its end. Then he must be humble before the *shaykh*, like a corpse in the hands of the washer, for the *shaykh* is responsible for his awaking, revival, and arrival at lofty stations. It is the *shaykh* who elucidated the path, illuminated the heart, discerned the pitfalls of the lower soul, offered cures for its illnesses, reinforced him with prayers and invocations, and made him arrive at this lofty station of the inspired soul. Obedience to the *shaykh* does not imply that one abandons his humanity and dignity. In the same way that one worships God with dignity, he also obeys with dignity.

Finally, it is imperative that the wayfarer does not make claims above the *shaykh*, even if he is addressed by an angel or made to see a certain vision. There are two reasons for this: the first is that the *shaykh* is the realized gnostic, experienced in the knowledge of the path and its pitfalls. Whereas the wayfarer has only recently been initiated into the stations of gnosis and inspiration. The *shaykh* is tried and true, but the wayfarer is still a novice. The second aspect deals with spiritual authority (*wilāya*) of the *shaykh* over the disciple. The disciple is born from the spiritual fatherhood of the *shaykh* who has authority over him, just as a father has a right over the son even if the son becomes self-sufficient.

When the agitation of the inspired soul starts to settle and no trace or memory of the commanding self remains, the wayfarer enters the fourth station of the tranquil soul (*al-nafs al-muṭmaʾinna*). The Quran states, "O tranquil soul, return to your Lord well-pleased, and pleasing to Him" (Q 89:27–28). The soul acquires tranquility from the incessant prompting of its carnal desires, but if there are still provocation from its lower aspect, then it regresses to the station of the reproachful soul. The tranquil soul is the first degree of human perfection.

When the tranquil soul develops further, extinguishing all of its desires, relinquishing attachment to stations and ambitions, it is called the contented soul (*al-nafs al-rāḍiya*). However, since traces of attachment remain, this annihilation (*fanāʾ*) must be followed by the state of subsistence (*baqāʾ*). So, it is the final station in *sulūk*, whereby human attributes are replaced by divine attributes.

After achieving this, the soul may attain a station where both God and the creation are pleased with it, so it is called the pleasing soul (*al-nafs al-marḍiya*). In this station, the soul beholds divine beauty, content in witnessing the divine attributes reflected within itself and thereafter, becoming the object of God's gaze and good pleasure.

Then if it is commanded to return to creation as a guide, it is called the perfected soul (*al-nafs al-kāmila*), which is the station of spiritual guardianship and the Pole (*quṭb*) of existence.

The Soul's Unknowability and Discipleship

Though the path to God is tread through self-knowledge, from another perspective, it is said that attaining complete knowledge of the soul is impossible because it originates from the divine spirit that God breathed into man, a reality that is fundamentally unknowable. God says, "He fashioned him and breathed into him from His Spirit" (Q 38:72), "placed on the earth a vicegerent" (Q 2:30), and "He taught Adam all the names" (Q 2:31). Human vicegerency is the manifestation of the all-comprehensive name *Allah*. Therefore, the Prophet's statement "He who knows himself knows his Lord" may be interpreted in an apophatic sense: if one were to realize the soul's true reality, then he will have come to know God's true reality. However, since absolute knowledge of God is impossible, knowledge of the soul is also impossible.

The second problem in knowing the soul is that the more one tries to know it, the more it eludes the seeker. The contemporary sage Akram Almajid writes:

> If the soul seeks, it seeks itself; and that is a loss, since every seeker of the self loses the self. He who seeks his self loses it, but he who loses his self finds it—in knowledge and reality—whether it is in the Intellect, imagination, or the senses, for all are one reality. Were it not for the manifestation of reality in the soul and the soul's transformation into a new creation thereby, it would never find itself, just like one seeking water in a mirage.[26]

The soul is elusive like a mirage, smoke diffused in a room, a water spill or subtle leak whose is source is impossible to find. It constantly deceives its owner, hiding or masquerading in various disguises. It feigns piety, faith, righteousness, sincerity, and justice, until it is ruled by the light of the intellect. Imam ʿAlī says, "The commanding, seducing soul flatters [its owner] like a hypocrite and adorns the garb of an agreeable friend, until it deceives and overcomes him like a pouncing enemy and dominating tyrant, driving him thereby into ruin."[27] When the soul deceives a person, it is to be expected, since its nature demands that it find strategies to attain its desire. Deception here means that the soul seeks one thing while the intellect seeks something else. God created the carnal appetites (*shahawāt*) and placed them within the soul. Were it not for desire, one could not subsist in the material world, for it is a person's mount, mover, and means of survival. Like the animal, its nature is attachment, irrespective of its being good or bad. So, if one trains it to pray, it attaches to prayer, and one orients himself towards spiritual perfections, then it attaches itself to its attainment. Sometimes, it attaches to a perceived goodness such as abstention, prayer, or some religious rite, even if it may be detrimental for that person. It is considered detrimental because of the *attachment*

26 Cited, with modifications, from Akram Almajid, *The New Creation*, trans. Mukhtar H. Ali (London: Sage Press, 2022), 198.

27 Āmidi, *Ghurar al-ḥikam*, no. 2106.

to the act and not the act itself. There are plenty of examples of ritualistic piety and religiosity that hinder spiritual development.

Knowing the soul through itself is impossible unless it is known through the intellect's light and the heart's insight. It is possible, however, to know certain of its aspects through contemplation and self-reflection, but only an expert guide such as the clairvoyant *shaykh* and sage can see its true nature. For this reason, Imam Zayn al-ʿĀbidīn said, "He who does not have a sage to guide him, perishes,"[28] for the *shaykh* is the guiding light of the intellect, the spiritual physician who diagnoses through clairvoyance (*firāsa*) and insight (*baṣīra*), then prescribes a remedy that corresponds to its real condition (*ḥaqīqa*). God may also directly inspire the soul of its true nature, as the Quran confirms, "By the soul and He who proportioned, He inspired it [with discernment] of its wickedness and its righteousness" (Q 91:8–9), and in some cases, by subjecting it to a trial.

The unknowability of the soul further provides evidence for the necessity of discipleship as Jesus declares, "Whoever holds on to his life loses it, and whoever renounces his life in this world will keep it for eternal life. Whoever desires to serve me, he must follow me; and wherever I am, there my servant will also be. Whoever serves me, my Father will honor him" (John 12:25–26). There is an inverse relationship between knowing the soul and transcending it. Just as one attains eternal life by renouncing it, one attains true knowledge of the soul through its effacement. In this case, it is the soul's annihilation (*fanāʾ*) in the light of the intellect, because after speaking about renouncing worldly life, Jesus enjoins his disciples to follow him wherever he may be. Since the prophet represents the intellect and the disciple represents the soul, only through the soul's surrender to the intellect does it become complete and thus honored by God.

One who strives to know God through the soul seeks the Absolute through the veils of contingency. Imam Jaʿfar al-Ṣādiq (d. 765) said:

> He who claims to know God through a veil, a form or a similitude is a polytheist, because a veil, form or similitude is other than Him, for He is One, Singular. How can He be Singular if one claims to know Him through something else? Only one who has come to know God through God knows Him. He who has not come to know Him through Him does not know Him, but only knows other than Him. The creatures do not perceive anything except through God and gnosis of God is not attained except through God.[29]

If God cannot be known through the soul, then how can God be known? Imam ʿAlī was asked, "How have you come to know your Lord?" He replied, "The way

28 Majlisī, *Biḥār al-anwār*, 78:159, no. 10.
29 Ibn Bābawayh, *al-Tawḥīd* (Beirut: Dār al-Maʿārif 2008), 143, no. 7.

He has made Himself known to me." The questioner asked, "How has He made Himself known to you?" He replied:

> He is unlike any form, nor sensed through the senses, nor compared to the people. He is near in His distance, distant in His proximity, above all things and nothing can be said to be above Him. He is before all things, and nothing can be said to be before Him. He is in all things but not in the way that something is inside of another. He is outside of all things but not in the way something is outside of another. Glory be to the One who is thus, and none is like so. He is the Origin of everything.[30]

Divine Trial and Discipleship

Having identified the stages of the soul's transformation towards perfection, it should be known that the soul will never attain perfection unless God Himself trains it. The Prophet said, "My Lord, do not entrust me to my soul even for the blink of an eye."[31] He relied entirely upon God to rectify, discipline, and transform the soul. With respect to God's training it, the Prophet said, "My Lord taught me conduct and perfected it within me."[32] This training has two aspects, one which relates to the divine names of majesty and the other to the names of beauty. God's training through the names of majesty often relate to His trial. He tests the soul for faith with tribulation, as the Quran states, "that He may try the believers with a fair trial" (Q 8:17). Or, as Imam ʿAlī says, "The believer's faith is not complete until he recognizes me through light, and if he knows me through light, then he is a believer whose heart God has tested for faith and expanded his breast for Islam. He has acquired gnosis of religion and so has come to perceive."[33] Thus, trials and tribulations are necessary for the soul's development because the soul straddles two dimensions in tension with one another, the material and the spiritual. The world is the abode of trial (*dār al-balāʾ*), as Imam ʿAlī says, "I swear by Him Who sent him [the Prophet] with the Truth, you shall indeed be mixed and intermingled and then separated in the sieve [of divine trial and tribulation]."[34] Imām Jaʿfar al-Ṣādiq states:

> It is mentioned in the Book of ʿAlī that among all mankind, the prophets undergo the severest of trials, and after them their inheritors [*awṣiyāʾ*], and after them the elect to the extent of their nobility. Indeed, the believer undergoes trial in proportion to his good deeds. So, he whose faith is sound and

30 al-Kulaynī, *al-Kāfī* (Tehran: Dār al-Uswa, 1991), 1:85, no. 2.

31 Abū Dāwūd, *Sunan* (Beirut: Dār al-Risala al-ʿĀlamiyya, 2009), no. 5090.

32 Qushayrī, *Risāla*, 316; ʿAbd ʿAlī b. Jumʿa Huwayzī, *Tafsīr nūr al-thaqalayn* (Beirut: Muʾassasat al-Tārīkh al-ʿArabī, 2001), 5:389, cited in Rayshahrī, *Mīzān al-ḥikma*, 1:78.

33 Ibn Abīʾl-Ḥadīd, *Sharh Nahj al-balāgha* (Beirut: Muʾassasat al-Aʿlamī liʾl-Maṭbūʿāt, 1995), 2: 450.

34 Raḍī, *Nahj al-balāgha*, sermon 16.

> whose deeds are good, his trials are also more severe. That is because God Almighty did not make this world a place for rewarding the believer and punishing the unbeliever. One whose faith is feeble and whose (good) deeds are few faces fewer tribulations. Verily, tribulations hasten towards the believer with greater speed than rainwater towards the earth's depths.[35]

God's trial is a part of the divine order (*sunna ilāhiyya*) that Jesus describes as the narrow gate: "Enter through the narrow gate. For wide is the gate and easy is the way that leads to destruction; those who enter it are many. But the gate is narrow and the way is difficult that leads to life, and those who find it are few" (Matthew 7:13–14). The Imams also indicated that "there is no constriction (*qabḍ*) and expansion (*basṭ*) in that which God has commanded or forbidden except that there is in it from God a trial and a decree."[36] "It is ineluctable that mankind should be purified, separated and sieved so that a great number is excluded by the sieve."[37] "You shall be purified in the way gold is purified."[38] "The greatness of man's reward goes with the greatness of suffering, and whenever God loved a people, He subjected them to suffering."[39]

Divine trial is a purification which culminates with the effacement of the ego, that is, annihilation of selfhood and the transformation of human attributes into divine attributes. It is also called voluntary death (*al-mawt al-irādī*), as the following *ḥadīth qudsī* alludes, "He who seeks Me, finds Me; he who finds Me, comes to know Me; he who comes to know Me, loves Me; he who loves Me is enthralled by Me; he who is enthralled by Me, I am enthralled by him; he whom I am enthralled by, I kill him; he whom I kill, I owe him blood-money; he to whom I owe blood-money, I am his blood-money."[40]

Just as God trains the soul through the names of majesty, He trains it through the names of beauty, as the Quran alludes, "He is the one who makes people laugh and weep" (Q 53:43). Since existence is circular, divine training must complete the circle of beauty and majesty. That is, just as God trains the soul through trial and hardship, so too must He train it through bounties and blessings. Without both types of training the wayfarer will not be complete and reach perfection. By extension, the *shaykh* trains the disciple through severity and hardship and through gentleness and kindness, but each according to his disposition and receptivity. This is because each person has a temperament governed by their natural elemental composition. Those whose character is stubborn are fire-like and change only through austerity and severity, like certain stones that melt only in severe heat. Those

35 Kulaynī, *al-Kāfī*, 2:259, no. 29.
36 Kulaynī, *al-Kāfī*, 1:152.
37 Kulaynī, *al-Kāfī*, 2:370, no. 2.
38 Kulaynī, *al-Kāfī*, 1: no. 4.
39 Kulaynī, *al-Kāfī*, 2:255.
40 Mīrzā Husayn Nūrī, *Mustadrak al-wasāʾil* (Beirut: Muʾassasat Āl al-Bayt li-Iḥyāʾ al-Turāth, 1987), 18:419.

whose character is earth-like are soft and sandy. They do not benefit from intense heat, rather only a certain amount of severity and austerity is beneficial. Those whose nature is water-like flee from the austerity of their teachers. Those whose nature is like wind and oil are consumed by fire and their personality becomes effaced by severity.[41]

Both disciples and *shaykhs* have an individual relationship to the divine names, some being governed by the names of majesty and others by the names of beauty, while some combine both. Furthermore, disciples each have an orientation to the *shaykh*, like the parts of a single tree. Some are like the trunk, while others are the branches, leaves, fruits, and so on. Since training disciples is a complex and subtle affair that deals with all aspects of the soul's development and the path to God, the true *shaykh*—like a prophet—is God's vicegerent. If it were possible to find God without the divine teacher (*ʿālim rabbānī*), Jesus would not have said to his disciple, "I am the way, the truth, and the life. No one comes to the Father except through me" (John 14:6).

During trials and hardship, one needs to take recourse in the *shaykh*. However, God's trial may come through the *shaykh* himself, and this is the most difficult type of trial. For example, the wayfarer may see something unbecoming of the *shaykh*, so his faith in him is tested. But as before, only the *shaykh* can remove doubts by distinguishing the divine and the human aspects of the *shaykh*. It may be that the perceived action is disapproved only in the disciple's eyes but not in God's. The disciple judges the act from his limited knowledge and intellect, but God knows its reality which is hidden from the disciple; and herein lies the test. In the Quran, Moses desired to learn from Khiḍr a certain type of hidden knowledge, Moses said to him, "May I follow you, so that you teach me some of the right guidance you have been taught?" In Sufi lore, Khiḍr is considered the consummate *shaykh* who demands from his disciple (Moses) total submission with respect to the Unseen, namely, the knowledge of right guidance, but one that opposes convention. Thus, he says, "You will not be able to bear patiently with me" (Q 18:67). Had Moses maintained the etiquettes of discipleship, he would not have been dismissed as he was when Khiḍr exclaims, "This is the parting of our ways. I will explain to you what you could not bear patiently" (Q 18:78).

Finally, God tested not only for man but also the angels, as Imam ʿAlī says,

> If God wanted to create Adam from a light whose brilliance would dazzle the eyes, whose beauty would amaze the intellects and whose fragrance would take one's breath away, He could have done so. And, if He had done so, all would have bowed before him in humility and the trial of the angels would have been lighter. But God, the Glorified, tests His creatures by means of things the real nature of which they do not know, to distinguish them through the trial, remove arrogance and to keep them away from vanity.[42]

41 Almajid, *The Law of Correspondence*, trans. Mukhtar H. Ali (London: Sage Press, 2021), 143.
42 Raḍī, *Nahj al-balāgha*, sermon 192.

Conclusion

The path to God is through knowledge and discipline of the soul. Although we identified seven distinct stations, it should be kept in mind that the human being is a single reality that manifests on various planes of existence, body, soul, heart, intellect, and spirit. There is a dynamic flow between the aspects of the soul, as there is between states and stations. Even if one reaches the tranquil soul—the first station of human perfection—it is possible to regress to previous stations or sink to the lowest station. Pure inerrancy belongs to God alone. Even prophets committed errors, if not sins, like our father Adam. The Quran says, "We had taken an oath earlier from Adam, but he forgot; he did not have resolve. . . . Adam disobeyed his Lord and erred" (Q 2:121). God created Adam with His "two hands" (Q 38:75), "taught Adam all the names" (Q 2:31), placed him on the earth as a vicegerent, and made him the proverbial *ka'ba* of angelic prostration; yet when God when tested him, he failed. Testing is God's way (*sunna*), as nothing is attained in this world or the next without discipline, study, and examination. Thus, He says, "Do people think that they will be left to say, 'We believe' and not be tested? We tested those before them, so that God will know for certain the truthful from the liars" (Q 29:3–4).

References

Abū Dāwūd. *Sunan*. Beirut: Dār al-Risāla al-ʿĀlamiyya, 2009.
al-ʿAjlūnī. *Kashf al-khafāʾ*. Beirut: Dār Iḥyāʾ al-Turāth al-ʿArabī, 1968.
ʿAlī b. Husayn (Zayn al-ʿĀbidīn). *The Psalms of Islam*. Translated by William Chittick. London: Muhammadi Trust, 1988.
al-Kulaynī. *al-Kāfī*. Tehran: Dār al-Uswa, 1997.
Almajid, Akram. *The Law of Correspondence*. Translated by Mukhtar H. Ali. London: Sage Press, 2021.
Almajid, Akram. *The New Creation*. Translated by Mukhtar H. Ali. London: Sage Press, 2022.
al-Nasāʾī. *Sunan*. Beirut: Dār al-Ḥaḍāra, 2015.
Āmidī, ʿAbd al-Wāḥid. *Ghurar al-ḥikam wa-durar al-kalim*. Tehran: Daftar-i Nashr-i Farhang-i Islāmī, 2000.
Āmulī, Ḥaydar. *Jāmiʿ al-asrār wa-manbaʿ al-anwār*. Edited by Henry Corbin and Osman Yahya. Beirut: Muʾassasat al-Taʾrīkh al-ʿArabī, 1969.
Ghazālī, Abū Ḥāmid al-. *Iḥyāʾ ʿulūm al-dīn*. Beirut: Dār al-Kutub al-ʿIlmiyya, 1986.
Huwayzī, ʿAbd ʿAlī b. Jumʿa. *Tafsīr nūr al-thaqalayn*. Beirut: Muʾassasat al-Tārīkh al-ʿArabī, 2001.
Ibn Abī'l-Ḥadīd. *Sharh Nahj al-balāgha*. Beirut: Muʾassasat al-Aʿlamī li'l-Maṭbūʿāt, 1995.
Ibn Bābawayh. *ʿIlal al-sharāʾiʿ*. Beirut: Dār al-Murtaḍā, 2006.
Ibn Bābawayh. *Kitāb al-Tawḥīd*. Beirut: Dār al-Maʿārif, 2008.
Ibn Bābawayh. *Maʿānī al-akhbār*. Beirut: Muʾassasat al-Tārīkh al-ʿArabī, 2009.
Kāshānī, Muḥsin Fayḍ. *al-Ḥaqāʾiq fī maḥāsin al-akhlāq*. Qum: Dār al-Kitāb al-Islāmī, 2002.
Majlisī, Muḥammad Bāqir. *Biḥār al-anwār*. Beirut: Dār Iḥyāʾ al-Turāth al-ʿArabī, 1983.
Makkī, Abū Ṭālib. *Qūt al-qulūb*. Beirut: Dār Kutub ʿIlmiyya, 1997.
Nūrī, Mīrzā Husayn. *Mustadrak al-wasāʾil*. Beirut: Muʾassasat Āl al-Bayt li-Iḥyāʾ al-Turāth, 1987.

Qayṣarī, Dāwūd al-. *Sharḥ Fuṣūṣ al-ḥikam*. Edited by Ḥasanzada Āmulī. Qum: Bustān-i Kitāb, 2002.
Qayṣarī, Dāwūd al-. *The Horizons of Being: The Metaphysics of Ibn al-ʿArabī in the Muqaddimat al-Qayṣarī*. Translated by Mukhtar H. Ali. Leiden: Brill, 2020.
al-Qushayrī. *al-Risāla al-Qushayriyya*. Cairo: Dār al-Kutub al-Ḥadītha, 2001.
Raḍī, al-Sharīf al-. *Nahj al-balāgha*. Edited by Subḥī al-Ṣāliḥ. Beirut: Dār Kutub al-Lubnānī, 2004.
Rayshahrī, Muḥammad. *Mīzān al-ḥikma*. Beirut: Dār Iḥyāʾ al-Turāth al-ʿArabī, 2001.

4 Necessitated Evil

An Islamic Neoplatonic Theodicy From the Ismaili Tradition

Khalil Andani

Introduction

The "problem of evil" presents as a universal dilemma touching at the heart of many monotheistic theologies. However, contemporary literature on God and the problem of evil disproportionately showcases Christian analytic theology both in terms of its formulation and potential solutions. Even the statement of the problem of evil smuggles in Christian presuppositions about God derived from analytic "perfect being" theology or premodern scholastic thought. A typical formulation of the logical problem proposes that: (1) God is omnipotent, omniscient, and omnibenevolent; (2) God is capable of eliminating evil (omnipotence); (3) God knows that evil exists in the world (omniscience); (4) God desires to eliminate all evil (omnibenevolence); (5) evil exists in the world; (6) it follows from these premises that God lacks either omnipotence, omniscience, or omnibenevolence; (7) therefore, God does not exist.[1]

Likewise, the spotlighted "solutions" to the problem of evil tend to be Christian theodicies or non-religious theodicies from the modern Euro-American philosophical tradition. The minimal token presence of non-Christian/non-Western voices merely fulfills a diversity quota. Such is the case in several notable publications like *The Problem of Evil: Selected Readings* edited by Peterson (no Muslim sources), *The Cambridge Companion to the Problem of Evil* edited by Meister and Moser (one essay about Islam), and *The Blackwell Companion to the Problem of Evil* edited by McBrayer and Howard-Snyder (one essay about Islam).[2] The token essays about Islamic theodicies in these volumes are highly selective in terms of what Islamic perspectives they feature. The few highlighted Muslim theodicies

1 Michael Tooley, "The Problem of Evil," in *Stanford Encyclopedia of Philosophy*, ed. Edward N. Zalta, https://plato.stanford.edu/archives/win2021/entries/evil/ (last accessed March 1, 2021).

2 Michael Peterson (ed.), *The Problem of Evil: Selected Readings* (Notre Dame: University of Notre Dame Press, 2017); Chad Meister and Paul K. Moser (eds.), *The Cambridge Companion to the Problem of Evil* (New York: Cambridge University Press, 2017); Justin P. McBrayer and Daniel Howard-Snyder (eds.), *The Blackwell Companion to the Problem of Evil* (New York: Wiley Blackwell, 2013).

DOI: 10.4324/9781003371670-5

often tend to be Sunni theological perspectives such as Ashʿarī and Muʿtazilī *kalām*. This is even the case with Sherman Jackson's masterful monograph, *Islam and the Problem of Black Suffering*, which only considers Sunni Muslim theodicies from the *kalām* tradition with no engagement with other Islamic theodicies.[3]

The present essay remedies this deficit by presenting an Islamic philosophical theodicy rooted in Islamic Neoplatonism. The currents of Islamic thought that employ Neoplatonic concepts have been labelled "Neoplatonism" by Western scholars. But the Muslim Neoplatonists designated their own discourse as *falsafa* and *ḥikma*, which may be found within a variety of Muslim intellectual traditions across sectarian lines. The theodicy offered in this essay is primarily rooted in Ismaili Muslim Neoplatonic metaphysics and the teachings of the contemporary Ismaili Imamate; but it could easily be grounded in the Peripatetic, Avicennan, Akbarian Sufi, or Ṣadrian traditions of Islamic thought. The essay demonstrates how Islamic Neoplatonism offers unique solutions to the so-called problem of evil that are not available to most contemporary theodicies stemming from analytic theology. The core elements of the Islamic Neoplatonic theodicy on offer in this essay are as follows:

1. God is absolutely simple and lacking in all internal boundaries, so all the divine attributes are negations of contingency, dependency, and limitation as opposed to real-distinct omni-properties or entitative attributes;
2. The verbal affirmation of God's "omnipotence," "omnibenevolence," and "omniscience" means that God is unrestricted and that He is the originator of all power, goodness, knowledge, and other great-making properties manifest in created contingent existence;
3. God, by virtue of His absolute simplicity and lack of constraints, necessarily originates a single, eternal, perfect, and "maximally excellent" originated being that is bereft of all evil as His direct effect: this first and perfect creation of God is called the First Intellect in Ismaili philosophy;
4. The First Intellect, as a created being that ontologically depends on God, is ontologically constrained and cannot produce a wholly perfect creation of its own; it only produces an effect that partakes in both perfection and imperfection; this effect is called the Universal Soul;
5. Unlike the First Intellect, the Universal Soul is in a state of potential perfection perpetually seeking actual perfection; the imperfect ontological status of the Universal Soul motivates it to engage in a goal-directed activity that produces the Cosmos and individual souls;
6. The Cosmos, including the world of humanity, is an expression of both perfection and imperfection; it is the manifestation of the Universal Soul's potential perfection in the process of seeking actualization; what appears as "evil" in the world is ontological privation, imperfection, deficiency, and disorder.

3 Sherman Jackson, *Islam and the Problem of Black Suffering* (New York: Oxford University Press, 2009).

7. Just as the imperfection or "evil" within the Universal Soul prompts it to seek out goodness through goal-directed efforts, the existence of evil can likewise motivate human souls—which are microcosmic parts of the Universal Soul—to strive for their own perfection through goal-directed action.
8. Individual souls can benefit through confronting internal and external evils *qua* imperfection by recognizing their inherent need to seek perfection and realizing their ontological dependence upon God and the perfections that emanate from Him. This recognition and realization, while prompted by the evil that befalls human souls, facilitates their goal-directed activity towards perfection.

I submit that this Islamic Neoplatonic theodicy offers a robust metaphysical and soteriological response to the problem of evil. This essay will proceed as follows. First, I will lay out the Islamic Neoplatonic theological and cosmological vision that forms the basis for my theodicy using Ismaili metaphysical texts. Second, I will apply the Islamic Neoplatonic model of reality to the problem of evil to expound my theodicy. My Islamic Neoplatonic theodicy comprises two components—a metaphysical or theological account of the "origins" of evil and a soteriological or teleological account of evil in terms of the "good" purposes it ultimately serves. In other words, the second component of my Islamic Neoplatonic theodicy is a soul-building theodicy that logically follows from my metaphysics. In laying out the metaphysics and proposed theodicy, I draw primarily on Ismaili Muslim philosophers including Abū Yaʿqūb al-Sijistānī (d. after 971), Ḥamīd al-Dīn al-Kirmānī (d. ca. 1020), Nāṣir-i Khusraw (d. ca. 1088), and Naṣīr al-Dīn al-Ṭūsī (d. 1274)—the last of whom was part of the Avicennan tradition as well.

Constructing an Islamic Neoplatonic Worldview from Ismaili Thought

The most historically dominant and enduring form of Ismaili philosophical theology was Neoplatonic metaphysics, theology, and cosmology. Ismaili theology shared this Neoplatonic orientation with many other important Islamic schools of thought, including the Peripatetic tradition, the tradition of Ibn ʿArabī (d. 1240) and his interpreters, and Twelver philosophical discourse associated with Mīr Dāmād (d. 1631) and Mullā Ṣadrā (d. 1640). While there are important differences among the many Muslim Neoplatonic schools—such as how to properly talk about God, the number of celestial intellects/souls, etc., these differences need not concern us. The following quotation reported from the hereditary Ismaili Imam ʿAbd al-Salām (ca. 15th century) summarizes the historical Ismaili account of the Neoplatonic worldview:

> The first thing that the Exalted God brought forth was the Command. As a result of the Command, the Universal Intellect was produced. The Universal Soul was produced as a result of the Universal Intellect and the hyle, or prime

> matter, the heavens, the four natures, minerals, plants and animals were produced as a result of the Universal Soul. In reality, the purpose of creating these substances is humankind's existence.[4]

Islamic Neoplatonic vocabulary continues to be evoked in the writings, speeches, and *farmāns* of the recent Ismaili Imams, Aga Khan III and Aga Khan IV.[5] The contemporary Ismaili Imams have also explicitly endorsed the historic Ismaili Neoplatonic corpus as a normative source of theological truth for contemporary Ismaili communities (see *farmāns* of Aga Khan IV in Karachi 2000 and Lisbon 2018).[6] Given my own positionality as a constructive thinker within the Ismaili tradition, I find it most appropriate to ground my Islamic theodicy in the worldview of Islamic Neoplatonism as this vision appears in Ismaili philosophy. In this section, I will offer some constructive arguments to support key premises of the Ismaili form of Islamic Neoplatonism.

The core principle of all Islamic Neoplatonic metaphysics is the absolute unity and unicity of God known as *tawḥīd*. All Islamic philosophers, whether Ismaili or non-Ismaili, agree that God is the absolutely independent, self-sufficient, unconditioned, necessary being (*wājib al-wujūd*) who creates and sustains all dependent realities, which are His creation. As the pure and unconditioned reality, God is absolutely simple—meaning that there no parts, distinctions, or ontological pluralities within God. The existence of any real parts, distinct aspects, or plurality within God logically entails the negation of God alone as an absolutely independent and self-sufficient reality.

This conclusion is obtained by the following argument (see Figure 4.1): to posit any real distinction within God entails an ontological difference between God's Essence (His Self or essential reality) and any posited real-distinct divine attribute or entitative property. In effect, this implies that each divine attribute is not identical to God's Essence and not identical to other divine attributes; even though these real-distinct attributes are said to be metaphysically connected to and inseparable from God's Essence and each other. This metaphysics of the Divine Essence vis-à-vis any real-distinct divine attribute leads to one of four metaphysical models of God:

1. God's Essence depends upon the collection of real-distinct divine attributes for its existence, and each real-distinct attribute is an uncaused independent reality: this entails that God's Essence is a contingent being who depends on His

4 Imam ʿAbd al-Salām, quoted in Shafique N. Virani, "The Right Path: A Post-Mongol Ismaili Treatise," *Iranian Studies* 43, no. 2 (2010): 206.

5 Khalil Andani, "Metaphysics of Muhammad: The Nur Muhammad from Imam Ja ʿfar al-Sadiq (d. 148/765) to Nasir al-Din al-Tusi (d. 672/1274)," *Journal of Sufi Studies* 8, no. 2 (2019): 99–175, 173–174.

6 The *farmāns* of the present Ismaili Imam are orally delivered to Ismaili-only audiences and then transcribed into *farmāns* books that are available in Ismaili prayer-houses called *Jamatkhanas*. While some *farmāns* have been published and distributed to the Ismaili community at large, other *farmāns* are only available in *Jamatkhanas* or in private collections of individual Ismailis. I am here referring to the Aga Khan's *farmāns* from a private unpublished collection.

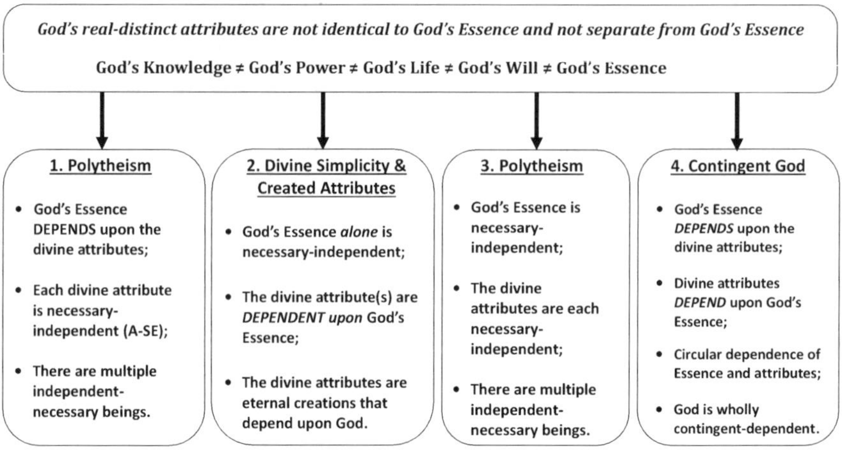

Figure 4.1 If God has real/entitative attributes distinct from His Essence

real-distinct attribute(s), which are themselves uncaused necessary beings possessing aseity—thereby positing a plurality of independent necessary beings or "gods" that constitute God's nature, amounting to a nested polytheism or ontological pluralism;

2. God's real-distinct attribute(s) are ontologically dependent upon God's Essence, which alone is the uncaused necessary being: this position actually entails Islamic Neoplatonic divine simplicity since only God's Essence is uncaused and independent and any so-called divine attributes turn out to be dependent contingent realities that lack aseity—which are properly called "creation;"
3. God's Essence and every real-distinct divine attribute(s) are all ontologically independent and uncaused realities: this also entails a plurality of independent necessary beings or "gods," which amounts to polytheism or ontological pluralism;
4. God's Essence and every real-distinct divine attribute(s) are all ontologically dependent on each other in a circular dependency structure (A depends upon B depends upon C depends upon A): this entails that either one of God's Essence and/or real-distinct attributes is uncaused and independent—since the law of transitivity means one member of the circular chain will depend upon itself; or the entire circular dependency structure consisting of God's Essence and real-distinct attributes depends upon an external reality, entail that God is dependent upon something else, which is a denial of God.

Therefore, the only logical conclusion is that God does not contain or possess real-distinct entitative attributes (known in *kalām* theology as *ṣifāt maʿnawiyya*) such as power, knowledge, life, goodness, etc. where such attributes are mutually distinct and distinct from God's Essence. For the Islamic philosophers, the common predications about God found in the Quran and Sunna and religious language are interpreted analogically or equivocally to maintain divine simplicity. For example, to the predication "God is knowing" (*Allāhu ʿālimun*) is commonly taken to mean that "God has knowledge" (*Allāhu lahu ʿilmun*), where knowledge (*ʿilm*) is a real entitative attribute distinct from and not numerically identical to God's Essence.[7] However, the Islamic philosophers understand "God is knowing" to properly mean that "God is the reality (*ḥaqīqa*) of knowledge" (post-classical Avicennan thought) or that "God is the originator of all knowledge, which He grants to the creaturely bearers of knowledge" (Ismaili thought). Therefore, God in His Essence neither possesses the entitative attribute of knowledge nor is He qualified by ignorance in the sense of lacking an entitative attribute that He could or should possess.[8] The same hermeneutic is applied to every positive divine predication—such as God's life, power, compassion, forgiveness, hearing, seeing, etc. including the so-called omni-properties asserted in perfect being theism. Accordingly, all Islamic philosophers including the Ismailis uphold strong divine simplicity—that God transcends multiplicity, parts, distinctions, entitative attributes, and limits. It necessarily follows from this fact that there is only one God *qua* absolutely simple unconditioned reality; the existence of two Gods *qua* necessary beings logically entails real distinctions within each necessary being, and this means that each God would be composed of real attributes, accidents, or parts in order to be differentiated from the other "gods." The negation of parts from God entails that God is absolutely single, immutable, eternally timeless, incorporeal, and incomparable to any created dependent reality.

The next metaphysical issue is the concept of creation. All monotheists maintain that God is the creator of all things, but this belief can be understood in many ways. In Islamic Neoplatonic philosophy, God's creation does not refer to a discrete temporal divine action that occurs in a specific moment. But rather, creation according to the Islamic philosophers is an eternal activity by which God eternally and continuously bestows existence to contingent dependent realities. Aga Khan III, the late Imam of the Ismailis, explains the meaning of creation as follows:

> The creation according to Islam is not a unique act in a given time but a perpetual and constant event; and God supports and sustains all existence at every moment by His will and His thought. Outside His will, outside His thought, all is nothing, even the things which seem to us absolutely

7 On this view, see Richard M. Frank, *Beings and Their Attributes* (Albany: SUNY Press, 1978), 15–16.

8 Nicholas Heer, "Al-Abharī and al-Maybudī on God's Existence: A Translation of a Part of al-Maybudī's Commentary on al-Abharī's *Hidāyat al-Ḥikma*," https://digital.lib.washington.edu/researchworks/bitstream/handle/1773/4887/abhari-sep.pdf?sequence=1&isAllowed=y (last accessed February 22, 2022); ʿAbd al-Karīm al-Shahrastānī, *Struggling with the Philosopher*, ed. and trans. Wilferd Madelung and Toby Mayer (London: I. B. Tauris in association with The Institute of Ismaili Studies, 2001), 43–48. Al-Maybudī equates the formula of identifying God's attributes with His Essence [*falsafa* articulation] and denying the existence of the attributes while affirming their effects [Ismaili articulation].

self-evident such as space and time. Allāh alone wishes: the Universe exists; and all manifestations are as a witness of the Divine will.[9]

In other words, for the Islamic philosophers of the Neoplatonic tradition, God is an eternal and continuous creator. Creation is an eternal divine action in which God perpetually bestows existence to everything other than Him. The premodern Ismailis such as al-Sijistānī, al-Kirmānī, Khusraw, and Ṭūsī designated God's eternal creative act as God's word (*kalimat Allāh*) or God's command (*amr Allāḥ*) based on the Quranic teaching that God creates by simply saying "Be."[10] Given that creation is an eternal dependency relation between created being and God, Islamic philosophers conceive the process of creation as a hierarchical manifestation of dependent realities as opposed to a temporal cosmogonic process. In this context, the Muslim Neoplatonists speak of the "first creation" (*al-mubdaʿ al-awwal*) of God as a dependent reality that receives existence directly from God by virtue of God's singular eternal act of origination. The first creation logically and ontologically precedes other dependent creatures which receive existence from God through various intermediaries. The technical term for God's first creation is the First Intellect or Universal Intellect. The First Intellect is a unified, incorporeal, eternal, and intellectual substance that perpetually contemplates the intelligible essences or forms of all things—such as universals, necessary truths, etc.

The Islamic philosophers maintain that there can be only one First Intellect, i.e., one direct creation of God, and that this First Intellect is an eternal and perfect creation. This is known as the "Rule of One." The logical basis for this claim is that only a single divine act or effect can proceed from an absolutely simple and unitary reality (God). If God directly originates a plurality of effects, i.e., two effects, then the existence of those two effects entails the real existence of two aspects within God—where God produces each effect in virtue of a different aspect of Himself. However, since God is absolutely simple without multiple aspects, He only produces a single effect by virtue of His pure singularity. Among the earliest Islamic philosophers to argue this position was the Ismaili thinker al-Kirmānī:

> It is impossible that two different things to be brought into existence except from two things that necessitate the existence of both. Whatever combines together two things is itself multiple and whatever is multiple is preceded [in existence] and has something that is prior to it. Since He [God], may He be praised, transcends being multiple or being conjoined to any attribute, the existence of two different things from Him is impossible; and since the

9 Sir Sultan Muhammad Shah Aga Khan III, *Memoirs of the Aga Khan,* quoted in Khalil Andani, "Evolving Creation: An Ismaili Muslim Interpretation of Evolution," *Zygon* 57, no. 2 (2022): 448.

10 Paul E. Walker, *The Wellsprings of Wisdom: A Study of Abū Yaʿqūb al-Sijistānī's Kitāb al-Yanābīʿ Including a Complete English Translation with Commentary and Notes on the Arabic Text* (Salt Lake City: University of Utah Press, 1994), 50–58, 100–109.

existence of two different things from Him is impossible, it follows that what comes into existence from Him is singular [*wāḥidan*].[11]

Ibn Sīnā argues for the same conclusion as follows: if God produces two effects—creation A and creation B—by virtue of His singularity, it follows that God produces A and not-A by virtue of the same aspect of Himself. However, by the inference of equipollence, this entails that God produces A and does not produce A in one and the same respect—a clear contradiction. Therefore, God only produces one direct creation—the First Intellect.[12]

A third argument for this conclusion—that God only produces one effect—is to analyze the logical entailment of the claim that God may directly produce more than one effect. Let us suppose that God directly originates two effects. Even if this were the case, it would still be *possible* for God to originate either (a) one direct effect, or (b) two direct effects. But this raises the question as to what it is about God that determines the actualization of one of these two possibilities over the other. Since God is absolutely simple and does not acquire new intentions or attributes at any time, it would follow that outcomes (a) and (b) cannot *both* be possible. One of them would be impossible, and the other would be necessary. If we assume that (a) God directly producing a single effect is necessary, then our argument for the Rule of One is confirmed. If, on the other hand, we assume that (b) is necessary—that God necessarily produces two direct effects—it would still require that (a) God producing one direct effect is possible; one of the preconditions for God actually originating two direct effects is God *possibly* originating one direct effect—because *two* direct effects is just the doubling of *one* direct effect. Therefore, if one supposes that (b) is necessary, it logically follows that both (a) and (b) are possible for God—but this is a contradiction. The absolute simplicity of God precludes both (a) and (b) being possible, and therefore, (b) must be impossible. If (b) is impossible, then (a) God directly originating one effect is necessary.

The simplicity of God further entails that God's creation of the First Intellect could not be any other way and is modally necessary (the same outcome in all possible worlds). The creation of the First Intellect is an act of Divine Will. However, contrary to many analytic Christian theologians, God's Will is not a libertarian choice where God contingently selects one possible world among others and is free to do otherwise. Rather, God's creation of the First Intellect is an act of God's Will, and God's Will is determined by God's Essence to be pure goodness and the apex of wisdom. God's unalterable will to create the First Intellect is still "free" because His act of willing the First Intellect is neither determined, influenced, or compelled by anything external to His Essence—unlike creaturely choices and actions.

11 Ḥamīd al-Dīn al-Kirmānī, *Rāḥat al-ʿaql*, ed. Musṭafā Ghālib (Beirut: Dār al-Andalūs, 1983), 201.

12 On this argument, which is known as "Rule of One," see Wahid M. Amin, "From the One, Only One Proceeds," *Oriens* 48, no. 1–2 (2020): 123–155; Davlat Dadikhuda, "Rule of the One: Avicenna, Bahmanyār, and al-Rāzī on the Argument from the *Mubāḥathāt*," *Nazariyat* 6, no. 2 (2020): 69–97. Thanks to Davlat Dadikhuda for clarifying the argument for me.

Everything that exists is due to God's Will, and God's freedom of the will is based on the principle that *God only does what He wills, and God refrains from what He does not will.* Al-Sijistānī expounds the nature of God's Will along these very lines:

> The Creator's Will is absolutely undivided (*ghayr munqasim*). Indeed, His Will is what manifests His wisdom and what that wisdom perfects until it attains to the uppermost limit of its intended telos. . . . Whoever describes the Will of God, the Exalted, as being similar to this [creaturely] will that deliberates (*mutaṣarrifa*) among opposing alternatives has ascribed incapacity and deficiency to the Creator, may He be exalted from that. . . . The Will of the Creator, may He be glorified and exalted, is not temporal and is neither due to need, habit, favor, or anger. But rather, His Will is pure goodness (*al-jūd al-maḥḍ*) with the manifestation of wisdom. Thus, He does not decide among opposing alternatives. But rather [His Will] is united with what He wills. We do not witness anyone who possesses a perfect will with a single position.[13]

There are numerous differences between God's Will and human will. Unlike human will—which is subject to various accidents like need, habit, emotion, space, and time—the Will of God is eternal and transcends these limits. While human will deliberates on a set of possible alternatives and can only choose one option, the Will of God does not select from a pool of choices: if God were a libertarian agent who picks one choice from several options, this would limit God to selecting one contingent outcome and necessarily forfeiting His other options. However, God's Will transcends such creaturely limits; it necessarily follows that God's Will is essentially undivided and singularly directed towards pure goodness and utmost wisdom; therefore, God's Will to create the First Intellect cannot have been otherwise and is modally necessary. Furthermore, the pre-existence of many possible worlds within God's Essence, such that He deliberatively selects one of them in a libertarian manner, introduces contingency and plurality within God and thereby violates God's absolute oneness.[14] Libertarian choices amount to brute contingency—because libertarian choices are not determined by anything in the agent and, therefore, amount to self-caused contingencies. Since both implications are logically impossible, it logically follows that God's creation of the First Intellect is a necessary divine action entailed by God's Essence.

The First Intellect as God's necessary and direct creation must be the most perfect contingent being in terms of completeness and actuality—a fact that will prove fruitful to resolving the problem of evil. The Ismaili philosophers al-Sijistānī and al-Kirmānī each offered arguments for the absolute perfection of the First Intellect as God's first creation. According to al-Sijistānī, God's creative action—known as

13 al-Sijistānī, *The Book of the Keys to the Kingdom*, ed. Ismail K. Poonawala (Tunis: Dār al-Gharb al-Islāmī, 2011), 266–267.

14 Athīr al-Dīn al-Abharī, *Hidāyat al-ḥikma* (Karachi: Maktab al-Madīna, 2009), 107–108.

His Will (*mashīʾa*), Command (*amr*), Origination (*ibdāʿ*)—is identical to God's goodness (*jūd al-bārī*), which is "Perfect Goodness" (*al-jūd al-tāmm*). This necessarily follows from the fact that God Himself is the "Perfectly Generous" (*al-jawād al-tamām*), and there cannot be any deficiency (*naqṣ*) or imperfection in what flows from the Perfectly Generous. Perfect Goodness, as God's act of creation, necessarily brings forth a perfect substance (*jawhar*) or an essence (*dhāt*) that is inclusive of all perfections and actualizes them to the maximal degree. As al-Sijistānī writes:

> The First Creation (*al-khalq al-awwal*) appeared (*ẓahara*) from Perfect Goodness (*al-jūd al-tāmm*) as something perfectly encompassing the entirety of hierarchically differentiated things. Had there been anything hidden from [its] knowledge of the hierarchically differentiated things and its encompassing them, then it would not be perfect; and if its perception of things is not from the aspect of hierarchical differentiation, then it does not deserve to be called "Intellect;" and if deserving this name were removed from it, its manifestation would be contrary to the Perfect Goodness from the Perfectly Generous (*al-jawād al-tamām*).[15]

In al-Sijistānī's formulation, God's eternal act of Will or Origination ("Perfect Goodness") produces a perfect essence and these two are eternally and ontologically united as one being—in the manner of existence and essence—to constitute the "Perfect Creation" (*al-khalq al-tāmm*) known as the First Intellect: "When the True Originator originated the first [being], He originated it perfect and without defect. He did not leave anything out of it."[16] Likewise, al-Kirmānī argues that the whatever comes into existence directly from God must be perfect without requiring anything else for its self-actualization. If God does not directly originate the First Intellect as a perfect being bearing all attributes of perfection, the First Intellect would be deficient in some respect. However, this would still require the prior existence of a creation that *is* truly perfect—since what is imperfect is posterior in existence to what is perfect.[17] He further argues that if the First Intellect were deficient, it would entail the existence of some other entity with God that caused Him to originate an imperfect deficient creation instead of a perfect creation.[18] Stated another way, if God does not create the First Intellect as the most perfect creation, then a true perfect creation would still be a possible creation that God *failed* to originate. Since God originates the first creation directly, His origination of an imperfect creation instead of a perfect creation entails that God is incapable of creating the perfect creation—because some limiting factor, external cause, or impediment has prevented God from originating a truly perfect creation; this entails the

15 al-Sijistānī, *Ithbāt al-nubuwwāt*, ed. Wilferd Madelung and Paul Walker (Tehran: Miras-e-Maktoob, 2016), 25.
16 Walker, *The Wellsprings of Wisdom*, 53.
17 Kirmānī, *Rāḥat al-ʿaql*, 181.
18 Kirmānī, *Rāḥat al-ʿaql*, 184–186.

impossible conclusion that God is both limited and internally complex—which violates His aseity and absolute unity. Therefore, the idea that God may create an imperfect creature is logically impossible, and it follows that the first creation of God is a wholly perfect and fully actualized creation.

Theologically speaking, the First Intellect possesses all great-making properties and perfections such as knowledge, power, life, consciousness, eternity, etc. as real internal attributes that are concomitants of its essence. The only perfection that the First Intellect lacks is aseity, since the First Intellect's eternally depends upon God for its eternal existence. Al-Kirmānī accordingly explains that the ontological essence of the First Intellect is perfect life (*al-ḥayāt*) from which the other attributes of perfection necessarily flow as its concomitant perfections: "The substance of this Origination is the substance of life and its essence is the essence of life. Life is the pre-eminent over the rest of these attributes. . . . It [First Intellect] is unified from the standpoint of its being an origination [of God] and a single thing and it is multiple from the standpoint of the attributes existing within it. Life is the substrate for whatever befits it on account of its degrees in what exists with respect to its perfections."[19]

The First Intellect is eternally in a state of blissful self-contemplation through which it recognizes God as its originator and attests to God's absolute oneness.[20] The First Intellect's essential perfection, self-contemplation, and recognition of God results in the overflow or emanation of existence and the production of its own effect. This emanated effect, which the First Intellect produces by the necessity of its own perfect nature, is called the Universal Soul—which is a spiritual and intellectual substance like the First Intellect. Insofar as the Universal Soul is an effect of the First Intellect, it is not identical to it and therefore lacks the essential perfections and actuality of the First Intellect.[21] The Universal Soul, having recognized its imperfection in comparison to its own cause, essentially desires to become perfect like the First Intellect. As a result, the Universal Soul receives as much emanation from the First Intellect as possible and then engages in goal-directed activity or teleological motion: it emanates Prime Matter and Form (including individual souls) and thereby produces the material spatio-temporal Cosmos. Time and space are the result of the Universal Soul's creative activity, which manifests the actualization of its potencies through the assistance of the First Intellect. The Universal Soul creates and regulates the Cosmos for the express purpose of actualizing its own latent perfection:

> Similarly, the [Universal] Soul derives benefit and sustenance from the Intellect and strives to attain perfection. The Soul is the constructor of the corporeal world [*khudāwand-i tarkīb-i jismānī*], and it is the Soul which

19 Kirmānī, *Rāḥat al-ʿaql*, 190–191.

20 Nāṣir-i Khusraw, *Six Chapters or Shish Faṣl*, ed. and trans. Wladmir Ivanow (Leiden: E. J. Brill for the Ismaili Society, 1949), 44.

21 Khusraw, *Six Chapters*, 44, 47–49.

> started the movement of this world. . . . The object of its producing this world was to produce souls, in order that in them the Soul itself would become perfect, and ultimately attain the position. of the Intellect.[22]

The soteriology of the Islamic Neoplatonic model is one where individual souls (as emanations and substantial parts of the Universal Soul) may realize and actualize perfection through attaining gnosis and perfecting their virtues. The perfected human soul is a mirror-like receptable for the emanations of perfect that flow from the First Intellect through the Universal Soul. Thus, the perfect human soul is an image of the First Intellect within the constraints of its own ontological plane.

Constructing an Islamic Neoplatonic Theodicy

Having laid the metaphysical groundwork of Islamic Neoplatonism from an Ismaili perspective, we are now in a position to construct an Islamic theodicy in response to the problem of evil. But is such a theodicy even possible? Evan Fales has presented an argument against the very possibility of theodicy. His argument runs as follows:[23]

1. There is a best possible world (or class of them).
2. This world is not such a world.
3. God would create only best possible worlds.
4. Therefore, God does not exist.

According to Fales, the "best possible world" that God can and must create is what he calls a "Perfect Creature." A Perfect Creature is a created being that has all the great-making properties of God as many theists ordinarily conceive Him, with the except of aseity. As Fales puts it, such a Perfect Creation would possess "perfect goodness, eternality or sempiternality and, perhaps, lack of any potentiality."[24] The Perfect Creature has the "maxima of creaturely power, knowledge, goodness;" it would be all-knowing and has power over everything other than God.[25] The only attribute that the Perfect Creature lacks is aseity, since it is created and sustained in existence by God. The crux of Fales' argument is that no such Perfect Creature exists because it is obvious that our physical world is imperfect; and that God would never fail to create the Perfect Creature. Therefore, he reasons, God does not exist. In his own words: "God—the God of theism—would in any case not have

22 Khusraw, *Six Chapters*, 49. I have modified the translation.

23 Evan Fales, "Theodicy in a Vale of Tears," in *Blackwell Companion to the Problem of Evil*, ed. Justin P. McBrayer and Daniel Howard-Snyder (New York: Wiley Blackwell, 2013), 349–362.

24 Fales, "Theodicy in a Vale of Tears," 358.

25 Fales, "Theodicy in a Vale of Tears," 360.

created a world such as ours, because it would have been possible for Him to create the very best, a PC world."[26]

Unlike many Christian and Islamic theological worldviews, the Ismaili Neoplatonic model can overcome Fales' challenge head-on. This is because Fales' anti-theodicy argument presupposes a generic kind of Christian theism where God directly creates the physical Cosmos without any intermediaries; he does not test his argument against non-Christian theistic worldviews. But the Islamic Neoplatonic paradigm rejects this binary theo-cosmology where God creates and acts directly upon the physical world without intermediary incorporeal causes. As shown earlier, Ismaili philosophers affirm that God necessarily and directly creates *only* a perfect creation or perfect world—this being the First Intellect. Therefore, the "Perfect Creature" that Fales expects a true God to create—a creature that is maximally good, powerful, knowing, eternal, and actual—directly maps on to the First Intellect as conceived by Ismaili philosophers. As al-Sijistānī and al-Kirmānī explain, the First Intellect is necessarily essentially perfect and contains all of the perfections or "goods" that most non-Neoplatonic theists ascribe to God. In the words of al-Kirmānī, the First Intellect is "entirely living, entirely powerful, entirely knowing, entirely eternal, entirely all-encompassing, entirely perfect, complete, and singular. It is the first existent, the real, and the originated being. So it is the first origination with respect to existence and [God's] will. . . . It is a singular essence to which these attributes are connected—some of which are due to its essence and some of which are due to its relationships with other things."[27] I would suggest that Ismaili Neoplatonic philosophy overcomes the first stage of Fales' theodicy challenge: God has created the Perfect Creature and the best possible world—this is the First Intellect. The second part of Fales' challenge requests an explanation for why—in addition to the Perfect Creature—there are also imperfect creatures in existence: "What is at stake here is whether God has sufficient reason to create other, less perfect worlds, *in addition to* His creation of (one or more) PCs. I believe not."[28] The remainder of this chapter addresses this issue by way of constructing an Islamic Neoplatonic theodicy.

An appropriate place to begin constructing an Islamic theodicy is to define the "good" within the Ismaili Neoplatonic framework. While it is common to hear that "God is good," strictly speaking, God does not possess "goodness" as an attribute; if this were the case, then God would have to conform to some external standard of goodness external to His Essence. In the Islamic Neoplatonic system, one may either identify "goodness" with God in the manner of Ibn Sīnā—such that God's Essence *is* goodness itself—or identify "goodness" with the First Intellect as the

26 Fales, "Theodicy in a Vale of Tears," 362.

27 Kirmānī, *Rāḥat al-ʿaql*, 189.

28 Fales, "Theodicy in a Vale of Tears," 361.

perfect creation of God. Naṣīr al-Dīn al-Ṭūsī and the Ismailis generally identify goodness and perfection with the essence of the First Intellect:

> It is clear that goodness is a concomitant of perfection and that perfection is a concomitant of goodness, and that evil is a concomitant of deficiency and deficiency is a concomitant of evil. Thus, absolute goodness lies where one finds absolute perfection, and pure evil lies where one finds absolute deficiency. So, wherever good is intermixed with evil, perfection and deficiency also are intermingled. For example, since the First Intellect is in essence superior to all existent things and more perfect in existence and higher in rank, absolute perfection belongs to it. Thus, wherever one finds it, there is absolute goodness.[29]

Ṭūsī defines goodness in terms of perfection and identifies the latter with the First Intellect. This follows from the prior argument showing that the First Intellect by logical necessity is the most perfect contingent being. This helps our theodicy directly meet the problem of evil: God directly creates a perfect creation that is perfectly good. God has eternally originated what philosophers call the "best possible world"—which is the First Intellect and all the perfections inhering within it. God does not create evil, nor does He create a rational creature capable of even doing evil. What, then, is evil? Evil according to Ṭūsī is imperfection and deficiency. Evil is the privation of goodness and has no positive ontological essence. He argues this by noting that the existence of any good or perfection like wealth or daylight requires a cause, while their privations like poverty or night do not require a cause: "Just as the absence of existence is non-existence, the absence of wealth is poverty and the absence of day is night, so the absence of good is evil."[30] Accordingly, the existence of any evil at any level of reality is at best a "partial evil;" there is no such thing as "absolute evil," which would be tantamount to sheer non-existence—and non-existence does not actually exist.[31]

If God does not actually create evil and only creates pure goodness, then whence evil? According to the Ismaili philosophers and other Muslim Neoplatonists, the existence of evil *qua* imperfection and deficiency comes from the Universal Soul (the second level of creation) and not the First Intellect (God's direct perfect creation): "And because the Universal Soul is inferior in essence, existence and rank to the First Intellect, and has one side turned towards perfection and another towards deficiency, in it perfection and deficiency are mingled."[32] The Universal Soul is the origin of "evil" only in the sense that it is relatively imperfect or deficient in

29 Naṣīr al-Dīn Ṭūsī, *The Paradise of Submission*, ed. and trans. Sayyid Jalal Badakhchani (London: I. B. Tauris in Association with The Institute of Ismaili Studies, 2005), 52.

30 Ṭūsī, *Paradise*, 53.

31 Ṭūsī, *Paradise*, 53.

32 Ṭūsī, *Paradise*, 52.

comparison to the absolute goodness of the First Intellect. At this point, one may ask: why must this be the case? Why can't the Universal Soul be totally perfect? The Universal Soul is the effect of the First Intellect, but it lacks the absolute perfection of the First Intellect. The First Intellect, being an effect of God that lacks aseity, does not possess the creative power to originate or sustain a perfect created being like itself; if the First Intellect had such power, it would be self-sufficient and identical to God. Accordingly, the "best possible world" that the First Intellect can produce is a creature that is potentially perfect but not actually perfect due to the existence of imperfection or deficiency within itself—this being the Universal Soul. Thus, evil is not a substance; it is an accident parasitic upon the existence of goodness: "Goodness emanates essentially from the Bestower of the good [*wāhib al-khayr*], whereas evil comes accidentally [*bi-ʿaraḍ*] along the way."[33] Thus, the existence of evil *qua* privation and imperfection is necessary because creation—even the most perfect creation—lacks the aseity and creative power of God. While God creates the First Intellect as the best possible world and perfect creation, the First Intellect produces the Universal Soul, a creation that is perfect in potentiality but imperfect in act, as the best possible world that it is capable of producing.

The Universal Soul's essential imperfection, which may be called evil, is the necessary condition for the Universal Soul's cosmogonic activities. The Soul's realization of its deficiency causes it to seek to remedy this defect or evil by directing itself towards the perfection and goodness of the First Intellect. In other words, the existence of relative evil serves as the sufficient reason why the Universal Soul desires perfection in the first place; one only desires what one does not yet have. Thus, the existence of relative evil, even at the cosmic level of the Universal Soul, plays an overall positive role in directing its bearer to desire goodness. The Universal Soul seeks out goodness and perfection by acting or moving—not physically but spiritually—towards its end-goal. In other words, the Universal Soul is perpetually moving from imperfection to perfection; the Soul's substance and activity is a teleology or a way of life. The teleological activity of the Universal Soul produces individual souls and constructs a Cosmos comprised of Prime Matter and the Form:

> Matter and form became necessary when the Universal Soul conceived the essence of the First Intellect and realised its perfection. From the realisation of the perfection of the Intellect, form, which comes from the category of perfection, came into existence. And when it [the Soul] conceived its own essence and realised its deficiency, matter, which comes from the category of deficiency, came into existence. These two conditions were inevitable for the Soul, because it has two aspects: one [pointed] towards unity, [i.e., the realm of the Intellect], and the other towards multiplicity.[34]

33 Ṭūsī, *Paradise*, 52.
34 Ṭūsī, *Paradise*, 22.

The individual souls and the Cosmos that the Universal Soul creates are reflections of the Universal Soul's ontological structure. Similar to the Universal Soul, the Cosmos manifests both perfection and imperfection, that is to say, both good and evil. The material dimension of the physical world issues from the Universal Soul's imperfection while the formal or qualitative dimension of the world expresses the Soul's perfections—which it receives from the First Intellect. In other words, the Universal Soul is unable to produce a fully perfect or purely good Cosmos; the most optimal world that the Soul can produce is a Cosmos containing perfections and imperfections.

> The action of the [Universal] Soul is of two kinds. One is perfect potentially but imperfect in realization, as in the case of the creation of the world which is potentially perfect, but only [gradually] comes into existence. . . . Therefore the action of the Soul in this world is only potentially perfect before its [final] realization. But in some other actions the Soul is perfect both potentially and actually, as in the case of the production of the souls of the Speaker Prophets, Founders and Imams who are human beings in reality by the forms of their own souls.[35]

This means that the imperfections of the Cosmos—which one would identify as natural and moral evil—are not the primary intention of the Universal Soul. Rather, they are the inevitable and necessitated byproducts of the Universal Soul's imperfect ontological status. The Universal Soul sustains and regulates the Cosmos in the most optimal manner possible for it. Therefore, the Universal Soul does not "intervene" in the world since it is doing its utmost best at any given time. Likewise, various evils in the world like natural disasters are not intentional actions of the Universal Soul:

> The Universal Soul lacks nothing she might want for the sphere to be at its utmost perfection and limit in its movements, and she arranges them however she wishes, determining according to what she learns from her own cause, which is the Intellect. . . . Soul has no need to change anything in their circumstances; nor is the compulsion that emerges in their movements and actions alien to the wishes of Universal Soul. . . . With respect to the occurrence of variances due to the motion of the sphere, as in the case of earthquakes, lightning, drought, epidemics, fire, flood, and the like, relating any one of these to a determination of the Soul at the time that it happens is extremely repugnant, since temporal determination at a specific time is a form of deficiency.[36]

In other words, the Universal Soul does not send down lighting or earthquakes to punish people. The Universal Soul is constantly receiving the best possible

35 Khusraw, *Six Chapters*, 52.
36 Walker, *The Wellsprings of Wisdom*, 74–75.

determination as guidance from the Intellect, which helps the Universal Soul guide all creatures towards their respective telos.

The foregoing discussion provided a metaphysical account of the existence of evil. This is summarized as follows: God only creates absolute goodness and perfection in the form of the First Intellect; the First Intellect produces an effect that is only potentially perfect and contains deficiency—this being the Universal Soul; the Universal Soul's ontological imperfection is the root of "evil" *qua* privation of goodness; the Universal Soul's internal "evil" prompts it to seek perfect goodness by engaging in goal-directed action—which is the production of the Cosmos; as a result, the Cosmos created by the Universal Soul manifests both perfection and imperfection. The Cosmos in its totality is the manifestation of imperfection in the process of actualizing perfection. The final part of our theodicy seeks to explain what positive role the existence of natural and moral evil *qua* imperfection plays in the Cosmos. In other words, this theodicy situates the existence of relative evil as part of the manifestation of a greater good.

As mentioned earlier, the Universal Soul creates the Cosmos in order to realize perfection by way of producing human souls that actualize spiritual perfections. The perfect human soul is one that is most receptive to the emanations of the Universal Intellect and reflections these benefits in the form of knowledge and virtue. In the view of Ṭūsī, the existence of evil *qua* deficiency helps the Universal Soul achieve its "good" end-goal in two ways. First, the existence of less perfect or deficient substances in the world serve as intermediaries and proximate causes for the manifestation of better substances.

> Divine wisdom has decreed that the things of this world that are precious and dear are derived from shabby things far removed from them in likeness. For example, gold and silver come from earth and stone, musk from the navel of the wild deer, amber from the excrement of aquatic beasts, honey from bees, sugar from cane, pearls from shells, silk from worms, linen from plants, and human beings from sperm. All spiritual and physical beings, from the First Intellect down to the Universal Soul, from all the spheres down to the elements, are means and intermediaries, for man to come into existence from non-existence.[37]

Thus, one reason why imperfection exists in the Cosmos is that the temporal order of manifestation is inverted in comparison to the spiritual world. In the spiritual world, perfection manifests first and imperfection appears after. But since the physical world is the reflection of the spiritual world within the mirror of Prime Matter, the order of manifestation is inverted such that the less perfect substances temporally precede the more perfect ones. Thus, things that

37 Ṭūsī, *Paradise*, 165.

are relatively imperfect or evil can be teleologically arranged towards a good purpose. As mentioned earlier, Ṭūsī affirms that evil is partial or relative and not total or absolute. For example, he explains that a housefire is a partial evil while the complete non-existence of fire is a total evil. Fire itself, in terms of its existence, is a good and only becomes evil accidently when actualized in the wrong circumstances. Therefore, the root of all partial evil is still goodness. Partial evil is really the result of a disorder—when things that are otherwise good are disordered or imbalanced.

A second reason why the existence of evil *qua* imperfection facilitates a greater good is that the experience of evil in its various forms may help awaken and prompt human souls to seek out goodness and perfection. This is a microcosmic recapitulation of what eternally happens in the Universal Soul. Just as the Universal Soul's recognition of its own imperfection or "evil" led to it being desirous of perfect goodness, the same may occur within individual human souls. Ṭūsī explains how human beings' experience and endurance of misfortunes and calamities facilitates their purification from certain vices of the soul:

> All these calamities, misfortunes, disasters and mishaps, if seen from the angle of reality, are but forms of God's all-embracing mercy, so that people in this world will not be overtaken with hubris, nor become afflicted with pride by the ridiculous vanities and garish ornaments of the deceitful devil in this perishable abode. It is by such [calamities] that arrogance, the spirit of rebellion, pride, sin and self-forgetfulness do not gain mastery over them, and it is through the descent [of such misfortunes] that they do not turn away from God Almighty, thus falling into the infernal abyss of satanic passions and desires. . . . And if life's vicissitudes were not there to polish the soul—according to the saying, "God be praised who has made misfortune to be the polisher of the free-born"—no intelligence of the Resurrection and the Hereafter [*ʿaql-i qiyāmatī-yi ākhiratī*] would ever evolve from potentiality to actuality.[38]

The human experience of moral and natural evil helps with "soul building"—the actualization of the human soul's capacities and perfections. In a sense, since all evil is partial and relative, one could say that the existence of certain evils—like suffering, loss of wealth, loss of status, grief, etc.—may in the long run end up warding off greater evils from the human soul such as hubris, pride, vanity, etc. In other words, the relative evils that befall a human being may serve to "polish" his or her soul and cleanse it of certain psycho-spiritual impurities. In this context, Ṭūsī further explains that the human being is best served by maintaining patience

38 Ṭūsī, *Paradise*, 166.

in the face of trials and calamities since such an orientation will ultimately benefit his soul:

> One of the extraordinary aspects of man's patience before adversity and his endurance of misfortune is that the greater his misfortune and the more hurtful the calamity which afflict him, the stronger becomes his faith in God Almighty and his certainty that therein lies his salvation in both worlds. The substance of his soul melts in the crucible of tribulation, so that all its impurities and deficiencies disappear, all his dross is consumed away in the fire, and he is left like refined and purified gold.[39]

These words of Ṭūsī regarding how natural calamities and sufferings can purify the human soul are further echoed in more recent statements of the Ismaili Imams. Aga Khan III made the following *farmān* to the Ismaili community in the prior century:

> The Imam will not attempt to stop the natural and fate- related difficulties and sufferings coming upon man. If the Imam does so, then the other world be here, that is, this world and the Hereafter would be same or nothing like the Hereafter would remain. Man should not be dismayed by the difficulties and sufferings befalling him in this world, but he should be pleased because by such natural sufferings, man's sins are washed away and the soul is released from sins. You should understand that by enduring the fate-related sufferings and difficulties which are preordained, the soul becomes pure, but the illnesses and sufferings which come as a result of your carelessness do not wash out your sins. However, God has given man intellect, which he should make use of and have the illnesses which come as a result of carelessness treated.[40]

In this quote, the Ismaili Imam differentiates between different kinds of evils and afflictions. Some evils are man-made and the effect of sheer human negligence. Other evils are preordained and exist due to cosmic necessity. The latter kind of evil, manifest in the form of calamities and difficulties, helps facilitate the purification and perfection of the human soul. However, the human being needs to orient itself properly in the midst of such evils to actually benefit from these misfortunes. In other words, the theodicy outlined in this essay needs to be embodied in a set of practical attitudes that a person can adopt in the course of everyday life.

The soul-making theodicies of Ṭūsī and Aga Khan III bear striking resemblance to the soul-making theodicy of the late John Hick. Mark S. M. Scott has expounded

39 Ṭūsī, *Paradise,* 168.

40 Aga Khan III, *Farmān* (Dar es Salaam: Private Collection, 13 July 1945).

Hick's theodicy in the following quote, which rings similar to the previous quote of the late Aga Khan:

> If the world were designed as a lavish "playpen," we would have no incentive for moral improvement. We would simply bask in the pleasures of our safe and carefree environment. God acts towards us not as a doting parent but as a Father who constructs a world that will "foster quality and strength of character" rather than grant our every wish: "This world must be a place of soul-making. And its value is to be judged, not primarily by the quantity of pleasure and pain occurring in it at any particular moment, but by its fitness for its primary purpose, the purpose of soul-making." Without danger, difficulty, and temptation we would never achieve moral victories or strive for excellence.[41]

Both Ṭūsī and Aga Khan III invite human beings to interpret everything that happens in daily life—whether seemingly positive or apparently negative—as a manifestation of God's mercy. Ṭūsī explains that people will interpret and perceive God's actions mediated through the Universal Intellect and Universal Soul differently based on their own degree of spiritual receptivity and development:

> The Almighty's dealings appear as tyranny to one who dwells in the levels of multiplicity [*darājat-i kathrat*] and from whom all true realities are veiled; they [appear as] justice to one in the darkness of whose soul a light has appeared, so that there is an even distribution between light and darkness; and it [appears] as grace to him the light of whose soul exceeds its darkness; and it is an all-encompassing mercy to that person whose soul is illuminated by the Light of God.[42]

Aga Khan III, in a public interview for European audiences, expresses this same Ismaili teaching in less theological and more practical language. He extolls his listeners to interpret everything that befalls them as a manifestation of goodness sent by God and bring oneself into harmony with existence:

> I should, first of all, advise my heirs to learn to desire the thing that happens, and not try to mold events to their desires. . . . It is not a sorry scheme of things, and the business, the duty of man, is to get himself into harmony with it. I would counsel my heirs to seek satisfaction, not in the flux of circumstances, but within themselves; I would have them resolute, self-controlled,

41 Mark S. M. Scott, "Suffering and Soul-Making: Rethinking John Hick's Theodicy," *The Journal of Religion* 90, no. 3 (2010): 313–314, 318. Thanks to the anonymous reviewer for bringing this piece to my attention.

42 Ṭūsī, *Paradise*, 75.

> independent, but not rebellious. Let them seek communion with that Eternal Reality which I call Allah and you call God! For that is the twin problem of existence to be at once entirely yourself and altogether at one with the Eternal. I say that you should endeavor to suit your desire to the event, and not the event to your desire. If a wall tumbles down and crushes my foot, I must say: "That is the best thing that could happen to me."[43]

The late Aga Khan's words point to a practical and embodied theodicy. His advice articulates the Islamic principles of contentment (*riḍā'*) and trust in God (*tawakkul*). His words prefigure some of the ideas in the popular book of Eckhart Tolle known as *The Power of Now*. The Aga Khan is inviting people to accept the existence of apparent evils and resituate them as manifestations of divine goodness. His exhortation to see events as "the best thing that could happen to me" ties back to the Neoplatonic metaphysics expounded earlier—that God only creates the best possible world, and that the Cosmos is always at its best possible state at any given moment.

Conclusion

The goal of this essay was to offer a Muslim theodicy rooted in the Islamic Neoplatonism espoused in the Ismaili tradition. The essay first presented a metaphysical account of what is called evil. In this account, God as the necessary and independent reality only creates what is absolutely good and perfect—the First Intellect—which may be identified with goodness itself. In this way, Ismaili Neoplatonic thought overcomes the challenge of Fales', which requires God to create a "Perfect Creature." Evil has no positive ontological status and is privative and accidental. God does not create evil. Evil *qua* imperfection is the necessary consequence of the fact that the perfect creation of God is itself *not* identical to God. Therefore, God's perfect creation known as the First Intellect—due to its being contingent and ontologically limited—cannot create a second perfect creation but only a potentially perfect creation—this being the Universal Soul. Evil initially appears as the relative imperfection of the Universal Soul, which lacks the absolute perfection of its cause. However, the Universal Soul interprets its imperfection or "evil" as a reason to seek out and desire the good. In this way, evil at the cosmogonic level serves as an occasion for the manifestation of goodness. The Universal Soul creates human souls and the Cosmos as an expression of its movement towards perfection. The Cosmos, as the product and manifestation of the Universal Soul, necessarily and inevitably contains both good and evil or perfection and imperfection. Even within the Cosmos, the various manifestations of evil including natural and moral evil are properly ordered towards the actualization of a greater good—the perfection of

43 Aga Khan III, "My Philosophy of Happiness, W. R. Titterton Interview," *The NanoWisdoms Archive*, www.nanowisdoms.org/nwblog/10494/ (last accessed March 1, 2021).

human souls. Every human soul can interpret its experience of evil as an occasion to redirect itself towards the goodness that emanates from God through the cosmic hierarchy.

Overall, an Islamic Neoplatonic theodicy fully solves the so-called problem of evil. God does not create evil; evil exists as a necessary consequence of creation not being equal to God; within creation, the existence of evil is made to serve a greater good—the first good being the production of the Cosmos by the Universal Soul, and the second good being the purification and perfection of human souls. The proper human response to evil, as a way of translating this theodicy, is to accept whatever happens as a mercy and grace from God. The human struggle through pain, suffering, and tribulation may help facilitate the soul's actualization of perfection. In this way, evil properly interpreted and ordered is just a lesser and dimmer manifestation of goodness. In this respect, the human being may experience a deeper happiness from the divinely bestowed goodness underlying his or her life struggles, as Aga Khan III once said: "Struggle is the meaning of life. Defeat or Victory is in the hands of God but struggle itself is man's duty and should be his joy."[44]

References

al-Abharī, Athīr al-Dīn. *Hidāyat al-ḥikma*. Karachi: Maktab al-Madīna, 2009.

Aga Khan III, Sir Sultan Muhammad Shah. *Farmān*. Dar es Salaam: Private Collection, July 13, 1945.

Aga Khan III, Sir Sultan Muhammad Shah. *Precious Pearls*. Karachi: Ismaili Association, 1961.

Aga Khan III, Sir Sultan Muhammad Shah. "My Philosophy of Happiness, W. R. Titterton Interview." *The NanoWisdoms Archive*. www.nanowisdoms.org/nwblog/10494/ (last accessed March 1, 2021).

al-Shahrastānī, ʿAbd al-Karīm. *Struggling with the Philosopher*. Edited and translated by Wilferd Madelung and Toby Mayer. London: I. B. Tauris in Association with the Institute of Ismaili Studies, 2001.

al-Sijistānī, Abū Yaʿqūb. *The Book of the Keys to the Kingdom*. Edited by Ismail K. Poonawala. Tunis:Dār al-Gharb al-Islāmī, 2011.

al-Sijistānī, Abū Yaʿqūb. *Ithbāt al-nubuwwāt*. Edited by Wilferd Madelung and Paul Walker. Tehran: Miras-e-Maktoob, 2016.

Amin, Wahid M. "From the One, Only One Proceeds." *Oriens* 48, no. 1–2 (2020): 123–155.

Andani, Khalil. "Metaphysics of Muhammad: The Nur Muhammad from Imam Jaʿfar al-Sadiq (d. 148/765) to Nasir al-Din al-Tusi (d. 672/1274)." *Journal of Sufi Studies* 8, no. 2 (2019): 99–175.

Andani, Khalil. "Evolving Creation: An Ismaili Muslim Interpretation of Evolution." *Zygon* 57, no. 2 (2022): 443–466.

Dadikhuda, Davlat. "Rule of the One: Avicenna, Bahmanyār, and al-Rāzī on the Argument from the *Mubāḥathāt*." *Nazariyat* 6, no. 2 (2020): 69–97.

44 Aga Khan III, *Precious Pearls* (Karachi: Ismaili Association, 1961).

Frank, Richard M. *Beings and Their Attributes*. Albany: SUNY Press, 1978.
Heer, Nicholas. "Al-Abharī and al-Maybudī on God's Existence: A Translation of a Part of al-Maybudī's Commentary on al-Abharī's *Hidāyat al-Ḥikma*." https://digital.lib.washington.edu/researchworks/bitstream/handle/1773/4887/abhari-sep.pdf?sequence=1&isAllowed=y.2009 (last accessed February 22, 2022).
Jackson, Sherman. *Islam and the Problem of Black Suffering*. New York: Oxford University Press, 2009.
Khusraw, Nāṣir-i Khusraw. *Six Chapters or Shish Faṣl*. Edited and translated by Wladmir Ivanow. Leiden: E. J. Brill for the Ismaili Society, 1949.
Kirmānī, Ḥamīd al-Dīn. *Rāḥat al-ʿaql*. Edited by Musṭafā Ghālib. Beirut: Dār al-Andalūs, 1983.
McBrayer, Justin P., and Daniel Howard-Snyder (eds.). *The Blackwell Companion to the Problem of Evil*. New York: Wiley Blackwell, 2013.
Meister, Chad, and Paul K. Moser (eds.). *The Cambridge Companion to the Problem of Evil*. New York: Cambridge University Press, 2017.
Peterson, Michael (ed.). *The Problem of Evil: Selected Readings*. Notre Dame: University of Notre Dame Press, 2017.
Scott, Mark S. M. "Suffering and Soul-Making: Rethinking John Hick's Theodicy." *The Journal of Religion* 90, no. 3 (2010): 313–314.
Tooley, Michael. "The Problem of Evil." In *Stanford Encyclopedia of Philosophy*, edited by Edward N. Zalta. https://plato.stanford.edu/archives/win2021/entries/evil/ (last accessed March 1, 2021).
Ṭūsī, Naṣīr al-Dīn. *The Paradise of Submission*. Edited and translated by Sayyid Jalal Badakhchani. London: I. B. Tauris in association with the Institute of Ismaili Studies, 2005.
Virani, Shafique. "*The Right Path:* A Post-Mongol Persian Ismaili Treatise." *Iranian Studies* 43, no. 2 (2010): 197–221.
Walker, Paul E. *The Wellsprings of Wisdom: A Study of Abū Yaʿqūb al-Sijistānī's Kitāb al-Yanābīʿ Including a Complete English Translation with Commentary and Notes on the Arabic Text*. Salt Lake City: University of Utah Press, 1994.

5 Seyyed Hossein Nasr's Metaphysical Theodicy

Justin Cancelliere

Introduction

Notwithstanding the recent mainstreaming of postcolonial thought,[1] it bears repeating that not every problem is a problem for everyone. In the case of what is today referred to as the problem of evil, some scholars suggest that, despite the ancient provenance of specifically theological discourses on evil that are in many respects continuous with modern ones, it took until the Enlightenment for there to emerge *arguments from* evil for the inexistence of God.[2] Given the degree and extent to which intellectually serious people have since found such arguments compelling, what explains their late arrival, historically speaking?

Of course, all such questions pertaining to the causes of modernization are exceedingly complicated, making detailed discussion of them beyond the scope of these introductory remarks. It will, however, be helpful for present purposes to sketch the basic types of responses that these questions most commonly receive. Have human beings always possessed the same innate capacities, or do these capacities themselves change over time? For some thinkers, ancient and medieval people were simply less capable of disinterested rationality—generally speaking, and for whatever reason—than modern people are,[3] whereas for others, historical variation in the productions of human intellectual activity are explainable with reference primarily to factors extrinsic to the aptitude for such activity itself. In short, one can view the issue most fundamentally in terms of either a development (for

1 See, e.g., Dipesh Chakrabarty, "The Idea of Provincializing Europe," in *Provincializing Europe: Postcolonial Thought and Historical Difference*, ed. Dipesh Chakrabarty (Princeton: Princeton University Press, 2000), introduction; Walter D. Mignolo and Catherine E. Walsh, "Eurocentrism and Coloniality: The Question of Totality of Knowledge," in *On Decoloniality: Concepts, Analytics, Praxis*, ed. Walter D. Mignolo and Catherine E. Walsh (Durham, NC: Duke University Press, 2018), chapter 9.

2 See, e.g., Michael W. Hickson, "A Brief History of Problems of Evil," in *The Blackwell Companion to The Problem of Evil*, ed. Justin P. McBrayer and Daniel Howard-Snyder (Chichester: Wiley-Blackwell, 2013), chapter 1.

3 In addition to well-known figures like Hume, Marx, and Freud, one could mention thinkers such as Marquis de Condorcet, Auguste Comte, E. B. Tylor, and Pierre Teilhard de Chardin.

DOI: 10.4324/9781003371670-6

good or for ill) or a uniformity, with the most nuanced perspectives naturally taking account of both aspects and giving each its due.

For the contemporary philosopher and scholar of Islam Seyyed Hossein Nasr, whose comments on the problem of evil form the subject of this essay, it is not that the ancients and medievals possessed a lower level of critical acumen than their modern counterparts and thus were unable to fully appreciate the potential scope of the problem of evil, and nor is it true that they were able to but opted not to express themselves openly. Rather, he makes the claim—radical by today's standards—that in the last analysis the problem of evil is only inaccurately considered a genuine problem to begin with,[4] which is to say that he views the emergence of what were referred to above as "arguments from evil" as symptomatic of an intellectual decline.[5]

Although Nasr does take the problem very seriously as a matter of both historical and contemporary significance,[6] he has not been shy to say that "if all men could be taught metaphysics . . . there would be no atheists and agnostics."[7] For Nasr, this conviction applies just as much to nonbelief caused by the existence of evil in the world as it does to any other line of reasoning that might cause a person to adopt skeptical attitudes towards God. In other words, Nasr's thought moves decidedly against the grain in associating metaphysics not only with the ability to resolve difficulties thought by many to be irresolvable, but also and above all with direct knowledge of and therefore certainty regarding the reality of the Divine. According to him, the heart of metaphysics consists not in discursive reasoning—what Plato called *dianoia*—but rather in what is termed gnosis, or the putatively divine form of knowledge typically described as non-dual in nature and therefore infallible.[8]

While it is true that epistemologies founded upon gnosis are not wholly unfamiliar to contemporary Westerners—this being due in large part to the impetus the 1960s and 1970s counterculture gave to the popularization of Eastern metaphysical

4 Seyyed Hossein Nasr, *The Garden of Truth* (New York: HarperOne, 2007), 55.

5 Nasr therefore distinguishes between a certain type of intellectual *sophistication* and what he takes to be *intellectuality* properly so-called.

6 Seyyed Hossein Nasr, *The Need for a Sacred Science* (Albany: SUNY Press, 1993), 9. See also Seyyed Hossein Nasr, *Knowledge and the Sacred* (Albany: SUNY Press, 1989), 143.

7 Seyyed Hossein Nasr, "Introduction," in *The Essential Frithjof Schuon*, ed. Seyyed Hossein Nasr (Bloomington: World Wisdom, 2005), 32. See also Nasr, *Need for a Sacred Science*, 9.

8 To forestall common misunderstandings regarding the notion of infallibility here, it is important to note that gnosis in the strictly metaphysical sense is said to have a single object, namely the Real Itself. So, for thinkers who view gnosis in the way that Nasr does, the gnostic's infallibility extends no further than the gnosis itself, which is to say that he or she, as an individual, is infallible neither epistemically nor, a fortiori, as regards character. According to Frithjof Schuon, one of Nasr's teachers: "The Intellect is infallible in itself, but this does not prevent the human receptacle from being subject to contingencies which, though they cannot modify the intrinsic nature of intelligence, can nonetheless be opposed to its full actualization and to the purity of its radiance" (Frithjof Schuon, "In the Wake of the Fall," in *Science and the Myth of Progress*, ed. Mehrdad M. Zarandi [Bloomington: World Wisdom, 2003], 24). See also René Guénon, *Introduction to the Study of the Hindu Doctrines*, trans. Marco Pallis (Hillsdale: Sophia Perennis, 2001), 76.

doctrines[9]—it goes without saying that the concept of gnosis taken as signifying a mode of knowing that is as real as it is valid remains at best marginal in mainstream philosophical and theological circles. As a general rule, then, contemporary discussion of the problem of evil tends to remain confined to the disciplines of philosophy of religion and philosophical theology, both of which conventionally take certain characteristically modern postulates at face value.

In the present context, one thinks in particular of the influence and significance of Kant—the "all-destroyer" as he came to be called by his contemporaries—whose self-styled "Copernican revolution" in metaphysics[10] proved so successful in causing many thinking people to abandon the traditional epistemologies that, if not overtly centered on gnosis, at least contained openings onto it.[11] Furthermore, it is important to mention the complicating factor of ambivalent or even hostile attitudes towards gnosis stretching back into pre-modern times, particularly among Christian authors who either felt threatened by it or—as in the case of what Nasr would characterize as the pseudo-gnosis of historical Gnosticism—had perfectly valid reasons for deeming it heretical.

In contrast to those contemporary thinkers who disregard gnosis in engaging with the problem of evil, Nasr places it at the heart of his theodicy, since for him no fully satisfactory theodicy is possible without it.[12] Insofar as one approaches the problem exclusively from the perspective of either exoteric theology or rationalistic philosophy, it is bound to remain insoluble according to Nasr,[13] who explains its historically corrosive effect on religious faith in the West in terms of a lack of access to sufficiently integral expositions of metaphysics, or to what he alternatively refers to as "sacred science" (*scientia sacra*).[14] Moreover, the qualification "integral" here is significant given the fact that anyone with a library card or an internet connection is now free to peruse the whole of Plato or Plotinus. For if, as Nasr claims, metaphysics involves more than just book learning, the situation arguably becomes one of compound ignorance whenever a human collectivity suffers from a dearth not only of people who are capable of penetrating down to the real

9 See, e.g., Harry Oldmeadow, *Journeys East: 20th Century Western Encounters with Eastern Religious Traditions* (Bloomington: World Wisdom, 2004), 269; Morgan Shipley, *Psychedelic Mysticism: Transforming Consciousness, Religious Experiences, and Visionary Peasants in Postwar America* (London: Lexington Books, 2015), 2; Paul Oliver, *Hinduism and the 1960s: The Rise of a Counter-Culture* (London: Bloomsbury, 2014).

10 See Immanuel Kant, *Critique of Pure Reason*, trans. and ed. Paul Guyer and Allen W. Wood (Cambridge: Cambridge University Press, 1998), 110.

11 Consider, for example, the way Plotinus approached and made use of Aristotle, or, moving in the other direction, as it were, the way St. Thomas Aquinas was influenced by Pseudo-Dionysius. For the latter, see Fran O'Rourke, *Pseudo-Dionysius and the Metaphysics of Aquinas* (Leiden: Brill, 1992).

12 Nasr, *Need for a Sacred Science*, 9. To be clear, one need not "possess" gnosis oneself to understand why there is evil in the world; a theoretical understanding of metaphysics suffices. But without the water of gnosis the flower of metaphysics eventually dries up and dies.

13 Nasr, *Knowledge and the Sacred*, 143.

14 Nasr, *Knowledge and the Sacred*, 143.

intentions underlying this or that text theoretically but also of those individuals who have assimilated the relevant truths existentially.

This point leads to the other half, so to speak, of Nasr's metaphysical theodicy, the import of which extends beyond the necessary doctrinal considerations into the practical concerns of human life. For Nasr, comprehensively addressing the problem of evil requires taking account of the human *experience* of evil. His theodicy therefore has much to say about how one should understand the reality of *suffering*. In fact, there is a sense in which Nasr is concerned more with suffering than he is with evil, since an evil in and of itself is just that, whereas an evil suffered with the right intention purifies the one afflicted by it. So even if, unlike some thinkers, Nasr does not find it necessary to appeal via the purificatory aspect of suffering to the providential role played by evil in the cosmos in order to "vindicate" God, the holism of his perspective nevertheless demands drawing the various connections that he takes to obtain between the objective and subjective aspects of any given phenomenon—in this case between evil as a fact about the world "out there" and evil as productive of suffering.

As for the contemporary relevance of Nasr's theodicy, it consists first and foremost, one might argue, in the timelessness of its essential content, which must always be relevant ipso facto, at least insofar as one affirms the principle of the "timeliness of the timeless,"[15] and specifically inasmuch as human beings are always and everywhere suffering. But regarding the question of relevance in its more extrinsic aspects, namely those pertaining to the social and political domains, one could mention the sense in which Nasr's approach to evil and suffering might serve as an antidote to hysteria, the destructive power of which doubtless becomes exacerbated in "information societies" and "internet cultures." Anyone who has lived and reached some degree of maturity will know the power of negative experiences and influences to consume a life and waste it. If a person were to understand not only why evil exists but also that it must exist, he or she would be in the best position possible to conquer it, since equanimity born of knowledge obviously conduces to effective action, and action in the absence of knowledge is effective only by accident, as it were.[16]

The following is divided into four sections. The first will outline Nasr's solution to the problem of evil; the second will present his views on suffering; and the remaining two will flesh out this presentation of his theodicy by exploring certain ways in which it might be elaborated upon—on the basis of his own principles—in order to account for aspects of the questions of evil and suffering that are only briefly addressed in his writings. In particular, I will examine the ability of Nasr's theodicy to account for evil insofar as it appears as an active force rather than as a privative phenomenon, and I will discuss the relationship between the problem

15 For which see M. Ali Lakhani, *The Timeless Relevance of Traditional Wisdom* (Bloomington: World Wisdom, 2010), vii.

16 See, e.g., Nasr, *Garden of Truth*, 91.

of evil and that of free will and predestination, which Nasr touches upon but does not develop.

Implications of Infinitude

In Nasr's exposition of metaphysical truth, God, who is the supreme Good, is said to be both absolute and infinite, with goodness in this context entailing munificence, absoluteness entailing oneness and simplicity, and infinitude entailing freedom from all limitation. For Nasr, reflecting upon these divine attributes taken together suffices to solve the problem of evil, which he views as proceeding from an insufficiently metaphysical conception of God's nature. In order to understand what he means, it will first be helpful to say more about how exactly he understands the nature of metaphysics.

According to Nasr, metaphysics is not properly speaking a branch of philosophy; rather, it comprises philosophy's very root as the highest of all sciences, which is to say that metaphysics is the science of ultimate reality.[17] In using the term science here, which Nasr intends in its pre-modern sense, he means to distinguish his conception of metaphysics from that of thinkers who see in it nothing beyond unverifiable speculation. For Nasr, there are two main problems with this view: first is its Kantianism, which he rejects,[18] and second is the notion that metaphysics is limited to mental activity alone.[19] As already mentioned, the heart of metaphysics as understood by Nasr is gnosis, which is a mode of knowing that transcends thought.[20] While gnosis in the broadest sense does admit of degrees,[21] the lower degrees derive their reality from—or deserve the designation "gnosis" on account of—their participation in the highest degree, which has as one of its preconditions the contemplative cessation not only of thought but also of the operations of the soul's other faculties, namely sensory perception, memory, imagination, and even intuition, which constitutes a kind of anticipation of gnosis.[22]

17 Nasr, *Knowledge and the Sacred*, 132.

18 Nasr, *Knowledge and the Sacred*, 42.

19 See, e.g., Nasr, *Knowledge and the Sacred*, 34, 132, 261, 313, 325.

20 For an excellent study of gnosis (*ma'rifa*) in the context of Islamic spirituality, see Reza Shah-Kazemi, "The Notion and Significance of *Ma'rifa* in Sufism," *Oxford Journal of Islamic Studies* 13, no. 2 (2002): 155–181.

21 Nasr does usually use the term gnosis in this broad sense and even simply identifies it with traditional metaphysics (see, e.g., Nasr, *Need for a Sacred Science*, 54; Nasr, *Knowledge and the Sacred*, 50n13). But it is clear from his writings that the essence of gnosis consists in the non-dual knowledge of the Divine, with which the transcendent center point of the human state mysteriously coincides (see Nasr, *Knowledge and the Sacred*, 1–4). As he says, "this knowledge . . . is strictly speaking not human" (*Knowledge and the Sacred*, 326).

22 For discussion of this possibility of man's becoming annihilated in God (*fanā'*), see Nasr, *Garden of Truth*, 134–136. For a concise statement of it, see Nasr, *Knowledge and the Sacred*, 326. The relationship between *fanā'* and subsistence in God (*baqā'*) is beyond the scope of this essay.

It can therefore be seen that insofar as metaphysics involves doctrines, or, more loosely, the human intellect's capacity for speculative theorizing, these aspects can only be "outward" vis-à-vis what is essentially an inexpressible "state" of consciousness.[23] When a metaphysician in the Platonic sense of the term thinks, it can only be either to clothe truths in mental forms for the sake of assimilating and expressing them[24] or to untie mental knots that obstruct the supra-rational realization of these truths to begin with, as in the "midwifery" of Socrates.[25] And given the fact that the attainment of this special sort of knowledge entails the extinction—however momentary[26]—of the subject that knows, it can also be seen that the object of gnosis necessarily appears from without as a kind of emptiness or void, hence the whole phenomenon of apophatic mysticism.

To return then to the abovementioned divine attributes upon which Nasr bases his theodicy, we are now in a good position to understand how his conception of God might differ from that of a theologian or rationalist philosopher, neither of whose methods go beyond the subject-object dichotomy presupposed by discursive thinking. For Nasr, the oneness of God demands the ultimately illusory nature of any and all dualities—a non-duality that, among innumerable other implications, entails God's not being limited by His own divinity, so to speak. When one thinks of God, it is natural to imagine Him as being somewhere "out there"—perhaps seated upon His throne at the summit of the cosmic hierarchy—which is not wrong from Nasr's point of view. But to stop there risks making an idol of the world, since to think of God only as He exists in relation to His creation contradicts His absoluteness.[27] In Nasr's metaphysics, God is absolute with a true absoluteness, which is to say that in and of itself the world is devoid of being. And God is infinite with a true infinitude, which is to say that He is not bound by His own unboundedness.

Now, in Nasr's explication of this second principle in particular, God's infinitude can be thought of in terms of possibility, in which case one can say that the Divine, which is All-Possibility, comprehends all that is possible, including the possibility of Its own negation,[28] or of the mysterious imposition of limits upon that which is always essentially free in Itself; such, for Nasr, is the origin of the world in God. From this metaphysical vantage point, which could be called emanationist,[29]

23 See Nasr, *Knowledge and the Sacred*, 134, 151.

24 See Nasr, *Knowledge and the Sacred*, 151–152.

25 See Plato, *Theaetetus*, 148e–151d, trans. M. J. Levett, revised Myles Burnyeat, in Plato, *Complete Works*, ed. John Cooper and D. S. Hutchinson (Indianapolis: Hackett, 1997), 165–168.

26 "Realization of the Self, being im-mediate, strictly speaking transcends time, arriving like a flash of all-illuminating light: The question of how much time is spent in that state of enlightenment is immaterial" (Reza Shah-Kazemi, *Paths to Transcendence: According to Shankara, Ibn Arabi, and Meister Eckhart* (Bloomington: World Wisdom, 2006), 43.

27 See Nasr, *Need for a Sacred Science*, 8.

28 Nasr, *Need for a Sacred Science*, 9–10; Nasr, *Knowledge and the Sacred*, 134; Nasr, *Garden of Truth*, 54.

29 Nasr does not deny creation *ex nihilo*, but he does explain it in metaphysical terms as referring to the existentiation of preexistent possibilities, which from the point of view of the created order do

the existentiation of the cosmos entails separation from its source, which in turn necessitates the appearance of evil—whether literally or figuratively at any given level of reality—since only God is good.[30] More specifically, Nasr characterizes the creation of the world as a "projection toward nothingness" and evil as "a kind of 'crystallization of nothingness,' real on its own level of existence but an illusion before God, who alone is Reality as such."[31] Correctly understanding evil from Nasr's point of view therefore requires avoiding two pitfalls—one being the denial of the reality of evil insofar as it is real, and the other being the false attribution of reality to it insofar as it is not. On the side of the subject, then, theodicy demands an epistemology based upon discernment between the Absolute and the relative, while on the side of the object it demands ontological hierarchy, or gradation in the category of being (*tashkīk al-wujūd*, in Islamic philosophical terms).

Here one might ask, however, why this particular possibility—that of cosmogenesis—is actually brought to pass, given the close conceptual relationship between possibility and contingency.[32] While Nasr's metaphysics does in fact distinguish between possibilities of manifestation and possibilities of non-manifestation,[33] the world belongs to the former category on account of God's goodness, as it is in the nature of the good to communicate and give of itself.[34] So while on the level of abstract attributes like absoluteness and infinitude their very meanings imply God's not being limited by them (which could be expressed by saying that the reality of the Absolute subsumes and encompasses that of the relative, and that the reality of the Infinite subsumes and encompasses that of the finite), on the level of God's positive qualities or perfections—for example goodness or beauty—there is a sense in which His own nature constrains Him to be just those things.[35] In a word, God cannot will not to be God,[36] but He is not "imprisoned in the castle of

indeed appear as "nothing" prior to their being made manifest. See Nasr, *Knowledge and the Sacred*, 232–233.

30 Nasr, *Need for a Sacred Science*, 10. In saying that only God is good, Nasr means that only God is good absolutely, since naturally not all separation from God (in the technical sense of an ontological disjunction) can be considered evil. For example, he says explicitly that "the element of evil [does not] appear in any of the worlds still close to the Divine Proximity" (*Knowledge and the Sacred*, 144). Moreover, he often speaks not of evil but of "what manifests itself as evil on a particular plane of reality," "what appears on the human plane as evil," "what theologically is called evil," etc. (*Knowledge and the Sacred*, 144; *Need for a Sacred Science*, 14n5; *Garden of Truth*, 54).

31 Nasr, *Need for a Sacred Science*, 10. See also Nasr, *Knowledge and the Sacred*, 144.

32 For which see Nasr, *Knowledge and the Sacred*, 139.

33 See Nasr, *Knowledge and the Sacred*, 140.

34 Seyyed Hossein Nasr, "Evil as the Absence of the Good," in *Voices of Islam*, ed. Vincent J. Cornell (Westport: Praeger, 2007), 2:134; Nasr, *Knowledge and the Sacred*, 134.

35 It is not that these qualities possess any reality apart from God such that a perfect being would be required to instantiate or exemplify them perfectly in order to be perfect. Rather, the divine Reality simply is what It is, and to speak of necessity in this context is simply to register this fact theoretically. For Nasr, it would be absurd to posit the existence of immutable criteria independent of God, since the root reality of every valid criterion is God Himself.

36 Nasr, *Knowledge and the Sacred*, 144.

transcendence"[37] either. God is not free not to create,[38] but it is He who imposes this limitation upon His own self in virtue of His freedom from all limitation. As Nasr has explained at length in various works, integral metaphysics distinguishes between two main levels or aspects of divinity—namely, God as pure Being, or the "personal God" of theology, and God as Beyond Being or the ultimately Real, which is metaphysically infinite[39]—and it is in fact the failure to make this distinction, according to Nasr, that leads to so many theological aporias, including the problem of evil.[40] From the perspective of the divine Essence, which is beyond both Being and, a fortiori, good and evil, God does not oppose the existence of evil as such.[41] But He does oppose all concrete evils on the level of His Will, which belongs not to the Essence but to its first determination as Being.[42]

Assuming now the metaphysical necessity of both the existence of the cosmos and the presence of evil in it, a further question may arise—namely, that of the amount as well as types and degrees of evil found in the world. Could not the world have less evil in it than it does, and could it not exclude the more heinous types of evil, and especially the most horrible degrees of any given type? Since this question will be revisited in the final section of this essay, I will only sketch some of the relevant principles here for the sake of rounding out our picture of Nasr's solution to the problem of evil.

First, from Nasr's point of view, God's creation is overwhelmingly good and beautiful, so someone pondering the problem of evil must account for the obvious fact of people's differing experiences of the world while at the same time striving for disinterestedness, which of course excludes any kind of relativism. According to Nasr, the more one is able to step back from the particularities of this or that limited experience—whether it be one's own or that of someone else with which one is preoccupied—the greater will be one's ability to concretely perceive the ultimate unreality of evil in the face of the Good.[43] Naturally someone immersed in evil will be tempted to see evil everywhere in spite of the fact that, as Nasr says,

37 Paul Eduaro Muller-Ortega, *The Triadic Heart of Śiva: Kaula Tantricism of Abhinavagupta in the Non-Dual Shaivism of Kashmir* (Albany: SUNY Press, 1989), 138.

38 "The Absolute and Infinite Reality . . . cannot but manifest and create" (Nasr, *Knowledge and the Sacred*, 144).

39 See Nasr, *Knowledge and the Sacred*, 136, 156n15. For extended discussion of the notion of metaphysical infinitude, see René Guénon, "Infinity and Possibility," in *The Multiple States of the Being*, trans. Henry D. Fohr; ed. Samuel D. Fohr (Hillsdale: Sophia Perennis, 2001), chapter 1.

40 See Nasr, *Need for a Sacred Science*, 9, 14n5. According to Nasr, "Integral metaphysics is fully aware of the necessity, on their own level, of the theological formulations which insist upon the hiatus between God and man or the Creator and the world. The metaphysical knowledge of unity comprehends the theological one in both a figurative and literal sense, while the reverse is not true" (*Knowledge and the Sacred*, 138).

41 Nasr, *Knowledge and the Sacred*, 144.

42 Nasr, *Knowledge and the Sacred*, 144.

43 See Nasr, *Garden of Truth*, 55–56.

"the ugly is passing accident, while . . . beauty is abiding substance."[44] Second, while Nasr affirms the doctrine of predestination, he does not take it to contradict free will, which, for him, people must have if moral evil is to have any meaning.[45] So if certain forms of moral evil are found in the world, an important part of the explanation is simply that God made man free to do as he pleases. Last, although Nasr says that it can be understood perfectly well why God, who is pure goodness, created a world in which there is evil,[46] it is not possible to understand an individual evil in and of itself,[47] since evil is not only characterized by ontological privation, which all things share vis-à-vis God,[48] but is also ontologically insubstantial[49]—a tenebrous mode of existence that manifests itself epistemically as unintelligibility. At best, man can only understand this or that evil in its providential context, for the goodness of God demands that all of what appears as evil contribute to and ultimately be effaced by a greater good.[50]

Nevertheless, human beings do not possess God's measures.[51] It is thus that, according to Nasr, the problem of evil is best solved by living a life that would make possible the dawning of sacred knowledge within one's own being.[52] As he says, "This realization or actualization is the best possible way of understanding the nature of the Good and the why of terrestrial human existence which, being removed from God, cannot but be marred by the fragmentation, dissipation, and privation that appears as evil and that is as real as that plane of reality upon which it manifests itself."[53]

Light Become Fire

If the key to Nasr's solution to the problem of evil lies in his conception of the divine nature, the key to his approach to suffering lies in his conception of the nature

44 Nasr, *Need for a Sacred Science*, 121. Elsewhere he explains that evil "remains always limited and bound while goodness is unlimited and opens unto the Infinite" (*Knowledge and the Sacred*, 145). See also Nasr, "Absence of the Good," 138. For the linguistic association between beauty and goodness and ugliness and evil in Arabic, see Nasr, *Knowledge and the Sacred*, 277n33.

45 Nasr, "Absence of the Good," 134.

46 Nasr, *Need for a Sacred Science*, 9.

47 Nasr, *Knowledge and the Sacred*, 145.

48 Nasr, *Knowledge and the Sacred*, 144.

49 Nasr, *Knowledge and the Sacred*, 145. See also Nasr, "Absence of the Good," 131; Nasr, *Garden of Truth*, 84.

50 Nasr, *Knowledge and the Sacred*, 145–146. In the Quran, the story of Moses and Khiḍr (18:65–82) serves as a kind of locus classicus for this point.

51 In the language of the Quran: "It may be that you hate a thing though it be good for you, and it may be that you love a thing though it be evil for you. God knows, and you know not" (Q 2:216). All translations of Quranic verses are taken from Seyyed Hossein Nasr, Caner Dagli, Maria Dakake, Joseph Lumbard, and Mohammed Rustom (eds.), *The Study Quran: A New Translation and Commentary* (New York: HarperOne, 2015).

52 Nasr, *Knowledge and the Sacred*, 145.

53 Nasr, *Knowledge and the Sacred*, 145.

of man. In Nasr's anthropology, the human state is fundamentally determined by two aspects or poles.[51] On the one hand, man is made in the image of God—a truth that Islam expresses through its doctrine of man's vicegerency (*khilāfa*), according to which man is the representative (*khalīfa*) of God on earth. On the other hand, man is only ever God's servant (*ʿabd*)—a status entailed by his utter poverty in the face of the Divine. For Nasr, the purpose of human life is fulfilled by giving each of these two aspects of the soul its due so that one recovers his or her primordial nature (*fiṭra*), which serves as a kind of gate opening out onto the liberating perfection exemplified for Muslims by the Prophet Muḥammad.[55]

Now given the fact that every positive quality admits of being inverted and made into a vice, man qua vicegerent is in danger of becoming proud, and man qua servant is in danger of becoming abject.[56] So vicegerency, which pertains to the "divine spark" within man,[57] and servitude, which pertains to his creatureliness, must interpenetrate and inform each other in order for this polarity to be resolved into a higher unity. At the same time, Nasr is careful to explain a certain asymmetry whereby servitude precedes and is presupposed by vicegerency.[58] From one point of view, all human beings are both representative and servant whether they are aware of it or not. But from another point of view, there is a sense in which all people are called to be servants, whereas not all people are called to be representatives.[59]

For the purpose of understanding Nasr's account of suffering, one could say that, from the first of these two perspectives, it is the unresolved tension between the divine and creaturely aspects of the human state that causes suffering in the most fundamental sense,[60] whereas, from the second perspective, it is caused by the need to sacrifice the lower self in order to attain to the higher self,[61] or rather the one, true Self, alienation from which renders all happiness fleeting and ultimately false. In short, man's vicegerency causes him to suffer through its perversion as vanity and pride, and his servitude causes him to suffer through his placing himself in the service of the wrong master, with the underlying ailment being one in any case. In the concise expression of Nasr: "The cause of all separation, division, otherness, and ultimately suffering is ignorance . . . and the cure knowledge."[62]

54 See, e.g., Seyyed Hossein Nasr, *The Heart of Islam* (New York: HarperOne, 2004), 13; Nasr, *Need for a Sacred Science*, 134.
55 See Nasr, *Garden of Truth*, 21–22.
56 For precisions on the notions of pride and humility, see Nasr, *Garden of Truth*, 126–127.
57 See, e.g., Nasr, *Garden of Truth*, 12.
58 Seyyed Hossein Nasr, *Islamic Life and Thought* (Chicago: ABC International Group, 2001), 16.
59 The intention here is to highlight the question of vocation in connection with the highest possibilities implied by the notion of vicegerency. Of course all people are so called in principle. For clarifications regarding the distinction between the common people (*ʿawāmm*) and the spiritual elite (*khawāṣṣ*), see Nasr, *Heart of Islam*, 177. See also Nasr, *Knowledge and the Sacred*, 319–320.
60 For the soul's yearning for peace "beyond all tension and duality," see Nasr, *Garden of Truth*, 78.
61 For which sacrifice see, e.g., Nasr, *Garden of Truth*, 97.
62 Nasr, *Knowledge and the Sacred*, 7.

As for all the forms of suffering imposed upon man from without, by his environment, these are explainable from two main points of view—one objective or macrocosmic and the other subjective or microcosmic—although in each case it is really just a question of starting points and emphases. From the objective point of view, which comprises an aspect of subjectivity, man's experience of the world must involve suffering on account of the world's ontological status, which entails not only biological imperfection and decay but also a multiplicity of goods both real and apparent. Insofar as man participates along with other animals in the state of embodiment, he will experience illness, injury, and death.[63] And insofar as he is distinct from other animals in possessing the freedom to choose, individual people are liable to suffer the negative consequences of any and all wrong choices, whether made by them or not. Alternatively, from the subjective point of view, which comprises an aspect of objectivity, the nature of the human state demands suffering in virtue of its imperative of perfection. In Islamic terms, man is unique among creatures on account of God's having "taught Adam the names" (Q 2:31). According to Nasr, "[This] means that God has placed within human nature an intelligence that is central and the means by which he can know all things. It also means that human beings themselves are the theophany, or visible manifestation, of all of God's Names."[64] Thinking in terms of the human vocation, then, one could say that the perfection of God demands the perfection of man. But since man is not one in the same way God is—obviously—his being qualified by God's perfections, of which the divine Names are descriptions, involves a passage or movement from potentiality to actuality.[65] In order to be perfect, man must be free, but freedom exercised by an imperfect creature in a domain characterized by multiplicity perforce involves the possibility of error, which, as already mentioned, forms one of the roots of suffering.[66]

Turning now from the fact of human suffering to the details of its role in the quest for happiness, it is first important to point out that Nasr's emphasis on knowledge should not be taken to imply any denigration of the spiritual significance of love. On the contrary, not only does Nasr draw explicit connections between love

63 See, e.g., Nasr, *Need for a Sacred Science*, 107.

64 Nasr, *Heart of Islam*, 13.

65 For Nasr's situation of this notion (*al-takhalluq bi-akhlāq Allāh*) vis-à-vis the concepts of annihilation in God (*fanā'*), subsistence in God (*baqā'*), and spiritual realization (*taḥqīq*), see Nasr, *Garden of Truth*, 135–136.

66 Regarding the question of animal suffering, which features prominently in certain formulations of the "evidential" problem of evil, it could be said that, just as man suffers along with other animals insofar as all animals are by definition both conscious and subject to the limitations of corporeality, so too—or even more fundamentally and profoundly—do non-human animals suffer on account of their ontological proximity to the human state, the reality of which they both manifest and participate in; cosmic centrality (that of the human state) entails both a maximum of blessing and a maximum of potential peril. It is also worth noting that, in Islam, it is believed on the basis of a hadith that animals will be resurrected and given just recompense on the Day of Judgment.

and suffering in the context of the spiritual life,[67] but he also explains how, at the highest level, the realities of knowledge and love coincide—an identity that entails their inextricability in the realm of relativity.[68] Thus, in interpreting his claim that the cause of suffering is ignorance and the cure knowledge, knowledge must be understood here as encompassing not only direct intellectual apprehension, which is non-discursive,[69] but also the concomitants of this apprehension on the level of the soul, both a priori and a posteriori. On the one hand, the notion of seeking of course implies desire, and in the case of the sincere search for true knowledge it further implies a love that is pure, or a purifying love, since knowledge is not something cheap.[70] On the other hand, the reality of attainment implies both compassion and generosity, since divine knowledge is intrinsically good, and the inward being of the true gnostic is not cluttered with anything that could obstruct the outward radiation of this good. As Nasr explains, "The heart of the saint is the source of a light resulting from his inner illumination and of a warmth issuing from the fire of the love of God. Knowledge and love at this level are united in a single reality, like the light and heat of a fire, the locus of this sacred fire being the heart."[71]

Now just as, subjectively speaking, the comprehensiveness of the human state demands the possibility of vice, so too does the totality of cosmic manifestation demand ambiguity on the level of objective phenomena. It is thus that fire can both benefit and harm, and that, by analogy, the imperishable fire comprising man's very center mysteriously becomes capable of burning him—a possibility opened up by

67 See Nasr, *Garden of Truth*, 64.

68 In *The Garden of Truth*—the work in which Nasr has the most to say about love—he says that without the fire of love life "becomes deprived of value" (61); that the Truth cannot be reached without love (70); and that the one who has not loved has not lived (70). For the relationship between knowledge and love, see, e.g., Nasr, *Knowledge and the Sacred*, 313–315.

69 Discussion of the modalities of such apprehension is beyond the scope of this essay. One could refer to the two primary, paradigmatic modes as "Platonic" and "Aristotelian," since in both cases intellection involves the collapse of the distinction between subject and object.

70 See Nasr, *Garden of Truth*, 60.

71 Seyyed Hossein Nasr, "The Heart of the Faithful Is the Throne of the All-Merciful," in *Paths to the Heart: Sufism and the Christian East*, ed. James S. Cutsinger (Bloomington: World Wisdom, 2004), 39. These notions of luminosity and radiation are helpful for appreciating the relevance of Nasr's theodicy to any and all people, regardless of the degree to which they are intellectually inclined. Some might wonder, for example, whether the consolation of the sage is a wholly private affair, or if it can be communicated in a compassionate way to those who lack it. From the point of view of Nasr's philosophy, a metaphysician may very well be blessed with the ability to convey beneficial knowledge to people in a language they can understand; there is nothing about essential truths that requires their being expressed in an arcane way. But prior to the question of any good deed for Nasr is always that of a person's underlying spiritual state, since, as it is said in Islam, "actions are according to their intentions." For him, the root precondition of all true service is being fully present—something only possible through spiritual realization. One need not understand metaphysics to benefit from someone who does and who has found peace through the "path of knowledge." Not all metaphysicians are saints, and not all saints are metaphysicians, but there are types of people for whom neither sainthood nor even posthumous salvation is possible without metaphysics.

the scission between subject and object, precisely. It is not without reason, then, that Nasr speaks not only of the fire of love but also of the fire of the passions.[72]

From the point of view of this symbolism, the crucial question for man in his quest for happiness is that of his well-faring in respect of the fire within him. For what does this fire burn, with what does he feed it, and in what manner does it finally burn *him*? Insofar as it burns with the love of God, man sacrifices himself at the altar of this love, which in consuming him frees him of the dross of his own separative existence.[73] For such a person, the alchemy of love makes a medicine of suffering regardless of its proximate cause. If it comes from without, then it aids the lover in abandoning that which will never fully satisfy him, and if it comes from within, it aids him in abandoning his own self for that which will.[74] Contrariwise, insofar as man succumbs to the fire of his passions, which he feeds with gratifications while heedless of God, he is really only feeding it with his self,[75] which in being so consumed is condemned to suffer in vain. For Nasr, whose perspective situates ascetical attitudes in the context of the path of knowledge,[76] man is not asked to completely suppress his appetites, which have positive functions in accordance with God's goodness and wisdom. But justice does demand disciplining them for the sake of placing them at the service of man's higher faculties. Man cannot escape being burned, since the fire of Reality is one.[77] But the lower modalities of this fire must be kept within their proper bounds lest their blaze blind him from the truth of his situation. In the case of the lover of God, then, he casts himself into the fire that liberates, whereas the lover of his own self casts himself into the fire of Hell,[78] "whose fuel is men and stones" (Q 2:24).

Inversion and Excess

In suffering on account of evils—whether those be found within us or outside of us, and whether they be evil literally or metaphorically—human beings doubtless experience certain evils not just as privations of this or that good but as active forces in their own right. For example, as we just saw, there obviously exists an active element in man's surrendering himself to his own passions. Not only does man

72 See Seyyed Hossein Nasr, *The Essential Seyyed Hossein Nasr*, ed. William Chittick (Bloomington: World Wisdom, 2007), 32–33; Nasr, *Garden of Truth*, 96, 116.

73 See Nasr, *Garden of Truth*, 70.

74 See Nasr, *Garden of Truth*, 63–64, 120.

75 See Nasr, *Garden of Truth*, 96. According to Q 10:44, "God does not wrong human beings in the least, but rather human beings wrong themselves."

76 See, e.g., Nasr, *Garden of Truth*, 131, 171.

77 Nasr occasionally refers to the classical Sufi tripartition of the stages of the acquisition of sacred knowledge (itself rooted in the Quran), according to which the path can be envisaged as proceeding from the "lore of certainty" (*ʿilm al-yaqīn*), or hearing about fire, to the "eye of certainty" (*ʿayn al-yaqīn*), or seeing fire, to the "truth of certainty" (*ḥaqq al-yaqīn*), or being consumed by fire (Nasr, *Garden of Truth*, 30–31, 33; Nasr, *Knowledge and the Sacred*, 325; Nasr, *Islam and the Plight of Modern Man* [Chicago: ABC International Group, 2001], 95n7).

78 See Nasr, *Garden of Truth*, 96.

harbor within himself "the self that incites to evil" (*al-nafs al-ammāra bi'l-sū'*), but he is also free, so that even his passive attitudes with respect to this self involve some degree of activity. In the context of Nasr's theodicy, which underscores the privative aspect of evil, how should we understand evil as it is sometimes encountered—namely, as consciously subversive or malicious? In what follows, I will address this question before turning to the relationship between theodicy and the free will/predestination problematic, the intention being to explore some ways in which Nasr's discussion of the problem of evil might be expanded upon and tested against certain objections.

Even though Nasr's focus on metaphysics, ontology, and cosmology in his explanation of evil very naturally results in a foregrounding of evil's ontological insubstantiality, his writings do contain keys for helping his readers understand how the relative reality of evil—a fact that he emphasizes repeatedly[79]—is able to be experienced so viscerally. For example, in *Knowledge and the Sacred*, Nasr writes that "the doctrine of *māyā* or *ḥijāb* . . . explains evil as privation and separation from the Good and also as an element contributing to a greater good, although within a particular ambience or plane of existence, evil remains evil as a result of either privation *or excess*."[80] Furthermore, in this same work he explains how the cosmogenic irradiation of Being entails not only the appearance of privative modalities for the possibilities contained *in divinis* but also the reflection and thus inversion of these same possibilities in the cosmic mirror, or "the mirror of nothingness."[81] Although in itself such inversion is neutral, Nasr explicitly identifies it as one of cosmological preconditions of human perversity,[82] from which point of view one might imagine the just-mentioned excess as a kind of caricature of the superabundant plenitude of Being Itself.

On a more basic level, though, excess in its negative sense refers to the blameworthy overstepping of a limit. When someone perpetrates excesses, what is the nature of the limit that is being transgressed? From the religious point of view, it is of course the limits established by God as expressed in His Law that are violated by the wrongdoer. But as Nasr points out, one can and must distinguish between specifically religious conceptions of evil, which are characterized by a certain degree of relativity, and the spiritual significance of evil, which is universal.[83] From this more fundamental perspective, the violation is against the limits set by the nature of the human state itself.[84]

79 Nasr, *Need for a Sacred Science*, 10; Nasr, *Knowledge and the Sacred*, 145; Nasr, "Absence of the Good," 133; Nasr, *Garden of Truth*, 83–84.

80 Nasr, *Knowledge and the Sacred*, 145 (emphasis added).

81 Nasr, *Knowledge and the Sacred*, 140, 201.

82 "The fall of man upon the earth, like the descent of a symbol from a higher plane of reality, means both reflection and inversion which in the case of man leads to perversion" (Nasr, *Knowledge and the Sacred*, 176).

83 Nasr, "Absence of the Good," 136. See also Nasr, *Garden of Truth*, 83–84.

84 Consider Q 2:57: "They wronged Us not, but themselves did they wrong."

As we just saw, the human vocation involves striving to perfect both servitude and vicegerency, which constitute the poles of man's primordial nature or *fiṭra*. To understand how it is that evil appears as an active force in the world in spite of having no real ontological foundation, it is necessary to situate these anthropological terms in their cosmological context. In Nasr's cosmology, all that is other than God (*mā siwā Allāh*) comprises at once mirrors reflecting His Face and veils hiding Its splendor.[85] The existentiation of the cosmos can therefore be envisaged in terms of a progressive veiling of the one, true Reality, with each veil becoming more and more opaque the closer this "tendency toward nothingness," as Nasr calls it, nears its terminus, which can never be reached precisely on account of its being nothing.[86]

To link now this notion of the veil (*ḥijāb*) with that of the *fiṭra*, or more specifically with that of man's vicegerency, we can start by saying that, normatively speaking, and considered in relation to the entelechies of other creatures, man's function in the cosmos is to manifest God in a central fashion, or to reflect not just one or more of the divine Names but the Supreme Name—*Allāh*—which contains all of the others.[87] The upshot of this divine intention in the domain of the limited and the multiple is that the reconciliation of all oppositions characteristic of divinity finds its reflection in the icon of man, who "squares the circle" of creation by manifesting that which is highest in the very midst of what is lowest. In thus fulfilling his purpose as the jewel in the crown of the cosmos, man renders the veil diaphanous or even transparent—a possibility affirmed by the famous *ḥadīth qudsī* according to which God Himself becomes the hearing with which His servant hears, the sight with which he sees, the hand with which he strikes, and the foot with which he walks.[88] As Nasr explains it: "The miracle of human existence is that man can undo the existentiating and cosmogonic process inwardly so as to cease to exist; man can experience that 'annihilation' (the *fanā'* of the Sufis) which enables him to experience union in the ultimate sense."[89] And while it is true that Islam's status as a path of moderation (*wasaṭiyya*) places providential limitations upon the outward unveiling of such realization, there were nevertheless exceptions that proved the rule, to say nothing of the immense spiritual radiance of the Prophet.

Now, if the highest possibilities of the human state involve the attenuation or even rending of the cosmic veil, the lowest possibilities involve its thickening to the point of absurdity, or, alternatively, its thinning in a way that is extraordinary but illicit or false. An example of the first would be the general ambience of a civilization in which the good is conceived of exclusively in material terms, and

85 Nasr, *Knowledge and the Sacred*, 190, 197.

86 See Nasr, *Knowledge and the Sacred*, 141.

87 For the most forceful and profound elaboration of Nasr's anthropology, see Nasr, "Man, Pontifical and Promethean," in Nasr, *Knowledge and the Sacred*, chapter 5.

88 See, e.g., Nasr, *Garden of Truth*, 38, 128.

89 Nasr, *Knowledge and the Sacred*, 326.

an example of the second would be the phenomena associated with the end times in various religious traditions—one thinks, for instance, of the experiential possibilities afforded by certain drugs, or of the wonders that will be performed by the Antichrist according to various prophetic narrations in Islam.[90]

As for the commission of genuinely wicked acts by individuals—and to return to the notion of the normative limits intrinsic to the human state—it is perhaps best understood in this context with the aid of geometrical symbolism, namely that of the circle. Given the fact that the microcosm and macrocosm mirror each other, one can imagine both the human state and the cosmos in their integrality as being each comprised of a series of concentric circles, with the center points symbolizing the human body and the corporeal plane of existence, respectively. Moving out from the center in all directions, the ontological modality of each world—human and cosmic—becomes increasingly subtle (moving in the "direction" of the immaterial) until one reaches the outermost circle, which in reality constitutes an unreachable limit. In man, the upward limit rejoins his innermost center, symbolized by the heart, where man is mysteriously capable of meeting his Lord; the lower limit represents his ability to sink to the "lowest of the low," in Quranic terms;[91] and the lateral limits represent the possibility of indefinite wandering—of spiritual lukewarmness, one might say—at least until the time of death. As for the cosmos, the upward limit indicates the divine Throne, the lower limit nothingness, and the lateral limits symbolize the indefinitude of manifestation, which reflects the infinitude of its Principle.[92]

Now, insofar as man is a creature, it is not possible for him to traverse all the levels of reality, regardless of the direction in which he sets off. Moving upward, in spiritual ascent, it is required of him that he progressively cast off his own limitations—a journey culminating in the abandonment of his very self, or in his dying before death.[93] Moving horizontally, the horizon recedes endlessly until he gives up and turns back out of fatigue or else gets stranded. And moving downward, in disobedience, his stubborn refusal to overcome himself, or his willful persistence in following his own desires without restraint and apart from any awareness of God, results in increasingly severe deformations of his inward substance the further he pushes down into darkness, as it were. When traveling upwards, each successive boundary is crossed via a death, in an aeviternal moment. But moving downwards, self-assertively clinging to life renders each boundary substantial. And just as physically colliding with something produces temporary disfigurement of the body, or extreme forms of physical exertion cause contortions in the

90 A veil can of course be either predominantly inward or predominantly outward in nature.

91 See Q 95:5.

92 For the metaphysical meaning of indefinitude, see René Guénon, "Infinite and Indefinite," in *The Metaphysical Principles of the Infinitesimal Calculus*, trans. Michael Allen and Henry D. Fohr; ed. Samuel D. Fohr (Hillsdale: Sophia Perennis, 2003), chapter 1.

93 The injunction "die before you die," which Nasr cites with some frequency, has been attributed to the Prophet of Islam. See, e.g., Nasr, *Garden of Truth*, 22–23; Nasr, *Need for a Sacred Science*, 33.

face, likewise does straining against the moral limits of the human state lead to grotesque caricatures of man's inherent qualities, and this really is the key to understanding how something that is most fundamentally defined negatively as the absence of something else is able to appear so convincingly as though it possessed reality in its own right.

To tie the foregoing together, man as vicegerent exists in a world of veils, and he himself is a veil. The more he fulfills the highest purpose of his existence by dying spiritually, the more transparent he becomes to the light of God's perfections. But the more he rebels against this purpose, the more his reflection of this light takes on a lurid or even abominable quality on account of the absurdity of the nothing's violent assertion of itself as though it were something, or of what amounts to "playing God." If evil often appears to us as an active force in the world, it is because the metaphysical opacity of the evil person obscures the true source of whatever power or presence appears in him, albeit by way of abuse and dissipation.[94] It is perhaps for this reason—the fact that the Light is one—that Meister Eckhart spoke of the blasphemer's praising God,[95] and that, in the language of the Quran, "there is no thing, save that it hymns His praise, though you do not understand their praise" (17:44).

Oneness and Totality

We saw earlier that Nasr explains the presence of evil in the world as a necessary concomitant of cosmogenesis. As he says, "To use the very term *world* implies already separation from God . . . [and] what we call evil is the result of this withdrawal and separation."[96] Taking this doctrine for granted, we then posed the question of whether the world might not have *less* evil in it than it does, or only certain types or degrees of evil. Surely, as mentioned, the postulate of human freedom is indispensable to any cogent response to this question. But we could have probed the initial cosmological picture a bit more, as it is not immediately apparent why separation would have to manifest itself as evil on any given level of reality, since celestial modes of existence and freedom of will in the most general sense are not mutually exclusive, to say the least.[97] Thinking in terms of geometrical symbolism again, could not the emanation of the cosmos, which can be envisaged as proceeding spherically out from its originary Center, have been halted before the

94 It is interesting that, in Arabic, the root of the word for unbelief or religious infidelity (*kufr*, from k-f-r) means to cover or hide, and the root of the adjective used to describe the false messiah or Antichrist (*dajjāl*, from d-j-l) means to deceive or misrepresent.

95 See Meister Eckhart, *The Complete Mystical Works of Meister Eckhart*, trans. and ed. Maurice O.C. Walshe (New York: Crossroad, 2009), 26; Meister Eckhart, *Meister Eckhart: Teacher and Preacher*, trans. Bernard McGinn (New York: Paulist Press, 1986), 216.

96 Nasr, *Garden of Truth*, 54.

97 One might also wonder about the distinction between evil and badness more generally, for which see Nasr, "Absence of the Good," 135.

conditions for the appearance of evil were met? Why did God not just make the world unambiguously paradisal from the start?

The most profound and purely metaphysical answer to this question is simply that God is one, for oneness implies totality. But one could also say, slightly less elliptically, that to say God is to say world, and to say world is to say man. As we have already seen, God creates because it is in His nature to do so, or because He is who He is, and His creation includes man on pain of the name *Allāh* not receiving its rights, so to speak. Furthermore, the world, which is finite, must be so indefinitely, since otherwise the sphere of the cosmos would be limited by nothingness, which is absurd. It would be as though the abovementioned logical possibility of a kind of paradisal orb were to be suspended in a void, with its inhabitants being able to stroll along its boundary and peer out into emptiness.[98] But such a world could not contain man, since the very nature of man is distinguished from the natures of other things precisely by its mysterious ability to encompass the extremes of manifested existence within itself—from nothing properly so-called to the "nothingness" of the Divine. So the world contains moral evil—including its most abhorrent forms—because it contains man, and it contains man because principial oneness demands manifested totality.

Now as satisfying as such explanations may be for readers who are predisposed to find traditional metaphysical doctrines compelling, some might wonder at what are liable to appear as cavalier appeals to necessity. When one studies metaphysics, it quickly becomes apparent that much hinges on the notion of necessity, which, after all, is intimately linked with that of truth. In saying that infinitude entails finitude, or that oneness demands totality, how should these metaphysical modes of implication be understood? Can things be other than they are? What is the relationship between necessity, possibility, and freedom? In the context of the problem of evil, God is absolved of evil by the freedom of man, but the nature of man is nevertheless determined by God. It is thus that theodicy is, as Nasr has noted, closely related to the problem of free will and predestination,[99] to which we now turn.

In Nasr's metaphysics, God is both pure necessity and pure freedom, and since only God is absolute, only He possesses these attributes in an absolute manner.[100] In the human domain, by contrast, there can be neither absolute necessity nor absolute freedom, since the world is relative by definition.[101] According to Nasr, the oneness of freedom and necessity on the divine level manifests itself as mutual limitation on the level of relativity. Man, then, is neither fully determined

98 From this point of view, the vastness of the physical universe reflects the fathomless interiority of man.

99 Nasr, *Knowledge and the Sacred*, 146.

100 Nasr, *Knowledge and the Sacred*, 146.

101 Nasr, *Knowledge and the Sacred*, 146.

nor fully free. Given the beauty of Nasr's exposition here, it is worth reproducing at some length:

> Man's freedom is as real as himself. He ceases to be free in the sense of independent of the Divine Will to the extent that he ceases to be separated ontologically from God. At the same time, man is determined and not free to the extent that an ontological hiatus separates him from his Source and Origin, for only God is freedom. Journeying from the relative toward the Absolute means at once losing the freedom of living in error and gaining freedom from the tyranny of all the psycho-material determinations which imprison and stifle the soul. In God there is pure freedom and pure necessity and only in Him is man completely free and also completely determined but with a determination which, being nothing but man's own most profound nature and the root of his being, is none other than the other face of freedom, total and unconditional.[102]

Regarding the relationship between the question of free will and predestination and the problem of evil, understanding it requires specifying the exact meanings of necessity and freedom as they relate to both God and man. Metaphysically speaking, necessity refers simply to Reality's being what It is, and freedom refers to Its illimitability. God exists by His very nature, and because He does not change, He cannot not be. Relying upon nothing, therefore, and possessing no partners in virtue of His oneness, God is exalted above anything that could place a limit upon His freedom. As for man, all of whose endowments of course come from God, his participation in divine freedom transpires within the limits of a predetermined destiny, since the changelessness and perfection of the Divine entail everything's already being accomplished in reality. From this lofty point of view, or at this level, which in theoretical Sufism is called *wāḥidiyya*, or oneness as inclusive of manyness, things simply are what they are, with the upshot for human freedom being that a person is only ever free to become what he or she always already is on the level of his or her unmanifested individuality. In this doctrine, which in the Islamic world found its most profound expression in the writings of Ibn ʿArabī (d. 1240) and his followers, the objects of God's knowledge are uncreated (*ghayr majʿūl*), and insofar as they enter into manifestation, God in His justice bestows upon them that which their own natures demand—no more and no less.[103]

Thus, if someone were to accept that it is man and not God who is responsible for moral evil but then wonder why God makes human nature to be what it is, one

102 Nasr, *Knowledge and the Sacred*, 146. See also Nasr, *Islamic Life and Thought*, 17.

103 See, e.g., Ṣadr al-Dīn al-Qūnawī, *al-Nuṣūṣ*, ed. Ibrāhīm Ibrāhīm Muḥammad Yāsīn (Alexandria: Munshaʾat al-Maʿārif, 2003), 52. Chittick has made his expert translation of this remarkable text available online: www.williamcchittick.com/wp-content/uploads/2019/05/Sadr_al-Din_Qunawi_The_Texts_al-Nusus.pdf (last accessed October 10, 2022).

answer is simply that human nature is not something made. God does not create the objects of His own knowledge; rather, He simply knows what He knows. It is also helpful to recall here the concept of divine wisdom for the obvious reason that, as already mentioned, man does not possess God's measures. In the context of Islam, one is reminded of the Quranic passage in which the angels question God's decision to make man His representative on earth: "And when thy Lord said to the angels, 'I am placing a vicegerent upon the earth,' they said, 'Wilt Thou place therein one who will work corruption therein, and shed blood, while we hymn Thy praise and call Thee Holy?' He said, 'Truly I know what you know not.' And He taught Adam the names, all of them" (2:30–31). All things—their good and their evil—are determined from the start, but man is free to fail to appreciate the fact, in which case he lives beneath himself and suffers on account of his ignorance. Being thus estranged from the paradise of his own primordial nature, which participates in divine knowledge, he forfeits his supreme opportunity, which is to abandon even that for God Himself, in whom alone evil is seen to have never really been.

Closing Remark

In his influential *Historical and Critical Dictionary*, the 17th-century philosopher Pierre Bayle (d. 1706) declared the presence of evil in a world created by a perfect divinity to be "not only inexplicable, but also incomprehensible."[104] As he explained, "All that can be opposed to the reasons why this being has allowed evil agrees more with the natural light and the ideas of order than do the reasons themselves."[105] Writing as he was on the cusp of the Enlightenment, Bayle's conclusion is unsurprising given the ascendance of a modus operandi that divorced reason from intellect not just in its most profound, purely Platonic sense, but even as it was somewhat more modestly understood by the scholastics (i.e., as a non-discursive faculty of contemplation).[106]

Given the degree to which the emergence of agnostic and atheistic approaches to the problem of evil was bound up historically with what are arguably severely impoverished epistemologies, this examination of Seyyed Hossein Nasr's metaphysical theodicy placed much emphasis on the gnostic heart of his integral theory of knowledge. For Nasr, it is not that gnosis affords access to truths about which God remains silent in His revelations. Rather, the crucial distinction is between

104 Pierre Bayle, *Historical and Critical Dictionary: Selections*, trans. Richard H. Popkin (Indianapolis: Hackett, 1991), 169.

105 Bayle, *Historical and Critical Dictionary*, 169.

106 I take the terms faculty and contemplation here to connote individuality and embodiment, albeit with the understanding that, as Aquinas taught, the activity of *intellectus* constitutes a human participation in angelic cognition. It is also worth noting that Aristotle's hylomorphism does not prevent him from affirming the separability and essential independence of intellect. See, respectively, Rik Van Nieuwenhove, "Contemplation, Intellectus, and Simplex Intuitus in Aquinas: Recovering a Neoplatonic Theme," *American Catholic Philosophical Quarterly* 91, no. 2 (2017): 199–225; Lloyd P. Gerson, *Aristotle and Other Platonists* (Ithaca: Cornell University Press, 2005), 152–172.

mediated and unmediated forms of knowing, since it is through neglect of the imperatives of the latter that scriptural exegesis risks losing touch with the deepest meanings contained in any given revealed text. From Nasr's point of view, it is not necessary to be a metaphysician nor, a fortiori, a realized saint to have "justified true belief" in God. On the contrary, in his conception of tradition, the continued radiation of the intellective heart of an integrally traditional civilization suffices to illuminate the totality of its aspects and dimensions. It is thus that even simple believers are blessed with participation in the certainties of the tradition as a whole. In the case of Islam, one imagines the happy end of those who with a full heart took God and His Prophet at their word, for "paradise is surrounded by hardships," and "truly with hardship comes ease" (Q 94:5–6).[107]

References

al-Qūnawī, Ṣadr al-Dīn. *al-Nuṣūṣ*. Edited by Ibrāhīm Ibrāhīm Muḥammad Yāsīn. Alexandria: Munsha'at al-Ma'ārif, 2003.

al-Qūnawī, Ṣadr al-Dīn. *The Texts*. Translated by William C. Chittick. www.williamcchittick.com/wp-content/uploads/2019/05/Sadr_al-Din_Qunawi_The_Texts_al-Nusus.pdf (last accessed October 10, 2022).

Bayle, Pierre. *Historical and Critical Dictionary: Selections*. Translated by Richard H. Popkin. Indianapolis: Hackett, 1991.

Chakrabarty, Dipesh. "The Idea of Provincializing Europe." In *Provincializing Europe: Postcolonial Thought and Historical Difference*, introduction. Princeton, NJ: Princeton University Press, 2000.

Eckhart, Meister. *Meister Eckhart: Teacher and Preacher*. Translated by Bernard McGinn. New York: Paulist Press, 1986.

Eckhart, Meister. *The Complete Mystical Works of Meister Eckhart*. Translated and edited by Maurice O. C. Walshe. New York: Crossroad, 2009.

Gerson, Lloyd P. *Aristotle and Other Platonists*. Ithaca: Cornell University Press, 2005.

Guénon, René. "Infinity and Possibility." In *The Multiple States of the Being*, translated by Henry D. Fohr; edited by Samuel D. Fohr, chapter 1. Hillsdale: Sophia Perennis, 2001.

Guénon, René. *Introduction to the Study of the Hindu Doctrines*. Translated by Marco Pallis. Hillsdale: Sophia Perennis, 2001.

Guénon, René. "Infinite and Indefinite." In *The Metaphysical Principles of the Infinitesimal Calculus*, translated by Michael Allen and Henry D. Fohr; edited by Samuel D. Fohr, chapter 1. Hillsdale: Sophia Perennis, 2003.

Hickson, Michael W. "A Brief History of Problems of Evil." In *The Blackwell Companion to The Problem of Evil*, edited by Justin P. McBrayer and Daniel Howard-Snyder, chapter 1. Chichester: Wiley-Blackwell, 2013.

Kant, Immanuel. *Critique of Pure Reason*. Translated and edited by Paul Guyer and Allen W. Wood. Cambridge: Cambridge University Press, 1998.

Lakhani, M. Ali. *The Timeless Relevance of Traditional Wisdom*. Bloomington: World Wisdom, 2010.

107 "Hardships" in the Hadith translates *makārih* (sing. *makrah*), which most literally means things that are loathed or hated but can also mean adversities, hardships, etc.

Mignolo, Walter D., and Catherine E. Walsh. "Eurocentrism and Coloniality: The Question of Totality of Knowledge." In *On Decoloniality: Concepts, Analytics, Praxis*, edited by Walter D. Mignolo and Catherine E. Walsh, chapter 9. Durham, NC: Duke University Press, 2018.

Muller-Ortega, Paul Eduaro. *The Triadic Heart of Śiva: Kaula Tantricism of Abhinavagupta in the Non-Dual Shaivism of Kashmir*. Albany: SUNY Press, 1989.

Nasr, Seyyed Hossein. *Knowledge and the Sacred*. Albany: SUNY Press, 1989.

Nasr, Seyyed Hossein. *The Need for a Sacred Science*. Albany: SUNY Press, 1993.

Nasr, Seyyed Hossein. *Islam and the Plight of Modern Man*. Chicago: ABC International Group, 2001.

Nasr, Seyyed Hossein. *Islamic Life and Thought*. Chicago: ABC International Group, 2001.

Nasr, Seyyed Hossein. "The Heart of the Faithful Is the Throne of the All-Merciful." In *Paths to the Heart: Sufism and the Christian East*, edited by James S. Cutsinger, 32–45. Bloomington: World Wisdom, 2004.

Nasr, Seyyed Hossein. *The Heart of Islam*. New York: HarperOne, 2004.

Nasr, Seyyed Hossein. "Introduction." In *The Essential Frithjof Schuon*, edited by Seyyed Hossein Nasr, 1–64. Bloomington: World Wisdom, 2005.

Nasr, Seyyed Hossein. *The Essential Seyyed Hossein Nasr*. Edited by William Chittick. Bloomington: World Wisdom, 2007.

Nasr, Seyyed Hossein. "Evil as the Absence of the Good." In *Voices of the Spirit*, edited by Vincent J. Cornell, vol. 2, 131–138. Westport: Praeger, 2007.

Nasr, Seyyed Hossein. *The Garden of Truth*. New York: HarperOne, 2007.

Nasr, Seyyed Hossein, Caner K. Dagli, Maria Massi Dakake, Joseph E. B. Lumbard, and Mohammed Rustom (eds.). *The Study Quran: A New Translation and Commentary*. New York: HarperOne, 2015.

Oldmeadow, Harry. *Journeys East: 20th Century Western Encounters with Eastern Religious Traditions*. Bloomington: World Wisdom, 2004.

Oliver, Paul. *Hinduism and the 1960s: The Rise of a Counter-Culture*. London: Bloomsbury, 2014.

O'Rourke, Fran. *Pseudo-Dionysius and the Metaphysics of Aquinas*. Leiden: Brill, 1992.

Plato. *Theaetetus*. Translated by M. J. Levett, revised by Myles Burnyeat. In *Complete Works*, edited by John Cooper and D. S. Hutchinson, 158–234. Indianapolis: Hackett, 1997.

Schuon, Frithjof. "In the Wake of the Fall." In *Science and the Myth of Progress*, edited by Mehrdad M. Zarandi, 1–27. Bloomington: World Wisdom, 2003.

Shah-Kazemi, Reza. "The Notion and Significance of *Maʿrifa* in Sufism." *Oxford Journal of Islamic Studies* 13, no. 2 (2002): 155–181.

Shah-Kazemi, Reza. *Paths to Transcendence: According to Shankara, Ibn Arabi, and Meister Eckhart*. Bloomington: World Wisdom, 2006.

Shipley, Morgan. *Psychedelic Mysticism: Transforming Consciousness, Religious Experiences, and Visionary Peasants in Postwar America*. London: Lexington Books, 2015.

Van Nieuwenhove, Rik. "Contemplation, Intellectus, and Simplex Intuitus in Aquinas: Recovering a Neoplatonic Theme." *American Catholic Philosophical Quarterly* 91, no. 2 (2017): 199–225.

6 Hume on Trial

Can Evil and Suffering Be Justified?

Muhammad U. Faruque

I

In the face of countless atheist attacks on the existence of God through the problem of evil, it has become almost a *façon de parler* for contemporary theist philosophers to first concede that the world is full of suffering and then offer various apologies in order to show how the concept of God can nonetheless be defended. As Meghan Sullivan and Paul Blaschko point out, we can think of these theist philosophers almost like a team of defense attorneys, offering alternative narratives and defenses, challenging the way in which Hume, Voltaire, and their numerous contemporary disciples use evil and suffering as an indictment of God's existence or goodness.[1] In fact, the situation can be best imagined as the following courtroom scenario:

> In his opening remarks, the atheist stands up and points to the sheer amount and degree of suffering in the world. He reminds the jury of particular instances of horrendous suffering, telling us stories so awful that we're tempted to turn away. "Now imagine God witnessing such suffering," he tells us. "If he exists, he's right there. He's perfect. He's all-powerful. He could stop this suffering at any moment. But he doesn't." The courtroom is silent. "The only explanation," the atheist concludes, "is that the God you've been led to believe in does not and cannot exist."[2]

The purpose of this article is not to offer another apology *à la* a defense attorney on behalf of those who see the trace of transcendence in nature, since the problem of evil is a doubly difficult problem for atheists if naturalism happens to be true (more on this later). Nevertheless, with the pandemic of COVID-19 unleashing its deadly consequences, which has already claimed over 15 million casualties all over the globe, the question of evil and suffering does make one wonder about its underlying purpose in human life. At the same time, it is also true that in recent years numerous people, especially in the West, have turned away from religion

1 Meghan Sullivan and Paul Blaschko, *The Good Life Method* (New York: Penguin Press, 2022), 203.
2 Sullivan and Blaschko, *Good Life Method*, 204.

DOI: 10.4324/9781003371670-7

as a result of what they see as pointless suffering all across life. This supposition of "pointless suffering"[3]—framed more distinctly as the "evidential problem of evil"—can be traced back to the influential writings of David Hume in the Enlightenment period, which find their modern, stronger formulations in such philosophers as William Rowe and Paul Draper.[4] The purpose of this article is, therefore, to engage and challenge this Humean tradition that on the surface seems to pose a serious dilemma for those who do not accept naturalistic explanations. In essence, I will argue that the Humean tradition misunderstands the meaning of suffering by assuming that the goal of creation should be a custom-made paradise populated by weak, hedonistic humans seeking to maximize their pleasure. Instead, this paper will argue that the telos of creation is the human being's spiritual development and ultimate perfection for which suffering in life can be a means to actualize one's latent spiritual and ethical flourishing. But let us proceed step by step.

II

The atheist, no doubt, would begin by pointing to the cases of what Marilyn Adams calls "horrendous evils," i.e., "evils the participation in which (that is, the doing or suffering of which) constitutes prima facie reason to doubt whether the participant's life could (given their inclusion in it) be a great good to him/her on the whole."[5] As indicated earlier, the atheist attempts to generate psychological discomfort in our mind by recounting stories of horrendous suffering in the world such as the Holocaust of 1939–1945 or the Boxing Day Tsunami of 2004 or horrific instances of child rape, so that we would be motivated to turn away from any meaningful explanation. For example, Rowe brings to attention the two well-known cases of horrendous evil (a horrendous evil may be either a moral evil or a natural evil):[6]

3 Whether it is "pointless" or not depends, of course, on a given perspective.

4 The evidential problem of evil—as opposed to the more ambitious logical problem of evil—explains to what extent certain instances, kinds, quantities, or distributions of evil constitute evidence against the existence of God. The logical problem of evil simply discounts the existence of God by arguing that evil is incompatible with a good, all-powerful God. See J. L. Mackie, "Evil and Omnipotence," *Mind* 64 (1955): 200–212; Alvin Plantinga, *The Nature of Necessity* (Oxford: Clarendon Press, 1974); Alvin Plantinga, *God, Freedom, and Evil* (Grand Rapids: Eerdmans, 1977); William Rowe, "The Problem of Evil and Some Varieties of Atheism," *American Philosophical Quarterly* 16 (1979): 335–431; William Rowe, "Evil and Theodicy," *Philosophical Topics* 16 (1988): 119–132; Paul Draper, "Pain and Pleasure: An Evidential Problem for Theists," *Nous* 23 (1989): 331–350. The origin of the "logical problem of evil" goes back to Pierre Bayle. Leibniz wrote his *Essais de Theodicée* (1710) in response to Pierre Bayle's treatment of the problem of evil in his *Dictionnaire historique et critique*. See Pierre Bayle, *Bayle Corpus—Oeuvres complètes*, ed. Antony McKenna and Gianluca Mori (Paris: Classiques Garnier Numérique, 2012); Leibniz, *Essais de théodicée: Sur la bonté de Dieu, la liberté de l'homme et l'origine du mal* (Chicago: ARTFL Project, 1996).

5 Marilyn Adams, *Horrendous Evils and the Goodness of God* (Melbourne: Melbourne University Press, 1999), 26.

6 See Rowe, "Evil and Theodicy," 119.

E1:

In some distant forest lightning strikes a dead tree, resulting in a forest fire. In the fire a fawn is trapped, horribly burned, and lies in terrible agony for several days before death relieves its suffering.[7]

E2:

This is an actual case reported in the *Detroit Free Press* on January 3, 1986. The case involves a five-year-old girl in Flint, Michigan, who was severely beaten, raped, and then strangled to death early on New Year's Day in 1986.[8]

The event runs as follows: "the girl's mother was living with her boyfriend, another man who was unemployed, her two children, and her nine-month-old infant, fathered by the boyfriend. On New Year's Eve all three adults were drinking at a bar near the woman's home. The boyfriend had been taking drugs and drinking heavily. He was asked to leave the bar at 8:00 p.m. After several reappearances he finally stayed away for good at about 9:30 p.m. The woman and the unemployed man remained at the bar until 2:00 a.m., at which time the woman went home and the man to a party at a neighbor's home. Perhaps out of jealousy, the boyfriend attacked the woman when she walked into the house. Her brother was there and broke up the fight by hitting the boyfriend, who was passed out and slumped over a table when the brother left. Later the boyfriend attacked the woman again, and this time she knocked him unconscious. After checking on the children, she went to bed. Later, the woman's five-year-old girl went downstairs to go to the bathroom. The unemployed man returned from the party at 3:45 a.m. and found the five-year-old dead. She had been raped, severely beaten over most of her body, and strangled to death by the boyfriend."[9]

The latter part of this paper will be devoted to discussing various assumptions underlying the aforementioned cases, but the first thing that comes to mind about these cases is the question of innocent or pointless suffering. In fact, Rowe goes on to claim that no good we can think of justifies God in permitting E1 and E2, which can be viewed as instances of horrendous evil occurring daily in our world. Whether one can agree with this or not (including framing the question in this way), the roots and form of such inductive arguments go back to Hume, who is the main target of my investigation. But it should be briefly noted that such cases of *apparently* pointless evil or suffering are also found in religious scriptures. For instance, the Q 18:65–82 mentions the story of Moses meeting a stranger (often

7 E1 is a hypothetical event, which Rowe takes to be a familiar sort of tragedy in nature.

8 Reported in Bruce Russell, "The Persistent Problem of Evil," *Faith and Philosophy* 6 (1989): 121–139.

9 Rowe "Evil and Theodicy," 120. Following Rowe (1988: 120), the case of the animal will be referred to as "E1," and the case of the little child as "E2."

identified as Khiḍr, who is a possessor of special knowledge) who baffles him by killing a boy and sinking a boat. The Qur'an graphically describes Moses' disgust at such acts: "You have certainly done a horrible thing" (Q 18:74).[10] In any case, let us return to Hume who, in his *Dialogues Concerning Natural Religion*, spells out four circumstances (or complaints) which determine all contexts for evil and suffering that we encounter in this world. As mentioned earlier, Hume's arguments wielded a great influence on contemporary philosophers, so it is worth quoting him at length before returning to E1 and E2:

> The *first* circumstance, which introduces evil, is that contrivance or economy of the animal creation, by which pains, as well as pleasures, are employed to excite all creatures to action, and make them vigilant in the great work of self-preservation. Now pleasure alone, in its various degrees, seems to human understanding sufficient for this purpose. All animals might be constantly in a state of enjoyment; but when urged by any of the necessities of nature, such as thirst, hunger, weariness; instead of pain, they might feel a diminution of pleasure, by which they might be prompted to seek that object, which is necessary to their subsistence. Men pursue pleasure as eagerly as they avoid pain; at least, might have been so constituted. It seems, therefore, plainly possible to carry on the business of life without any pain. Why then is any animal ever rendered susceptible of such a sensation?[11]

As we shall soon see, all these circumstances that Hume enumerates are interrelated. The first circumstance expresses the wish that if only living beings were incapable of pain, life would have been much more comfortable. In particular, if only animals were moved to action by a lessening of pleasure rather than by being driven through a feeling or a sensation of pain in order to maintain their basic needs, such as thirst, hunger, weariness, etc.! The hedonic tone in these desires is manifestly clear, but Hume does not seem to understand that both pain and pleasure are relative. In other words, a given unpleasant experience (e.g., hunger) may seem less unpleasant once we become accustomed to it, e.g., those who fast regularly or fast for a prolonged period as they do during the month of Ramadan. But Hume does note that this particular desire to eliminate pain is connected to the second circumstance, which has to do with the general laws of nature:

> But a capacity of pain would not alone produce pain, were it not for the *second* circumstance, *viz*., the conducting of the world by general laws; and this seems no wise necessary to a very perfect being. It is true; if everything were conducted by particular volitions, the course of nature would be perpetually

10 All translations from the Quran are taken, with modifications, from Muhammad Pickthall, *The Meaning of the Glorious Qur'an* (Chicago: Kazi, 1996).

11 David Hume, *Dialogues Concerning Natural Religion*, ed. D. Coleman (Cambridge: Cambridge University Press, 2007), XI, 81.

> broken, and no man could employ his reason in the conduct of life. But might not other particular volitions remedy this inconvenience? In short, might not the deity exterminate all ill, wherever it were to be found; and produce all good, without any preparation or long progress of causes and effects? . . . A being, therefore, who knows the secret springs of the universe, might easily, by particular volitions, turn all these accidents to the good of mankind, and render the whole world happy, without discovering himself in any operation. . . . A few such events as these, regularly and wisely conducted, would change the face of the world; and yet would no more seem to disturb the course of nature or confound human conduct, than the present economy of things, where the causes are secret, and variable, and compounded.[12]

Again, the appeal to the deity here is that if only the management of the world had been administered on the basis of a voluntaristic will to avoid all pain and suffering! Hume does grant that you cannot completely run the world haphazardly, for that would lead to a total chaos. So he respects the necessity of putting the laws of nature in place. But he wonders why it is that an omnipotent deity, who knows all the secrets of the universe—including what is in everyone's mind, cannot make use of His "particular volitions" to neutralize all would-be evils. For instance, He could have secretly the changed the minds of 9/11 hijackers so that they would be prompted not to demolish the World Trade Center at the last moment. And a great evil could have been avoided. Similarly, He could have also influenced the decision of the gunman who massacred innocent worshippers at the mosque in Christchurch, New Zealand. The point being that one can think of numerous such cases where all that was asked of God was a little interference here and there so that the world would have been a slightly better place.

It is interesting that Hume's appeal to such voluntaristic exercise of the Divine Will has a parallel in the Ash'arite-Mu'tazilite debate on the question of evil in relation to divine justice. The Mu'tazilite theodicy begins with the premise that it is impossible for God to perform a bad act or to omit an obligation (*taklīf*).[13] According to the Mu'tazilites, human actions are the result of autonomous will and power. If human actions are determined by God, it would be unjust of Him to either reward or punish His creatures based on their actions.[14] This is so because if God is the sole agent of every action, which includes both good and bad, He would end

12 Hume, *Dialogues Concerning Natural Religion*, XI, 81–82.

13 The Ash'arites reject the Mu'tazilite notion of *taklīf* and argue that God is not bound by any such obligations. For the Mu'tazilite notion of *taklīf*, see Sophia Vasalou, *Moral Agents and Their Deserts: The Character of Mu'tazilite Ethics* (Princeton: Princeton University Press, 2008), 32, 48.

14 The Ash'arites believe humans acquire their "acts," while God creates them—a theory known as "*kasb*." For more information, see Daniel Gimaret, *Théories de l'acte humain en théologie musulmane* (Paris: J. Vrin, 1980); Ayman Shihadeh, *The Teleological Ethics of Fakhr al-Dīn al-Rāzī* (Leiden: Brill, 2006); Muhammad Faruque, "Does God Create Evil? A Study of Fakhr al-Dīn Rāzī's Exegesis of *Sūrat al-falaq*," *Islam and Christian–Muslim Relations* 28, no. 3 (2017): 271–291.

up punishing the bad person for a crime that He Himself has implanted in them in the first place. Thus, God's justice requires humans to have free choice and control over their actions.[15] The Mu'tazilites also believe that the creation of the world is ultimately beneficial for humans despite any suffering that may exist in it, since it gives them an opportunity to attain reward that far exceeds the suffering. Furthermore, the Muʿtazilites affirm that the moral value of an act is objective and within the reach of reason. In other words, ethical terms such as "good" or "bad" refer to real and objective properties of acts. The Ashʿarites, who reject ethical realism, affirm God's unlimited omnipotence and will. In their view, God's actions are not restricted by ethical considerations. The Ashʿarites embrace the doctrine of divine voluntarism that places God above the constraints of human reason. Unlike the Muʿtazilites, they reject belief in free will and assert that all things are determined by divine decree.

Although Hume was not exactly an Ashʿarite, the Ashʿarite undertone of his reasoning is not difficult to trace.[16] At any rate, the consequences of implementing Hume's recommendations would be that moral qualities would hardly have any value. Freud, theft, robbery, murder, deceit, hate crime, racism, etc. would have little negative consequences, since everyone is going to know in advance that no one is going to be harmed in the end because of God's secret interference. And if Hume argues that he does not require God to do it every time, his critic will ask, "How does Hume know that God is not already interfering every now and then, which is the reason the extent of these evils is within the limits?" So we will have to start all over again.[17] But more important, for Hume the telos of creation seems to be to maximize pleasure and remove pain, which would render meaningless such values as self-sacrifice, care for others, compassion, and the capacity to love. For instance, it is difficult to see how without challenges and obstacles one would be able to develop such spiritual qualities as compassion and selfless, unconditioned love. Most of all, such a custom-made paradise, I would argue, would defeat the very purpose of creation, which is about actualizing the perfections latent in the

15 Atheist philosophers such as Mackie and Antony Flew (at the time Flew was still an atheist) recently argued that God could have constituted human nature in such a way that human beings would always "freely" choose the good. But as others pointed out, the concept of good makes little sense without any reference to temptation, fear, lust, envy, anxiety, etc. Moreover, it makes no sense to call a person morally good if that person is by self-constitution incapable of being tempted. More important, the idea of loving someone (e.g., God) does not sound intelligible if there is not the freedom to not love as well. Thus, the Muʿtazilite notion can still be defended. For more information, see Ninian Smart, "Omnipotence, Evil, and Superman," *Philosophy* 36 (1961): 188–195; Antony Flew, "Are Ninian Smart's Temptations Irresistible?" *Philosophy* 37, no. 139 (1962): 57–60; John Hick, *Evil and the God of Love* (London: The Macmillan Press, 1977), 266–277.

16 It is not unrelated that Hume and Ashʿarism also overlap when it comes to their respective versions of occasionalism. See, e.g., Steven Nadler, "'No Necessary Connection': The Medieval Roots of the Occasionalist Roots of Hume," *The Monist* 79, no. 3 (1996): 448–466.

17 Moreover, can Hume guarantee that even such infrequent divine interferences would not lead to a total chaos in both the natural world and the moral life?

human self rather than producing weak, hedonistic human beings who might succumb to temptations easily. We will come back to this particular point, but for now, let us continue to deal with Hume's circumstances:

> But this ill would be very rare, were it not for the *third* circumstance which I proposed to mention, *viz.* the great frugality, with which all powers and faculties are distributed to every particular being. So well adjusted are the organs and capacities of all animals, and so well fitted to their preservation, that, as far as history or tradition reaches, there appears not to be any single species, which has yet been extinguished in the universe. . . . In order to cure most of the ills of human life, I require not that man should have the wings of the eagle, the swiftness of the stag, the force of the ox, the arms of the lion, the scales of the crocodile or rhinoceros; much less do I demand the sagacity of an angel or cherubim. I am contented to take an increase in one single power or faculty of his soul. Let him be endowed with a greater propensity to industry and labour; a more vigorous spring and activity of mind; a more constant bent to business and application. Let the whole species possess naturally an equal diligence with that which many individuals are able to attain by habit and reflection; and the most beneficial consequence, without any allay of ill, is the immediate and necessary result of this endowment. Almost all the moral, as well as natural evils of human life arise from idleness; and were our species, by the original constitution of their frame, exempt from this vice or infirmity, the perfect cultivation of land, the improvement of arts and manufactures, the exact execution of every office and duty, immediately follow; and men at once may fully reach that state of society, which is so imperfectly attained by the best regulated government.[18]

Once again, Hume's complaint here is related to the first two circumstances he delineated earlier: if only human beings were endowed with superabundant abilities beyond a strict minimal survival limit! We are too meagerly endowed with powers and, in particular, with our capacity for perseverance and success. If only there were no illnesses, idleness, attention deficit disorder (ADD), mental agitation, lack of self-confidence, and ailments of all sorts! How many of us have fallen behind deadlines in the wake of COVID-19 and have had to suffer both mentally and otherwise? And all Hume demands is a sort of upgrade on our abilities and natural gifts, not that we should have to have "wings of the eagle, the swiftness of the stag, the force of the ox, the arms of the lion, the scales of the crocodile, and so on."

A good response to such wish-fulfillment would be to suggest watching the film *Bruce Almighty* (2003).[19] The film offers an excellent thought-experiment on the various circumstances that Hume has laid out. Following his dismissal from job,

18 Hume, *Dialogues Concerning Natural Religion*, XI, 82–84.
19 *Bruce Almighty*, directed by Tom Shadyac (Universal Pictures, 2003).

Bruce Nolan (Jim Carrey) lashes out at God and complains that He is the one who is responsible for all his misfortunes. Bruce then receives a surprising message, which ultimately takes him to a place where he meets God (Morgan Freeman). Following a rather rough introduction, God offers to give Bruce His powers to prove that He is managing the affairs of the world correctly. Endowed with divine powers, Bruce starts to use them for personal gain and various wish-fulfillments, e.g., he gets his job back. He soon finds ways of using his powers to cause miracles to occur at otherwise mundane events that he covers as a reporter. He also begins to hear voices in his head, which God explains are prayers, meant for God, but which Bruce now must deal with. Since the prayers are too many to handle individually, Bruce creates a program that automatically answers every prayer with an "Yes." But he soon discovers that the city has fallen into chaos due to his actions, since people have prayed for all sorts of things without realizing their consequences. Eventually, Bruce goes back to God and asks Him to take back His powers. The film ends on a good note, showing how Bruce's own wishes have been fulfilled the moment he decides to submit to God's will. The moral of the story is obvious (i.e., "Be careful what you wish for!"), so I will proceed to analyze Hume's fourth circumstance (or complaint):

> The *fourth* circumstance, whence arises the misery and ill of the universe, is the inaccurate workmanship of all the springs and principles of the great machine of nature. . . . One would imagine, that this grand production had not received the last hand of the maker; so little finished is every part, and so coarse are the strokes, with which it is executed. Thus, the winds are requisite to convey the vapours along the surface of the globe, and to assist men in navigation: But how oft, rising up to tempests and hurricanes, do they become pernicious? Rains are necessary to nourish all the plants and animals of the earth: But how often are they defective? How often excessive? Heat is requisite to all life and vegetation; but is not always found in the due proportion. On the mixture and secretion of the humours and juices of the body depend the health and prosperity of the animal: But the parts perform not regularly their proper function. What more useful than all the passions of the mind, ambition, vanity, love, anger? But how oft do they break their bounds, and cause the greatest convulsions in society? There is nothing so advantageous in the universe, but what frequently becomes pernicious, by its excess or defect; nor has nature guarded, with the requisite accuracy, against all disorder or confusion. The irregularity is never, perhaps, so great as to destroy any species; but is often sufficient to involve the individuals in ruin and misery.[20]

At first blush, what Hume is suggesting here might sound quite reasonable. That is, what we observe in nature as ordained by Providence may be just enough to keep us going, but could the universe not have been less hostile or contain less

20 Hume, *Dialogues Concerning Natural Religion*, XI, 84–85.

evil than what we encounter at present? Granted, we need fire for survival, but need there be giant wildfires that destroy town after town causing havoc? Granted, there are viruses and diseases that humans have to fight against, but should there be something like the COVID-19 pandemic that claimed millions of lives, including children? Granted, human life would not make sense without such emotions as love, anger, ambition, etc., but how often do they lead to horrendous forms of suffering, as one sees in the case of E2? And what about animal suffering such as the case of a fawn trapped in a forest fire and horribly burned due to a lightning strike (i.e., E1)?[21] All this is to say, Hume and his followers grant that some evil is unavoidable, but need there be such pointless evils as E1 and E2? What does this say about the nature of God?

III

Unlike his modern followers, Hume does not reject the existence of God because of evils in the world. He rather concludes by saying that God must be impersonal and does not care about human suffering in the world.[22] It is interesting that long before Hume, in around 1000 BC, a Babylonian priest named Saggil-kinam-ubbib composed a poem entitled "Theodicy," in which he reaches a very similar conclusion.[23] The poem was composed in the form of a dialogue and can be summarized as follows. The character identified as Sufferer was orphaned at an early stage and seemed to find no way out of his suffering. He tried to be more religious and pious, but it did not ameliorate his situation. Moreover, he argues that the rich and the powerful always turn the situation in their favor, and many criminals seem to get away with their crimes. Furthermore, those who neglect God seem to be rich, while those who pray seem to be poor. All of these, the Sufferer argues, show that

21 For example, J. S. Mill says, "[T]hose who flatter themselves with the notion of reading the purposes of the Creator in his works, ought in consistency to have seen grounds for inferences from which they have shrunk. If there are any marks at all of special design in creation, one of the things most evidently designed is that a large proportion of all animals should pass their existence in tormenting and devouring other animals. . . . If a tenth part of the pains which have been expended in finding benevolent adaptations in all nature . . . what scope for comment would not have been found in the entire existence of the lower animals, divided, with scarcely an exception, into devourers and devoured, and a prey to a thousand ills from which they are denied the faculties necessary for protecting themselves!" See J. S. Mill, *Three Essays on Religion*, ed. Louis J. Matz (New York: Broadview Press, 2009), 99–100. This is a highly subjective appraisal. If animals do not devour each other at a certain rate, what is going to control animal overpopulation? Also, if we are so concerned with animal pain, why is it that billions of people still choose to consume animal meat? This, of course, does not mean we should not be concerned with animal pain. On the contrary, the Islamic tradition offers a treasury of ethical resources in order to deal with animals and their welfare. Many Islamic philosophers such as Mullā Ṣadrā even affirm "animal resurrection." See, Mullā Ṣadrā, *al-Shawāhid al-rubūbiyya*, ed. Jalāl al-Dīn Āshtiyānī (Mashhad: Chāpkhānah-yi Dānishgāh-i Mashhad, 1967), 261–335.

22 Hume, *Dialogues Concerning Natural Religion*, XI, 85.

23 W. G. Lambert, "The Babylonian *Theodicy*," in *Babylonian Wisdom Literature* (Oxford: Oxford University Press, 1960), 63–90.

God does not prevent evil in society. In response, the character identified as Friend argues that many of these events are a fact of common destiny, implying that many people go through both happiness and suffering in their life. For him, wealth and prosperity can also be the result of one's piety. More important, he argues that it is often difficult for humans to make sense of the divine mind, but wrongdoers will certainly face a terrible outcome. In the end, without rejecting the existence of God, they both agree that God does not care much about human suffering.[24]

The point of this analysis is to show that while the problem of suffering is an ancient issue, it did not necessitate people to disbelieve in God across most of the known cultures. So it is rather strange that Hume's successors and atheist philosophers would use the problem of evil to argue against God's existence.[25] But to be fair to contemporary Humeans, they only claim the non-existence of God in probabilistic terms or using inference to the best explanation. For instance, philosophers such as Rowe also use the Bayesian approach to argue that it is unlikely that God exists.[26] One cannot help noting the *irony* in applying such approaches, since Bayesian probability originates with Thomas Bayes—an 18th-century clergyman and a mathematician—who tried to prove the existence of God through his novel statistical method![27] Moreover, it does not help to reduce and quantify a multidimensional philosophical issue to a set of probability claims and assign various quantitative values.

IV

Be that as it may, we are now in a position to offer a response to the Humean understanding of evil and suffering. Let us first uncover the assumptions in the Humean approach:

- The assumption of anthropomorphism, i.e., attributing arbitrary human characteristics to God (or expecting God to behave like humans);
- The assumption of the "pleasure principle," i.e., the instinctive seeking of pleasure and avoiding of pain, as the defining characteristic of the self;[28]

24 Lambert, "Babylonian Theodicy," 86–87.

25 One wonders if there is a psychological reason behind it. Could it be the horrible memory of the World War II? One is reminded of the following utterance by a Holocaust victim: "If there is a God, He will have to beg my forgiveness." See Jennifer Lassley, "A Defective Covenant: Abandonment of Faith Among Jewish Survivors of the Holocaust," *International Social Science Review* 90, no. 2 (2015): 1–17. See also, Zachary Braiterman, *(God) After Auschwitz: Tradition and Change in Post-Holocaust Jewish Thought* (Princeton: Princeton University Press, 1998), which considers the collapse of theodicy and the strategic reinvention of tradition by critically appraising theological and textual revision in the post-Holocaust writings of Jewish thinkers.

26 William Rowe, "The Evidential Argument from Evil: A Second Look," in *The Evidential Argument from Evil*, ed. Daniel Howard-Snyder (Bloomington, IN: Indiana University Press, 1996), 262–285. See also, Michael Tooley, *The Problem of Evil* (Cambridge: Cambridge University Press, 2019), 37ff.

27 Thomas Bayes, "An Essay Towards Solving a Problem in the Doctrine of Chances," *Philosophical Transactions of the Royal Society of London* 53 (1763): 370–418.

28 The expression is from Freudian psychology, but its usage in this chapter has little relationship to it.

- The assumption that the world is full of suffering, or at the very least, life contains more suffering than joy;
- The assumption of a mechanistic worldview, all of nature works according to mechanical laws, and everything in the material world can be explained in terms of the arrangement and movements of its parts.

Before discussing the problems with each of these assumptions, let us grant, for the sake of argument, that they are all true and that God's existence is highly unlikely. One now wonders how atheism would make sense of the horrible cases of E1 and E2. The atheist would invoke "natural selection," which involves survival of the fittest. According to the standard scientific account, the earth is approximately four and a half billion years old, and in this long period innumerable organisms and species have competed and struggled for survival. In this cruel and blind system of the evolutionary process, only the stronger survive, but even they will eventually perish, often in a helpless manner. Regarding the cruelty of nature, philosopher Holmes Rolston III speaks of such evils as predation, parasitism, selfishness, randomness, blindness, disaster, indifference, waste, struggle, suffering, and death.[29] And Richard Dawkins concurs by affirming that natural selection is a very unpleasant process.[30]

In a recent article, Yujin Nagasawa has coined the term *systemic evil* to refer to the entire biological system characterized by the cruelty and blindness of the evolutionary process.[31] In such a paradigm, instances of horrendous evil such as E1 and E2 are simply unfortunate consequences of the systemic evil of nature, period (since it is pointless to question a blind process). While E2 is a combination of both moral and natural evil (natural evil because the man in question is, after all, a product of nature), allowing us to hold the offender accountable for his actions, we can easily think of cases which involve a more complicated scenario. For example, think of someone who has a sibling on the autism spectrum (henceforth case X). Her situation is such that she is unable to communicate with others, since due to hearing issues she never managed to learn a language. In other words, she is both deaf and dumb. In addition to the communication problem, she also suffers from several physical and mental disorders. At times her behavior turns so violent and hyper that she starts banging her forehead against the wall to the point of being covered in blood. Let us also imagine that the parents have availed themselves of all the possible treatments, but her situation did not improve. How can we now justify this situation in terms of the blind processes of nature, except to say that they are what they are, i.e., selfish, random, and indifferent? It is thus not difficult to see how in atheistic naturalism the problem of systemic evil leads one to a dead end.

29 Rolston, Holmes III, "Does Nature Need to Be Redeemed?" *Zygon* 29, no. 2 (1994): 212.

30 Frank Miele, "Darwin's Dangerous Disciple: An Interview with Richard Dawkins," *Scepsis* 3, no. 4 (1995), https://scepsis.net/eng/articles/id_3.php/ (last accessed March 20, 2022).

31 Yujin Nagasawa, "The Problem of Evil for Atheists," in *The Problem of Evil: Eight Views in Dialogue*, ed. N. Trakakis (Oxford: Oxford University Press, 2018), 151–175.

Added to these examples are the extreme cases of Hitlers and Mussolinis, whose crimes should far exceed merely a mortal death.

This then brings us back to the sphere of transcendence, where the problem of evil and suffering fares much better. But the reason why the problem of evil baffles the minds of so many people today has to do with a flawed understanding of the nature of God and of the purpose of creation, including human beings' place in it. The God that is presupposed in Humean approaches to evil is a father-like figure who looks at His creation in terms of human emotions. And when atheist philosophers acknowledge that God can be conceived in terms of being itself, i.e., as Ultimate Reality, they think such a notion of God is irrelevant in discussions of evil and suffering since humans cannot relate to (or worship) such a meta-personal deity. Recall that Hume himself reaches a deistic conception of the divine. So it is imperative that we clarify what we mean by "God."

God is the Supreme Principle, Who is at once Absolute, Infinite, and the All-Perfect.[32] And being Absolute, It is also Beyond-Being, which is beyond any name, form, or conceptualization. That is, the Absolute as such is beyond any determination or manifestation, and yet the infinity or the all-possibility of the Absolute implies that It cannot but give rise to the cosmos or the world. Consequently, the Absolute qua Beyond-Being self-determines Itself into Being, which engenders cosmic existence or the world of becoming. Therefore, attributes such as omniscience, goodness, or omnipotence pertain to Being rather than to Beyond-Being. In other words, there is a distinction between the "Personal God" and meta-personal divinity in that the former enters into a relationship with Its manifestation, whereas the latter is beyond all relationalities. Moreover, Beyond-Being is absolute necessity in itself, whereas Being is absolute necessity in relation to the cosmos but not in relation to Beyond-Being. In fact, Being is the first self-determination of Beyond-Being or the Absolute as such, arising due to Its inner infinitude, and thus opening the door to the overflowing of endlessly inexhaustible ontological possibilities. And it is here that the metaphysical roots of evil are to be found. So the more fundamental question is not "Why does a good God create a world in which there is evil?," rather "Why does a Perfect (and Good) God create an *imperfect world*?" Islamic philosophers such as Ibn ʿArabī and Mullā Ṣadrā respond to this question by arguing that it has to do with divine infinitude, which implies infinite possibilities, including the possibility of negating God's own goodness.[33] Rūmī

32 This view is shaped by my study of Islamic metaphysics, particularly as it is represented by the School of Ibn ʿArabī.

33 For Ibn ʿArabī's reflections on evil, see Özgür Koca, "Ibn ʿArabī (1165–1240) and Rūmī (1207–1273) on the Question of Evil: Discontinuities in Sufi Metaphysics," *Islam and Christian—Muslim Relations* 28, no. 3 (2017): 293–311. Mullā Ṣadrā explains evil through his gradational ontology (*tashkīk al-wujūd*), which is the most appropriate way of thinking about God's providential care in its totality—distinguishing between the contingent effects of God in their undifferentiated reality from the differentiated details of the hierarchy of the cosmos. For Mullā Ṣadrā, the created order is a direct manifestation of the overabundant mercy of God, and hence it remains unaffected by the

expresses the same truth in a more poetic (but profound) manner when he says that "divine infinitude" mirrors the case of a perfect painter who must be able to paint an ugly painting, so as to show that she possesses all levels of perfection as an artist.[34]

So Hume is partially right to surmise that God qua Beyond-Being is unrelated to the world. But his mistakes lie in failing to distinguish between Beyond-Being and Being, and the fact that they, nevertheless, constitute a single reality. This is not difficult to understand once we take into consideration the fact that God's reality is also defined by His names and attributes. In terms of Islamic metaphysics, one would say that the Divine Essence (*al-dhāt al-ilāhī*) or Beyond-Being is beyond all names and attributes (as It contains them in an undifferentiated manner), whereas Being (*al-wujūd*) contains all the divine names and attributes in a differentiated manner.[35] And it is important to note that these names and attributes are characterized not only by unity and uniformity but also by opposition, diversity, and contrariety. Hence just as God is named as "the guide" (*al-hādī*), He is also named as "the one who misguides" (*al-muḍill*). Similarly, God is both the forgiver (*al-ghaffār*) and the avenger (*al-muntaqim*), the giver of life (*al-muḥyī*) as well as the giver of death (*al-mumīt*), the all-merciful (*al-raḥmān*) and the one who can harm and cause distress (*al-ḍārr*), the manifest (*al-ẓāhir*) and the hidden (*al-bāṭin*), and so on. So the apparent discord, strife, and suffering that one observes in the world emanate from the opposition and diversity of the divine names, which is to say that asking God to create a world without any evil is akin to *asking God to stop being God*, that is, the Infinite cannot but manifest Its inexhaustible possibilities.[36] But it is important to note that God's attributes of mercy and compassion trump His attributes of majesty, such as being vengeful, so that Ultimate Reality is not envisaged in term of a dualistic tension between good and evil. Regardless, let us pause to see how all these views challenge the narrow, anthropomorphic conception of God, which is the target of atheist philosophers.

V

In the narrow, anthropomorphic view, God is conceived in terms of His attributes of benevolence and goodness. But the view of God presented here suggests that He can sometimes misguide, and even cause harm. In addition, the Quran also calls

---

particular occurrences of evil such as the earthquake or the atrocious act of a despot, since in the final analysis, the relative existence of evil facilitates a greater good. For more information, see Sajjad Rizvi, "Considering Divine Providence in Mullā Ṣadrā Šīrāzī (d. 1045/1636): The Problem of Evil, Theodicy, and the Divine Eros," *Oriens* 49, nos. 3–4 (2021): 318–369.

34 See Koca, "Ibn ʿArabī (1165–1240) and Rūmī (1207–1273), 305." See also, Nasrin Rouzati, "Evil and Human Suffering in Islamic Thought—Towards a Mystical Theodicy," *Religions* 9, no. 47 (2017): 1–13.

35 See e.g., Dāwūd al-Qayṣarī, *Maṭlaʿ khuṣūṣ al-kalim fī maʿānī Fuṣūṣ al-ḥikam (Sharḥ Fuṣūṣ al-ḥikam)*, ed. Jalāl al-Dīn Āshtīyānī (Qum: Būstān-i Kitāb, 2008).

36 On the other hand, if the world is all-perfect, it would already be God.

God "the best of plotters" (*khayr al-mākirīn*).[37] So someone might object to all this by arguing that "plotting" and other attributes expressing a negative relationship imply deceit, deception, and harm, and these can hardly be qualities of a good God. If God plots, then He schemes; and if He schemes, then this implies some sort of deceitful activity, which means He cannot be God. Now one may argue that "plotting" can sometimes be motivated by love and care of people. For example, in order to make it on time for the lecture, a professor had to come up with a "plot" with his wife of how they would divert their one-year-old's attention to another part of the house so that he could escape. Simply trying to leave the house was not an option for this professor, since that would make the child sad, which would then require the professor to console his child, which would mean he would likely be late for the lecture. Or worse, he would have to drive faster than usual to work, thereby putting himself and others at risk on the road.[38] In a nutshell, plotting need not always be evil, and if this is true on the human plane, how much truer it would be on the divine plane. But let us reemphasize that God has both "personal" and "meta-personal" aspects. The meta-personal aspect explains the metaphysical roots of evil, while the personal aspect explains how God is involved with His creation.

Now someone might still object that this way of looking at things already presupposes the existence of God, whereas one is meant to argue for or against the existence of God based on the phenomena of evil—and not the other way round. This is a false reasoning. The Humean tradition sets up the problem of evil in such a unilateral way that its opponents have no choice but to put all their eggs in one basket. To wit, the atheist points out some examples of evil in the world and then argues that since these evils seem pointless, they must make the existence of God unlikely, Who is supposed to be good and benevolent. This way of setting up the issue then compels the theist philosopher to seek a "justification" at any cost. Hence, various "justification" stories have been suggested such as open theism, which states that God does not know the future, or the acknowledgement thesis, which acknowledges that God can be "imperfect," or an appeal to the human inability to fathom the divine mind. Needless to say, none of these proposals are satisfactory. But what is left undiscussed in all of this is that the theist or non-theist philosopher does not need to consider the existence or the non-existence of God in relation to the problem of evil. The theist or non-theist philosopher can prove the existence of God through various traditional arguments, which do not require discussing evil. In other words, the evidential problem of evil does not by itself invalidate the traditional arguments for God's existence, and the theist has every reason to seek their certitude from them when discussing evil. What this means is that once the theist has certitude about God's existence through the traditional cosmological or ontological arguments, the problem of evil ceases to be a threat to God's existence; the issue then rests on how to best explain evil in the overall scheme of divine

37 Q 3:54 and 8:30.

38 Adapted from Mohammed Rustom, "On Listening: Hearing God's Voice in the Face of Suffering," *Sacred Web* 45 (2020): 36–43.

providence. This is perhaps the reason why, in the Islamic tradition, the "problem of evil" is not presented as a *problem* but rather as an instrument to bring about the human's spiritual development and ultimate perfection.[39] I shall soon discuss the spiritual meaning of suffering and return to the cases of E1, E2, and X, but before that, a short detour to a philosophical argument for the existence of God is in order.

As is well-known, there are various ontological, cosmological, teleological, aesthetic, logical, and moral arguments for God's existence. In my opinion, they all have to be considered in relation to, and not in isolation from, one another. This is because arguments for God are often related to one's given notion of God, and different religious/metaphysical traditions offer varied conceptions of Ultimate Reality. In any event, given the wide range of arguments for God's existence in the Islamic tradition, I will now provide a short reconstruction of Avicenna's famous position wherein he offers what can be called the most sophisticated "onto-cosmological" proof.[40] This argument can be framed in terms of the key question, "Can contingent beings be self-caused, even though their series may involve an infinite chain?" In response, physicists such as Stephen Hawking may invoke the "no boundary proposal" (i.e., space-time not delimited by any original singularity) to affirm a self-caused universe, but the empirical validity of such a speculative and extrapolative (based on our understanding of current physical theories) theory is widely doubted.[41] For Avicenna, however, the contingent can only become necessary through another entity, and this is perhaps the most significant bone of contention between contemporary naturalists and traditional philosophers. For a naturalist, it is fine to imagine a contingent initial natural causal state (contingent either because the existence of the entities involved in that initial state is contingent or because at least some of the properties of the entities involved in that initial state are contingent). But for Avicenna and many others in the Islamic tradition, contingent beings, by definition, lack "eternal necessity," which necessitates their existentiation through something that must have eternal necessity in itself. And only being or existence (*wujūd*) fits the bill. Take any entity, e.g., a triangle, and you will find it possesses an "essential" but not "eternal" necessity. That is, in every possible world, the definition of a triangle will hold, but that does not necessitate its "eternal" existence.

39 That it was not presented as a "problem" can be gleaned from the works of such influential philosophers as Avicenna, Suhrawardī, and Mullā Ṣadrā. That is, Avicenna et al. discuss "evil" in the context of "divine providence" (*al-ʿināya al-ilāhiyya*). See Avicenna, *The Metaphysics of the Healing*, trans. M. E. Marmura (Provo: Brigham Young University Press, 2005), 339–346; Mullā Ṣadrā, *al-Ḥikma al-mutaʿāliya fi'l-asfār al-ʿaqliyya al-arbaʿa*, ed. Gholamreza Aavani et al. (Tehran: Bunyād-i Ḥikmat-i Islāmi-yi Ṣadrā, 2003), 7:71ff.

40 See Avicenna, *al-Ishārāt wa'l-tanbīhāt*, ed. Sulaymān Dunyā (Cairo: Dār al-Maʿārif, 1957–1060), 3:15–27. For the standard commentaries on the *Ishārāt*, see Fakhr al-Dīn al-Rāzī, *Sharḥ al-Ishārāt wa'l-tanbīhāt*, ed. ʿAlī Riḍā Najafzādah (Tehran: Anjuman-i Āthār wa-Mafākhir-i Farhangī, 2005); Ṭūsī's commentary is included in the Sulaymān Dunyā edition cited above.

41 For an illuminating discussion of the issues of the "origin of the universe" from a physicist's point of view, see Hawking's colleague George Ellis's article "Before the Beginning: Emerging Questions and Uncertainties," in *Toward a New Millennium in Galaxy Morphology*, ed. D. L. Block et al. (Dordrecht: Springer, 2000), 693–720.

Yet, even if we grant an infinite chain of contingent beings, the series cannot become necessary except through another. For brevity of space, I will skip over the other premises, but this argument, which I call the "argument from contingency," proves that the series of a chain of contingent beings necessarily terminates in that whose existence is necessary in itself, i.e., God.[42]

VI

With the existence of God now established, we can proceed to discuss the goal of creation in Islamic metaphysics, which would deconstruct the second assumption in Humean approaches to evil, namely the pleasure principle. According to Ibn ʿArabī, God wanted to see His own infinite reality in an all-inclusive object encompassing the totality of His never-ending self-manifestation, so that He would have objective self-knowledge.[43] So God brings into existence a comprehensive being, identified as the perfect human (*al-insān al-kāmil*) so that He may see His own perfection in the mirror of the former. Accordingly, Adam or the prototype of the perfect human was created in the form of the name *Allah* (i.e., the Absolute), which contains the perfection of all the divine names and attributes. Now it may be asked at this point, why did God, whose Essence already contained infinite perfection, wish to see Himself in the mirror of another being? Did not God already "see" His perfection before the creation of the perfect human? In response, the Sufis would say that even though God did witness Himself (i.e., His names and qualities) *before* the creation of the perfect human, this witnessing was through His own Essence and not through an external form. For the act of seeing oneself in oneself is different from the act of seeing oneself in another being, which would be like a mirror to the former. In the case of the former, i.e., seeing oneself in oneself, the witnessing takes place without any intermediary, whereas in the case of the latter, the act of seeing is materialized through an intermediary, which is the reality of the perfect human. Moreover, although this act of vision is still within the Divine Essence in the sense that nothing can be outside of God, yet it is an outward projection of the Divine Self manifested in "external reality." Thus, the perfect human is the very mirror through which the Divine Essence manifests Itself. As is known, Adam forgets to abide by the divine command at some point and, consequently, falls from paradise. But for Ibn ʿArabī, Adam's banishment from paradise should be understood as a descent from place and not from level. That is, the expulsion from paradise allowed Adam (i.e., humanity in general) to realize his own latent capacity for "wholeness and perfection" and thereby rise above all created beings to become a symbol of God's own perfection, love, and goodness. Since every

42 Also, most of the historical arguments tend to prove God's existence from the radical contingency of the world. This is evident whether one is considering the world in terms of the Aristotelian notions of potentiality and actuality or the Neoplatonic notion of composite or the Avicennan/Thomist conception of a composite of essence and existence.

43 Ibn ʿArabī. *Fuṣūṣ al-ḥikam*, ed. A. E. Afifi (Beirut: Dār al-Kitāb al-ʿArabī, 2002), 48–49.

human self contains the seed of the perfect human (by being born into the human state), the goal of life is to actualize self-perfection and be a perfect mirror where the Divine can behold Its reality. In simple terms, this is about knowing and loving God inasmuch as it is about God's knowing and loving Himself through us. Since God is the source of all love, peace, and beauty, it is only by participating in His reality that we can come to fulfil the deepest meaning of life.

Yet, as numerous Sufi philosophers have stated, what comes as a "veil" (*ḥijāb*) between the perfect human and the reality of God is our egocentric self with all its selfish desires and machinations (i.e., the pleasure principle). Sufis further argue that it is hard to overcome this egocentric self except through profound suffering, since most of us take it to be our real self. Therefore, in the spiritual universe, pain and suffering allow us to ascend to reality. From Rūmī's perspective, the most important phase in our spiritual journey involves knowing the self and ultimately recognizing that we have been separated from our original source *in divinis*. By employing the symbolism of the "reed" as the lament of the perfect human, Rūmī in his *Masnavī* illuminates for the reader that this existential separation is the primary cause of our suffering in this life.[44] Humans tend to forget their divine origin and busy themselves with worldly attainments; so in order to awaken them from the state of forgetfulness, suffering can be an elixir which is both alchemical and transformative.

The positive value of suffering can be gleaned from other contexts as well.[45] For instance, suffering helps us bond with God and remain inwardly content, even in the midst of a great trial. Rūmī gives us a fascinating juxtaposition between the hard-hearted Pharaoh and those who are stricken with grief. God gave Pharaoh the empire of the world, but He did not grace him with pain, suffering, and hardship. Pharaoh thus never experienced a single moment of suffering—a state that would impel him to call upon God for help. After all, grief is worth more than all of this world; and this is because it causes the grief-stricken to call upon God fervently, thereby drawing them closer to the divine.[46] At the deepest level, however, suffering brings about a hidden mercy from the treasury of divine possibilities. This is to say that God cannot "be" God if people are not needy.[47]

44 See Baḥr al-ʿUlūm, *Tafsīr-i ʿirfānī-yi Masnavī-yi Maʿnawī* (Tehran: Intishārāt-i Īrān Yārān, 2006), 1:2–4.

45 For instance, suffering leads to spiritual growth, self-purification, and inner peace, see Muhammad Faruque, "Untying the Knots of Love: The Qur'an, Love Poetry, and Akkad's The Message," *Journal of Islamic and Muslim Studies* 5, no. 2 (2020): 112–128.

46 Rūmī, *Masnavī-yi maʿnawī*, ed. and trans. by R. A. Nicholson as *The Mathnawí of Jalálu'ddín Rúmí* (London: Luzac, 1924–1940), book 3, verses 200–207.

47 One is also reminded of the story of Job in the Bible. By the standards of his day, Job's suffering can only be a sign that he is a great sinner. Resisting that implication, however, he demands that God explain why he, a good man, is being so badly treated. Moreover, he argues that his case shows that God is not governing the world through justice, and he argues that the prosperity of the wicked and the suffering of the righteous in general are further evidence of God's not showing justice. When He replies to Job, God speaks of His wisdom and providence in creating and maintaining

This view of suffering is very much in synchrony with the Quranic perspective, which presents evil and suffering as part and parcel of life. There are numerous verses in the Quran which talk about the *dunyā* or the earthly life with its "abode of trials and suffering" and an "abode of false pleasure." For instance, Q 2:155–157 presents a view of life in which trials, disappointments, and suffering are very much the reality of the earthly life:

> And surely We shall try you with something of fear and hunger, and loss of wealth and lives and crops; but give glad tidings to the steadfast, who say, when a misfortune strikes them: Lo! we are God's and Lo! unto Him we are returning. Such are they on whom are blessings from their Lord, and mercy. Such are the rightly guided. (Q 2:155–157)

In other places, the Quran talks about the trials and intense emotional challenges that most prophets or prophetic figures have faced during their lives.[48] Similarly, the *dunyā* is presented as a place where people run after vain glory and false pleasure:

> Know that the life of this world is mere play, and idle talk, and spectacle, and boasting to one another, and rivalry in respect of wealth and children. . . . And in the hereafter, there is grievous punishment, but also forgiveness from God and His good pleasure, whereas the earthly life is but a playful illusion (Q 57:20)[49]

One thus wonders why it is that the same Creator who created the world also cautions us against this world. The answer lies in the Sufi idea of "appearance and reality" (*ṣūra wa-maʿnā*), which tells us that life in this world is to be negated insofar as it hides us from the reality of God. In other words, when we identify with our egocentric self and become oblivious to our inner reality as defined by the perfect

---

the universe, implying that human knowledge of things is limited. Job realizes his mistakes and repents. In response to Job's suffering, Carl Jung contends that it is pointless to test Job when God already knows that Job will turn out to be faithful in the end. Moreover, in making Job suffer, Jung opines, God has actually exposed Himself to be lacking moral consciousness, justice, goodness, and all other related divine attributes. One can respond to this by asking whether it make sense to psychologize God and project one's own insecurities on Him, especially when we do not yet know the range of interpretations that these kinds of parables might offer. See Carl Jung, *Answer to Job*, trans. R. F. C. Hull (London: Routledge and Kegan Paul, 1954), 3–92.

48 See, e.g., Aḥmad Samʿānī, *The Repose of the Spirits: A Sufi Commentary on the Divine Names*, trans. William Chittick (Albany: SUNY Press, 2019), 42–43.

49 One indirect indication of this is the comparatively higher rates of depression, suicide, and other DSM-5 mental disorders in rich and affluent countries. That is, materialism cannot be our answer to peace and happiness. In fact, it leads to both self-alienation and alienation from nature. See, for example, A. M. Ruscio et al., "Cross-Sectional Comparison of the Epidemiology of DSM-5 Generalized Anxiety Disorder Across the Globe," *JAMA Psychiatry* 74, no. 5 (2017): 465–475.

human, God's reality remains hidden from us. So the important question is not why there is suffering in this world, rather whether God has given us enough means to overcome these evils and suffering.

In light of the doctrine of the perfect human, the answer is in the affirmative because, being created in the image of God, we already contain all the spiritual resources to overcome every challenge, except that these inner resources are veiled by our egocentric self. In other words, God has already given us all that Hume was asking for. But Hume's mechanistic outlook made him ask God to artificially place such traits as speed, patience, and resilience in him. That is, instead of seeking these traits *within* himself, he was looking elsewhere. All this is to say, the telos of creation is not the weak, hedonistic, egocentric self. Nor it is matter or the physical cosmos with its imperfections, which are necessitated by the divine infinitude. Rather, from God's point of view, it is the perfect human who is the *raison d'être* of the universe.

One may thus grant that evil and suffering in a religious universe can be a source of great spiritual reckoning and spiritual development. Perhaps in such a context suffering does make sense, for the most part. But the skeptic may still wonder about the cases of E1, E2, and X since they do not serve any spiritual purpose, or so it appears. Could God not prevent these horrendous evils? At this point in our foray into the problem of evil in this chapter, we have come a long way to see that such questions are ill posed. It is a pessimistic outlook that always finds the glass half empty. Recall that one of the assumptions underlying the Humean approach to evil is to claim that the world is full of suffering and that cases such as E1 and E2 are fairly common, which yield no spiritual benefit. Yet this is an assumption that can never be proven statistically. This is because suffering is not "measurable." But more to the point, it is simply not possible to interview the world's eight billion people in order to show that more than half the population actually believe that their life—as far as they can see it—contains more pain and suffering than peace and happiness. It might seem difficult to believe, especially since we are constantly inundated with terrible news across the globe, but the media hardly documents all the happy moments that people experience all over the world, even in the midst of tragedies. Take the example of the *Late Show* host Stephen Colbert, whose life has been shaped by tragedy. When he was barely ten years old, his father and two of his older brothers died suddenly in an aviation accident. The subsequent investigation revealed that avoidable crew errors led to the accident, which killed 72 of the 82 people on board. When asked how such a tragedy would not destroy any certitude that God exists, Colbert explains that his basic disposition towards the world is gratitude. "I'm very grateful to be alive," he says. "And so that act, that impulse to be grateful, wants an object. That object I call God." In fact, Colbert goes a step further and asserts that every punishment from God can be seen as a gift.[50] I would venture to say such an attitude is fairly

50 Sullivan and Blaschko, *Good Life Method*, 153–154.

widespread across the world, where most people still believe in God and find meaning through God amid suffering.

VII

It is, nonetheless, possible to find more specific explanations for tragic incidents such as E1 and E2 (I believe I have already offered more general answers). Recall the story of Moses and Khiḍr, where Moses was horrified to see his companion killing a boy and sinking a boat for no reason. However, Khiḍr later reveals that he killed the boy because his parents were true believers, whereas he would grow up to be a disbeliever and pressure his parents into defiance and disbelief. Moreover, he knew that God would favor the parents with a more virtuous and caring child. As for the boat, Khiḍr informs Moses that there was a tyrant ahead of the people who owned the boat, and this tyrant seizes every good boat by force. But it is important to emphasize that not anyone can take on the role of Khidr in the Quran and justify apparently "unlawful" actions in the name of some future catastrophe. One has to take into consideration the underlying intention behind such stories in sacred scriptures. Regardless, it matters little whether or not skeptics and atheists find these explanations plausible, since it would not do to expect God to behave like humans. Nonetheless, the story of the boy shows that he was saved from future sins that would have sullied his destiny (i.e., more suffering). Similar explanations can be offered for the boat incident, and by analogy for E1 and E2. Moreover, when it comes to cases such as E1, E2, or X, one has to consider the totality of their existential return to God, which involves all the stages of their journey, in addition to their earthly life. It would be premature to judge an affair either good or evil based on the appearance of the earthly life alone, whose temporal scale is insignificant compared to the everlasting life of the spirit (notice that none of these explanations/resources are available to the atheist in their materialist ontology). Moreover, as we explained before, demanding a secret interference by God *à la* Hume would only exacerbate the situation, since we cannot foresee all the ripple effects because of a given interference. If it is objected that the issue lies with the form and intensity of evil, and not with evil as such, it may be replied that God cannot alter the laws of nature, which He Himself has put in place. That is, the nature of fire is to burn, and it will not distinguish between a saint and a sinner when it comes to burning things. Likewise, God need not change the rule of the principle of non-contradiction (PNC) or make a triangle with four sides. Similarly, He cannot artificially change the nature of the egocentric self, which is prone to evil (called *al-nafs al-ammāra* or the evil-prone self in the Quran), but He has given us the necessary intelligence, agency, and discernment to choose right from wrong and journey towards realizing our true self, which is free of all pain and suffering. All in all, it thus seems unreasonable to think that when it comes to evil God owes us everything, whereas we owe Him nothing. So when confronted with evil and suffering, instead of asking "Where is God?," it makes more sense to ask, "Where are you?"

References

Adams, Marilyn. *Horrendous Evils and the Goodness of God*. Melbourne: Melbourne University Press, 1999.

Avicenna. *al-Ishārāt wa'l-tanbīhāt*. Edited by Sulaymān Dunyā. Cairo: Dār al-Ma'ārif, 1957–1960.

Avicenna. *The Metaphysics of the Healing*. Translated by M. E. Marmura. Provo: Brigham Young University Press, 2005.

Baḥr al-'Ulūm. *Tafsīr-i 'irfānī-yi Masnavī-yi Ma'nawī*. Tehran: Intishārāt-i Īrān Yārān, 2006.

Bayes, Thomas. "An Essay Towards Solving a Problem in the Doctrine of Chances." *Philosophical Transactions of the Royal Society of London* 53 (1763): 370–418.

Bayle, Pierre. *Bayle Corpus—Oeuvres Completes*. Edited by Antony McKenna and Gianluca Mori. Paris: Classiques Garnier Numérique, 2012.

Braiterman, Zachary. *(God) After Auschwitz: Tradition and Change in Post-Holocaust Jewish Thought*. Princeton: Princeton University Press, 1998.

Draper, Paul. "Pain and Pleasure: An Evidential Problem for Theists." *Nous* 23 (1989): 331–350.

Ellis, George. "Before the Beginning: Emerging Questions and Uncertainties." In *Toward a New Millennium in Galaxy Morphology*, edited by D. L. Block et al., 693–720. Dordrecht: Springer, 2000.

Faruque, Muhammad. "Does God Create Evil? A Study of Fakhr al-Dīn Rāzī's Exegesis of *Sūrat al-falaq*." *Islam and Christian—Muslim Relations* 28, no. 3 (2017): 271–291.

Faruque, Muhammad. "Untying the Knots of Love: The Qur'an, Love Poetry, and Akkad's the Message." *Journal of Islamic and Muslim Studies* 5, no. 2 (2020): 112–128.

Flew, Antony. "Are Ninian Smart's Temptations Irresistible?" *Philosophy* 37, no. 139 (1962): 57–60.

Gimaret, Daniel. *Théories de l'acte humain en théologie musulmane*. Paris: J. Vrin, 1980.

Hick, John. *Evil and the God of Love*. London: The Macmillan Press, 1977.

Hume, David. *Dialogues Concerning Natural Religion*. Edited by D. Coleman. Cambridge: Cambridge University Press, 2007.

Ibn 'Arabī. *Fuṣūṣ al-ḥikam*. Edited by A. E. Afifi. Beirut: Dār al-Kitāb al-'Arabī, 2002.

Jung, Carl. *Answer to Job*. Translated by R. F. C. Hull. London: Routledge and Kegan Paul, 1954.

Koca, Özgür. "Ibn 'Arabī (1165–1240) and Rūmī (1207–1273) on the Question of Evil: Discontinuities in Sufi Metaphysics." *Islam and Christian—Muslim Relations* 28, no. 3 (2017): 293–311.

Lambert, W. G. "The Babylonian *Theodicy*." In *Babylonian Wisdom Literature*. Oxford: Oxford University Press, 1960.

Lassley, Jennifer. "A Defective Covenant: Abandonment of Faith Among Jewish Survivors of the Holocaust." *International Social Science Review* 90, no. 2 (2015): 1–17.

Leibniz. *Essais de théodicée: Sur la bonté de Dieu, la liberté de l'homme et l'origine du mal*. Chicago: ARTFL Project, 1996.

Mackie, J. L. "Evil and Omnipotence." *Mind* 64 (1955): 200–212.

Miele, Frank. "Darwin's Dangerous Disciple: An Interview with Richard Dawkins." *Scepsis* 3, no. 4 (1995). https://scepsis.net/eng/articles/id_3.php/ (last accessed March 20, 2022)
Mill, J. S. *Three Essays on Religion*. Edited by Louis J. Matz. New York: Broadview Press, 2009.
Mullā Ṣadrā. *al-Shawāhid al-rubūbiyya*. Edited by Jalāl al-Dīn Āshtiyānī. Mashhad: Chāpkhānah-yi Dānishgāh-i Mashhad, 1967.
Mullā Ṣadrā. *al-Ḥikma al-muta ʿāliya fī ʾl-asfār al- ʿaqliyya al-arba ʿa*. Edited by Gholemreza Aavani et al. Tehran: Bunyād-i Ḥikmat-i Islāmi-yi Ṣadrā, 2003.
Nadler, Steven. "'No Necessary Connection': The Medieval Roots of the Occasionalist Roots of Hume." *The Monist* 79, no. 3 (1996): 448–466.
Nagasawa, Yujin. "The Problem of Evil for Atheists." In *The Problem of Evil: Eight Views in Dialogue*, edited by N. Trakakis, 151–175. Oxford: Oxford University Press, 2018.
Pickthall, Muhammad. *The Meaning of the Glorious Qur'an*. Chicago: Kazi, 1996.
Plantinga, Alvin. *The Nature of Necessity*. Oxford: Clarendon Press, 1974.
Plantinga, Alvin. *God, Freedom, and Evil*. Grand Rapids: Eerdmans, 1977.
al-Qayṣarī Dāwūd. *Maṭla ʿ khuṣūṣ al-kalim fī ma ʿānī Fuṣūṣ al-ḥikam (Sharḥ Fuṣūṣ al-ḥikam)*. Edited by Jalāl al-Dīn Āshtīyānī. Qum: Būstān-i Kitāb, 2008.
al-Rāzī, Fakhr al-Dīn. *Sharḥ al-Ishārāt wa'l-tanbīhāt*. Ed. ʿAlī Riḍā Najafzādah. Tehran: Anjuman-i Āthār wa-Mafākhir-i Farhangī, 2005.
Rizvi, Sajjad. "Considering Divine Providence in Mullā Ṣadrā Šīrāzī (d. 1045/1636): The Problem of Evil, Theodicy, and the Divine Eros." *Oriens* 49, no. 3–4 (2021): 318–369.
Rolston, Holmes III. "Does Nature Need to Be Redeemed?" *Zygon* 29, no. 2 (1994): 205–229.
Rouzati, Nasrin. "Evil and Human Suffering in Islamic Thought—Towards a Mystical Theodicy." *Religions* 9, no. 47 (2017): 1–13.
Rowe, William. "The Problem of Evil and Some Varieties of Atheism." *American Philosophical Quarterly* 16 (1979): 335–341.
Rowe, William. "Evil and Theodicy." *Philosophical Topics* 16 (1988): 119–132.
Rowe, William. "The Evidential Argument from Evil: A Second Look." In *The Evidential Argument from Evil*, edited by Daniel Howard-Snyder, 262–285. Bloomington, IN: Indiana University Press, 1996.
Rūmī. *Masnavī-yi ma ʿnawī*. Edited and translated by R. A. Nicholson as *The Mathnawí of Jalálu'ddín Rúmí*. London: Luzac, 1924–1940.
Ruscio, A. M. et al. "Cross-sectional Comparison of the Epidemiology of DSM-5 GeneralizedAnxiety Disorder Across the Globe." *JAMA Psychiatry* 74, no. 5 (2017): 465–475.
Russell, Bruce. "The Persistent Problem of Evil." *Faith and Philosophy* 6 (1989): 121–139.
Rustom, Mohammed. "On Listening: Hearing God's Voice in the Face of Suffering." *Sacred Web* 45 (2020): 36–43.
Sam ʿānī, Aḥmad. *The Repose of the Spirits: A Sufi Commentary on the Divine Names*. Translated by William Chittick. Albany: SUNY Press, 2019.
Shihadeh, Ayman. *The Teleological Ethics of Fakhr al-Dīn al-Rāzī*. Leiden: Brill, 2006.
Smart, Ninian. "Omnipotence, Evil, and Superman." *Philosophy* 36 (1961): 188–195.
Sullivan, Meghan, and Paul Blaschko. *The Good Life Method*. New York: Penguin Press, 2022.
Tooley, Michael. *The Problem of Evil*. Cambridge: Cambridge University Press, 2019.
Vasalou, Sophia. *Moral Agents and Their Deserts: The Character of Mu'tazilite Ethics*. Princeton: Princeton University Press, 2008.

7 Cultivating Prayerful Presence at the Bedside

From Mastery Towards Mystery

Hina Khalid

Introduction

The COVID-19 pandemic embedded one mantra in our quotidian existence: "social distancing." Our habitual interactions had to conform to a new normal, as spontaneous somatic gestures like handshakes and hugs were ruled out as off-limits. Several studies have addressed the detrimental psychological effects of such modes of physical distancing, ranging from the phenomenon of "touch hunger,"[1] as tactile contact in both social spaces and health care settings was curtailed or minimized, to the instances of "prolonged grief disorder,"[2] as individuals could not be present with their loved ones during their final moments. In this chapter, I take this phenomenon of corporeal isolation as a theological occasion to reflect on the significance of human embodiment, and on the role of bodily afflictions in the nurturance of virtue in individual and interpersonal domains. Specifically, I consider the spiritual import of both the embodied phenomenology of illness, as that which confirms our status as creatures, and the embodied accompaniment by caregivers of the ill person, as that which instantiates the divine love and compassion in worldly settings. Drawing on certain crucial Sufi insights, I will argue that our engagements with our own finitude, and our finite modes of being present to one another, mediate the infinite reality. This mediation is reflected in the words of Daniel P. Sulmasy, "We need to know where God is to be found in the experiences both of being ill and of being healers."[3] In thus discerning, in our explorations of suffering, the divine reality on the multiple sites of human fragmentation, we are returned in a chiastic manner to this divine reality[4] who inhabits our worldly afflictions and inspires our practices of care through loving presence.

1 Joanne Durkin, Debra Jackson, and Kim Usher, "Touch in Times of COVID-19: Touch Hunger Hurts," *Journal of Clinical Nursing* 30, no. 1–2 (2021): 4.

2 Batya Swift Yasgur, "A Time to Grieve: Addressing Bereavement Challenges During the COVID-19 Pandemic," *Psychiatry Advisor*, www.psychiatryadvisor.com/home/topics/general-psychiatry/a-time-to-grieve-addressing-bereavement-challenges-during-the-covid-19-pandemic/ (last accessed April 12, 2022).

3 Daniel P. Sulmasy, *The Healer's Calling: A Spirituality for Physicians and Other Health Care Professionals* (New York: Paulist Press, 1997), 4.

4 In the words of Frithjof Schuon, "To speak of a 'spiritual anthropology' is already a tautology—for by definition man entails spirit—but it is justified in a world which, having forgotten the

DOI: 10.4324/9781003371670-8

I begin, in the first section, with a reflection on the sacredness of the body as it is understood in the Islamic spiritual tradition, which sets forth the body as a finite locus of the divine presence, and as a corporeal constellation of the divine signs.[5] This lays the foundation for my subsequent reflections on the nature of bodily illness and disease—for, indeed, if the body is the site of a sacrality that becomes progressively unveiled, it is also the site of modes of suffering that fragment our everyday existence. Interlacing these existential modalities of sacrality and suffering, Sufi writers have variously conceptualized bodily affliction as a soteriological crucible for cultivating spiritual virtues, and, more specifically, the divine attributes. Across these sections, I will formulate and foreground this body-spirit nexus in this way: paradoxically, it is precisely through our experience of our embodied *creature*liness—as crystallized in our decentering encounters with illness and ultimately, with our own mortality—that we reflect something of the *divine* in whom we gradually become recentered.

Building on this principle of the finite as the fitting habitat of the infinite because it is the mutable matrix within which the infinite chooses to become housed, I then reflect on what it means to be present in a bodily manner *with* and *to* the one who is ill or sick, because such human co-presence is a mode of concretely manifesting, in and through our creaturely habitations, God's own compassionate outreach to the world. I argue that the practice of visiting and being *with* the sick, the virtues of which are enshrined in the Hadith literature, bodies forth an ethic of "mystery" over "mastery"—in this vision, the other is not an object to be finally controlled or domesticated but a fellow creature who is enfolded in, and forever journeying towards, the inexhaustible infinite. In the conclusion, I will offer a reflection on the vitally embodied nature of Islamic burial practices—as somatic modes which further reinforce the divinely endowed sacrality of the fragile body. Thus, this chapter itself is formulated as a journey through the spiritual significance of three embodied "moments"—beginning with the individual *experiencing* of bodily illness, moving to the bodily *accompanying* by the caregiver of the ill person, and concluding with the final bodily *returning* of the individual to her home in God.[6]

---

divine, no longer knows what is *human*" (emphasis mine) (Frithjof Schuon, *From the Divine to the Human: A New Translation with Selected Letters*, ed. Patrick Laude [Bloomington: World Wisdom, 2013], 66).

5 Scott Kugle, *Sufis and Saints' Bodies: Mysticism, Corporeality, and Sacred Power in Islam* (Chapel Hill: The University of North Carolina Press, 2007), 29.

6 Of course, the experience of illness does not necessarily entail death (for the individual may be cured). However, in attending to the aspects of death and burial rites, the embodied ethic of "mystery" over "mastery" is, I argue, further enriched—for death is, by definition, that embodied reality that we cannot finally "master." As the Quran asserts on several occasions, such as Q 4:78 and Q 29:57, death is an ontic fact from which no human person can escape. In any case, I would suggest that *any* experience of illness or disease, whether curable or terminal, inasmuch as it entails a phenomenological intimacy with our bodily limitations and vulnerabilities, "gestures" towards the creaturely horizon of death.

Sacred Somatics: The Finite as the Habitat of the Infinite

Sufi writers have variously articulated the spiritual meaning of the body, seeing human materiality not as an encumbrance which should be ascetically denied or erased in the pursuit of truth, but "more subtly as a sign" of the non-material divine.[7] Such visions of sacral embodiment, as Seyyed Hossein Nasr has pointed out, challenge certain popular as well as scientistic notions of the body as a mere aggregate of its biophysical components.[8] In these conceptions, the body is viewed as a "mere machine" rather than, as many religious traditions would affirm, as a divine gift which is infused with traces of the transcendent.[9] This mechanistic diremption of the physical from the spiritual is, Nasr notes, symptomatic of a broader epistemic milieu according to which nature at large is regarded as denuded of sacred, significatory vitality and is reduced to a passive backdrop against which the drama of human existence can unfold. Several commentators have identified this view of the world and of the human body as the subtle metaphysics undergirding various strands of modern natural science and modern medicine, wherein the world and the body stand before us as "manipulable object[s],"[10] and as devoid of teleological purpose and meaning. The finite world and our bodily existence are, in other words, not seen as pointing *beyond* themselves to a transcendent source whose signs shimmer ever-presently in the immanent.

This intersection of the transcendent and the immanent, and the spiritual and the material, is vividly limned in the Quranic vision of a cosmos which is, at all moments, "engaged in a joyful act of [divine] praise" (Q 17:44).[11] The finite world, in other words, is translucently "brimming" over with the infinite, such that spatiotemporal materiality continually reflects as well as expresses the eternal light. With regard to the human person, this "theophanic indicativity,"[12] to invoke Tim Winter's phrase, of the physical is enfleshed in God's inbreathing of spirit into the body. When God fashioned Adam, the Quran tells us, God breathed into him *of my spirit* (Q 15:29), and this ontic elevation of the human person beyond the singularity of mere materiality became the basis of the angels' prostration before Adam. In this life-infusing encounter that is said to be "more intimate than a kiss,"[13] God expresses the divine proximity to the human being. Like a humble clay vessel, the human body assumes its shape and integrity "by being hollowed from inside," such that what may appear to be unreachably transcendent (the divine spirit) comes to

7 Kugle, *Sufis and Saints' Bodies*, 29.
8 Seyyed Hossein Nasr, "The Wisdom of the Body," in *Religion and the Order of Nature* (New York: Oxford University Press, 1996), 236.
9 Nasr, "The Wisdom of the Body," 261.
10 Jeffrey P. Bishop, *The Anticipatory Corpse: Medicine, Power, and the Care of the Dying* (Notre Dame: University of Notre Dame Press, 2011), 21.
11 Abdal Hakim Murad, "Creation Spirituality," in *Travelling Home: Essays on Islam in Europe* (Cambridge: The Quilliam Press, 2020), 114.
12 Murad, "Creation Spirituality," 112.
13 Kugle, *Sufis and Saints' Bodies*, 30.

rest in our bodily midst.[14] Scott Kugle highlights the central paradox of this anthropocosmic vision in this way: on the one hand, the body is ineluctably material (Q 15:28) and is thus transient, fragile, and vulnerable to spatiotemporal limitations, but, on the other hand, it is materiality suffused with and energized by spirit, and is therefore "eternal, unbounded by space, opening into the infinite."[15]

This "opening" outwards of the embodied human *beyond* herself is specifically intimated in the Hadith, "Allah created Adam in His *ṣūra* (image/form)."[16] In Sufi metaphysics, this notion of a divine imprint came to denote the archetypal fullness of the human being as the locus of all divine names,[17] and in Sufi ethics, it would designate the spiritual telos of human existence, as expressed in the Prophetic injunction to "qualify yourselves with the qualities of God." The ethical thus becomes the efflorescence or activation, as it were, of the metaphysical, as the spiritual aspirant seeks to gradually inculcate the divine qualities in their own selves. This entanglement of the divine and the human, as mediated through the inspirited human body, is articulated in the following statement by the 14th-century Sufi, Ḍiyā' al-Dīn Nakhshabī (d. 1350):

> The sages have said, "knowledge of one's own self gives evidence for knowledge of the divine creator," but in the way of contrasts, not of equivalence. Those who know their true nature as temporal beings understand their Lord, who is beyond time. Those who understand themselves to be of contingent being recognize their Lord who is the necessary being. . . . Recognize your own self in reality/if you wish to know all else in totality. . . . If you wish to arrive at an understanding of the deepest symbolic meaning of your own self, just take a look at your own bodily form (*ṣūra*). Let your gaze alight upon the inner meaning of each part, from the top of your head to your last toe-nail. You will see that your existence is the setting for several thousand precious essences, like jewels, that you call your organs and limbs. It is bedecked with rare gems of universality and possessed of the radiant beauty of comprehensive totality.[18]

Two points are especially worth noting in this passage: firstly, in qualifying the assertion of spiritual authorities that self-knowledge betokens knowledge of the divine (adapted, presumably, from the Hadith, "Knowledge of one's self gives knowledge of one's Lord"), Nakhshabī asserts that this insight is established not through *equivalence*, but through *contrasts*. In other words, to know oneself as a creature *in* time is to know the God who transcends time, and to know one's

14 Kugle, *Sufis and Saints' Bodies*, 30.

15 Kugle, *Sufis and Saints' Bodies*, 30.

16 Toshihiko Izutsu, *Sufism and Taoism: A Comparative Study of Key Philosophical Concepts of Ibn 'Arabī and Lao-Tzu and Chuang-Tzu* (Lahore: Suhail Academy, 1983), 225.

17 Izutsu, *Sufism and Taoism*, 230.

18 Kugle, *Sufis and Saints' Bodies*, 29.

ontological precarity is to know the divine aseity. And yet, despite her frailty and essential vulnerability, the human person is presented here as a cipher to the entire universe: to know oneself *truly* is to know "the totality" of everything else. Thus, Nakhshabī sets forth a crucial interrelation between the body of the human and the "body" of the cosmos: if one wishes to know the inner symbolism of one's own self, one need only attend to one's physical form, for, in the manner of a microcosm, the body enfolds the mysteries of the whole. A deep synergy exists between the microcosm of the human body and the macrocosm, so that "jewels" of our bodily lineaments irradiate the light of the universe which is reflected in those very jewels.[19] The body, in this way, "speaks" realities beyond its immediate actuality, as reinforced in the Islamic conception that each limb and organ will testify before God on the Day of Resurrection (Q 36:65; Q 40:21), whilst, in this world, every bodily part "praises God separately and in its own way."[20]

This notion of physicality as redolent with the sacred runs through the writings of various other Muslim philosophers and mystics who have theorized the body as a locus of the divine wisdom—which, when understood and inhabited in a God-attuned way, conduces to one's spiritual realization.[21] For instance, around four centuries before Nakhshabī, the Ikhwān al-Ṣafāʾ (Brethren of Purity) devoted 3 of their 51 epistles to matters of the body, endowing each part with an inner meaning and value. They analogize the intricacy and interdependence of the body's components to a house made of variegated elements, all of which cohere to form the whole.[22]

Reflecting the microcosm-macrocosm syzygy delineated earlier, the authors establish a series of correspondences between the body and the world of nature itself: thus, the body is akin to the earth, the bones resemble mountains, the hair is like plants, and the breath wafts like the wind. In thus delineating the mysteries of the body, the Ikhwān highlight that the purpose of their analogical explorations is not to glorify the body for its own sake but precisely to illuminate "the signs of

19 There is a striking parallel here with the cosmology of Hua-Yen Buddhism, which draws on the Indic motif of Indra's Net to imagine the universe as a "net of dazzling jewels, infinitely complex and totally interdependent" (Barry McDonald, "Preface," in *Seeing God Everywhere: Essays on Nature and the Sacred*, ed. Barry McDonald (Bloomington: World Wisdom, 2003), 15).

20 Nasr, "Wisdom of the Body," 256.

21 Nasr, "Wisdom of the Body," 252. As Ingrid Mattson notes, "the culprit in Sufi practices is rarely the body but is the *nafs* . . . (that is) each person's lower self, which must be tamed or even killed to liberate the human spirit to begin its ascent toward God." The main dichotomy in Islamic spirituality is thus, Mattson affirms, "between *nafs* ("self") and *rūḥ* ("spirit"), rather than between body and soul." Eschewing a Cartesian dualism between the material and the immaterial, we might say that Islamic thought instead tends towards a distinction between *forms* of embodied living—a self-oriented mode (governed by the impulses of the *nafs*) and a God-directed one (guided by the higher imperatives of the *rūḥ*) (Ingrid Mattson, " 'The Believer Is Never Impure': Islam and Understanding the Embodied Person," in *Treating the Body in Medicine and Religion: Jewish, Christian and Islamic Perspectives*, ed. John J. Fitzgerald and Ashely John Moyse [London: Routledge, 2019], 73).

22 Nasr, "Wisdom of the Body," 253.

God and His Secrets," of which the human body is a focal prism.[23] The finite, in other words, is only properly understood when it is regarded as "emplaced" in, and dynamically pointing towards, its infinite milieu.

That the human body is the diaphanous site of the divine reality is further echoed by the mystic and philosopher Ibn ʿArabī (d. 1240), who, like the Ikhwān al-Ṣafāʾ, adopts the imageries of part and whole to highlight the body's role in the cosmic order. In Ibn ʿArabī's theological anthropology, which we cannot discuss in detail here, the human person is "endowed with a perfect 'comprehensiveness,'"[24] owing to her synthesizing of the divine names in herself, and stands, on account of this integrative wholeness, as God's vicegerent (*khalīfa*) on earth.[25] Ibn ʿArabī writes that when God created this *khalīfa* (i.e. the human person), in whom all the divine attributes inhere (and are awaiting, to use our earlier terminology, their concrete "activation" in the ethical life of the individual), God built for her a city wherein to abide with various "workers" and "masters." This city is the body, and it consists of "four pillars [which correspond] to the four elements" and a center, which is the heart.[26] To return to the image of the bodily vessel vitalized by the divine breath, Ibn ʿArabī foregrounds the sacrality of the body by appealing to the Quranic account of Adam's creation—into the corporeal city of the body, God blows His enlivening spirit, and thus the body becomes, in all of creation, "the seat of the highest reality" (namely, the divine spirit or *rūḥ*).[27]

Crucially, alongside this attestation of the divine breath, Ibn ʿArabī elaborates on another somatic image of the Quran to highlight the cosmic status of the human person, namely, God creating Adam "with both His hands."[28] That Adam is the recipient of the divine touch is symbolic of the exaltation of human beings in the hierarchy of existence, for the human being *alone* is "touched" by the divine hands.[29] This is why, for Ibn ʿArabī, God specifically foregrounds this haptic, creative exchange as God chastises Iblīs for his arrogant refusal to submit to Adam: "What prevented you from prostrating to that which I created *with My hands*?" (Q 38:75). The imageries of the divine breath and the divine touch thus synergize to emphasize the human as the apex of creation: if, as noted earlier, the angels prostrate to Adam because of the spirit which in-breathes his body (which bestows upon him divine-like qualities),[30] in relating the remonstration of Iblis, the Quran adduces the touching of the human by God to accentuate Iblīs' error. Interestingly, Ibn ʿArabī draws our attention to the shared trilateral root of the Arabic terms

23 Nasr, "Wisdom of the Body," 255.
24 Izutsu, *Sufism and Taoism*, 227.
25 For a comprehensive account, see Izutsu, *Sufism and Taoism*, 218–246.
26 Nasr, "Wisdom of the Body," 256.
27 Nasr, "Wisdom of the Body," 256.
28 Izutsu, *Sufism and Taoism*, 231.
29 Izutsu, *Sufism and Taoism*, 231.
30 Seyyed Hossein Nasr, *Ideals and Realities of Islam* (Chicago: ABC International, 2000), 5.

for "human being" (*bashar*) and "touching" (*mubāshara*) to emphasize that what makes the human *human* is precisely this divine touch:

> And since He created Adam with both His hands, He named him *bashar*, because of His "touching" [*mubāshara*] him directly with the two hands that are attributed to Him, the word "touching" being taken here in a special sense which is applicable to the Divine Presence. He did so as an expression of His special concern with this human species.[31]

This conception of the divine touch is, I suggest, a particularly fertile image in relation to human practices of being present to the ill person: if the divine touch, like the divine breath, conveys God's closeness to the human person, we might see our own modes of touch, which embody our loving presence to another, as participations in, and reflections of, God's primordial creative touch, which constitutes the human *as* human. Reinforcing this fleshly finitude as central to what it is to be human, Kugle highlights that the name *Adam* derives from the word for "earth" or "dust" in Hebrew, and in Arabic, it shares a root with *adīm*, meaning "skin" or "surface."[32] Thus, Kugle notes:

> The linguistic logic is that dust is the surface of the earth, the skin of the earth, from which Adam was made. Adam's taking his name from the skin of the earth signifies the human materiality that . . . both hide[s] and reveal[s] what is inside while giving the body an appearance to the outside world.[33]

In this way, the body evinces our elemental connection with the universe—both in its comprehensive totality (enfolding, as the Sufis affirm, all the layers of the cosmos) and in its basic materiality (constituted, as we are, of the clay of the earth).[34] Inwardly and outwardly, the human person is colored in the cosmic hue. This anthropocosmic affinity is, crucially, not a fact that can be apodictically grasped but is an insight to be dynamically cultivated through our embodied engagements: thus, for instance, Sufi writers have repeatedly emphasized that the movements of the ritual prayer are not superfluous embellishments to the inner meaning of submission to God but are enwoven *with*, and generative *of*, that meaning.

Each motion of the prayer is imbued with its own cosmic connotation, pointing towards, as well as enacting, the cyclical rhythms of the universe and its multiple realms of being. The upright position in which one begins the prayer is

31 Izutsu, *Sufism and Taoism*, 231.
32 Kugle, *Sufis and Saints' Bodies*, 2.
33 Kugle, *Sufis and Saints' Bodies*, 2.
34 The Quran highlights the fact of human materiality as pertinent to each stage of the human being's life journey: we are created from the earth, shall return to it upon death, and be finally re-enlivened from it at the resurrection (Q 20:55). Thus, the body is integral to our being not only in our earthly life but also in our eschatological fate.

representative of the dignified rank that the human being holds in creation, as God's appointed *khalīfa*. This vicegeral verticality is, however, counterpoised through the bowing and prostrating positions, as the worshipper is progressively brought closer to the "skin of the earth" and finally touches her head to the ground. If the posture of standing forth before God enacts what is distinctively human (for only the human being can stand upright), the other motions of the prayer too are correlated with specific realms: the horizontal *rukūʿ* (bowing) embodies the horizontal plane of motion that animals inhabit, the act of sitting (*julūs*) typifies the stability and equipoise of the mineral realm, and the humbling prostration (*sujūd*) evokes the earthly entanglement of plants, whose roots sink deep into the soil.[35]

In short, the act of prayer, in which all parts of our body are aligned, coordinated, and unfurled to the divine presence, gently "propels" the human person through a vast tapestry of existence, and re-integrates her, through her recitation of the divine word, into that cosmic litany that is always already unfolding in and around her. Ingrid Mattson highlights a crucial dimension of the bodily embeddedness of Muslim worship—although the validity of the ritual prayer is determined by the intention one *brings* to the act of worship (according to the oft-cited Hadith, "Actions are [judged] by their intentions"), this intentionality does not reduce the specific bodily configuration to an external hollow container of one's internal devotional state. For, in the Islamic conception, one's intention is not a disembodied abstraction but a concrete "act of will and is followed by the act of *imagining the body in motion*."[36] This is why a person who is bedridden, for instance, is enjoined to visualize herself as enacting the motions of the prayer, alongside reciting the correct verses.

This spiritual elasticity of the worshipping and worshipful body is also reflected in other styles of Islamic devotional praxis, such as the incantatory ritual of *dhikr* (invocation or remembrance) and the sacred soundscape of *samāʿ* (a term which means "listening" and encompasses practices such as singing, listening to music, and dancing to attain union with the divine). In both modalities, as with the ritual prayer, one's bodily motions are integral to the cultivation of a spiritual openness and receptivity to the divine—a receptivity into which the entire created order is gathered up or recapitulated. Across the terrains of Sufi practices, even the act of silent *dhikr* (i.e., the inward recitation of sacred verses, in which one does not move the tongue or the body) demands scrupulous attention to one's corporeal state.[37]

Thus, Sufi texts affirm that the practitioners of this *dhikr* must, mutely and motionlessly, direct specific utterances to distinctive parts of the body: as one manual notes, the *lā* or "negation" of the *shahāda* (the attestation of divine unity) begins at the navel and rests eventually at the right breast.[38] The celebrated dance

35 William Chittick, "The Bodily Gestures of the *Ṣalāt*," in *In Search of the Lost Heart: Explorations in Islamic Thought*, ed. Mohammed Rustom, Atif Khalil, and Kazuyo Murata (Albany: SUNY Press, 2012), 23–26.

36 Mattson, " 'The Believer Is Never Impure'," 77. Emphasis mine.

37 Shahzad Bashir, "Movement and Stillness: The Practice of Sufi *Dhikr* in Fourteenth-Century Central Asia," in *Meditation in Judaism, Christianity and Islam*, ed. Halvor Eifring (London: Bloomsbury Academic, 2013), 203.

38 Bashir, "Movement and Stillness," 203–204.

of the whirling dervishes similarly involves a specific bodily configuration which aligns one's inner and outer worlds: the right palm is turned upward to receive the divine blessings from heaven, and the left palm is turned downward to transmit those blessings to the earth.[39] The body and the cosmos are thus harmonized in a mellifluent adoration of God, as the practitioner enacts the human vocation of standing at the dynamic intersections of the heavenly and the earthly, and the transcendent and the immanent.

Crucially, this dance is sometimes referred to as *muqābala*,[40] which means "meeting face to face"—the ceremony constitutes a spiritual choreography in which one *truly* witnesses the "face," the inner reality, of one's human others and the "face" of the divine other. The ritual prayer too is oriented to a witnessing of the divine for, as the Hadith affirms, "Prayer is the ascension (*miʿrāj*) of the believer." Just as the Prophet ascended bodily to the heavens to behold God, so too does prayer, enacted in and through our bodies, repristinate our spiritual gaze towards the divine face, which is visible, as the Quran tells us, "wheresoever you turn" (Q 2:115). So central is the bodily orientation in the forming, informing, and reforming of one's spiritual life that several saints have affirmed that the act of remembering God should pervade the entire body. As asserted by the *ṭarīqa* of the jurist and Sufi Ibn Idrīs (d. 1837), the recitation of the *shahāda* should imbue each glance and perfuse each passing breath.[41] We may articulate prayer's situatedness in, and saturation of, the material body, a motif that is integral to the theoretical and the practical frameworks of Sufism, in the contemporary idiom of Sulmasy:

> Prayer requires that one's body *be* somewhere, be it in the office, the car, or the home. Prayers also take place *in* bodies; genuine prayers involve all of us. When we really pray, we pray with our lymph and with our bones. Genuine prayer is something that gets underneath our fingernails like rich, black, fertile soil. We breathe prayer into our lungs like mountain air. We swim in it like water. Prayer involves giving our entirety to God; minds, souls, and bodies. . . . Every last tendon is God's.[42]

Embodied Suffering: Actualizing Divine Virtues Through Creaturely Conditions

So far, we have seen that the fact of human embodiment is central to the cosmic and spiritual imaginations of the Islamic tradition, wherein the body is regarded as a shimmering site of the indwelling divine presence. Uniquely encasing the divine breath, and lovingly "touched" by the divine hands, the body becomes a receptacle

39 Fatimah Mohammed-Ashrif, "Visions of Beauty: Exploring Aesthetics as a Starting Point for Meaningful Inter-Religious Encounter, True-Seeing, Truth-Seeking, and Personal Transformation," *CrossCurrents* 68, no. 3 (2018): 366.
40 Mohammed-Ashrif, "Visions of Beauty," 366.
41 Kugle, *Sufis and Saints' Bodies*, 270.
42 Sulmasy, *The Healer's Calling*, 73–74.

of the sacred and bears witness to our ontological kinship with all of material creation. If this conception of the in-spirited human body (wherein, to use our earlier terminology, materiality "opens out" towards spirit) constitutes the bedrock of Sufi metaphysical anthropology, this truth is physically enacted, as we have explored, across the multiform modes of Muslim devotion and most vividly in the ritual prayer. The purpose of this discussion, in the previous section, was to highlight a crucial paradox which will inform our subsequent explorations: namely, the finite (referring here specifically to the fleshly or the material) serves as the matrix of the infinite, and so our distinctly *creaturely* faculties become sacred spaces in which we may progressively reflect and realize the divine. If prayer constitutes one embodied locus where this sacrality is unfurled, we now explore how the embodied experience of illness/disease too has been understood, across the Islamic tradition, as a somatic site of witnessing and knowing the divine. To thus articulate the leitmotif of this section: if our bodies are never simply manipulable, inert "matter" but dynamically gesture beyond themselves, so too do our experiences of bodily affliction furnish vistas of spiritual perfection through re-centering in God.

We will explore the contours of this "re-centering" through the prism of three distinct, but interrelated, virtues: namely, servitude (*ʿubūdiyya*), patience (*ṣabr*), and gratitude (*shukr*). Mohammed Ghaly, in his seminal work *Islam and Disability*,[43] characterizes these three attributes as the cardinal traits which are re-iterated across Islamic mystical texts, and which are specifically invoked as the virtuous concomitants of one's trials and tribulations. Whilst these traits are linked, in these texts, to sufferings in a general sense (thus including, but not limited to, bodily diseases and afflictions), our concern here is the specific state of bodily disease and the cultivation of virtues *through* this embodied state. This is because the consideration of embodied illness crystallizes even more vividly the argumentative thread running through this chapter: that which is finite (the bodily) mediates and reflects the infinite (the spiritual). To reiterate this finite-infinite nexus: the encounter with our own finitude (which, as we affirmed in note 6, is intimated in *all* experiences of bodily disease, whether curable or not) can inspire a more God-centered way of acting and being. Moreover, building on our discussion of the macrocosmic salience of the human body, we may argue that there is something uniquely *cosmic* about the experience of embodied illness and afflictions: not all creatures can experience, for instance, the emotional pangs of regret and the crippling effects of chronic self-doubt, but all creatures will succumb to death (or, indeed, it may be more accurate to say that whilst we *cannot* be sure that all creatures undergo certain forms of complex psychological distress, we *know* that all creatures will, by virtue of their finitude, suffer an end to their embodied existence).[44]

43 Mohammed Ghaly, *Islam and Disability: Perspectives in Theology and Jurisprudence* (London: Routledge, 2010).

44 Much depends, of course, on how we define psychological pain and suffering—for this definition will determine the forms of suffering that we meaningfully attribute to animals. The specific question of animal pain and suffering has received some scholarly attention in recent years—for a

This turns us, then, to the first of our triad: namely, the virtue of *ʿubūdiyya*, which bears a distinctly cosmic aspect. *ʿUbūdiyya*, which means "servitude," is limned in Sufi texts as an essential trait on the spiritual path, referring to the state of complete reliance on, and an attitude of perfected servanthood towards, the eternal Lord. *ʿUbūdiyya* is thus intricately connected to the attribute of *faqr*, which denotes one's creaturely "poverty," expressed through one's ontological dependence on the eternally rich God (Q 35:15). The Ashʿarite theologian, al-ʿIzz b. ʿAbd al-Salām (d. 1262), noted that the realization of one's servitude to the divine is one of the most important benefits of one's suffering, which reattunes the human person to the abiding truth that she is always in existential need of God.[45] Indeed, the experience of sickness disabuses us, and often in an immediate and visceral way, of the illusion of "control"—illness and disease have the quality of a sudden interruption or imposition, frustrating the projected trajectories of our lives and the habitual patterns of our living. In these moments or stages of rupture, we come to inhabit, even to "feel," our fundamental finitude—a reality we often lose sight of when we become immersed in the hurly-burly of the everyday world. To suffer an illness or disease is to be reminded that we are, despite our pretensions, radically limited beings, and this human-shaped limitation attests to the essential vulnerability of our bodies, and our varying ventures, to death.

Crucially, returning to the passage by Nakhshabī cited earlier, which sets forth human temporality as the worldly correlate of the divine eternality, Sufi authors have often asserted that to know oneself as an *ʿabd*, namely, as fragile and fleeting, is to already begin to know the God who transcends these fragmentations of finitude.[46] This contradistinction of worldly boundedness and the divine imperishability points us to the essentially *cosmic* nature of the status of *ʿubūdiyya*—it is a universal state of *all* things at *all* moments. Insofar as they are always reliant on God for their fundamental existence, all spatiotemporal beings submit to God (Q 16:49) and, as noted previously, sing forth praises of the divine. In other words, every creature, by virtue of its very *being*, is an innate *ʿabd* (servant) of God. It is humans alone who fall away from this state of perpetual and worshipful submission, for their faculty of free will allows the possibility of a volitional estrangement from their God.

Although, owing to their creatureliness, human beings are *always* the ontologically poor servants of God, they do not always indwell this state *consciously* and *heart*-fully.[47] We might term this a distinction between an *existential ʿubūdiyya*, which pertains to all creatures, including human beings, in every moment, and an *enacted ʿubūdiyya*, which is performed by all non-human creatures in every

---

theologically inflected evaluation, see Aaron S. Gross, *The Question of the Animal and Religion: Theoretical Stakes, Practical Implications* (New York: Columbia University Press, 2015).

45 Ghaly, *Islam and Disability*, 55.

46 In this vein, the Sufi writer al-Qushayrī quoted his spiritual master, "just as 'lordship' is an eternal quality of God, so is 'servitude' a quality of man that stays with him as long as he lives" (Ghaly, *Islam and Disability*, 55).

47 Martin Lings, *What Is Sufism?* (Cambridge: Islamic Texts Society, 1993), 47.

moment, who inhabit a constant state of prostration and praise, but which human beings frequently veer away from. In this way, our calling unto, and our glorification of, the divine, which should synchronize with the cosmic chorus of creaturely submission, often falls silent in the clamor of our projected autonomy.

And yet, in sincere and focused moments of prayer, we embody something of this enacted *ʿubūdiyya* (indeed, the Arabic term for worship, *ʿibādā*, shares the same trilateral root as *ʿabd*), thus inhabiting, as we have explored, our creaturely affinity with, and dynamic "containment" of, the entire cosmos. This form of attentively enacted *ʿubūdiyya* is also crucially intertwined with the Prophetic *miʿrāj* (of which prayer is said to be a microcosmic instantiation). Sufi writers have often foregrounded the Quranic appellation for the Prophet, "His servant" (*ʿabduhu*) (Q 17:1), which is employed in the account of the Prophet's ascension, seeing in this divine designation the ethical and the spiritual summit of the human person.[48] To formulate this motif of the intercalation of human fragility in the divine plenitude as an axiom, human fulfilment rests in the recalibration of one's existential *ʿubūdiyya* into a loving relationality with the divine. This attunement is paradigmatically crystallized in the *miʿrāj* and is reiterated on earth in prayer, wherein, following the ascensional archetype, one may both see God and hear God.

In the light of our discussion so far, we may now directly address this question—in what way is this strain of servanthood cultivated through suffering, and more specifically, through illness and disease? The great Sufi scholar, al-Qushayrī (d. 1072), wrote that *'ubūdiyya* is the cornerstone of relation with the divine for those afflicted with bodily impairments or other forms of suffering and who are seeking spiritual nourishment. Elaborating the modality of this nourishment, al-Qushayrī quotes the saying of a Sufi master, who, when asked about the fulfilment of servanthood, affirmed: "[It is] when a man surrenders himself completely to his [divine] master and has patience with Him in the tribulations He imposes."[49] As we noted previously, illness and disease experientially focalize the essential vulnerability of the human condition (the "existential" *ʿubūdiyya*), and we might view the attitude of surrender as the befitting *response*, or practical "outworking" of this creaturely truth (the "enacted" *ʿubūdiyya*). In other words, to realize the inner meaning of bodily suffering, the experience of one's finitude vis-à-vis the divine reality must effloresce into a loving submission *to* that divine reality. The phenomenology of this enacted *ʿubūdiyya* is vividly expressed in the following meditation of Rūmī (d. 1273), where he claims that the nihilating power of suffering is a soteriological window unto the divine plenitude:

> Between God and His servant are just two veils; and all other veils manifest out of them: they are health, and wealth. The man who is well in body says, "Where is God? I do not know, and I do not see." As soon as pain afflicts him,

48 Annemarie Schimmel, *And Muhammad Is His Messenger: The Veneration of the Prophet in Islamic Piety* (Chapel Hill: The University of North Carolina Press, 1985), 246.

49 Ghaly, *Islam and Disability*, 56.

he begins to say, "O God! O God!," communing and conversing with God. So you see that health was his veil, and *God was hidden under that pain*. As much as man has wealth and resources, he procures the means to gratifying his desires, and is preoccupied night and day with that. The moment indigence appears, his ego is weakened and he goes round about God.[50]

Rūmī here directly entwines the modalities of material poverty and spiritual poverty—the loss of wealth correlating to the former, and the loss of health instantiating the latter. Where our wealth and health are intact, we may fail to direct our attention to anything beyond these bounties, which are, as Rūmī so colorfully emphasizes, precarious. Though not articulated in precisely these terms, Rūmī's point is that material prosperity and bodily well-being are more conducive to the generation of *shirk*,[51] since our return to God is then mediated through the multiple folds of worldly intermediaries. Material destitution and ill-health remove these intermediaries and cauterize the specters of *shirk* as well, thus generating the immediacy of spiritual richness. That God is "hidden" under, or remains implicit in, the pain of illness and disease articulates the notion that bodily suffering irradiates a spiritual plenitude by recentering the individual in her essential servanthood. Much as the ritual prayer, which percolates through our limbs and our heart, betokens a death to one's egoic identity and a spiritual rebirth into a deeper truth,[52] illness and disease too dissolve the veil of self-sufficiency and unveil the human person's creaturely ephemerality. In thus concretely inhabiting her unity with God's creation, the individual is drawn yet closer to God, and this proximity is enacted, as Rūmī affirms, through an intimate dialogue or communion with the divine (much as, in his ascensional encounter, the Prophet speaks to God). In this existential entanglement, the servant calls upon the God who first called the servant into being (and, as the Sufis affirm, who *continues* to call the servant into being), shattering her self-aggrandizing conceptions of control.[53] To echo the idiom of Rūmī, the serv-

50 Safaruk Chowdhury, *Islamic Theology and the Problem of Evil* (Cairo: AUC Press, 2021), 41. Emphasis mine.

51 For a Sufi interpretation of the sin of *shirk*, see William Chittick, *The Sufi Doctrine of Rumi* (Bloomington: World Wisdom, 2005), 82. In Sufi terms, the cardinal sin of associating partners with God denotes the error of seeing *anything* in existence as possessing its own reality/aseity.

52 The Prophet's ascension too, of which prayer is an intimate echo, symbolizes a "spiritual death [to the ego] and rebirth [in God]" (Omid Safi, *Memories of Muhammad: Why the Prophet Matters* [New York: HarperOne, 2009], 168). On this interplay of death and rebirth, many Sufis have maintained that the prostration is, paradoxically, where the human being is at her spiritual summit as she "falls," or metaphorically "dies" into, her cosmic kinship with the world, and into a recognition of her essential nothingness before the divine splendor; see Chittick, "Bodily Gestures of the *Ṣalāt*," 26.

53 That suffering is specifically connected to the greater likelihood of the sufferer to *call* upon God is limned elsewhere by Rūmī in his *Masnavi*, where he writes that God longs to hear the yearnings of His servants, for these sighs and cries are like gentle melodies and "fragrances" rising up to the divine. Through her heartfelt supplication, the individual is brought closer into loving relationship with God. Rūmī foregrounds this point through an avian allegory: "It is on account of their sweet voices, that choice parrots and nightingales are jailed in cages, ugly owls and crows are never jailed

ant thus "goes round about" God, encircling the God who primordially encircles the servant.

Rūmī's elaboration of the divine reality, who is somehow concealed under our bodily suffering, returns us to the crucial principle of Sufi anthropology outlined earlier—namely, that the telos of the spiritual path, in a conscious imitation of the words and the life of the Prophet, is to cultivate in oneself the divine qualities. These qualities are, crucially, not to be understood as adventitious superimpositions on our humanity but as the very fulfilment, through an ongoing unfoldment, of that humanity—indeed, these qualities are customarily understood as latent possibilities lodged in our primordial nature (*fiṭra*).[54] This microcosmic capacity reinforces the truth, which we noted earlier, that human beings alone can embody and refract *all* the divine attributes. Here, then, is a way to rearticulate the leitmotif of this chapter: the finite serves as a fitting conduit to the infinite, and the mutable body is the temple of the immutable spirit.[55] This paradoxical copresence of two categorically distinct realities is exemplified in the three qualities we are discussing in this section—if the virtue of *ʿubūdiyya*, our first quality, is intrinsically a *creaturely* value, which confirms our ontological *distinction* from God, the virtues of *ṣabr* and *shukr*, which we will now explore, are archetypally *divine* qualities, through which we reflect something of God's inexhaustible fullness. Indeed, among the 99 divine names are *al-Ṣabūr* (the Patient) and *Al-Shakūr* (the Grateful).

In elaborating the meaning of these divine attributes, the great theologian al-Ghazālī (d. 1111) affirms that the former refers to God's utter transcendence of any inclination to haste, such that God meticulously disposes each affair "in its proper time, in the way it which it needs to be and according to what it requires."[56] God's "patience" betokens, in other words, an ontological seasonability and a forbearing attentiveness to the *particularity* of each thing's unfolding. God's "gratitude" refers to the divine largesse in bestowing boundless rewards upon His righteous servants—unlike humanly exchanged gifts, which are packaged with the finitude of a transactional logic, there is no end to the divine gift that is the "happiness of paradise."[57] Ghazālī thus states that God *alone* is "absolutely grateful,"[58] where this gratitude implies not a need or privation in God which is somehow fulfilled by human devotion but denotes precisely the obverse mode of superabundant generosity—in response to our good deeds of just "a few days,"[59]

in cages. . .. [T]he disappointments of the pious, be sure, are appointed for this wise purpose. Just as birds send forth mellifluous tunes in times of distress, so too are our pleas unto God imbued with a soft beauty" (Jalāl al-Dīn Rūmī, *Masnavi*, trans. E. H. Whinfield [1898], www.sacred-texts.com/isl/masnavi/msn06.htm [last accessed February 14, 2022]).

54 Murad, "Creation Spirituality," 114.

55 Nasr, "Wisdom of the Body," 237.

56 al-Ghazālī, *The Ninety-Nine Beautiful Names of God*, trans. David B. Burrell and Nazih Daher (Cambridge: Islamic Texts Society, 1992), 149.

57 Ghazālī, *The Ninety-Nine Beautiful Names of God*, 101.

58 Ghazālī, *The Ninety-Nine Beautiful Names of God*, 101.

59 Ghazālī, *The Ninety-Nine Beautiful Names of God*, 101.

God pours forth an infinite stream of blessings and compassion. Such is the breadth and depth of the divine gratitude that, as several Hadiths indicate, even when an ill person can no longer enact a virtuous deed in its full measure, she goes on receiving the divine reward as though she were performing this action.[60] Ghaly delineates this principle by giving the example of a person who is now deaf but who had once listened to a specific portion of the Quran every day. The plenitude of the divine munificence means that this individual would continue to receive God's reward as though she were still engaging in this holy habit.[61]

How, then, are these divine attributes of patience and gratitude enkindled, and kept ablaze, in the human person across the volatile vales of suffering? The virtue of patience (*ṣabr*) is extolled in several Quranic verses and prophetic narrations,[62] and across many Sufi life worlds, it has been delineated as a station (*maqām*) on the spiritual path, arriving at which the aspirant bears hardship with equanimity and self-restraint, secure in the knowledge that all things proceed from, are energized by, and return to God. This attitude of patient forbearance and temperance is, crucially, not only applicable to encounters with afflictions and trials, but it pertains equally to one's experiences of fortune and felicity. These modalities of serene submission to, and patient poise before, both sufferings and joys might be understood as two distinctly situated responses to the *same* central truth: namely, that God alone is the enduring reality, and all else is subject to the vicissitudes of time.[63] By thus guarding against despair during difficulties and against pride in times of prosperity, one "enacts" one's ontological lightness:[64] we meet all circumstances, congenial as well as sorrowful, with the humility befitting a perfect servant of the divine, aware of the radical precarity of our being that rests like "a feather on the breath of God."[65]

60 One such Hadith is, "No Muslim would be visited with an affliction in his body save God would order the Guardians (Angels) who guard him by saying, 'Write down for My servant every day and night the equal [reward] of the good [*khayr*] he was doing as long as he is confined in My fetter [i.e., sickness]'" (Ghaly, *Islam and Disability*, 45).

61 Ghaly, *Islam and Disability*, 45.

62 As the Quran affirms in Q 2:153–57, "O all you who believe, seek your help in patience and prayer; surely God is with the patient. . . . Surely We will try you with something of fear and hunger, and diminution of goods and lives and fruits; yet give thou good tidings unto the patient who, when they are visited by an affliction, say 'Surely we belong to God, and to Him we return': upon those rest blessings and mercy from their Lord, and those—they are truly guided."

63 Ira M. Lapidus, "The Meaning of Death in Islam," in *Facing Death: Where Culture, Religion, and Medicine Meet*, ed. Howard M. Spiro, Mary G. McCrea Curnen, and Lee Palmer Wandel (New Haven: Yale University Press, 1996), 149.

64 This sentiment is powerfully embodied in the following prayer of ʿAlī b. al-Ḥusayn, the Prophet's great grandson: "O God, bless Muhammad and his Household, make me laud Thee, extol Thee, and praise Thee in all my states so that I rejoice not over what Thou givest me of this world nor sorrow over that of it which Thou withholdest from me!" (Imam Zayn al-ʿĀbidīn, *The Psalms of Islam*, trans. William Chittick [London: Muhammadi Trust, 1988], 102).

65 Rowan Williams, *A Silent Action: Engagements with Thomas Merton* (London: SPCK, 2013), 75.

In the context of suffering, patience is understood as the integral virtue of enduring one's afflictions with faith and fortitude and attaining the rewards of this mode of waiting on God. For this reason, several Muslim writers have set forth intricate methods of cultivating and sustaining this virtue across the world, which is a moral sanatorium for returning to the divine. The Hanbali theologian and jurist, Ibn al-Qayyim (d. 1350), for example, noted that to cultivate patience, one should act as though one already possesses it—and over time, it will become an embodied habit ingrained in the existential fabrics of one's nature.[66] Especially in times of great suffering, patience may be instilled if one attends hopefully to the rewards that lie ahead—and if one cannot look towards the eschatological horizon of divine mercies in the hereafter, one can anchor one's trust in the ever-merciful God for a more immediate period of ease here in the world. In an evocative image, Ghazālī analogizes *ṣabr* to a tree: *maʿrifa*, or spiritual insight, constitutes the stem; *ḥāl*, or a spiritual state/consciousness, constitutes the branches; and *ʿamal*, one's concrete deeds/actions, constitutes the fruits. Ghazālī extends this arboreal motif in his important work entitled *The Book of Patience and Gratitude*, where he affirms that:

> We do not know when God will make the means of sustenance easy. . . . We must empty the place (the heart) and wait for the descent of mercy at the appointed time. This is similar to preparing the earth, clearing it of weeds and sowing the seeds. And yet, all this will be to no avail without rain.[67]

The divine mercy is presented here as rain, which fecundates the soil of our hearts in which patience may become deeply rooted. Whilst we may attentively tend the ground in anticipation of God's merciful outpouring, the precise timing of this divine downpour is beyond our control. The fruits of patience thus involve a steadfast waiting on God—just as rain issues forth spontaneously from the sky, so too does God's mercy take the form of what Neil Douglas-Klotz terms "sacred surprise."[68]

With regard to illness and disease, this Godward anticipation may involve, to adopt Ibn al-Qayyim's guidelines, the hope for a time of worldly relief (a time which, like that of the unbidden rain, one cannot forecast with precision), or, indeed, the trust in God's promise of eternal felicity for those who remain patient through life's turbulences (a felicity whose experiential summit is God's proximity and pleasure (Q 3:15; Q 9:72)). Particularly in the intractable context of a terminal illness, we might say that the expectation of the divine showering of mercy is gently "deferred" to the afterlife, as one is confronted with the reality that one will

66 Ghaly, *Islam and Disability*, 57.

67 Safia Aoude, "The Concept of *ṣabr* in Islamic Spiritual Care: Definitions and Contextual Adaptations," unpublished, 1–17, www.academia.edu/25631939/The_concept_of_ṣabr_in_Islamic_spiritual_care_definitions_and_contextual_adaptions (last accessed January 12, 2022).

68 Neil Douglas-Klotz, *The Sufi Book of Life: 99 Pathways of the Heart for the Modern Dervish* (New York: Penguin, 2005), 201.

not be cured here below.[69] One is patient before a terrain of existential uncertainty, indwelling a "quiet horizon of hope"[70] as one entrusts oneself to the One to whom all things return. Patience is thus enwoven with trust (*tawakkul*)[71]—both virtues synergistically denote a tranquil "reposing" in the divine, with the assurance that one is never forgotten to the God to whom even the falling of a leaf is known (Q 6:59).

This mode of patient, heartful resting in and with God is articulated beautifully in Q 52:48–49, where God, speaking of those who deny the message of divine oneness, instructs the Prophet to wait patiently for the divine command. God assures the Prophet of His unwavering presence to him, asserting that the Prophet remains beheld by God's gaze. In situations where our patience too is put to the test, such as sickness and disease (and quintessentially, terminal illness), we might say that we are called on to enact our own *imitatio Muḥammadī*[72] and to recall that we too are lovingly "held" in the divine sight. In thus bodying forth something of the Prophetic patience, we ultimately mirror the archetypal patience of the divine, who felicitously and forbearingly unfolds all things and who rewards our emulation thereof.

Crucially, it is not only that God is the transcendental prototype of patience, and the One who mercifully brings the seeds of our patience to full fruition; indeed, the Quran also affirms that patience is itself implanted in us *by* God. Our active tilling of the soil of our hearts does not nullify the truth that all things have their origin in God, and so what God, as *Al-Shakūr*, superabundantly *rewards* as the seedlings of patience is, paradoxically, His own divinely granted *viriditas*. As the

69 This is not to say that the divine "shower" of mercy can only manifest in the form of heavenly reward—there are many mercies and blessings along the way even if one is not cured in the "physical" sense. Indeed, to anticipate our discussion in the next section, we might say that those who accompany the terminally ill person on their journey are themselves one of the divine outpourings of compassion.

70 Sioned Evans and Andrew Davison, *Care for the Dying: A Practical & Pastoral Guide* (Norwich: Canterbury Press, 2014), 133.

71 As Aoude writes, the "Quranic concept of patience is paradigmatic, especially in connection with the Quranic concept of trust (*tawakkul*)." Aoude quotes Alexander C. Scott, who elaborates this conjunction of patience and trust in the worldview of the ʿAbd al-Razzāq al-Kāshānī (d. 1330), a crucial Persian figure in the school of Ibn ʿArabī: "al-Kashani understands patience and trust not only to be 'distinguishing marks of the person of faith' but as stations (*maqamat*) and states (*ahwal*) of the interior mystical journey to the goal of unqualified profession of divine oneness (i.e., *tawhid*). For this author, as for many Sufis before and after him, trust and patience become two of the key ingredients in the alchemy of spiritual purification and the achievement of human perfection" ("The Concept of *ṣabr* in Islamic Spiritual Care," 4). The synthesis of patience and virtue is often understood as the state of what Sufis call a *qalb salīm* (sound heart), a phrase employed in Q 26:89, where "healthy" denotes a sense of wholeness and tranquility with God. We encounter the paradox then, that although one is ill/sick bodily, if one "can see the will of Allah even in times of adversity and tribulation," one may in fact be "healthy" in the true sense of the term (Aziz Sheikh and Abdul Rashid Gatrad, *Caring for Muslim Patients* [Abingdon: Radcliffe Medical Press, 2000], 37).

72 Annemarie Schimmel, *Gabriel's Wing: A Study into the Religious Ideas of Sir Muhammad Iqbal* (Leiden: Brill, 1963), 120.

Quran instructs in Q 16:127, again addressing the Prophet regarding those who oppose the message of Islam, "Be patient, for *your patience is from Allah*." Ibn al-Qayyim cites this verse to encourage the suffering individual to remember that she has no power *herself* to acquire patience, and that all virtues flow forth from the font of divine mercy.[73] To return to Rūmī's image, God thus utterly "encircles" the servant, infusing and energizing her with the embodied forbearance which He germinates into a tree of paradisal bliss.

On this note of the act of God's giving *to* the servant, we turn to our final virtue of gratitude (*shukr*), conceived in the Islamic imagination as the appropriate spiritual response to the plenteous divine gifts. This quality ordinarily pertains to a particular blessing/favor (*ni ʿma*),[74] such that one expresses one's gratefulness to the infinitely generous God for this bestowal of fortune. Whilst gratitude is thus the befitting attitude in times of joy and comfort, Sufi writers have often stressed that the spiritual summit of *shukr* lies, paradoxically, in cultivating gratitude in the midst of one's afflictions. This may take the form of expressing one's gratitude for the previous blessings of God, which often our tribulations bring to relief for us for the first time. Or, indeed, it may involve a grateful recognition of the blessings that one continues to be showered with, even as one is traversing a trackless desert.

One instance of this embodiment of *shukr* in the context of bodily illness/disease appears in the oft-cited account of the early Muslim jurist, ʿUrwa b. al-Zubayr (d. 713). It is narrated that ʿUrwa had developed gangrene in his leg, and the doctors advised him that it should be amputated, lest the gangrene spread through the rest of his body and kill him. ʿUrwa agreed to undergo the operation, and when it was over, he picked up the amputated leg and kissed it, declaring: "I swear by the One who mounted me on you, I never used you to walk to any place of wrong action or to any place where God would not like me to be."[75] He then instructed that the leg be washed, perfumed, enshrouded, and buried in the cemetery. We note here, to reiterate a crucial motif of this chapter, the tenderness of this embodied encounter, where the body and its individual parts are reverentially "entrusted" to the God who created and *gifted* them to the human being. Indeed, the ascription of a somatic identity *to* his removed leg (which he addresses as "you"), characterizing it as an integral part he has carried only on noble and Godward paths, recalls the Islamic principle that the body is given to us as an *amāna* (trust), and that, in response to this sacred bestowal, all limbs will attest before God on Day of Judgement.[76] The decay and burial of this limb enlivens in ʿUrwa a humble gratitude for all that God has sustained of his bodily form—it is reported that one of ʿUrwa's friends came to visit him following his operation, and demanded, "Show me the affliction for which I have come to console you." ʿUrwa revealed his stump, and

73 Ghaly, *Islam and Disability*, 58.
74 Ghaly, *Islam and Disability*, 60.
75 Ghaly, *Islam and Disability*, 60.
76 Nasr, "Wisdom of the Body," 237.

his friend affirmed, "God has saved most of you: your sanity, your tongue, your eyesight, your two hands, and one of your two legs." ʿUrwa replied: "Nobody has consoled me as you have."[77] The loss of a limb, in other words, only highlighted to ʿUrwa the blessings that God yet continued to pour over him, cementing for him the theological truth that, to employ the Quranic idiom, he is never "lost" to the intimate gaze of God.

This account furnishes us with an instance of recognition of, and gratitude for, the abundant divine favors *in spite of* one's affliction. However, Sufi writers have frequently affirmed that the fulfilment of gratitude is to thank God *for* the affliction itself, which demands a more refined spiritual sense and active "reposing" in the divine.[78] Thus, Ibn al-Qayyim asserts that one way to cultivate gratitude during suffering is to keep in mind that "blessings always assume the guise of afflictions."[79] Here, the blessing is concealed *in* the affliction itself, and the process of spiritually discerning this veiled bounty is described in this way: to see the beauty in the trial is to "imagine the rose from the thorn and to imagine the non-visible part to be the whole."[80] In other words, to arrive at the apex of gratitude is to see the rose not as an attractive appendage to the thorn but as implicitly enfolded *in* the thorn, and thus to see one's experiences of privation as already brimming over with a spiritual fullness. This station of perfected gratitude is, in the Sufi worldview, enwoven with the virtue of love (*ḥubb*) for God, for the true lover, as poets like Ḥāfiẓ have effusively expressed, welcomes all things that come from the beloved. In the idiom of the 11th-century Sufi and theologian al-Hujwīrī (d. 1072), unadulterated love for God (which bears no taint of self-interest and is not motivated by any prospect of divine favors) is embodied in one's praise of, and gratitude towards, God even in times of suffering, for whatever is sent forth by the beloved is itself to be loved.[81] Just as God, who is the paragon of *shukr*, gratefully receives every one of our small good acts, in inhabiting the divine-human entanglement, our spiritual vocation is similarly to express gratitude for *all* that God gives us.

This fractal-shaped interplay of divine gratitude and human gratitude bespeaks, more generally, the ontological circularity of love—as Ghazālī emphasizes, God superabundantly rewards those who do good, and such individuals are described in the Quran as particularly *beloved* to God (Q 2:195); correlatively, our gratitude to God in times of both our delight and our distress flows forth from a *love* for God

77 Ghaly, *Islam and Disability*, 60.

78 As Schimmel affirms, the "Quranic pairing of the concepts of the 'patient' and the 'thankful' person eventually becomes the basis for Sufi teaching that while patience in adversity is undoubtedly a virtue, an even greater virtue lies in the capacity to go beyond patience and actually express genuine thankfulness to God for the purgative opportunities inherent in every trial" (Quoted in Aoude, "The Concept of *ṣabr* in Islamic Spiritual Care," 4).

79 Ghaly, *Islam and Disability*, 61.

80 Ghaly, *Islam and Disability*, 61.

81 Ghaly, *Islam and Disability*, 61. Embodying this principle is another prayer of ʿAlī ibn al-Ḥusayn: "Let my gratitude to Thee for what Thou hast taken away from me be more abundant than my gratitude to Thee for what Thou hast conferred upon me!" (Imam Zayn al-ʿĀbidīn, *Psalms of Islam*, 289).

for His own sake. Regarding this dynamic spiral which structures and energizes the divine-human relationality, we may note that the paradox we delineated earlier regarding the virtue of patience—namely, that we are rewarded for that which God Himself gives us—is reiterated in the context of our humanly nourished and embodied gratitude. This paradox is articulated by Ghazālī in these terms: when God is grateful for a good action, He *praises* this action; yet, in thus praising the "works of His servants," Ghazālī notes, "He praises His *own* work, for their works are His creations."[82] For Ghazālī, this spiral of divine giving and praising evinces the superlative munificence and gratitude of God—if, in our quotidian contexts, we regard as thankful the one who receives something and praises the giver, then the one who *gives* that very favor which He praises "is even more deserving of being called grateful."[83]

When we thus turn our hearts towards God in gratitude for our afflictions alongside our joys, not only do we finitely reflect the infinite stream of divine generosity, but that gratitude itself becomes "saturated" with God, because it is issuing forth *from* God. As Ghazālī affirms, an individual's "gratitude *itself* is another blessing [from God] following the blessing for which he gives thanks."[84] God graciously entrusts the patient and grateful servant with the very qualities through which she may *return* to God—this reciprocity of the divine-human giving, such that we *give* to God that which God gifts us, is elegantly hinted at in Q 52:48–49, which we explored earlier. In enjoining the Prophet to remain patient, these verses set forth what we might term a "whorl of witnessing"—God assures Muhammad that he is never forgotten by God but remains constantly within God's sight; he is then instructed to glorify God as he moves through the world and to praise God during part of the night and with the fading of the stars at dawn. To thus summarize the purport of the divine and human gratitude, as intimated in these verses: in response to God's primordial "witnessing" of the servant, to praise or express gratitude to God constitutes an embodied form of reciprocally "bearing witness" to the divine benefactions, by which the individual both *reflects* God and devotionally reorients herself *to* God.

Embodied Healing: Reflecting the Compassionate Presence of God

In short, then, illness and disease, as understood across Sufi lifeworlds, represent a spiritually transmutative experience by which the embodied sufferer may realize and properly inhabit her divine milieu. We have explored how this realization is *enacted* through the channels of three virtues—servitude, patience, and gratitude—all of which inculcate in the individual a sense of her creaturely status as a finite recipient of the infinite divine mercy. Put differently, the singularity of suffering

82 Ghazālī, *The Ninety-Nine Beautiful Names of God*, 101. Emphasis mine.
83 Ghazālī, *The Ninety-Nine Beautiful Names of God*, 101.
84 Ghazālī, *The Ninety-Nine Beautiful Names of God*, 102. Emphasis mine.

has an atomizing momentum as well as a universalizing teleology—it pulverizes the individual's sense of self-sufficiency, but precisely this existential erosion can provide the directionality for a return to the ineffaceable presence of God. In this vein, Safaruk Chowdhury, in his significant work *Islamic Theology and the Problem of Evil*, describes illness as affording a transformative opportunity for "virtue-building and cognitive illumination,"[85] by which the individual is drawn to a more complete understanding of both themselves and the divine reality. Chowdhury articulates the existential modalities of this spiritual refinement in terms that echo the central paradox of this chapter—bodily afflictions and disease instill in the individual the moral qualities to become both "a better *servant* of God" and a true *khalīfa*, namely, a "temporal *representative*" of God.[86] The spiritual synergy of both *submitting to* and *reflecting* the divine plenitude is embodied, as we have noted, in the three virtues discussed previously—*ʿubūdiyya* is innately a creaturely attribute, whilst *ṣabr* and *shukr* have their transcendental archetypes in the divine. This inner realignment with one's divine origin is vividly articulated in God's utterance to the sick person, "O my servant! Health unites you with yourself, but sickness unites you to me"[87]—where this "union" denotes both, what we might call, a *devotional* union (as the suffering individual submits in creaturely humility *to* God) and a *reflective* union (as the individual embodies, and thus re-presents, certain qualities of God). In both cases, through the embodied encounter with her constrictions and finitude, the individual is, so to speak, stretched Godward, propelled by the reciprocal dynamism of the divine-human relation.

If illness and disease are thus intended to orient us more fully to the divine, they are also, crucially, events of opening outward to our fellow human *others*. As Ahmed Ragab has emphasized in his study of Islamic conceptions of "patienthood," the experience of sickness necessarily "entails a set of relations, rituals, and interactions" that inform how one inhabits sickness as a "locus of social experience and communication."[88] In the Muslim worldview, the journey through an illness, curable or terminal, is not meant to be undertaken alone—hence the recurrent emphasis in the Hadith literature on visiting and caring for the sick. In this section, we explore these relational dimensions of illness and delineate the ways that being finitely *present to* the sick person participates in, and mirrors, the infinite divine compassion. I frame this discussion of the interpersonal implications of illness within the broader theological concept of hospitality, as elaborated by Mona Siddiqui, who situates human benevolence against the metaphysical backdrop of God's primordial "hospitality."[89] In and through our embodied, attentive *accompaniment* of the ill person, we refract something of God's omnipresence

85 Chowdhury, *Islamic Theology and the Problem of Evil*, 38.

86 Chowdhury, *Islamic Theology and the Problem of Evil*, 38. Emphasis mine.

87 Fazlur Rahman, *Health and Medicine in the Islamic Tradition* (New York: Crossroad, 1989), 59.

88 Ahmed Ragab, *Piety and Patienthood in Medieval Islam* (New York: Routledge, 2018), 1.

89 Mona Siddiqui, *Hospitality in Islam: Welcoming in God's Name* (New Haven: Yale University Press, 2015).

to His creatures, and in this way, illness becomes perfused with the potency of both "horizontal" and "vertical" relationality. Articulating this intersection of the horizontal and the vertical, which we develop in this section, Ghaly draws on the conception of Zuhayr Muḥammad al-Zamīlī, who affirmed that it is not only the sick person who is "tested" by her sickness, but also her family and indeed, society at large, for whom caring *for* the sick individual assumes a distinctive ethical-spiritual valence.[90]

The lineaments of this modality of care are enfolded in Siddiqui's elaboration of "hospitality" as it is developed across Muslim literature. In its general sense, Islamic hospitality refers to the virtue of giving "voluntarily and without compensation."[91] Siddiqui traces this ethos of "welcome and generosity" to the Arabic word *ḍıyafa*, a term which is invoked in the Hadith, "There is no good in the one who is not hospitable."[92] In many religious traditions, Siddiqui notes, the act of hosting the guest or accommodating the stranger is imbued with spiritual meaning, for the stranger is often regarded as a locus of the divine presence. In the Biblical and Quranic narratives, for instance, Abraham graciously hosted three visitors, providing them with food and shelter, unaware that they were angels in guise. In the Quran, more specifically, this ethic of reaching out to the unknown other is crystallized in the multiple injunctions to give charity, to feed the poor, and to look after widows, travelers, and orphans. The virtue of giving *from* one's wealth and treating the vulnerable with generosity and compassion pervades the Quran, and such hospitality actively subverts the transactional economy of exchange: it must be given without expectation of a reward (Q 76:8–9). As Siddiqui foregrounds, this scriptural altruism goes beyond the specificities of institutionalized charity, and involves a deep-rooted, sacred responsibility to protect and serve others.[93]

In this way, the Islamic imperative of self-giving action transcends certain diluted conceptions of hospitality in terms of a "quaint sentimentality" or an incidental reception of others into our dwellings.[94] When revered and enacted as a divine duty, hospitality is not simply about "making physical room for others in our homes, but it is essentially an attitude to life . . . we need to make room for others in our hearts and minds, and with our words."[95] As the Quran affirms in Q 2:263, "A kind word with forgiveness is better than almsgiving followed by injury." At the heart of hospitality is thus a radical regard and compassion for others on the level of their fundamental humanity; indeed, whereas contemporary understandings of hospitality veer towards exclusivity (insofar as we invite into our hearts and hearths only those who are already known to us or those whom we wish to know),

90 Ghaly, *Islam and Disability*, 48.

91 El-Sayed El-Aswad, "Hospitality," in *Encyclopedia of Islam and the Muslim World*, ed. Richard C. Martin (New York: Macmillan, 2003), 462.

92 Siddiqui, *Hospitality in Islam*, 11.

93 Siddiqui, *Hospitality in Islam*, 29.

94 Siddiqui, *Hospitality in Islam*, 30.

95 Siddiqui, *Hospitality in Islam*, 18.

the scriptural emphasis is often placed on those who are "nameless strangers and not just invited guests."[96] Through this mode of compassionate outreach to the "nameless" other, our self-identifying tendencies become dissolved, for the vulnerable stranger is, in her anonymity, "disruptive" of our everyday affectivities which extend only to the perimeter of the known.

This decentering disruption, however, marks an affective integration on a deeper level, drawing us towards greater openness, love, and generosity. The notion that "true" hospitality is enacted towards those whom one does not know personally is reflected in the Islamic tradition on visiting the sick, which, as Ragab's analysis of the Hadith commentaries reveals, "was not seen as a personal duty that drew from a person's relationship to the sick. Instead, it was either a communal obligation that ensured that the sick would be visited, a *sunna* [Prophetic practice], or a recommended act that individuals were encouraged to engage in."[97] In extending ourselves in compassion towards the other, we crucially mirror something of God's primordial "hosting" of His servants through the act of creation, which emerges not through any lack or poverty in the heart of God, but flows forth, as Ibn ʿArabī and other Sufis put it, from the superabundant compassion/mercy (*raḥma*) of God. This generative hospitality which brings the world into being unfurls into God's continued hospitality by way of sustaining and providing for His creation (Q 35:3). Offering hospitality thus becomes a human way to imitate the cosmic generosity of God; if God's ontological gift is, fundamentally, the gift of *Himself* to creation,[98] when we too offer ourselves *to* the other whom we usher in, we become, by extension, multiple finite loci of God's metaphysical "welcoming" of the world.

Hospitality then, in its true sense, denotes a fundamental *orientation* towards others—that is, a state of *being* characterized by benevolence and self-giving, in an echo of the perpetually reverberating *raḥma* of God. This attitudinal hospitality which should suffuse our entire being involves, crucially, not only the generous and loving treatment of others who arrive in our midst (such as the unexpected traveler or stranger) but demands also an active *going out* to the other in humility and compassion. The sacrality of this human-to-human outreach is focalized in the Prophetic traditions narrating the virtue of visiting the sick, which, reflecting a crucial theme of this chapter, highlight the deeply *embodied* nature of offering comfort and healing to the other. Indeed, these traditions, which Ragab foregrounds in his study of Islamic medical literature, attest that each embodied *act* of visitation (referred to in this literature as *ʿiyāda*)[99] bears its distinctive spiritual meaning.

96 Siddiqui, *Hospitality in Islam*, 30.

97 Ragab, *Piety and Patienthood*, 118.

98 Siddiqui, *Hospitality in Islam*, 129. As the Hadith of the Hidden Treasure articulates, the world arises out of God's longing "to be known;" creation is thus "the work of divine love, [as well as] divine self-love," by which God mercifully breathes the world into being (Siddiqui, *Hospitality in Islam*, 133).

99 In Islamic medical literature and beyond, this term "became a specific term for visiting a patient to fulfil the religious obligation or follow the *sunna* of the prophet" (Ragab, *Piety and Patienthood*, 121).

Firstly, this "hospitable" *going out* of oneself in service of the one in need must be accompanied by a righteous intention—one must not expect a recompense from the patient but must trust in the merciful rewards of God, *al-Ṣabūr* and *al-Shakūr*. As one tradition states: "Whoever visits a sick person, hoping for God's reward and the accomplishment of God's promise, God assigns him 70,000 angels to pray for him until he returns to his home."[100] In another narration which similarly weaves a heavenly halo around the visitor, a supernal caller declares, "May you [i.e., the visitor] and your steps be blessed, and may you find your place in heaven."[101] This motif of a spiritual envelope is reiterated in the Prophetic statement that a visitor "walks under a shade from heaven" as he journeys towards the dwelling of the sick person, and in another tradition, we are told that "a visitor wades in mercy up to his knees, and when he sits, mercy covers him all."[102] As Ragab identifies, in all of these narrations, "emphasis is placed on the *process* of visiting—leaving the house, walking to the sick, sitting there."[103] The infusion of physical motions with spiritual richness creates what Ragab calls a "pietistic cosmology,"[104] wherein the embodied acts of going *to* and being *with* the other are at all moments saturated with the divine presence.

Reaffirming this centrality of the body, the Prophet emphasized the importance of gently touching the sick person as an act of consoling and companioning:

> It is of the completion of visiting the sick that you extend your hand to him, ask him how he is, put your hand on him. And it is of the completion of your greeting him that you shake his hand.[105]

Ibn Baṭṭāl (d. 1057), the commentator on Hadith literature, similarly wrote that placing one's hand on the patient is a "sign of care" and a way to *feel* how much the patient is struggling.[106] Returning to Ibn ʿArabī's symbolic interpretation of Q 38:75, we may here view this humanly enacted touch as a finite mirroring of the primordial divine touch which affirms the dignified rank of the human being in the cosmic matrix. By extending a compassionate hand to the other, we reflect the tender, divine outreach or touch, which gently affirms and *bears witness to* the other's humanity (we recall here that the Arabic terms for "human being" and "touch" share the same root).

Touch constitutes, in other words, a concrete instantiation of one's hospitality, betokening a loving and attentive presence *to* and *with* the human other. In this way, human touch participates in, and reflects, the creative touch of God. Crucially,

100 Ragab, *Piety and Patienthood*, 118.
101 Ragab, *Piety and Patienthood*, 118.
102 Ragab, *Piety and Patienthood*, 118.
103 Ragab, *Piety and Patienthood*, 118.
104 Ragab, *Piety and Patienthood*, 118.
105 Ragab, *Piety and Patienthood*, 119.
106 Ragab, *Piety and Patienthood*, 121.

touch denotes participation in a deeper sense too—as Ibn Battal identified, to touch the sick person physically is to be "touched" or moved by their pain inwardly, and in this sense, the caring touch enacts *compassion* as an embodied mode of "suffering with" the other. To illustrate this participatory potency, we may draw on Aristotle, who, in reflecting on the human sensorium, highlighted the *essentially* reciprocal nature of touch. For Aristotle, touch is the sense most integral to embodied experience—it belongs universally to all living sentient beings, which is not the case with the other senses.[107] Moreover, tactile power is not limited to a specific bodily area, as is the case with the other senses—for this reason, we "touch *continuously*, if nothing else at least the ground with our feet."[108] Crucially for our purposes, touch is ineluctably inflected by mutuality—to see is not necessarily to be *seen* by what I see, but to touch is "immediately to be touched by what I touch—what I contact by means of touch comes into contact with me."[109]

The mutuality of the physical touch and the mutuality inherent in *compassion* are thus concentered—as the hospitable reaching *out* to the other is enacted through one's accompaniment *of* the other. To truly be *with* the sick person is to share in their suffering, and indeed, to be transformed by the encounter. Chowdhury proffers an elegant interpretation of this transformation, drawing on the Hadith wherein God, in response to a question from Adam about why God created people with various disparities (such as rich and poor, healthy and unhealthy), affirms that He desired "that the one who was granted favors should praise Me and thank Me."[110] The ordinary mode, Chowdhury notes, in which this narration and those similar to it are interpreted is that God decrees certain types of suffering to specific individuals so that other individuals can express their gratitude to God for not being among those who are ordained such afflictions. Such traditions are thus understood as setting forth a juxtaposition of states, where one's own good fortune is thrown into sharp relief by the recognition of its contrary (namely, the state of suffering).[111]

However, Chowdhury affirms, this principle of gratitude can be interpreted in another way: it does not involve a merely "superficial recognition" of one's prosperity vis-à-vis the other, but it entails gratitude *for* the other *in* and *of* herself, for she brings to the individual the opportunity for "healing, instruction and deep realization."[112] Developing this motif with specific reference to the issue of disability, Chowdhury affirms that "persons with disability *give* and the nondisabled *receive*,"[113] for the former draw the latter towards a recognition of their own existential fragility and vulnerability, and towards an insight into the divine plenitude.

107 Jean-Louis Chrétien, *The Call and the Response*, trans. Anne A. Davenport (New York: Fordham University Press, 2004), 92.
108 Chrétien, *The Call and the Response*, 90.
109 Chrétien, *The Call and the Response*, 85.
110 Chowdhury, *Islamic Theology and the Problem of Evil*, 47.
111 Chowdhury, *Islamic Theology and the Problem of Evil*, 47.
112 Chowdhury, *Islamic Theology and the Problem of Evil*, 48.
113 Chowdhury, *Islamic Theology and the Problem of Evil*, 47–48. Emphasis mine.

The implicit sense of hierarchy between the giver who is replete with riches and the receiver who is impoverished is reversed—here, the one who is vulnerable, and to whom society owes an obligation of care (as stipulated in Islamic ethics), is regarded as a catalyst of our spiritual insight. Ghazālī articulates this reversal in the context of almsgiving: one must give charity with an attitude of utter humility, by guarding against the self-aggrandizing pride which often attends, and always nullifies, our good deeds. This self-effacing subjectivity can be cultivated by purging oneself of the belief that one is better than the poor man and *instead* by seeing the poor man as our true benefactor. This is because, by accepting the giver's gift, the poor man has enabled the giver to humbly discharge an obligation towards God, and to attain spiritual purity in the process.[114]

In the context of being present *to* and *with* the sick, we might articulate this reversal of the roles of giver and receiver in this way:

> The intervention [i.e., the act of visiting the sick] God is demanding . . . is not to be executed from a position of sterile, disinterested self-reflection and concern, or independence, power, privilege and security but rather a sense of duty that is, of course, axiomatically grounded in the desire for God, but also from the realization that *those commanded to help are vulnerable themselves*. God subjects one group to encounter the vulnerabilities of another group in order to bring the former to comprehend their own vulnerability and thereby activate a deep love and empathy towards the latter group.[115]

When we *go out* to visit the sick person and encounter them in their fragility, our sense of self-sufficiency is slowly eroded, as we refract something of the divine self-giving in worldly milieus. In this hospitable outreach, the "artificial boundary between the guest [the sick person] and the host [the visitor]" is dissolved,[116] such that the host "recognizes the value and dignity" of the guest, along with "the responsibilities to tend to her needs; and she comes to appreciate the gift she receives in knowing and serving the other."[117] Part of this reversal of roles in the embodied encounter between host and guest, visitor and patient, involves the recognition that the sick person is, in some sense, closer to the divine, and thus, alongside the traditions that enjoin the *visitor* to pray for the patient, we find narrations that advise the

114 al-Ghazālī, *The Mysteries of Almsgiving*, trans. Nabih Amin Faris (Lahore: Sh. Muhammad Ashraf, 1980), 37.

115 Chowdhury, *Islamic Theology and the Problem of Evil*, 48. Emphasis mine.

116 Chowdhury, *Islamic Theology and the Problem of Evil*, 49. In another context, but reflecting the same principle, a dance therapist in the field of palliative care writes, "The therapist may believe that *he* or *she* is doing something for the client, when in truth I believe that it is the other way around. My clients have been my most valuable teachers" (Christina M. Puchalski, *A Time for Listening and Caring: Spirituality and the Care of the Chronically Ill and Dying* (Oxford: Oxford University Press, 2006), 289).

117 Chowdhury, *Islamic Theology and the Problem of Evil*, 51.

visitor to ask the *patient* to pray for them.[118] The sick person, who resides "in the confines of the divine presence,"[119] becomes the "giver" of divine blessings *to* the visitor. Indeed, this unshakeable divine "with-ness" is reinforced when God affirms that He abides in the dwellings of the sick person, and a failure to visit the suffering individual is thus a failure to visit God:

> On the Day of Judgement, God says, "O Son of Adam, I have fallen sick and you did not visit me." [The servant] would say, "O Lord! How could I visit you when you are the Lord of all the living?" God says: "Did you not know that my servant so and so has fallen sick and you did not visit him? Had you visited him, you would have found me there."[120]

In other words, the infinite dynamically indwells the finite, such that wherever we embody a compassionate presence to the other, we are not only *reflecting* the creative love of God but are also *encountering* God. So central is this modality of "with-ness" that one is enjoined in a Hadith to accompany the sick person even when they can no longer be cured—"when one of you visits the ill, then reassure him regarding his lifespan. Indeed, that will not repel anything, but it will comfort his soul."[121] The sense conveyed here by "lifespan" returns us to the theme of creaturely finitude articulated earlier—the sick person should not despair because their life, and indeed all finite life, is mysteriously and lovingly enfolded and comprehended by God. With this insight into the unswerving divine omnipresence, even when one cannot "repel" a disease, one can still offer comfort and healing to the soul. In this sense, the other is not an object to be "grasped" or controlled but is to be gently affirmed and accompanied in their suffering.[122] When all efforts at cure have been exhausted, one can simply *be* there with the patient, both reflecting and receiving God's solicitude.

This divine proximity, which we mirror in our earthly enactments of "hospitality" is colorfully articulated by Rūmī who, in relating the account of an individual insistently calling on God in prayer and seemingly receiving no response, narrates the eventual divine declaration: "Under every 'O Lord!' from you are many *labbayks* from Me."[123] *Labbayk*, meaning "Here I am," is the announcement that Muslims make during the pilgrimage as they stand before God and submit themselves

118 Ragab, *Piety and Patienthood*, 120.
119 Ragab, *Piety and Patienthood*, 120.
120 Ragab, *Piety and Patienthood*, 120.
121 "Hadith 2087 of Chapters on Medicine by Jami Al Tirmizi," *Islamic Finder*, www.islamicfinder.org/hadith/tirmidhi/medicine/2087/?language=fr (last accessed January 11, 2022).
122 In Puchalski's words, "Spiritual care is the practice of compassionate presence. It is the ability to love another without judgement, prejudice, or a preconceived expectation of something in return. It is the act of sitting with the ill and dying in moments of deep and profound sadness and grief, sharing the pain with them" (Puchalski, *A Time for Listening and Caring*, 40).
123 Mohammed Rustom, "On Listening: Hearing God's Voice in the Face of Suffering," *Sacred Web* 45 (2020): 42.

to Him. In Rūmī's narrative, it is not principally the human being who declares her presence before God, rather, it is God who perpetually announces His royal "here-ness." Our embodied accompaniment *of*, or "here-ness" *with*, the suffering other reattunes us to this primordial divine "here-ness," and in this sense, as Siddiqui affirms, "hospitality" becomes "an act of worship, [and is] thus challenging, humbling, and spiritually transformative."[124] Enfolded and energized by God, this interaction with the other constitutes a mystery, in the sense affirmed by the French philosopher Gabriel Marcel (d. 1973):

> A problem is something which I meet, which I find complete before me, but which I can therefore lay siege to and reduce. But a mystery is something in which I myself am involved, and it can therefore only be thought of as a sphere in which the distinction between what is in me and what is before me loses its meaning and its initial validity.[125]

Conclusion

Running through our discussion in the previous three sections is the motif that the Islamic ethos of encounter with God and engagement with fellow human beings can be characterized as the cultivation of an attitude of "mystery" and the rejection of attempts at "mastery." This motif of volitional abnegation within a sacral envelope is, of course, most powerfully bodied forth in the final creaturely destination of all beings—death. Therefore, it is fitting to conclude our explorations of the theme of embodied illness and care with a reflection on the ways that dying and death also affirm the sacrality of the material, and on the ways that this sacrality is enacted through, to explicate the Persian verb for "bury," the final *entrustment* of the individual to the earth. This beautifully evocative expression returns us to the notion of the body as a trust from God, which is gently companioned on its way and finally committed to the clay. As part of the "hospitable" presence to the sick (or, in this case, the dying) person, those at the bedside are encouraged to gently prompt the patient to recite the *shahāda* (or attestation of faith), which is itself an embodied declaration that one entrusts oneself to the divine unity, and thus "lean[s] back into the arms of [divine] surrender."[126] Those present will often also recite certain verses or chapters from the Quran, saturating the soundscape of the dying patient with God's revelation.[127]

124 Siddiqui, *Hospitality in Islam*, 17.

125 Gabriel Marcel, *Being and Having*, trans. Katherine Farrer (Glasgow: The University Press, 1949), 117.

126 Puchalski, *A Time for Listening and Caring*, 330.

127 Regarding this auditory accompaniment of the dying person, some Sufi masters have written that the ear is the organ with the strongest connection to the heart (Bashir, "Movement and Stillness," 209). Indeed, this pre-eminence of hearing seems to be affirmed by the facts of biology itself—our sense of hearing is "the first to develop in utero and the last to leave before dying" (Puchalski, *A Time for Listening and Caring*, 321).

The tenderness of such an earthly "embalming" of the individual with the divine word is poignantly encapsulated in the accounts of the Prophet's own final illness and death. It is narrated that, as the Prophet lay on his deathbed, he recited Q 113 and Q 114 (collectively known as the *mu'awwidhatayn*, or the "The Two Suras for Seeking Refuge") and then breathed these words over his body. As he gradually became weaker, his wife Aisha used to recite these verses and blow her breath over him—however, she would make him rub his body with his own hand, for the *baraka* (blessings) lay in his sacred touch. Suffused with the divine, to accompany the dying person in this sonorous space is to "tread on sacred ground."[128]

This space is, indeed, variously sacralized—mirroring the bodily dynamics of prayer, the bed of the dying patient is turned towards Mecca, effecting a "facing" that is both inward and outward. As the body is prepared for burial, it is treated with gentleness and dignity; indeed, a crucial aspect of this ritual is the washing of the body, and fragrance is rubbed onto the seven bodily parts that touch the ground in prostration. In this way, the body is prayerfully readied and nourished for its onward journey, as it goes on to rest in what Ibn 'Arabī calls the divine "womb" of the grave.[129] The individual is entrusted to, and "held" within, this maternal matrix until she is raised before the sight of her Lord. On this mode of "witnessing," it is said that, when the Prophet died, his closest companion, Abū Bakr al-Ṣiddīq, entered the Prophet's home, unveiled the Prophet's face, gazed at the Prophet, and gently kissed his forehead. We might say that this final, embodied display of tenderness and love, mediated through the faculties of sight and touch, shares in and reflects the ever-luminous gaze and ever-faithful touch of God, which, as we have explored, bespeak the divine care and guardianship of His servants. Abū Bakr beholds the Prophet for the last time and, in doing so, attests that the Prophet will not be forgotten to him, much as the unceasing divine witnessing evinces God's indissoluble and merciful "remembrance" of creation. Our own remembrance of our loved ones is inextricably connected to the fact of embodiment, a fact which God graciously preserves in the afterlife—as expressed in Ingrid Mattson's beautifully perceptive comment:

> While the promise of an embodied afterlife can give rise to fear, it also gives hope to those who have lost loved ones to death. When the living mourn the dead, it is the embodied person they used to embrace and gaze upon whom they long to see once more. The loss is felt in each of the senses: the bereaved want to hear the laugh of their beloved, to touch their body, to gaze upon their face, to smell their hair, to taste their salty skin in a kiss. They do not miss a spirit or soul; they miss an embodied person. For the Muslim, the vivid Quranic descriptions of reembodied persons in the afterlife can be a great comfort.[130]

128 Puchalski, *A Time for Listening and Caring*, 128.
129 William Chittick, "Death and the World of Imagination: Ibn al-'Arabī's Eschatology," *The Muslim World* 78, no. 1 (1988): 64.
130 Mattson, "'The Believer is Never Impure,'" 69.

In sum, we have seen that the embodied experience of illness and disease, and the bodily accompaniment of the other through their suffering, are infused with spiritual meaning, and this inner import of the material is finally focalized in the creaturely destiny of death. By setting out the metaphysical foundations of human embodiment in our first section and exploring how this sacrality is *enacted* in various styles of worship, we then reflected on the reality of illness and the virtues that Sufis have seen as integral to embodied afflictions. These qualities illuminated for us a central thematic strand of this chapter: namely, that the human being is both the servant *and* the vicegerent of God, and thus finds her fulfilment in a simultaneous submission *to* and embodiment *of* the divine plenitude. A crucial facet of this divine fullness is God's omnipresence to the world, reflecting what Siddiqui refers to as God's metaphysical "hospitality," and we argued that our own embodied, relational modes of being present to and with the suffering other mediates and mirrors this loving divine outreach to the finite. In *going out* to visit the suffering patient, we *receive* them in their fullness and gently affirm our "with-ness"—where this human-to-human "with-ness" also becomes an encounter with the divine, who abides in the dwellings of the vulnerable. We "touch" and *are* "touched" by the patient's pain, and, as the Hadith narrates, when the other is beyond the possibility of cure, we can yet offer comfort and consolation to their soul. In the final "touching" to prepare the body for burial and in commending the person to the earth, we *bodily* bear witness to the fact that all things, in life and in death, belong wholly to God. There is a tender beauty in this "letting go" of the individual, safely entrusting her to her earthly womb—much like the beauty of running one's hand through a gently flowing stream, a touch whose sensorial serenity lies in the interplay of approaches and retreats, of proximity and distance, and of being together and departure.

References

Aoude, Safia. "The Concept of *ṣabr* in Islamic Spiritual Care: Definitions and Contextual Adaptations." 1–17. Unpublished. www.academia.edu/25631939/The_concept_of_ṣabr_in_Islamic_spiritual_care_definitions_and_contextual_adaptions (last accessed January 12, 2022).

Bashir, Shahzad. "Movement and Stillness: The Practice of Sufi *Dhikr* in Fourteenth-Century Central Asia." In *Meditation in Judaism, Christianity and Islam*, edited by Halvor Eifring, 201–212. London: Bloomsbury Academic, 2013.

Bishop, Jeffrey P. *The Anticipatory Corpse: Medicine, Power, and the Care of the Dying*. Notre Dame: University of Notre Dame Press, 2011.

Chittick, William. "Death and the World of Imagination: Ibn ʿArabī's Eschatology." *The Muslim World* 78, no. 1 (1988): 51–82.

Chittick, William. *The Sufi Doctrine of Rumi*. Bloomington: World Wisdom, 2005.

Chittick, William. "The Bodily Gestures of the *Ṣalāt*." In *In Search of the Lost Heart: Explorations in Islamic Thought*, edited by Mohammed Rustom, Atif Khalil, and Kazuyo Murata, 23–26. Albany: SUNY Press, 2012.

Chowdhury, Safaruk. *Islamic Theology and the Problem of Evil*. Cairo: AUC Press, 2021.

Chrétien, Jean-Louis. *The Call and the Response*. Translated by Anne A. Davenport. New York: Fordham University Press, 2004.

Douglas-Klotz, Neil. *The Sufi Book of Life: 99 Pathways of the Heart for the Modern Dervish*. New York: Penguin, 2005.
Durkin, Joanna, Debra Jackson, and Kim Usher. "Touch in Times of COVID-19: Touch Hunger Hurts." *Journal of Clinical Nursing* 30, no. 1–2 (2021): 4–5.
El-Aswad, El-Sayed. "Hospitality." In *Encyclopedia of Islam and the Muslim World*, edited by Richard C. Martin, 462–464. New York: Macmillan, 2003.
Evans, Sioned, and Andrew Davison. *Care for the Dying: A Practical & Pastoral Guide*. Norwich: Canterbury Press, 2014.
Ghaly, Mohammed. *Islam and Disability: Perspectives in Theology and Jurisprudence*. London: Routledge, 2010.
al-Ghazālī, Abū Ḥāmid. *The Mysteries of Almsgiving*. Translated by Nabih Amin Faris. Lahore: Sh. Muhammad Ashraf, 1980.
al-Ghazālī, Abū Ḥāmid. *The Ninety-Nine Beautiful Names of God*. Translated by David B. Burrell and Nazih Daher. Cambridge: Islamic Texts Society, 1992.
Gross, Aaron S. *The Question of the Animal and Religion: Theoretical Stakes, Practical Implications*. New York: Columbia University Press, 2015.
Imam Zayn al-ʿĀbidīn. *The Psalms of Islam*. Translated by William Chittick. London: Muhammadi Trust, 1988.
Islamic Finder. "Hadith 2087 of Chapters on Medicine by Jami Al Tirmizi." www.islamicfinder.org/hadith/tirmidhi/medicine/2087/?language=fr (last accessed January 11, 2022).
Izutsu, Toshihiko. *Sufism and Taoism: A Comparative Study of Key Philosophical Concepts of Ibn ʿArabī and Lao-Tzu and Chuang-Tzu*. Lahore: Suhail Academy, 1983.
Kugle, Scott. *Sufis and Saints' Bodies: Mysticism, Corporeality, and Sacred Power in Islam*. Chapel Hill: The University of North Carolina Press, 2007.
Lapidus, Ira M. "The Meaning of Death in Islam." In *Facing Death: Where Culture, Religion, and Medicine Meet*, edited by Howard M. Spiro, Mary G. McCrea Curnen, and Lee Palmer Wandel, 148–159. London: Yale University Press, 1996.
Lings, Martin. *What Is Sufism?* Cambridge: Islamic Texts Society, 1993.
Marcel, Gabriel. *Being and Having*. Translated by Katherine Farrer. Glasgow: The University Press, 1949.
Mattson, Ingrid. "'The Believer Is Never Impure': Islam and Understanding the Embodied Person." In *Treating the Body in Medicine and Religion: Jewish, Christian and Islamic Perspectives*, edited by John J. Fitzgerald and Ashely John Moyse, 64–83. London: Routledge, 2019.
McDonald, Barry. *Seeing God Everywhere: Essays on Nature and the Sacred*. Bloomington: World Wisdom, 2003.
Mohammed-Ashrif, Fatimah. "Visions of Beauty: Exploring Aesthetics as a Starting Point for Meaningful Inter-Religious Encounter, True-Seeing, Truth-Seeking, and Personal Transformation." *CrossCurrents* 68, no. 3 (2018): 358–371.
Murad, Abdal Hakim. "Creation Spirituality." In *Travelling Home: Essays on Islam in Europe*, 109–118. Cambridge: The Quilliam Press, 2020.
Nasr, Seyyed Hossein. "The Wisdom of the Body." In *Religion and the Order of Nature*, 235–262. New York: Oxford University Press, 1996.
Nasr, Seyyed Hossein. *Ideals and Realities of Islam*. Chicago: ABC International, 2000.
Puchalski, Christina M. *A Time for Listening and Caring: Spirituality and the Care of the Chronically Ill and Dying*. Oxford: Oxford University Press, 2006.
Ragab, Ahmed. *Piety and Patienthood in Medieval Islam*. New York: Routledge, 2018.
Rahman, Fazlur. *Health and Medicine in the Islamic Tradition*. New York: Crossroad, 1989.

Rūmī, Jalāl al-Dīn. *Masnavi*. Translated by E. H. Whinfield, 1898. www.sacred-texts.com/isl/masnavi/msn06.htm (last accessed February 14, 2022).

Rustom, Mohammed. "On Listening: Hearing God's Voice in the Face of Suffering." *Sacred Web* 45 (2020): 36–43.

Safi, Omid. *Memories of Muhammad: Why the Prophet Matters*. New York: HarperOne, 2009.

Schimmel, Annemarie. *Gabriel's Wing: A Study into the Religious Ideas of Sir Muhammad Iqbal*. Leiden: Brill, 1963.

Schimmel, Annemarie. *And Muhammad Is His Messenger: The Veneration of the Prophet in Islamic Piety*. Chapel Hill: The University of North Carolina Press, 1985.

Schuon, Frithjof. *From the Divine to the Human: A New Translation with Selected Letters*. Edited by Patrick Laude. Bloomington: World Wisdom, 2013.

Sheikh, Aziz, and Abdul Rashid Gatrad. *Caring for Muslim Patients*. Abingdon: Radcliffe Medical Press, 2000.

Siddiqui, Mona. *Hospitality in Islam: Welcoming in God's Name*. New Haven: Yale University Press, 2015.

Sulmasy, Daniel P. *The Healer's Calling: A Spirituality for Physicians and Other Health Care Professionals*. New York: Paulist Press, 1997.

Williams, Rowan. *A Silent Action: Engagements with Thomas Merton*. London: SPCK, 2013.

Yasgur, Batya Swift. "A Time to Grieve: Addressing Bereavement Challenges During the COVID-19 Pandemic." *Psychiatry Advisor*. www.psychiatryadvisor.com/home/topics/general-psychiatry/a-time-to-grieve-addressing-bereavement-challenges-during-the-covid-19-pandemic/ (last accessed April 12, 2022).

8 The Gifts of Suffering and the Virtues of the Heart

Atif Khalil

Introduction

After a tsunami struck Japan in 2011, I vividly recall an interview of an elderly man as he stood over the ruins of his hometown. Overcome by grief, he informed the reporter that the flood had killed not only his wife but also his children, their spouses, and his grandchildren. The tragedy took from him everything dear to his heart, leaving him shattered and alone to deal with the aftermath of the catastrophe. The story of the man—a modern version of Job—as it was recounted in the short news clip, could not but elicit profound feelings of compassion and sympathy from its global audience. It was also a story that, for those with religious and theological sensibilities, brought home what has often been identified in Western thought as the "problem of suffering."

More than 80 years ago, C. S. Lewis sought to respond to the challenge posed by this problem through a Christian framework for a modern audience in his book *The Problem of Pain*, with arguments that echoed lines of reasoning we would expect to find from representatives of other monotheistic religions as well that believe in an overarching benevolent, omnipotent deity. The heart of the issue, as Lewis laid it out in the opening of the short work, rested on acknowledging that God is both good and all-powerful. Now if He is good, then He would want us to be happy; and if He is omnipotent, He would be able to make it so. But since we are not happy, He must not be good, or He must not be omnipotent (or both). However, if He is lacking in either goodness or power, then He would be deprived of His most essential qualities. We would be better off, on philosophical grounds, in discarding belief in such a self-contradictory being altogether. This, in its most simplified form, was the crux of the argument, at least as far as Lewis spelled it out. He then began his response by attempting to excise both of these terms (*goodness* and *omnipotence*) of their more popular meanings; otherwise the problem, in his own view, remained unanswerable.[1]

1 C. S. Lewis, *The Problem of Pain* (London: William Collins, 2015), reprint, 16. The problem was articulated in the early Church by the theologian Lactantius (d. 340 CE), who had himself relied on its formulation by Epicurus (d. 270 BCE). Robin Ryan, *God and the Mystery of Human*

DOI: 10.4324/9781003371670-9

Lewis may have been correct in assuming that the dilemma was for the most part a Christian one. Certainly, in Islam the theological energy of the tradition went by and large into other areas of inquiry, such as the ontological status of the Quran or the debate around free will and predestination, both of which stemmed from revelation's emphasis on divine unity, in the case of the former, and divine omnipotence, in the case of the latter. The problem of suffering (or for that matter, evil),[2] was never a major one to begin with, largely because the theological axioms of the tradition never brought it to the fore with any force. And the fact that the standard Sunni position, particularly as it was articulated by the Ash`aris or even for that matter the Hanbalis, took pains to preclude human conceptions of goodness and justice from determining how we might understand or think about divine goodness and divine justice (unlike the dominant traditions in the West), served in many ways to prevent the problem from making significant inroads into Muslim tradition.

The existence of suffering, however, was undeniable, and there is no question that there was significant intellectual energy expended into understanding not so much how its presence might be reconciled with the existence of a good God, but rather the wisdom behind its existence, why we experience it, and the gifts it has to offer. And no one addressed these more concrete concerns more thoroughly than the representatives of the Islamic spiritual tradition of *taṣawwuf* or *iḥsān*. The aim of our present inquiry is to turn to this tradition and explore, meditate, and reflect over how its authorities sought to guide the wayfarer through the adversities of life. The practical focus of their texts, concerned as they are first and foremost with *ʿilm al-muʿāmala* ("the science of practical conduct"), led their authors to focus principally on the appropriate responses to hardship and to learn how to recognize its gifts.

The Fall, Paradise Lost, the *Dunyā*, and the Abode of Trial

The philosophically minded contemplatives of Islam often remind us that we suffer here for the simple reason that we are in the *dunyā*, a realm that stands in the lowest rung of the cosmic hierarchy. If, metaphysically speaking, God occupies the summit of the great chain of being, with an essence in which consciousness, being, and bliss (*wijdān, wujūd, wajd*) converge, then the further one moves away from this apex, the more one descends into ignorance, non-being, and the absence of bliss. Thus, while our world carries traces of the Godhead, being at once an outpouring or radiation of It, it is not the center itself, and by virtue of its ontological distance, it must be marked by pain and heartache. This is why Ibn ʿAṭāʾ Allāh (d. 1309) declares in one of his aphorisms, "Do not be surprised by the

Suffering: A Theological Conversation Across the Ages (New York: Paulist Press, 2011), 9. Often, the presence of divine omniscience is included in the problem, since God's perfect knowledge, along with His omnipotence, would, or so it is argued, confer upon Him the ability to create a world without suffering.

2 The two problems here being largely intertwined.

appearance of sorrows, so long as you are in this world, for they manifest nothing except what is in keeping with its nature"[3]—the nature here being one of distance and separation from the divine center. Along similar lines, Jaʿfar al-Ṣādiq (d. 765) once remarked, "He who seeks that which was not created, tires his soul to no avail." When pressed to explain to what he was alluding, he replied, "repose in the world (*rāḥa fī'l-dunyā*)."[4] To seek freedom from suffering in this rung of the cosmic hierarchy is therefore to seek the impossible, since suffering is woven, in a sense, into its very fabric. Any freedom must be sought either from above, after death, or from within, in the present moment, since the Heart in its interiority provides access to the highest plenums of existence. Outwardly, however, we can only encounter no more than transient reflections of them, like glimmerings of sunlight on a stream.

The doctrine of the Fall in the Abrahamic religions captures the idea of this separation quite fittingly. When Adam and Eve were exiled from Paradise, the world into which they were sent could not offer them, in their existential excommunication, what they experienced in their homeland, being as they were now in the abode of *ghurba*. Indeed, it is a curious feature of the language of the Quran that when it speaks of the pleasures and pains of the afterlife, of the Garden and the Fire, it uses two words: *saʿāda* and *shaqāwa*. The former is usually translated as "felicity" and the latter as "wretchedness."[5] And yet one of the rare instances where *shaqāwa* is used to describe the suffering of this world occurs when it speaks of the anguish experienced by Adam and Eve in their banishment from God, from their origin, from their homeland, and also (in the Islamic texts at least), from each other.[6] This

3 Ibn ʿAbbād, *Sharḥ al-Ḥikam al-ʿAṭāʾiyya*, ed. Muḥammad Riḍā b. Muḥammad Bashīr al-Qahwajī (Damascus: Dār al-Farfūr, 2003), 119 (aphorism no. 24).

4 Cited in Ibn ʿAbbād, *Sharḥ*, 120 (commentary on aphorism no. 24).

5 "The terms *the wretched* and *the felicitous* refer to the damned and the saved, respectively; these are among the most commonly used terms for these two groups in Islamic texts;" Seyyed Hossein Nasr, Caner Dagli, Maria Dakake, Joseph Lumbard, and Mohammed Rustom (eds.), *The Study Quran: A New Translation and Commentary* (New York: HarperOne, 2015), 585 (commentary on Q 11:105). The root s-ʿ-d (from which we get *saʿāda*) is used twice in the Quran, in both instances to refer to felicity, happiness, and joy in the afterlife. In Q 11:105 we read, "Among them will be the wretched and the felicitous"; and in Q 11:108 we read, "And those who are felicitous will be in Paradise." As for the root sh-q-w/y, it appears on 12 occasions, in all but two instances to refer (explicitly or implicitly) to the state of the wretched in the afterlife (Q 11:105, 11:106, 20:123, 23:106, 87:11, 92:15) or to *not* being in such a state in this world (Q 19:4, 19:32, 19:48). As for the two instances where it is used to describe a condition in this world, the first of these occurs in Q 91:12, in reference to the unlawful killing of the She-camel by the people of Thāmud. The verse reads, "When the most wretched of them rushed forward [or was deputed]." *Wretched* here, however, may well refer to the individual's future state, in the afterlife. In his commentary on the verse, Rāzī refers to this person, possibly identified as Qudār b. Sālif, as "the most wretched of the ancients by the verdict of the Prophet;" *al-Tafsīr al-kabīr* (Beirut: Dār al-Kutub al-ʿIlmiyya, 1990), commentary on Q 91:12. The English translators tend to render *ashqā* here as "the most wicked [of them]." For the other instance, see ensuing note.

6 "Let him [Iblis] not expel the two of you [Adam and Eve] from Paradise, so that you would become wretched" (Q 20:117).

is why Muslim tradition notes that the reason Jabal ʿArafāt east of Mecca is known as the Mount of Recognition is because it is where Adam and Eve finally met, recognizing each other after two centuries of separation.[7] This is not to say that we are not incapable of experiencing great anguish in this world, as the history of our species bears ample witness, or, for that matter, the tumultuousness of our own private lives. Relatively speaking, however, these pains cannot compare to the possibilities of wretchedness after death, nor to that initial experience in the wake of the Fall, of the trauma of Paradise lost so vividly recounted in the literature of the Western religions.

Intertwined into the story of the Fall is the idea, central to the Quran, that the *dunyā* is the abode of Trial (*ibtilāʾ*).[8] As the Quran states, "We created the human being from a drop of thickened fluid, to try to him (*nabtalīhī*). Thus, We have given him hearing and sight" (Q 76:2). And in the chapter of the Cave we read, "We have made that which is on the earth an adornment, to try them, to see which of them is best in conduct" (Q 18:7). To exist in this world is therefore to exist in a realm marked by hardships that accompany divinely ordained tests—tests meant to try, develop, and ripen the soul. In a sense, our mettle is continuously tested here, and this will continue into our final breaths. This is one reason why this world is not the domain of *shaqāwa* proper, since the general usage of the term in the Quran implies a state of a decisive finality and even hopelessness (even though divine mercy, unperceived, may still have the final say).[9] In worldly trials, however, there is always light at the end of the tunnel, and one can reach out to it through whatever it may be that the trial is summoning one to. While this may not entirely alleviate the intensity of its suffering, inwardly one may nevertheless find some measure of comfort knowing that one has done the best they could, without despairing, surrendering to the providence that brought it to one's doorstep. Besides, a conviction that *how* we respond to trials will determine our posthumous states—our stations after death, our ranks in the afterlife—lightens their weight immeasurably, since an interiorized, contemplative religiosity always calls us to keep our eyes set on the larger scheme of things, beyond what we may see through the very narrow gaze of our terrestrial field of vision, concerned only with our fleeting welfare in the here and now.

7 See John Penrice, *Dictionary and Glossary of the Koran* (London: Curzon Press, 1971), reprint, 96 (s.v. ʿ-r-f).

8 For an excellent study of the concept of *balāʾ/ibtilāʾ*, see Nasrin Rouzati, *Trial and Tribulation in the Quran: A Mystical Theodicy* (Berlin: Gerlach Press, 2015). Colin Turner's observation in the foreword is worth repeating: "The concept of the test is fundamental to the very act of creation itself" (ix). For a useful though dated treatment on suffering in Islam, see Montgomery Watt, "Suffering in Sunnite Islam," *Studia Islamica* 50 (1979): 5–19. See also Muhammad Faruque's more focused article, "Does God Create Evil? A Study of Fakhr al-Dīn al-Rāzī's Exegesis of *Sūrat al-Falaq*," *Islam and Christian Muslim Relations* 28, no. 3 (2017): 271–291.

9 On this theme, see William Chittick, *Imaginal Worlds: Ibn al-ʿArabī and the Problem of Religious Diversity* (Albany: SUNY Press, 1994); Mohammed Rustom, *The Triumph of Mercy: Philosophy and Scripture in Mullā Ṣadrā* (Albany: SUNY Press, 2012), chapters 6–7.

The Gifts of Tribulation, Surrender, and the Virtues of the Heart

This brings us to the main theme of our inquiry: without suffering, we would be deprived of the opportunities to cultivate the virtues of the Heart. Indeed, few if any of them could sprout without the waters of pain. One of the most defining of them is *ṣabr* (patience, forbearance, steadfastness),[10] the ideal response to *ibtilāʾ*, and about which a hadith states, "[It] is one of treasuries of paradise."[11] Usually paired in Sufi ethics with gratitude (*shukr*), the classical authorities debated among themselves over which of these qualities was more eminent. One argument ran that since thankfulness was an effortless response to blessings, while patience an effortful response to trials, the latter was superior. After all, it included the virtue of *mujāhada* or "struggle," required a laborious and taxing exercise of self-will, and came far less naturally. Another line of reasoning drew more directly from the Quran: revelation says to the grateful, "We shall surely give you more" (Q 14:7), but it says about the people of *ṣabr*, "Verily God is with the patient" (Q 8:46). Since intimacy with Him (literally "with-ness," *maʿiyya*) is far more valuable than any of His gifts—the grateful receive *from Him* while the patient receive *Him*—it stands to reason that *ṣabr* occupies pride of place.[12] Yet another argument for its superiority rested on the grounds, once again scriptural, that God says, "We shall confer upon the patient their rewards without limit" (Q 39:10). There is no other virtue, the exegetical authorities stressed, about which such a promise is made, the recompense of which is not bound by any constraints whatsoever.[13] This was why Fakhr al-Dīn al-Rāzī (d. 1209) in his famous commentary declared (drawing on a hadith), that when those who lived in relative ease (*ʿāfiya*) will see the rewards laid out on the Scales of Judgement, with no end in sight, for those who endured great trials, they will long to return to the world to undergo even more suffering than those afflicted with tribulations, that they might realize patience in all its modes.[14]

Another virtue that grows out of the soil of suffering is *tawakkul*, literally "reliance" on or "trust" in God.[15] The *mutawakkil* or trustor recognizes, sometimes after a period of defiance or resistance to divine decree, that what God chooses for us

10 Literally, *ḥabs al-nafs*, "holding the soul back," from what it might otherwise have a natural inclination to, whether it be complaint or anxiety. See Atif Khalil, "On Patience (*ṣabr*) in Sufi Virtue Ethics," in *Mysticism and Ethics in Islam*, ed. Bilal Orfali, Atif Khalil, and Mohammed Rustom (Beirut: American University of Beirut Press, 2022), 71–78.

11 al-Ghazālī, *Iḥyāʾ ʿulūm al-dīn* (Aleppo: Dār al-Waʿī, 1998), 4:96.

12 Qushayri, *Risāla*, ed. ʿAbd al-Ḥalīm Maḥmūd and Maḥmūd b. Sharīf (Damascus: Dār al-Farfūr, 2002).

13 The other instances of *bi ghayr ḥisāb* ("without limit," "without reckoning") in the Quran involve God's unconstrained bestowal of provision or sustenance (*rizq*). "He gives to whom He wills, without reckoning" (Q 2:212, 3:37, 24:38; cf. 3:27). The expression is also used in one instance (Q 38:39) in the context of describing the permission Solomon was granted by God to give of the gifts He had given him.

14 See his commentary upon Q 39:10 in *al-Tafsīr al-kabīr* (Beirut: Dār al-Kutub al-ʿIlmiyya, 1990).

15 For more on *tawakkul*, see Atif Khalil, "Ibn al-ʿArabī and the Sufis on Trust in God (*tawakkul*)," *Journal of the Muhyiddin Ibn ʿArabi Society* 71 (2022): 87–105.

is better than what we might choose for ourselves, since, like children, we fail to discern long-term consequences, preferring at all costs the sweet pleasures of the fleeting moment or the immediate future to necessary but painful surgical divine interventions. The compassionate, corrective trial, which forces us to undergo what we find unnecessarily distressing, contains concealed within it a wisdom, the knowledge of which we may only see when the veils are lifted, after death. Trusting in the omniscience behind God's oversight of our affairs, the trustor lets go, allowing the divine Trustee (*al-Wakīl*) to do what faith has always summoned him to. After all, we read in the Quran, "And in God let the faithful put their trust."[16] Outlining the characteristics of this virtue, itself a fruit of faith, one of the early gnostics observed: "From the reality of trust is that the servant of God abandon his own love for what God loves, his own choice for God's choice, his own calculating direction (*tadbīr*) for God's direction, through an independence from himself, while gazing at the flow of divine ordinances."[17]

Tawakkul, in this sense, is often born of a trial from which we cannot find a means of escape. Exasperated by futile attempts to free ourselves of its grip, we may find ourselves forced, in the end, to hand the reins of control over to the One in whose hands, paradoxically, they always were. It is this intentional, conscious, and volitional act that comprises the essence of trust and brings with it freedom from anxiety in the midst of the very trial. This is why the gnostic quoted earlier also said, "Concerns do not find a way into the [hearts of] the people of trust."[18] Once rooted, the virtue may even remain when the trial that bore it comes to pass—this itself being one of the gifts of the trial, with a sign of its internalization being that one not immediately turn in the face of every new hardship to desperate pleas of petition, neither to God, much less His creatures, for deliverance. Sometimes, the trustor may even sense, in her deeper recesses, an internal rebuke in response to a prayer to have it lifted: one movement of the heart, inspired by the *nafs*, may be checked by a higher movement, inspired by the spirit (*rūḥ*). Here, the suppliant may simply call out, tired of resisting destiny, "Do what You know is best." In this respect, *tawakkul* is closely bound to another central virtue of the spiritual life: *riḍā*, namely contentment, satisfaction, or good pleasure. It is to this state we are to aspire in this world, with *sa'āda*, felicity or happiness, understood as the gratification of every desire, reserved for the next world,[19] at least as far as the outward circumstances of our existence are concerned.

The loftiness of this quality of *riḍā* in Sufi ethics is drawn attention to by Makkī (d. 996) in the context of highlighting a debate that took place in early Islam on the status of three people. One of them anticipates and even yearns for death, because death, for him, opens the gate for an encounter with the divine Beloved. The second

16 Q 3:122, 3:160, 5:11, 9:51, 14:11, 39:38, and 64:13.

17 Attributed by Abū Ṭālib al-Makkī to one of the *'ārifīn*. See Abū Ṭālib al-Makkī, *Qūt al-qulūb*, ed. Maḥmūd al-Riḍwānī (Cairo: Dār al-Turāth, 2005), 2:910 (chapter on *tawakkul*).

18 Makkī, *Qūt al-qulūb*, 2005, 2:910.

19 "They shall have all that they desire, and with Us is more" (Q 50:35).

desires a prolonged life in order to accumulate as many virtuous deeds as possible over his brief journey through the world. And the third man leaves the matter entirely to God, saying to himself, "If He wills, He can give me life for as long as it pleases Him; and if He wills, He can give me death tomorrow." Where do each of these people stand, both in relation to God, and in relation to each other? For Makkī, the lowest rank belongs to the one who wishes for a long life. The nobility of this rank—and it is still a noble one—rests on the man's desire to accumulate as many beautiful deeds as possible, before the final accounting, and not out of a wish to delay the return simply to enjoy the fleeting pleasures of this world. Such a person stands at the station of hope or *rajāʾ*, since he hopes for a grace through which God will enable him to live a life of holiness and piety. The second rank, continues Makkī, belongs to the one who longs for death, not because of the toils and hardships of life, let alone suicidal inclinations, but out of a pining to return to God, to the ultimate object of his love and affection. Such a man stands at the station of *tashawwuq*, of longing, desire, and yearning, consumed as he is by a love for his Maker. The supreme degree, however, belongs to the one who leaves the decision to God, since he occupies, according to Makkī, the *maqām* or station of *riḍā*, being content and pleased with what God decrees for him. His state is like that of the soul before it entered the world: just as one did not choose to come into the *dunyā*, let alone when to enter it, the one marked by *riḍā* foregoes the decision, returning to an almost primordial state of complete and total surrender to God. Makkī goes on to declare that there is no fourth rank, and that the spiritual aspirant should aim to stand on one of the three rungs. That he unhesitatingly accords the supreme state to the station of *riḍā* illustrates the value attached in Sufi ethics to overcoming the desire to control our destiny, sometimes rooted in a subtle and even rebellious self-willing that may, in its origin, be retraced to the first sin of Adam and Eve. This was an act that marked the first rupture between what professor Chittick in his studies of Ibn ʿArabī (d. 1240) has identified as the "prescriptive" and "engendering command," namely what God commands us for our salvation, but which may not necessarily come to pass, and what He commands through His creative fiat, His *kun fa-yakūn*, and which *does* come to pass.[20]

Trials, Divine Decrees, and Human Petitions

Thus far, we have drawn attention to the importance placed on passively acquiescing to fate and divine decree. But the matter, as one might expect, is not so straightforward, and to suggest otherwise would be to distort the complex and variegated teachings found in the tradition, which, taken as a whole, never encourages one to adopt a course of complete stoicism. To be clear, one need not, as a law of the

20 That is to say, the *amr takwīnī* (engendering command) and *amr taklīfī* (prescriptive command). See, for example, William Chittick, *Sufi Path of Knowledge: Ibn al-ʿArabī's Metaphysics of Imagination* (Albany: SUNY Press, 1989), 292–293.

path, avoid every supplication or *du'ā* which aims to thwart a trial. The Quran, we know, is not devoid of accounts of men and women of great sanctity—from Job to Mary—who sought divine help to be released from the clutches of a crushing predicament. Indeed, at times it is impossible to resist such a prayer. There are occasions when the soul, unrestrained and unrestrainable, cries out to God with all its might for release. A story from the life of Junayd (d. 910) illustrates this very point. A woman who had lost her son once came to him, imploring him for a prayer. The holy man counseled her to be patient, and so she left, heeding his advice. After some time had elapsed, she came back, with the same plea. He advised her as he had done before, "Be patient," and so she departed once again. Finally, after some period she returned, more desperate than ever, lamenting her inability to exercise patience any longer. "If the matter is as you claim, then go," he said. "Your son has returned." Perplexed, she left, only to find, to her astonishment, that her son had indeed found his way back. When she inquired how he knew, Junayd answered with the verse, "Does He not respond to the desperate one when he calls upon Him, and removes for him his affliction?" (Q 27:62). Her state of *iḍṭirār* (abject need, desperation) had reached a point where, the Sufi master felt, a divine response was inevitable.[21]

It is significant to note from this story, one that carries echoes of the account of Joseph in the Quran, that Junayd did not instruct her to passively accept her fate. He told her to be patient, but with a patience that did not preclude praying for deliverance from her affliction. What parent, after all, would not do all that lay within their power for the safe return of a lost child? It is only natural and human to desire the well-being of our friends and family, especially those whom we love most. It is also natural, for that matter, to desire our own welfare. And this is one reason why Ibn ʿArabī unreservedly declares that patience does not necessarily entail avoiding complaint (*shakwā*) altogether—it only entails not raising our grievances to others. One may, however, do so with God, as Job himself did when he prayed, "Affliction has come over me, and You are the most merciful of the merciful" (Q 21:83). To ask God to remove a trial (*balā'*) as the Israelite prophet had done, does not deprive one of the virtue of patience, nor does such a petition reveal a deficiency in one's own state.[22] On this matter Ibn ʿArabī is explicit. In fact, he goes so far as to state that God afflicts us so that we might turn to Him in humble petition, to lift those very trials[23]—trials that bring us to the prayer rug, broken, in a state of abject need, reminding us of our own utter dependence on Him.

One of the spiritual benefits of seeking release from a tribulation is that it forces the suppliant to set his life in order, not only with God but others, at least if he wants his petitions answered. The desperation elicited by the *ibtilā'* forces the one tried to make far-reaching changes that he might otherwise not have had the least

21 Qushayrī, *Risāla*, 456.

22 Ibn ʿArabī, *al-Futūḥāt al-makkiyya*, ed. Aḥmad Shams al-Dīn (Beirut: Dār al-Kutub al-ʿIlmiyya, 1999), 3:310.

23 Ibn ʿArabī, *Futūḥāt*, 3:310.

inclination to. He may be so comfortably ensconced in heedlessness, devoid of any higher concerns, that the trial was the only way for God to awaken him out of his slumber. Our Sufi authors would probably have little reason to contest C. S. Lewis's famous observation that "God whispers to us in our pleasures . . . but shouts in our pain: it is his megaphone to rouse a deaf world. A bad man, happy, is a man without the least inkling that his actions . . . are not in accord with the laws of the universe."[24] The trial may thus rouse the one tried, catalyzing a process of reform that compels him to make concrete changes out of a hope that God pull him out of his misery. Even before he turns his attention to weeding out subtler vices of the soul, there are more rudimentary actions of the limbs, rules of outward behavior, to which the petitioner will feel compelled by a universal power far beyond his reach to conform. Otherwise, his prayers—and he would be the first to recognize this—would amount to no more than empty words. We dislike empty speech, and no sincere person turning to God would expect God to accept it as well. On this point, the Sufis and the *ʿulamāʾ* are unanimous: a genuine effort to bring one's life into agreement with what God wants of us, through His prescriptive command, forms a prerequisite for His response, at least in the way we may want it. It is not enough to simply raise one's hands and petition. As one early authority declared, "How can you expect the answering of [your] prayer, when you have blocked its pathway with sin?"[25] And in ʿAbd al-Qādir al-Jīlānī's (d. 1166) *Ghunya*, we find an articulation of the same sentiment:

> Petitionary prayer has rules of propriety and conditions. These are the means through which one elicits a response and obtains the object of his desire. He who observes and fulfils them is among those who have been responded to, while he who remains heedless of them or fails to meet their conditions, is among those who transgress with respect to what is required by petitionary prayer.[26]

This does not mean that God never answers the prayers of those who stubbornly refuse to change, since, in the final order, "the wind blows where it pleases," and with God all things are possible. It may be that answering the petition of such person on the part of God amounts, in its own way, to a greater affliction. Or it may simply be an illustration of a divine compassion that, unlike our own, remains unbound by limits. This is one reason why the Sufi authorities remind us that we should never lose hope, since God even answered the prayer of Iblīs when he sought respite (Q 7:14–15). But they also stress that if we genuinely wish to be delivered of an affliction, it lies in our own interests to create the conditions, within the powers vested in us, for its removal.

24 Lewis, *The Problem of Pain*, 91.

25 Qushayrī, *Risāla*, 463.

26 The saying is attributed it to an anonymous earlier figure. ʿAbd al-Qādir al-Jīlānī, *Ghunya*, ed. Yūsuf b. Maḥmūd al-Ḥājj Aḥmad (Damascus: Maktabat al-ʿIlm al-Hadīth, 2001), 409.

When Ya'qūb b. al-Layth (d. 879), the founder of the Saffārid dynasty, succumbed to an illness which none of his physicians could cure, they summoned the saintly Sahl al-Tustarī (d. 896) to his court, in the hopes that due to his piety, his prayers for the ruler might be answered. When the request was placed before him, he informed Ya'qūb that as long there were victims unfairly detained in his prisons, his own prayers would be useless, that God's justice would not permit it. Compelled by need and realizing the extent of a crime to which he had previously given little thought, he had no choice but to free them all. Sahl then prayed, and the man was cured of his malady.[27] The affliction, in the end, was a gift, opening up a pathway for the deepening of his own conscience and a recognition of his misdeeds, not to mention the internalization of a state of *faqr*, of impoverishment before God—yet another virtue of heart. In a sense, one might argue that we are all little Ya'qūbs governing our tiny fiefdoms, with trials that descend when necessary to set our lives in order. The counsel of Sahl may, in our own cases, either well up from our own hearts, or appear through the mouth of another in a form so compelling that we cannot, in all sincerity and true to our conscience, refuse it.

To Pray, or Not to Pray?

From our preceding treatment of how we should respond to afflictions, there is no doubt something of a tension within the Sufi tradition, at least on the surface, regarding whether or not one should seek release from trials through prayer. Some masters clearly emphasized the need to surrender to God's will, to accept destiny and acquiesce to what has been ordained. Thus, Wāsiṭī (d. 936) declared, "To choose what had been coming to you from pre-eternity (*azal*) is better than to object (through petitions) to the present moment."[28] And Dhū'l-Nūn (d. 859) is said to have informed an old man who requested a prayer from him, "If something has been preordained by God for you, then many unspoken prayers have already been heard: otherwise, what use has the drowning person for shouting? Only that he is sooner drowned, and more water comes to his throat."[29] Such an approach seemed the swiftest and most direct way to develop patience, trust, contentment, and similar qualities. Yet others emphasized the necessity of petitionary prayer in virtually all conditions because it revealed "neediness of servitude,"[30] thereby allowing one to cultivate the virtues of *faqr* and *fāqa*. For this faction, there lay a danger in not regularly turning to God through petitions, since such a state could reflect subtle, deeply seated feelings of self-sufficiency and independence. This was one reason why Ibn 'Arabī (not necessarily an advocate of this second view) argued, somewhat counter-intuitively, that when one supplicates, one should *not* begin with the

27 Qushayrī, *Risāla*, 460.

28 Qushayrī, *Risāla*, 456.

29 Cited in Annemarie Schimmel, *Mystical Dimensions of Islam* (Chapel Hill: University of North Carolina Press, 1975), 156.

30 Qushayrī, *Risāla*, 456.

needs of others, out of a sense of altruism, but oneself, since to do otherwise suggests that one stands *less* in need of divine aid and guidance than others do. When the Quran chastises those who "withhold their hands" (Q 9:67), a passage often interpreted to refer to those who refuse to *give*,[31] at least some advocates of the second view argued it referred to those who refuse to *ask*, to those who hold their hands back from petitionary prayer, from beseeching divine aid.[32]

The adoption of either one of these approaches too stringently and dogmatically presented obvious problems. With respect to the proponents of the first view, few as they were, their attitude could not, as Schimmel observed, be "regarded as typical for the Sufis in general," because the Quran instructs us to seek divine help on a regular basis.[33] And since the meditations of the Sufis were themselves not only concordant with but drawn from the well-springs of Muslim revelation, such an approach could not gain a strong foothold in the religious consciousness of the community.[34] The danger in the second view, however, of continuously seeking a way out through prayer of every hardship and unease, of every trifling inconvenience, was that it prevented one from benefitting from the gifts brought about through trials, from learning how to surrender to an omniscient power and sacrifice one's own will before the altar of God's will.

One method of reconciling the two perspectives, the merits of each of which were self-evident in their own right, lay in encouraging the afflicted one to combine both approaches, to petition through the tongue while remaining satisfied in the heart.[35] But the problem here was rather simple: since a genuine prayer of petition requires complete presence of heart (*ḥuḍūr al-qalb*), the articulation of a sincere feeling of need, how effective could such a request actually be? Certainly, the feeling of *iḍṭirār*, a powerful and even cosmic effectuating force (as we saw in the story of Junayd) would be altogether absent. The best resolution, the one that appears to have come to dominate the tradition, was the view enunciated by Qushayrī in his *Treatise*. Since, as he writes, "the moments vary," one should observe what is demanded by each of them. In certain circumstances, one cannot, as noted earlier, help but pray for release from the crippling effect of a trial. And yet in others, one may discern the profound benefits of the tribulation, recognize one's capacity through divine grace to endure it, and leave, in the end, the matter to God, trusting in His final judgement. This nevertheless raises the question of how precisely one is to know which course of action to take. Qushayrī (d. 1074) recommends that one observe the heart, paying attention to the direction to which it leads. One way

31 See the commentary upon Q 9:64 in Nasr et al. (eds.), *The Study Quran*, 524. Another interpretation (attributed to al-Qurṭubī) is that it refers to those who refused to go out in battle.

32 Qushayrī, *Risāla*, 455.

33 Schimmel, *Mystical Dimensions of Islam*, 156.

34 This view was not entirely without basis in the Hadith literature. As a divine report through the Prophet states, "As for the one who does not petition Me because of his preoccupation with My remembrance, I give him more than I give to the one who petitions;" Qushayrī, *Risāla*, 456.

35 Qushayrī, *Risāla*, 457.

is to discern whether the petition elicits a state of contraction (*qabḍ*) or expansion (*basṭ*). If it is the former, then one should hold oneself back from the request; and if it is the latter, one may proceed, with the ease with which the prayer flows out of one's heart a sign that this is in fact what the moment is summoning one to.[36] As Ibn ʿAṭāʾ Allāh declares in one of his aphorisms, "When He lets loose your tongue in prayer, then know He desires to give you."[37] Conversely, the incapacity to petition, either simply due to a hardness of heart which alienates one from God, or the heart's own resistance to asking for ease when the benefit of the trial is recognized in the interior recesses of the self, may be a sign that its removal was never part of the divine design to begin with.

The Gifts of the Pandemic

We began our reflection on the problem of suffering by drawing attention to the tragedy of the Tsunami that hit Japan and many of the surrounding countries of the Far East more than a decade ago. Years later, we would witness, and continue to witness, a different but more far-reaching global crisis.

From its beginning, one of the curious features in our public conversation about the pandemic, particularly in the West, was the virtual absence of any deeper meditation on the meaning of the tribulation. The questions that guided our analyses were almost always invariably framed along purely mechanistic, material, and "worldly" lines: Why, for example, did the Chinese not report COVID-19 to the global community as soon as it appeared? Why did Trump not take the threat seriously, despite the early forecast of a potential health crisis by American medical intelligence reports? Why did things go so bad in Italy? How long would it take before a vaccine would appear? What would be the short- and long-term economic implications of worldwide quarantining? Who was ultimately responsible?

No one asked, behind the endless array of pontifications for which all kinds of experts were drawn from the international community, whether there might be some wisdom behind the crisis at all, whether it might be teaching us something about the direction in which the world was going. Were we really, to use Trump's words, at "war with a foreign virus," or might the virus even have been a friend, to help set the balance of the earth in order, through surgical incisions that no oligarchy or group of nations could successfully bring about on their own? By reframing our angle of inquiry, there were more penetrating questions that could have been, and certainly may still be, explored.

The need to reframe our default modes of inquiry, as we have seen in this short chapter, is a recurring motif in Sufi literature. This is because the human being in a fallen state looks at the world through the eyes of *baṣar*, outward sight, whereas the

36 Qushayrī, *Risāla*, 457.

37 Ibn ʿAbbād, *Sharḥ*, 251 (aphorism no. 102). Ibn ʿAbbād corroborates the aphorism through the hadith, "He who is given petitionary prayer is not deprived of a response."

sage looks at it through the eyes of *baṣīra*, insight. And through *baṣīra*, as we have also seen, an outward trial may very well turn out to be an inward blessing, bringing to us a gift that we might be too blind or stubborn to see. External appearances, as we know, are all too deceiving.

What then, if any, might the gifts of the pandemic have been? While it lies beyond the scope of this treatment to explore the question in any depth, there are a few we may draw attention to, in passing.

For one thing, as the onset of the pandemic brought the economic and industrial juggernaut of the modern world to a halt, we saw some of the positive ecological effects of this slowing down on the environment, all the way from Italy to China. News outlets, for example, reported that as the waters of Venice's canals began to clear up and detoxify, dolphins started to appear in unprecedented numbers. In fact, pollution levels in regions under quarantine reached an all-time low. It was as if nature was teaching us that there is perhaps no better remedy for our dismal ecological predicament than to seriously slow down and curtail the technological and industrial pace of our lives; that we should adopt simpler, less ecologically corrosive, more nature-friendly, forms of living; and that there are few things worse for the natural environment than for us to collectively pursue unrestrained material progress. The words of climate scientist Peter Gleick (founder of the Pacific Institute in Berkeley, California) on the effects of COVID-19 are worth sharing in this context:

> As for the environmental benefits we see from the slowdown of day-to-day life and economic activity in terms of improving air quality and other slight benefits, it's a good sign. . . . But it would be nice if we could improve our environment without having to cripple our economy.[38]

Clearly, a global system in which the environment can only be salvaged through a "crippling of the economy" is unsustainable. The issue cannot be reduced to a question of the economy or the environment, since we are, after all, a part of the environment. Only far-reaching changes to our modes of life, our relation to nature, and our preoccupation with industrial and technological growth can save us from what may be our own inevitable end.[39]

Another gift of the pandemic was that it revealed to us how closely we are all interconnected to each other—how the well-being or suffering of one person effects the well-being or suffering of another. Few things demonstrated this as vividly as the contagiousness of COVID-19, especially as new variants emerged. The rich and well-do-to could no longer ignore the fate of the poor and the exposed,

38 "Why We React Fast to Pandemics but Slow to Climate Change," www.theweathernetwork.com/nu/news/article/why-we-react-fast-to-pandemics-coronavirus-but-slow-to-climate-change (last accessed July 27, 2022).

39 This question has already been extensively explored, for those unfamiliar, by S. H. Nasr in his many works on the environment.

since the virus was transmitted through the vast web of relationships that we are all, inescapably, bound to. Such are the conditions, whether we like it or not, of life in the global village of the 21st century. It is worth noting, in this context—to return again to C. S. Lewis—an observation of his in the *Screwtape Letters*, namely, that the philosophy which governs hell stands at the very opposite of such a reality. Here, what is good for you is not necessarily good for me, and what is bad for you is not necessarily bad for me. "The whole philosophy of Hell," asserts the devil in Lewis's work, "rests on the recognition of the axiom that one thing is not another thing, and, specially, that one self is not another self. My good is my good and your good is yours. What one gains another loses."[40] The pandemic, on the other hand, taught us the antithesis of this doctrine. It brought home, very concretely, the need to love one's neighbor as one oneself, a "virtue of the heart" not only in Christianity, but also Islam. Indeed, we find in some Sufi accounts an exhortation to love the other even more than we love ourselves, through the altruistic virtue of *īthār*, of preferring others to ourselves, not only in worldly but even after-worldly matters.[41] If anything, the pandemic forced us (or at least some of us) to more fully acknowledge our interdependence and reconsider the values of self-interest and self-preference that guide the lives of so many of us in the modern world, particularly in the absence of sacred traditions that place self-transcendence squarely at the center of human purpose and teleology.

Yet another gift was that that pandemic reminded us of our own frailty as a species. We pride ourselves in our fallen state—as promethean men and women, to use the expression of S. H. Nasr—in our mastery over the earth. Standing at the summit of the ecosystem, through our technology and instrumental rationality, we easily forget just how feeble we are. That such a materially and physically insignificant phenomenon as a virus (and a relatively mild one at that) could cripple our governments as severely as it did, for at least two years, was a reminder that "the human being was created weak" (Q 4:28); it was a reminder not to "walk proudly on the earth" (Q 17:37). And that it was a virus that brought about such a turn of events, an entity that brings us to about as close as we may get to an unseen reality, at the material level, without entering in the realm of the *ghayb* proper, the actual unseen realm, also appears to have been, in a subtle way, a reminder of the extent to which our lives are effected by truly unseen powers. It was as if we were being taught, through analogy, that the *ʿālam al-ghayb* has the final say over the *ʿālam al-maḥsūsāt*, and that in the final scheme of things, the world of the senses is subordinate to the world above.

40 C. S. Lewis, *The Screwtape Letters* (New York: HarperOne, 1996), reprint, 71–72.

41 Consider the following saying attributed to Abū Yazīd (d. 874): "[H]e is my disciple who stands on the brink of Hell and takes by the hand everyone being conveyed to Hell and dispatches him to Heaven, and then enters Hell in his place." Farīd al-Dīn ʿAṭṭār, *Memorial of the Saints*, abridged trans. A. J. Arberry (London: Arkana Penguin, 1990), reprint, 120. On the Bodhisattva-like quality of a certain class of saints, see the chapter by Michel Chodkiewicz entitled, "The Double Ladder," in *Seal of the Saints: Prophethood and Sainthood in the Doctrine of Ibn ʿArabī*, trans. Liadain Sherrard (Cambridge: Islamic Texts Society, 1993), 147–173.

References

ʿAṭṭār, Farīd al-Dīn. *Memorial of the Saints*. Abridged translation by A. J. Arberry, reprint. London: Arkana Penguin, 1990.
Chittick, William. *The Sufi Path of Knowledge: Ibn al-ʿArabī's Metaphysics of Imagination*. Albany: SUNY Press, 1989.
Chittick, William. *Imaginal Worlds: Ibn al-ʿArabī and the Problem of Religious Diversity*. Albany: SUNY Press, 1994.
Chodkiewicz, Michel. *Seal of the Saints: Prophethood and Sainthood in the Doctrine of Ibn ʿArabī*. Translated by Liadain Sherrard. Cambridge: Islamic Texts Society, 1993.
Faruque, Muhammad. "Does God Create Evil? A Study of Fakhr al-Dīn al-Rāzī's Exegesis of *Sūrat al-Falaq*." *Islam and Christian Muslim Relations* 28, no. 3 (2017): 271–291.
al-Ghazālī, Abū Ḥāmid. *Iḥyāʾ ʿulūm al-dīn*. Aleppo: Dār al-Waʿī, 1998.
Gleick, Peter. "Why We React Fast to Pandemics but Slow to Climate Change." www.theweathernetwork.com/nu/news/article/why-we-react-fast-to-pandemics-coronavirus-but-slow-to-climate-change (last accessed July 27, 2022).
Ibn ʿAbbād. *Sharḥ al-Ḥikam al-ʿAṭāʾiyya*. Edited by Muḥammad Riḍā b. Muḥammad Bashīr al-Qahwajī. Damascus: Dār al-Farfūr, 2003.
Ibn al-ʿArabī. *al-Futūḥāt al-makkiyya*. Edited by Aḥmad Shams al-Dīn. Beirut: Dār al-Kutub al-ʿIlmiyya, 1999.
al-Jīlānī, ʿAbd al-Qādir. *al-Ghunya*. Edited by Yūsuf b. Maḥmūd al-Ḥājj Aḥmad. Damascus: Maktabat al-ʿIlm al-Ḥadīth, 2001.
Khalil, Atif. "Ibn al-ʿArabī and the Sufis on Trust in God (*tawakkul*)." *Journal of the Muhyiddin Ibn ʿArabi Society* 71 (2022): 87–105.
Khalil, Atif. "On Patience (*ṣabr*) in Sufi Virtue Ethics." In *Mysticism and Ethics in Islam*, edited by Bilal Orfali, Atif Khalil, and Mohammed Rustom, 71–78. Beirut: American University of Beirut Press, 2022.
Lewis, C. S. *The Screwtape Letters*, reprint. New York: HarperOne, 1996.
Lewis, C. S. *The Problem of Pain*, reprint. London: William Collins, 2015.
Makkī, Abū Ṭālib al-. *Qūt al-qulūb*. Edited by Maḥmūd al-Riḍwānī. Cairo: Dār al-Turāth, 2005.
Nasr, Seyyed Hossein, Caner Dagli, Maria Dakake, Joseph Lumbard, and Mohammed Rustom (eds.). *The Study Quran: A New Translation and Commentary*. New York: HarperOne, 2015.
Penrice, John. *Dictionary and Glossary of the Koran*, reprint. London: Curzon Press, 1971.
Qushayrī. *Risāla*. Edited by ʿAbd al-Ḥalīm Maḥmūd and Maḥmūd b. Sharīf. Damascus: Dār al-Farfūr, 2002.
Rāzī, Fakhr al-Dīn al-. *al-Tafsīr al-kabīr*. Beirut: Dār al-Kutub al-ʿIlmiyya, 1990.
Rouzati, Nasrin. *Trial and Tribulation in the Quran: A Mystical Theodicy*. Berlin: Gerlach Press, 2015.
Rustom, Mohammed. *The Triumph of Mercy: Philosophy and Scripture in Mullā Ṣadrā*. Albany: SUNY Press, 2012.
Ryan, Robin. *God and the Mystery of Human Suffering: A Theological Conversation Across the Ages*. New York: Paulist Press, 2011.
Schimmel, Annemarie. *Mystical Dimensions of Islam*. Chapel Hill: University of North Carolina Press, 1975.
Watt, Montgomery Watt. "Suffering in Sunnite Islam." *Studia Islamica* 50 (1979): 5–19.

9 Cain, Systemic Evil, and Our Inhumanity

Martin Nguyen

Between the primordial disobedience of Satan and the tyranny wrought by the House of Pharaoh lies another Quranic narrative of significance: the story of the two sons of Adam (Q 5:27–32). In this tragic tale that cleaves close to the beginnings of humankind, revelation discloses something significant about our nature. It is a story that speaks to our persistent susceptibility and inclination to evil in its many forms, violence-unto-death especially. For Ali Shariati (d. 1977) the narrative occupied a prominent place in the revolutionary repertoire that he cultivated against the oppressors of his time.[1] As he attests, "Man begins with the struggle between spirit and clay, God and Satan, within Adam. But where does history begin? What is its point of departure? The struggle between Cain and Abel. . . . One killed the other, and the history of humanity began."[2] Revelation, of course, is never constrained in its address to particular moments in history. Its reach is extensive and persistent. The story of the two sons of Adam, then, is as resonant now as it was in Shariati's time and at the moment of historical disclosure. It is a story that strikes at the root of what it means to be human.

In Q 5, revelation relates: "Recite to them, with truth, the account of the two sons of Adam. When they each made a sacrifice, it was accepted from one of them, but it was not accepted from the other, who said, 'Surely I will kill you.' [The other] said, 'God only accepts from the reverent'" (Q 5:27). Though unnamed in the Quran, the exegetical tradition identifies the sons as Hābīl and Qābīl, otherwise known as Abel and Cain, respectively. According to the verse, Abel and Cain, brothers to one another, have turned to God in order for each to proffer a sacrifice. The sacrifices, however, are not received as equal. Abel, fastidiously aware of the Divine, has offered a sacrifice with the utmost reverence or *taqwā* since he is numbered among "the reverent" or *al-muttaqīn* in the verse. Because of the keenness

1 For example, see his lecture, Ali Shariati, "The Philosophy of History: Cain and Abel," in *On the Sociology of Islam: Lectures by Ali Shari'ati*, trans. Hamid Algar (Berkeley: Mizan Press, 1979), 97–110; Ali Shariati, *Man and Islam*, trans. Fatollah Marjani (Houston: Free Islamic Literatures Inc., 1981), 17–28; Ali Shariati, *Hajj*, trans. Somayyah Yaser (Bedford: Free Islamic Literatures Inc., 1977), 101, 124–146.

2 Ali Shariati, *On the Sociology of Islam: Lectures by Ali Shari'ati* (Berkeley: Mizan Press, 1979), 99.

DOI: 10.4324/9781003371670-10

of his faith, God accepts Abel's offering. The sacrifice presented by Cain, however, is rejected. His sacrifice is judged differently. There is a difference in quality and sincerity. Enraged by being passed over, Cain boils over into violence, declaring to his brother Abel: "'Surely I will kill you'" (Q 5:27). The elder son of Adam *names* something unprecedented, the forcible taking of another human being's life. Through this act of naming, Cain's dire imagining is ushered into a reality. From thought, to word, to action, he wills himself towards the murder of his brother.

In the face of such fell fury, Abel replies: "'God only accepts from the reverent'" (Q 5:27). His words seek to return them to that moment of sacrificial judgement. While interpreters of this verse have dwelt long on identifying the exact sacrifices left unsaid in the Quran, Abel (and the Quran for that matter) cares little whether what was offered was the fat of the flock, the harvest of the land, or otherwise.[3] The difference that distinguishes the two brothers is not the sacrifices themselves, but the disposition of faith with which the sacrifice was delivered.

Assaulted with the promise of his own violent death, Abel names *taqwā* in response. For to be among *the reverent, al-muttaqīn*, is to be in possession of *taqwā*, an essential principle that revelation emphasizes repeatedly.[4] Abel approaches the Divine with *taqwā*—an upright devotion informed by sincerity, humility, and mindfulness. He likewise replies to Cain with *taqwā* as well. Like a precarious flame within, *taqwā* is a state of vigilant piety that must be continually tended and protected.

In contrast, Cain's inner flame is all but extinguished. Cain comes before God askew and astray. The disposition of his faith, more than his sacrifice, is found unbefitting. Cain has made other than the Almighty the axis and orientation of his life. His focus is intensely and narrowly upon himself, his passed-over sacrifice, his bitter rejection,

3 The Quran explicitly omits any mention or reference to the sacrifices themselves. In contrast, the Biblical account in the book of Genesis relates: "In the course of time Cain brought to the Lord an offering of the fruit of the ground, and Abel for his part brought the firstlings of his flock, their fat portions;" Genesis 4:3–4, in Bruce Metzger and Roland E. Murphy (eds.), *The New Oxford Annotated Bible with the Apocryphal/Deuterocanonical Books, New Revised Standard Version* (New York: Oxford University Press, 1994), 6. Among the wide array of possible sacrifices that Muslim scholars cite (and which are resonant with what is preserved in the Biblical tradition), see the commentary upon Q 5:27 in Seyyed Hossein Nasr, Caner Dagli, Maria Dakake, Joseph Lumbard, and Mohammed Rustom (eds.), *The Study Quran: A New Translation and Commentary* (New York: HarperOne, 2015), 289.

4 *Taqwā* and its various lexical derivatives (from *ittaqā*, the form VIII verb of w-q-y) appear myriad times throughout the Quranic text. Take for instance: "Surely the noblest of you before God are the most reverent [*atqākum*]" (Q 49:13), or literally "those who have the most *taqwā*." William Chittick offers "God-wariness" as a possible translation: "Understanding *taqwā* as 'God-wariness' . . . makes *taqwā*'s orientation toward God explicit, brings out the implication of being aware and mindful, and avoids the negative and sentimental undertones of words such as 'piety,' 'dutifulness,' and 'righteousness;'" William Chittick, *In Search of the Lost Heart: Explorations in Islamic Thought*, ed. Mohammed Rustom, Atif Khalil, and Kazuyo Murata (Albany: SUNY Press, 2012), 13. When this consciousness of the Divine is expressed as a command, *ittaqū*, it is a call to fear God or to take heed rather in the sense that one must remain ever mindful of the Almighty in all that one does.

and this perceived injustice done cruelly to himself. Utterly powerless before God and God's judgement, Cain lashes out at the only other person present, Abel.

With ungodly resolve and a furious cruelty, Cain slays his brother, even as Abel promises to never raise his hand in response. Whereas moments before, Cain was merely the executor of a rejected sacrifice, he becomes in this instant the executor of a sacrificial abomination—a diabolic inversion of the ritual order. Instead of approaching with devotion and mindfulness, he turns away in arrogance and rage. Instead of a labored sacrifice, Cain slaughters his brother. Yet the fratricide is not offered for the sake of God. Instead, Cain, in the heat of the moment, forsakes the Divine so that he can take Abel's life for his own perverse sake. Out of this abomination, Cain has fashioned a new face for death for all of humankind. By the hand of a first son of Adam, uncalled-for blood is sown into the soil of the world. Fast has the fear of the angels come to pass: " 'Will You place therein one who will work corruption therein, and shed blood?' " (Q 2:30).

As the life of Abel departs this world, the monstrosity of murder enters it. Long shall it tarry until the end of days, and greedily shall it gather multitudes to its insatiable maw. From this moment hence, the sons and daughters of Adam, all of humankind to follow, will know the power of violence-unto-death, wielding it against others, those they deem lesser and different. This is not the violence of storms and natural disasters. Nor is it the violence of a predator slaying its prey. This is *human* violence. Since Cain first tilled it, this field of violence has never fallen fallow. How quickly after the fall from Paradise did Satan's shadow engulf the line of Adam on this earth.

The transgressions of Cain reveal a potential latent within us all. If Adam and Eve, the first of us, mark our beginnings upon this earth, then Abel and Cain, the first generation after, mark what we might become while we dwell herein. Abel and Cain represent two distinct currents coursing within human nature. In Abel is a force that takes God as its center. In Abel is the enabling of our *fiṭra*, that natural sense of belonging to the Divine. Here is our inclination to good and righteous action personified—a theo-centrism traced through faithful commitment and reverence.

In Cain, however, is a drive centered upon the self, one that is susceptible to the lure and ease of arrogance-unto-violence and violence-unto-death. When fueled and fed, it drives us only farther astray.[5] Through Cain our *fiṭra* is stunted and stymied. This is our inclination to wickedness and acts of transgression, as the

5 In the *Masnavī*, Rūmī offers a similar reading of the brothers. Cain is reduced to a "crow-intellect" (*ʿaql-i zāgh*) that roves everywhere but to the Divine, a term that also plays upon the notion that Cain learned to bury his murdered brother from observing a crow do similarly (see Q 5:31). In a contrast, Rūmī characterizes Abel as possessing an "Intellect whose sight does not rove" (*ʿaql-i mā zāgh*), likening it to the Prophet Muhammad's unflinching gaze in Q 53:17, "His sight did not swerve" (*mā zāgha al-baṣar*); see Jalāl al-Dīn Rūmī, *The Mathnawí of Jalálu'ddin Rúmí*, ed. and trans. Reynold A. Nicholson (London: Luzac, 1924–1940), book 4, lines 1301–1312. Cain can be said to represent the partial and roving intellect, and Abel the complete and unswerving Intellect. For these types of intellects, see Mohammed Rustom, "The Ocean of Nonexistence," *Mawlana Rumi Review* 4, no. 1 (2013): 192–193.

Quran discloses: "'Truly the self commands to evil'" (Q 12:53).[6] By virtue of our creation, each of us bears within the self the human and the inhuman, Abel and Cain respectively. The pull of Abel and Cain are both simultaneously felt, existing in tension and tandem within our personhood. Each roils against the other in a lifelong struggle for preeminence. While we may continually strive to assert the human, we must never lose sight that the inhuman perpetually persists as well—both in ourselves and in every "other" we encounter.[7]

We witness in Cain, then, our human susceptibility to succumbing to wiles upon the way. Although Satan may not be invoked explicitly anywhere in this passage of the Quran, the temptation to evil that he represents is palpable. The Quran describes the culminating moment as follows: "Then [Cain] made the killing of his brother agreeable to himself; so he killed him and became among the losers" (Q 5:30). Quite literally "his self" (*nafsuhu*), or the base nature of his soul, prompted him to carry out this act of fratricide. Cain's conviction to murder his brother emerged from out of the viler depths of a self run amok. It struck not from without but arose from within. Satan may have said, "'I will come for them from the front and behind, from their right and their left'" (Q 7:17), but the Prophet Muhammad discloses that the impulse to evil also pulses within: "Truly Satan flows in the blood of the son of Adam."[8] Nigh none can escape this weakness, as the Prophet declares elsewhere, "Satan touches every son of Adam on the day their mother gives birth to them."[9] As terrible as Cain's transgression was, Cain haunts us for another reason. His failings reveal the enormities to which each of us is possible of falling, in our own fashion. The unbridled self, a state to which we are all susceptible, lies at the root of evil's enactment. As Aleksandr Solzhenitsyn so poignantly put it, "But the line dividing good and evil cuts through the heart of every human being. And who is willing to destroy a piece of his own heart?"[10] Indeed, only through the intervention of the Divine—the angelic removal of the black stain from his heart—was the Prophet Muhammad freed from the pull of this deviating inner impulse.[11]

6 The speaker here is identified by the exegetical tradition as either Zulaykhā, the Potiphar's wife who tried to seduce Joseph, or more likely Joseph himself. See the commentary upon Q 12:53 in Nasr et al. (eds.), *The Study Quran*, 604–605.

7 In articulating an ethics of recognition, Viet Thanh Nguyen compellingly argues that it is critical to take ownership of our inhumanity, collectively and in its many particularities whether animated with ourselves or within others: Viet Thanh Nguyen, *Nothing Ever Dies: Vietnam and the Memory of War* (Cambridge, MA: Harvard University Press, 2016), 71–100.

8 See the commentary upon Q 114:5 in Nasr et al. (eds.), *The Study Quran*, 1584 (for references to the many places in which this tradition and its variants can be found in Hadith literature, see Nasr et al. (eds.), *The Study Quran*, 1906, s.v. "114:5c."). The term "son of Adam" is not a specific reference to Abel, Cain, or otherwise, but a designation for human beings in general.

9 The Prophet then goes on to name Mary and Jesus as exceptions. For the paper trail on this Hadith, Peter J. Awn, *Satan's Tragedy and Redemption: Iblīs in Sufi Psychology* (Leiden: Brill, 1983), 47, n. 131.

10 Quoted in Nguyen, *Nothing Ever Dies*, 72.

11 In the devotional biographies of the Prophet Muhammad's life, known as the *sīra* literature, an account is frequently related where two angels appear before the Prophet Muhammad, calmly

The figure of Cain, however, can be read with relevance beyond the individual self. Ali Shariati, for example, reads Cain socially across human history. As he declares, "Abel disappeared, and Cain came to the forefront of history, and there he still lives."[12] According to Shariati, Cain represents a recurrent and entrenched exploitative social system or as he puts it, "Throughout history, the children of Cain have been the rulers of mankind."[13] Read as a primordial paradigm, Cain embodies, then, the structural oppression that so frequently overtakes human societies. In his own life, Shariati witnessed several such manifestations. While studying abroad in Paris, he witnessed from within the very belly of the occupying French empire the unfolding Algerian War for Independence.[14] Then, back in his homeland of Iran, Shariati saw in the Pahlavi regime yet another historical instantiation of the "structure of Cain."[15] This repressive regime, while assuming outwardly a commitment to modernization, progress, and reform, sought inwardly to magnify its power through the systematic suppression of any and all opposition. It did so, according to Shariati, through the corruption and exploitation of the political, economic, and religious spheres of everyday life.[16] As a result, wide swaths of the populace were presented with a terrible choice: resist and suffer deprivation, depredation, and terror or acquiesce and be spared from the worst. It should be little surprise then, that so many of us succumb to the allure interwoven into systemic evils. What would we not give to feel safe, secure, singular, and even superior?

Yet it is from choosing the path of least resistance, the path that prioritizes narrow self-interests, that wickedness cascades into a torrent. Systemic evil might flow stronger when a hard-hearted Pharaoh assumes the lead, but that torrent was brought into being and is kept coursing across a land by the manifold acts of acquiescence and "minor" malice made every day by people committed to the security and benefit of themselves at the cost of others. Each one is a Cain who has surrendered to the whims of the self, rather than to the righteous will of God. Better to slay a brother and let the lesser burn than to fall short and suffer oneself, or so sayeth the aspect of Cain that burns within. More than this, one wrong begets another until evil has spilled over into another generation to the perpetual generation of itself. Fazlur Rahman duly notes, "A part of humanity influencing others in evil ways through

remove his heart, wash it in pure snow in order to cleanse it of a black spot, and then restore it. See Martin Lings, *Muhammad* (Cambridge: Islamic Texts Society, 1991), 25–26.

12 Shariati, *On the Sociology of Islam*, 100.

13 Shariati, *Hajj*, 101.

14 Georg Leube, "The Liberties of a Transmitter: Frantz Fanon According to Shariati," in *Ali Shariati and the Future of Social Theory: Religion, Revolution, and the Role of the Intellectual*, ed. Dustin J. Byrd and Seyed Javad Miri (Leiden: Brill, 2017), 157–169; Kingshuk Chatterjee, *'Ali Shari'ati and the Shaping of Political Islam in Iran* (New York: Palgrave Macmillan, 2011), 77–78.

15 Shariati's critique of socio-political formations is extensive. He states, "Slavery, serfdom, feudalism, bourgeoisie, industrial capitalism, and—as its culmination—imperialism, all belong to the structure of Cain;" Shariati, *On the Sociology of Islam*, 113.

16 Shariati, *Hajj*, 101–106; Shariati, *On the Sociology of Islam*, 115; Shariati, *Man and Islam*, 19–20.

example, pressure, or even education is a frequent theme in the Qur'ān."[17] Systemic evil is an all-too-common feature of social life. It is within such bedeviled societies, so many "Houses of Pharaoh," that we find ourselves dangerously intertwined and entangled today. We must confront and contend with these manifold shares of inhumanity, especially as they solidify into particular forms of structural oppression across time and the span of this world. As Viet Nguyen poignantly remarks, "Identifying with the human and denying one's inhumanity, and the inhumanity of one's own, is the ultimate kind of identity politics. It circulates through nationalism, capitalism, and racism, as well as through the humanities. Reminding ourselves that being human also means being inhuman is important simply because it is so easy to forget our inhumanity or to displace it onto other humans."[18]

References

Awn, Peter J. *Satan's Tragedy and Redemption: Iblīs in Sufi Psychology*. Leiden: Brill, 1983.

Chatterjee, Kingshuk. *'Ali Shari'ati and the Shaping of Political Islam in Iran*. New York: Palgrave Macmillan, 2011.

Chittick, William. *In Search of the Lost Heart: Explorations in Islamic Thought*. Edited by Mohammed Rustom, Atif Khalil, and Kazuyo Murata. Albany: SUNY Press, 2012.

Leube, Georg. "The Liberties of a Transmitter: Frantz Fanon According to Shariati." In *Ali Shariati and the Future of Social Theory: Religion, Revolution, and the Role of the Intellectual*, edited by Dustin J. Byrd and Seyed Javad Miri, 157–169. Leiden: Brill, 2017.

Lings, Martin. *Muhammad*. Cambridge: Islamic Texts Society, 1991.

Metzger, Bruce, and Roland E. Murphy (eds.). *The New Oxford Annotated Bible with the Apocryphal/Deuterocanonical Books, New Revised Standard Version*. New York: Oxford University Press, 1994.

Nasr, Seyyed Hossein, Caner Dagli, Maria Dakake, Joseph Lumbard, and Mohammed Rustom (eds.). *The Study Quran: A New Translation and Commentary*. New York: HarperOne, 2015.

Nguyen, Viet Thanh. *Nothing Ever Dies: Vietnam and the Memory of War*. Cambridge, MA: Harvard University Press, 2016.

Rahman, Fazlur. *Major Themes of the Qur'ān*. Minneapolis: Bibliotheca Islamica, 1994.

Rūmī, Jalāl al-Dīn. *The Mathnawí of Jalálu'ddin Rúmí*. Edited and translated by Reynold A. Nicholson. London: Luzac, 1924–1940.

Rustom, Mohammed. "The Ocean of Nonexistence." *Mawlana Rumi Review* 4, no. 1 (2013): 188–199.

Shariati, Ali. *Hajj*. Translated by Somayyah and Yaser. Bedford: Free Islamic Literatures Inc., 1977.

Shariati, Ali. "The Philosophy of History: Cain and Abel." In *On the Sociology of Islam: Lectures by Ali Shari'ati*, translated by Hamid Algar, 97–110. Berkeley: Mizan Press, 1979.

Shariati, Ali. *Man and Islam*. Translated by Fatollah Marjani. Houston: Free Islamic Literatures Inc., 1981.

17 Fazlur Rahman, *Major Themes of the Qur'ān* (Minneapolis: Bibliotheca Islamica, 1994), 59.

18 Nguyen, *Nothing Ever Dies*, 72.

10 Practical Muslim Theodicy

A Ghazalian Perspective on Emotional Pain

Joel Richmond

Introduction

Many of al-Ghazālī's ideas regarding self-restraint relate not only to holding back the soul from desire, but also to developing correct thinking and modifying one's inner dialogue. Nowhere is this better demonstrated than in his thoughts on the proper response to life's tribulations.[1] Before turning to al-Ghazālī directly, however, it is helpful first to explore some relevant theories of theodicy and explanations of evil that preceded his own response to the question of suffering.

Modern writers in the philosophy of religion, those dealing with the various problems of evil, rarely consider, if at all, the contributions to this subject by non-Western religious thinkers. Only on rare occasions do they engage or build upon earlier theodicies written by the Church Fathers. One example of a solution that does slightly consider other traditions is John Hicks' famous "Soul-Making Theodicy," developed upon the earlier articulation of theodicy as found in the writings of St. Irenaeus (d. 203).[2] Without the unnecessary human evolutionary premises that are added to the argument by Hick, the solution to the problem of why it is that God allows evil in the world is strikingly in line with al-Ghazālī's own solutions. The conclusion of Hick's soul-making argument is to state that the many evils that we find in the world, whether found in human morality or even natural disasters, all

1 For al-Ghazālī's best of possible worlds theodicy, see Eric L. Ormsby, *Theodicy in Islamic Thought: The Dispute Over al-Ghazâlî's "Best of All Possible Worlds"* (Princeton: Princeton University Press, 1984). Ormsby offers a summary of al-Ghazālī's view of suffering and gratitude on p. 254. See also Stephen R. Ogden, "Problems in al-Ghazālī's Perfect World: Objections and Counter-Objections to his Best Possible World Thesis," in *Islam and Rationality: The Impact of al-Ghazali: Papers Collected on His 900th Anniversary*, ed. Georges Tamer (Leiden: Brill, 2015), 2:54–88; Eric L. Ormsby, *Ghazali: The Revival of Islam* (London: Oneworld, 2008), 132–134. To the best of my knowledge, Ormsby is the first author to use the term "practical theodicy" in Islamic studies. See his note in al-Ghazālī, *Love, Longing, Intimacy and Contentment*, trans. Eric L. Ormsby (Cambridge: Islamic Texts Society, 2016), 126.

2 See John Hick, "An Irenaean Theodicy," in *Encountering Evil: Live Options in Theodicy*, ed. Stephen T. Davis (Louisville: Westminster John Knox Press, 2001), 38–52. For Hick's thought on other traditions, see Adnan Aslan, *Religious Pluralism in Christian and Islamic Philosophy: The Thought of John Hick and Seyyed Hossein Nasr* (Richmond: Curzon, 1998).

DOI: 10.4324/9781003371670-11

take place in order to allow finite persons to respond and learn to be more virtuous while working towards perfection through enduring these obstacles. Evil in the world is not without a purpose because it allows for human sanctification through the awareness of evil and its opposite, goodness. The other aspect of Hick's theodicy is the soteriological premise, which is that persons can continue to soul-build in the afterlife, a premise that is not shared by al-Ghazālī, at least not explicitly.[3] In his earlier formulation of this line of thinking—more to do with the problem of pain and suffering, and also more overtly Christian in its response—Hick expressed that our own modes of experiencing pain are usually self-regarding while they should be recognized as part of the gift of life that God has given us. In other words, our experience of suffering should be intertwined with the virtue of gratitude that allows us to recognize the limits of suffering. The argument mirrors al-Ghazālī's earlier explanations in many ways, as we will see.[4]

In Islamic philosophical thought, as demonstrated in the writings of Avicenna, the subject of evil was dealt with in a different manner than what we might first expect when looking for a theodicy. Although he does not explain how we might react to the trials of evil, he does explain why evil ultimately comes to exist in the world. For Avicenna, the reality of evil is first understood as a metaphysical and cosmological problem, while secondly, it is a failure of the rational soul to recognize its higher purpose. Here we will only focus on the former, as it suits our immediate purpose. Ayman Shihadeh, Shams C. Inati, and Marwan Rashed have all recently explored Avicenna's metaphysical ideas regarding evil, so it is useful to return to what they have uncovered, while comparing their results with my own interpretation.[5]

All these researchers agree that Avicenna took over and continued to build upon Neoplatonic ideas regarding the emanation of goodness from the first principle: he argues that the Necessary Existent, unmotivated by a final cause, is the reason why

3 John Hick, "Soul-Making Theodicy," in *God and the Problem of Evil*, ed. William L. Rowe (Malden: Blackwell, 2001), 265–281. For the problem of universal salvation in Islamic thought, see Mohammad Hassan Khalil (ed.), *Between Heaven and Hell: Islam, Salvation, and the Fate of Others* (New York: Oxford University Press, 2013); Mohammad Hassan Khalil, *Islam and the Fate of Others: The Salvation Question* (New York: Oxford University Press, 2012); Mohammed Rustom, *The Triumph of Mercy: Philosophy and Scripture in Mullā Ṣadrā* (Albany: SUNY Press, 2012), chapters 6–7.

4 John Hick, *Evil and the God of Love* (New York: Harper & Row, 1966), 255–261, 318–336; John Hick, "Soul-Making and Suffering," in *The Problem of Evil*, ed. Marilyn McCord Adams and Robert Merrihew Adams (Oxford: Oxford University Press, 1990), 174.

5 Ayman Shihadeh, "Avicenna's Theodicy and al-Rāzī's Anti-Theodicy," *Intellectual History of the Islamicate World* 7, no. 1 (2019): 61–84; Shams C. Inati, *The Problem of Evil: Ibn Sina's Theodicy* (Albany: SUNY Press, 2000); Marwan Rashed, "Théodicée et Approximation: Avicenne," *Arabic Sciences and Philosophy* 10 (2000). See also Carlos Steel, "Avicenna and Thomas Aquinas on Evil," in *Avicenna and His Heritage*, ed. Jules Janssens and Daniel De Smet (Leuven: Leuven University Press, 2002), 171–196; Muhammad Faruque, "Does God Create Evil? A Study of Fakhr al-Dīn al-Rāzī's Exegesis of *Sūrat al-Falaq*," *Islam and Christian-Muslim Relations* 28, no. 3 (2016): 1–21; Mohammed Rustom, "Devil's Advocate: ʿAyn al-Quḍāt's Defence of Iblis in Context," *Studia Islamica* 115, no. 1 (2020): 75–79.

goodness, convertible or co-extensive with existence itself, overflows throughout the cosmos.[6] It would not be wrong to say that existence and goodness are, for Avicenna, what in later medieval philosophy are called transcendentals.[7] In Avicenna's metaphysics, actualized possible existents proceed first as the quiddities of celestial intellects, and secondly proceed all the way to our own sublunar realm, causing not only the plenitude of separate actualized beings, but also the privation of these beings in their material realities as they are found. It is the privation in separate beings that results in various descending levels of the cosmos, ultimately reaching matter. It is privation itself that Avicenna initially designates as evil.[8]

In his various treatises, Avicenna gets considerably more specific regarding how and in what manner contingent existence results in evil. In the metaphysics section of his *Book of Healing*, he speaks about two divisions of evil that come into existence. There is first, essential evil (*al-sharr bi'l-dhāt*), and second, there is accidental evil (*al-sharr bi'l-ʿaraḍ*).[9] He says that essential evil is a privation in things which prevents their nature from reaching their primary perfections.[10] Thus, the evil of blindness would be that it prevents the eye from achieving its natural primary perfection, or, in other words, its teleological purpose of sight.[11] In contrast, his description of accidental evil is far more subtle. It is called "accidental evil" when a thing, good in itself, causes harm or corruption for something other than itself. An example of this relative evil would be a cloud or a mountain blocking sunlight from reaching fruits. The fruits ultimately depend on the sun for growth and nourishment. As a relation, the clouds and mountains become an evil for the fruits, while remaining a good in another respect according to their own specific natures.[12] The clouds and mountains are the cause of accidental evil and harm to the fruits, while the impediment of nutrition to the fruits remains an essential evil for the fruits themselves, according to what their primary perfection requires.

To fully understand the inner obstacles on the way to felicity in regard to these points and their remedy, we also need to know what al-Ghazālī sees as good and evil in the realm of theology. It is worth briefly outlining what exactly "evil" means for al-Ghazālī in a theological context. The question is approached in his major theological writings such as *al-Iqtiṣād fī'l-iʿtiqād* and *al-Maqṣad al-asnā'*, as well as in his major work on legal theory, *al-Mustaṣfā min ʿilm al-uṣūl*. In

6 Inati, *Problem of Evil*, 64–65; Shihadeh, "Avicenna's Theodicy and al-Rāzī's Anti-Theodicy," 63–65; Rashed, "Théodicée et Approximation," 225–226.

7 For a thorough understanding of the transcendentals and their implications, see the many contributions in Scott Charles MacDonald (ed.), *Being and Goodness: The Concept of the Good in Metaphysics and Philosophical Theology* (Ithaca: Cornell University Press, 1991).

8 Avicenna, *The Metaphysics of the Healing*, trans. Michael E. Marmura (Provo: Brigham Young University Press, 2005), 339.

9 Avicenna, *The Metaphysics of the Healing*, 340. See also Inati, *Problem of Evil*, 66; Shihadeh, "Avicenna's Theodicy and al-Rāzī's Anti-Theodicy," 65.

10 Avicenna, *The Metaphysics of the Healing*, 340.

11 Avicenna, *The Metaphysics of the Healing*, 340.

12 Avicenna, *The Metaphysics of the Healing*, 341.

later Ashʿarī theology, the theological school of which al-Ghazālī was a major representative, the question of evil takes a number of dimensions to do with both God and the human being. Most of the context is formed through the encounter of the Muslim communities with the early theological school of Muʿtazilism. The Muʿtazilites had several intricate beliefs regarding the nature of evil, broadly described as relating to questions of whether God is willing to commit evil, the nature of evil itself, and what constitutes evil in the case of human action. Here, we will put aside the question of evil in human action and law.

The Ashʿarī school is widely thought to take a position of anti-theodicy on the question of whether God is willing to commit evil. Anti-theodicy means precisely that God is under no obligation to act towards creation according to the human conception of justice. The central idea is that creation is God's property, and He can do with it whatever He so wills, with no injustice done on His part. Therefore, the attribution of evil to God is rendered incoherent. Many scholars have taken this position to mean that the Ashʿarī school altogether dispensed with the problem of evil as a whole.[13] The need to question God's omnipotence by the human scale of justice seemed to the majority of Ashʿarites to be an affront to His power. The various texts on this issue argue that it is impossible for the human mind to find the purpose of why God allows certain evils, why He acts justly, or why He behaves with perceived injustice towards His creation.[14] Abū'l-Ḥasan al-Ashʿarī (d. 935–936) devoted an entire section of his *al-Ibāna* to "the question concerning the torture of infants," taking aim at those who thought it was impossible or unjust for God to do so if He wished.[15] Even al-Ghazālī was willing to argue along these lines in defense of the Ashʿarite position.[16] We could say that he approached one aspect of the problem of evil from an Ashʿarite theological perspective and another according to what he determined from moral psychology. The latter has more to do with the proper human response in the face of perceived evils and where to find meaning in disappointing and horrific events.

Changing Perceptions of Evil

The topic of good and evil is not so clear-cut and simple, primarily because the perception of evil in the world is often subjective. Al-Ghazālī, when discussing gratitude shows that, what can be considered good from one perspective can also

13 On the question over whether God can do evil and also whether the Ashʿarīte school had disposed of theodicy as a problem, see Khaled El-Rouayheb, "Must God Tell Us the Truth? A Problem in Ashʿarī Theology," in *Islamic Cultures, Islamic Contexts: Essays in Honor of Professor Patricia Crone*, ed. Behnam Sadeghi, Asad Q. Ahmed, Adam J. Silverstein, and Robert G. Hoyland (Leiden: Brill, 2015), 411–429.

14 Mohammed Ghaly, *Islam and Disability: Perspectives in Theology and Jurisprudence* (London: Routledge, 2010), 24.

15 Abū'l-Ḥasan al-Ashʿarī, *The Elucidation of Islām's Foundation*, trans. Walter C. Klein (New Haven: American Oriental Society, 1940), 112–113; Ghaly, *Islam and Disability*, 24.

16 Ormsby, *Theodicy in Islamic Thought*, 47, 237; Ghaly, *Islam and Disability*, 176.

be deemed evil from another. It is in this dimension where the realm of human virtue fits into the picture. He shows that much of self-restraint has to do with correcting one's false perception of events in the world. Al-Ghazālī thinks that many misfortunes can befall a person in life, and this situation demands the constant need for the virtue of patience. Many terrible events do not involve human choice and must only be seen as opportunities for the exercise of patience, despite their awful and devastating nature for human emotions. Having patience in these trials is the most challenging and excruciating part of life, and overcoming these tests is one of the highest stations of patience. Moreover, al-Ghazālī believes that all afflictions are ultimately sent directly from God, so one must imitate the prophets in bearing misfortunes. The rewards for patience are many, but regarding the death of a child, an illness, or the loss of wealth, the reward is freedom from any reckoning on the Day of Judgement.[17]

The solution to how one must deal with misfortune is very Stoic in al-Ghazālī's teaching.[18] He puts an objection in the mouth of a questioner asking how it is possible to achieve such a high degree of patience when there is no choice regarding unfortunate events. Like a Roman Stoic, al-Ghazālī says that one does indeed have a choice in how he reacts to the misfortune; even though one cannot control events of the external world and their consequences, one can restrain the measure of anguish one feels over these predestined matters. In reacting to events, the various expressions of pain that can be outwardly shown is a matter that can, and should be, controlled through patience. The reaction of the Muslim is to have contentment with the decree of God. He or she must believe that the blessings that were given as a loan in the world were taken back in accord with the perfect justice of God. Because God's decree gives the allowance for misfortunes, the proper reaction is to continue in one's usual way of life, undisturbed and without the expression of despondency towards the world.[19] This is also the advice given in the *Book of Contentment*, which we will return to later.[20]

Al-Ghazālī relates one example of the highest degrees of patience: when the suffering individual cannot be identified as having any unusual behaviour from those around him. The suffering that takes place in the heart should not take the sufferer beyond the limits of patience. Although it is natural to feel pain or even weep, these emotions should not be allowed to overtake the person beyond certain limits. He makes it a point, however, that the normal expression of pain may even be necessary under certain circumstances, just as those who undergo a painful medical procedure might gasp and weep, so might the person who is undergoing misfortunes.[21]

17 al-Ghazālī, *Iḥyā' 'ulūm al-dīn* (Jeddah: Dār al-Minhāj, 2011), 7:246–247.
18 For suggested Stoic influences on al-Ghazālī's teaching on gratitude, see Simon Van den Bergh, "Ghazālī on 'Gratitude Towards God' and Its Greek Sources," *Studia Islamica* 7 (1957): 77–98.
19 Ghazālī, *Iḥyā'*, 7:250.
20 Ghazālī, *Iḥyā'*, 8:525.
21 Ghazālī, *Iḥyā'*, 7:251–252.

Although al-Ghazālī does admit that pain in the soul is to a certain extent inevitable, he also insists that there is great reward in restraining and concealing emotional distress, and its source, if possible, from the sight of others. It is common for all people to long for a past that cannot be retrieved and to a future that has already been decided by God; in either case, both varieties of mental wanderings are spent in vain, for nothing can be changed, and the short time in life will eventually get squandered by negative thinking.[22] Patience is also required when incoming thoughts inspired by the devil are met with in life. Patience is necessary for everyone in all states and actions, but even if one were to leave the presence of others and society, one would still require the virtue in the face of the devil's mental suggestions to the soul. According to al-Ghazālī, patience with various negative thoughts will only cease with death, so one must continually implore God for success against this obstacle.[23] In all cases, every type of pain must be suppressed through one demonstrating the station of patience.

The reader is given more information regarding misfortunes and tribulations in the *Book of Patience and Gratitude*, where the station of patience is given even more consideration.[24] There, al-Ghazālī answers the question of why he has joined together the two stations of patience and gratitude and how they form a unity on the path. To begin, he presents a series of seemingly paradoxical questions to do with trials in life and the practice of patience and gratitude. He asks, for example:

> Perhaps you will say: what has been mentioned regarding blessing indicates that there is a blessing from God in every existent. But this would indicate that trials do not exist. So, what is the meaning of patience? If trials do exist . . . then what is the meaning of having gratitude in trials?[25]

Other paradoxical questions are given in this section, but we should start with his reply to this one first, as it allows for new distinctions and provides us with an answer to solve all the others. First, al-Ghazālī replies that he does indeed believe that there is a difference between blessings and trials in life, and he further qualifies this dichotomy by introducing elements of relativity into the human perception of various events. His initial solution is to argue that there is a difference between an absolute blessing and a relative blessing. The absolute blessing would be felicity in

22 Ghazālī, *Iḥyā'*, 7:253.
23 Ghazālī, *Iḥyā'*, 7:256.
24 There have been a number of noteworthy articles on the concept of gratitude in Islam. For some recent contributions, see Ida Zilio-Grandi, "The Gratitude of Man and the Gratitude of God: Notes on *Šukr* in Traditional Islamic Thought," *Islamochristiana* 38 (2012): 45–62; Atif Khalil, "On Cultivating Gratitude in Sufi Virtue Ethics," *Journal of Sufi Studies* 4, no. 1–2 (2015); Atif Khalil, "The Embodiment of Gratitude (*shukr*) in Sufi Virtue Ethics," *Studia Islamica* 111 no.2 (2016): 159–178.
25 Ghazālī, *Iḥyā'*, 7:420. My translations in this chapter from Ghazālī's *Book of Patience and Gratitude* are adapted from an already existing complete translation of the work: al-Ghazālī, *Patience and Thankfulness*, trans. H. T. Littlejohn (Cambridge: Islamic Texts Society, 2010).

the afterlife and the encounter with God. In contrast, a relative blessing would be something, such as financial success, due to its ability to benefit one's religion or corrupt it. The same rule applies to the trials of life, for an absolute trial would be the loss of felicity, while a relative trial would be occasions like a loss of wealth, disease, and the experience of fear; these latter situations are relative trials because they lead only to pain in this world, while they might also be the cause of felicity in the hereafter.[26]

The subject is qualified to a greater degree when al-Ghazālī further explains the moments when patience and gratitude are not appropriate responses to misfortunes and trials. He mentions that only absolute gratitude should reflect absolute blessing. Furthermore, it is also wrong for an individual to be patient with disbelief and disobedience. It is faulty reasoning for a person to bear patiently with any trial or suffering if they can potentially remove the source of the pain or bring it to an end. For these reasons, when we have patience in the world, it can only be for what is not an absolute trial. What is not an absolute trial can also be considered a great blessing when it leads to something better in this life or the next. In this series of arguments, many examples are given. Let us suppose that a man and his children are murdered because of his wealth. What seemed to be a blessing—wealth—turned into a curse. The same is true for blessings other than wealth, as every blessing can, in its own way, change its nature over the course of time.[27]

In fact, al-Ghazālī argues, anything but faith and good character may become a trial for persons, while their opposites may become a blessing. Even knowledge, which is also an attribute of God, can become a curse for some people. A person's ignorance of the time of their death prevents them from falling into despondency and losing their enthusiasm for life. The ignorance of the many evil thoughts of others is also a blessing, for if a person were aware of all the wicked thoughts of others, he would not be able to function in society. The veil that prevents one from knowing the negative thoughts of others also comes to save one from falling into hatred, jealousy, and many other bad character traits, so it must, once again, be considered one of the blessings found in ignorance. Ignorance of another's faults is a blessing because it would result in hatred for the person, and that very same hatred would bring with it dire consequences in the hereafter. The opposite is also true for knowing the good qualities of another. Here al-Ghazālī's example is quite inventive. He says if that person happens to be a saint, and one was to harm him, the injurious person's punishment would be less than if the saint was known. That is, if one knowingly harmed a saint, with full knowledge that he or she was a saint, then the resulting consequence would bring with it a more painful punishment. Once again, in this case, ignorance is better than knowledge.[28] Many more examples are given in the text as to why ignorance might become superior to knowledge in certain situations.

26 Ghazālī, *Iḥyā'*, 7:420–421.
27 Ghazālī, *Iḥyā'*, 7:421.
28 Ghazālī, *Iḥyā'*, 7:422–423.

Eric Ormsby has previously dedicated an entire monograph to a fierce debate between al-Ghazālī's commentators on one specific sentence found in the *Revival*. The debate was centered on al-Ghazālī's claim about the world that "there is not in possibility anything whatever more excellent, more complete, or more perfect than it is."[29] One aspect of this debate is that al-Ghazālī conceives of Divine wisdom as permeating the lowest and highest of existents in the cosmos. There are, in fact, many instances in al-Ghazālī's works which either state this idea explicitly or simply allude to it. Ormsby has already explained the significance of this debate, as it was found in Islamic theology before al-Ghazālī's time.[30] We can see in his discussion of gratitude that he also continues this line of thought. He affirms that the trials of life are all a testament to God's wisdom in every case. There is not any event that does not manifest or testify to this wisdom in some manner or another. Additionally, he adds that every perceived trial or evil found in the universe contains some form of blessing. He says: "It is true what we have said: that God did not create anything except that in it is wisdom. And He did not create anything except in it [can be found] a blessing."[31] It is because of this witnessing of Divine wisdom that al-Ghazālī wants to remind the reader that there is an opportunity for gratitude in every sort of trial that life can deliver.

He gives five additional reasons why someone should feel gratitude during any affliction or tribulation. The first reason is that, for every possible trial or illness a human can be accosted with in life, there are far worse tribulations that they could be experiencing. A person should be thankful because for each perceived trial in the world, God could potentially increase it in severity if He so wills.[32]

The second reason why one should have gratitude in tribulation is that the perceived misfortune did not bring about a loss in one's faith and religion.[33] This reflects the reoccurring theme in the work that the hereafter is everything, while the present life is nothing in comparison. It should be obvious that al-Ghazālī sees the loss of religion to be the greatest calamity a person could undergo because felicity itself depends on the preservation of religion.

The third reason is that it is better to be punished in this world than in the afterlife. In the hereafter, the punishment received cannot be treated in the same way as it could be in this world, so one should not have anything less than complete gratitude towards God for bringing about the trial before the time of death, as it is less severe, even though it may not seem so at the time. There is no longer the opportunity for people to console each other in the hereafter because life has ended and with it any chance for repentance. If they were punished on earth, it is less likely that a believer would be punished a second time in the afterlife.[34]

29 Ormsby, *Theodicy in Islamic Thought*, 35.
30 Ormsby, *Theodicy in Islamic Thought*, 44–58.
31 Ghazālī, *Iḥyāʾ*, 7:424.
32 Ghazālī, *Iḥyāʾ*, 7:424.
33 Ghazālī, *Iḥyāʾ*, 7:425.
34 Ghazālī, *Iḥyāʾ*, 7:427.

The fourth reason has to do with God's attributes of knowledge and will. Al-Ghazālī says that each tribulation has already been written in the Mother of the Book (*umm al-kitāb*) mentioned in Q 13:39. This unseen celestial book contains all that will come to pass from the beginning to the end of creation, so one cannot run from what it contains of God's will. Gratitude comes with the knowledge that the trial, or part of the trial, will eventually come to an end.[35] Here, we can see how the solution given is once again to provide a contrast with the continuous tribulation of the afterlife, an event that much of humanity will eventually undergo.

The fifth reason is that the reward for suffering a trial is greater than the trial itself when eternal life is the measure. This can be seen from two aspects: the first understanding is that any part of an individual's body may come to sow the seeds of destruction if used in the wrong way. We already saw that al-Ghazālī believed that even ignorance could be beneficial in some circumstances; in the same manner, he indicates that the intellect itself could be a cause for someone's destruction in the hereafter. We might suppose that it could lead to the sin of pride if the person were knowledgeable. The clever scheming of intelligence could be forbidden if directed towards wrong ends.

Al-Ghazālī compares the discipline of a child to the situation of receiving trials from God. In the same way as the child will dislike punishment but will later thank his parents when grown, the believer will be shown in the afterlife that trials throughout life have delivered him from great destruction and were ultimately to his own benefit.[36] He points out that the vast majority of sins have their root in a desire for the goods of the world, while most of the salvific virtues result from turning the heart towards God and to the promise of the hereafter. Thus, there is reason to be thankful in misfortune because it shows the world to be the prison that it really is. Misfortune shows the servant that the world is not worth desiring and that death, as the inevitable certainty, should be welcomed as a release from this temporary prison.[37]

Al-Ghazālī also has more problematic explanations of suffering that are difficult to comprehend. However, these arguments show that the positing of the afterlife as the realm of justice and mercy is a constant theme and solution in al-Ghazālī's practical theodicy. He says that the suffering of one group of people in the afterlife provides a contrast that brings about salvific joy in the saved. The people who suffer in the fire of the hereafter for their unbelief and sin are put there to increase the unending happiness of those placed in the garden.[38] This is how al-Ghazālī sees God's justice and wisdom playing out among humanity. It is obvious for him that there is no justice in the physical world for most criminals, unbelievers, and

35 Ghazālī, *Iḥyāʾ*, 7:428.
36 Ghazālī, *Iḥyāʾ*, 7:428.
37 Ghazālī, *Iḥyāʾ*, 7:429.
38 Ghazālī, *Iḥyāʾ*, 7:423. On this same explanation as found in Ghazālī's *Book of Divine Unity and Trust in God* (book 35 of *Iḥyāʾ*), see Ogden, "Problems in al-Ghazālī's Perfect World," 70.

tyrants, so the afterlife provides a place where justice is shown to these groups, while those mysteriously deserving of it are receptive to God's mercy, living in the bliss of the Garden. The felicity experienced by believers is directly related to the virtue of gratitude that al-Ghazālī is so focused on teaching in the proceeding chapters. His argument is supported by the fact that people do not normally rejoice and show gratitude for blessings that are accorded to everyone universally. The light of the sun, or the beauty of the stars, do not automatically cause the feeling of gratitude because they are always available. It is only when some are deprived of these blessings that others can feel gratitude for what they have been given. For al-Ghazālī, this shows the wisdom of God in providing the allowance for some people to suffer in this world.[39] In any case, the scenario painted in these passages is especially frightening for those who believe in the Day of Judgement spoken of so frequently in the Qur'an.

Al-Ghazālī also tells us to react to our own suffering by believing that the trials of life are brought about for the purification from previous sins. This is hardly his own idea, and many reports and narratives are put forth to support his argument.[40] I do not think that, for al-Ghazālī, this way of thinking—explaining why certain people suffer—is meant to be an all-encompassing solution to the many problems of evil. The narrations all relate that the believers suffer most for the expiation of their sins in this world. They suffer on earth so they will not have to be punished a second time in the afterlife. The argument is not put forth to give reasons for why all people suffer, including the innocent; instead, it is designed to explain to believers the cause of their own suffering in life. For example, a Muslim might wonder, despite one's conviction of faith, why God would send great tribulations to the believers, trials which are comparably more severe than what the unbelievers experience. This is an intelligible solution and has much in common with other explanations of the problem of suffering that we find in the history of world religions. As already mentioned, this does not explain why animals or even innocent children suffer, so it might not satisfy certain Muʿtazilites. Still, it does allow the believer to regain control of their emotions and prevent themselves from having resentment against God.[41] The other benefit of the belief is that it allows the Muslim to feel that their suffering could perhaps be a blessing from God, which, as a solution, remains consistent with al-Ghazālī's other arguments in the text. This popular argument, commonly referred to even among modern Muslims, may be one reason we see such strong resilience of Muslims even in our own times.

From these discussions, it would be easy to conclude that it is better to ask God for tribulations to be purified from sin before death. Yet, al-Ghazālī is adamant that

39 Ghazālī, *Iḥyāʾ*, 7:423.
40 Ghazālī, *Iḥyāʾ*, 7:431–440.
41 On the view of suffering according to the Muʿtazilites, see Sherman Jackson, *Islam and the Problem of Black Suffering* (New York: Oxford University Press, 2009); Margaretha T. Heemskerk, *Suffering in the* [sic] *Muʿtazilite Theology: ʿAbd al-Jabbār's Teaching on Pain and Divine Justice* (Leiden: Brill, 2000).

this is the wrong way of viewing the situation. According to traditions coming from the Prophet, it is not permissible for one to seek out tribulation for any reason. In fact, one is commanded to seek refuge in God from the many diverse types of trials that could be brought about in life. The person seeking anything but blessing is acting only out of ignorance because many reports teach people to seek out well-being (*ʿāfiya*) in all states and affairs.[42]

Contentment with Trials

Turning to the *Book of Contentment (riḍāʾ)*, we can see that many of these arguments are further substantiated by new ways of considering suffering and perceived evils. There is a report of the Prophet "that he asked a group of his companions, 'What are you?' They answered, 'Believers.' He asked, 'What is the mark of your belief?' They replied, 'We endure patiently in affliction and we give thanks in well-being and we are content with whatever God decrees.' He exclaimed, 'Believers, by the Lord of the Kaʿba!'"[43] This tradition and others, further supported by verses of the Qur'an, are used by al-Ghazālī to show the connections between the stations of patience, gratitude, and contentment, especially in the face of tribulation. Before describing *riḍāʾ* in the works of the early Sufis, Atif Khalil describes this station in the following manner:

> The early Sufi moral psychologists were acutely aware of the difficulties the soul faced in realizing a state of *riḍāʾ* in all of its worldly affairs. It was acknowledged that to the extent that *riḍāʾ* is a natural response to circumstances that are pleasing to the soul, it is not the consequence of any real moral struggle or effort, and therefore not a particularly distinctive virtue. The litmus test lies in being able to exhibit a genuine state of satisfaction in the face of the bitter blows of fate, in response to those circumstances of loss that naturally elicit distress, anxiety, suffering and pain.[44]

For al-Ghazālī, the key to unlocking the door to endurance in suffering is to develop a love for God. It is only love that can penetrate the heart of the servant, allowing them to continue unharmed through any type of trial in life and to experience the absence of pain and turmoil. One relevant example is that a true lover will not feel any sensitivity to pain; they can be wounded in battle without being immersed in suffering or even realizing they are injured. The main lesson to be taken away is that when one is mentally preoccupied with a specific task or affair, the ability to feel pain or suffering is drastically reduced.[45] Furthermore, when a

42 Ghazālī, *Iḥyāʾ*, 7:441.
43 Ghazālī, *Iḥyāʾ*, 148.
44 Atif Khalil, "Contentment, Satisfaction and Good-Pleasure: *Riḍāʾ* in Early Sufi Moral Psychology," *Studies in Religion* 43, no. 3 (2014): 5.
45 Ghazālī, *Iḥyāʾ*, 8:538.

person is directed towards a specific goal, they are willing to endure any necessary pain to fulfill their aim.[46] This is even more the case when a lover is absorbed by love for the beloved.

Finally, we can once again touch on the question of why there is evil in the world according to al-Ghazālī. This is a problem that al-Ghazālī rarely engages with, except in an allusive manner. The question is directly related to theodicy but does not get answered in a way most people would hope for. As with so many instances in the *Revival*, he repeats that this question is connected to the mystery of predestination and thus cannot be spoken of in a work explaining the proper methods of Islamic *praxis* (*muʿāmala*).[47] Although it is by no means spelled out, we can assume that al-Ghazālī is referring to the theological idea that all things are created through God's will. In this sense, all things, both good and evil, are known and willed by God according to His wisdom.

It is quite apparent that al-Ghazālī has thought out these problems thoroughly and is able to solve many practical problems of suffering simply by positing the hereafter as the realm where the human being is recompensed through God's mercy and justice. He reminds the reader that when spiritual stations are considered, the state of poverty or sickness may be a prevention of a person growing prideful, or even leaning into the realm of disobedience.[48] When viewed from the world, each of these states falls into the realm of relativity, for blessings can be seen as trials, while great tribulations can be seen as blessings. Only God can see the complete picture of how these states relate to the provision of spiritual virtue or eventual destruction. The final goal of success on the path is the main reason why the chapter that follows patience is on gratitude, for if there is success over tribulation and desire, then this is the most direct reason for thankfulness. It is only one reason why the books are paired. Because gratitude is also a form of patience and contentment, all these stations are inseparably linked together. The spiritual benefit of each of these stations is that they allow a person to restrain their negative emotions and instead direct their attention to God.

References

al-Ashʿarī, Abū'l-Ḥasan. *The Elucidation of Islām's Foundation*. Translated by Walter C. Klein. New Haven: American Oriental Society, 1940.

al-Ghazālī. *Patience and Thankfulness*. Translated by H. T. Littlejohn. Cambridge: Islamic Texts Society, 2010.

al-Ghazālī. *Iḥyāʾ ʿulūm al-dīn*. Jeddah: Dār al-Minhāj, 2011.

al-Ghazālī. *Love, Longing, Intimacy and Contentment*. Translated by Eric L. Ormsby. Cambridge: Islamic Texts Society, 2016.

46 Ghazālī, *Iḥyāʾ*, 8:539.
47 Ghazālī, *Iḥyāʾ*, 8:560.
48 Ghazālī, *Iḥyāʾ*, 7:422.

Aslan, Adnan. *Religious Pluralism in Christian and Islamic Philosophy: The Thought of John Hick and Seyyed Hossein Nasr*. Richmond: Curzon, 1998.

Avicenna. *The Metaphysics of the Healing*. Translated by Michael E. Marmura. Provo: Brigham Young University Press, 2005.

El-Rouayheb, Khaled. "Must God Tell Us the Truth? A Problem in Ashʿarī Theology." In *Islamic Cultures, Islamic Contexts: Essays in Honor of Professor Patricia Crone*, edited by Behnam Sadeghi, Asad Q. Ahmed, Adam J. Silverstein, and Robert G. Hoyland, 411–429. Leiden: Brill, 2015.

Faruque, Muhammad. "Does God Create Evil? A Study of Fakhr al-Dīn al-Rāzī's Exegesis of *Sūrat al-Falaq*." *Islam and Christian-Muslim Relations* 28, no. 3 (2016): 1–21.

Ghaly, Mohammed. *Islam and Disability: Perspectives in Theology and Jurisprudence*. London: Routledge, 2010.

Heemskerk, Margaretha T. *Suffering in the* [sic] *Muʿtazilite Theology: ʿAbd al-Jabbār's Teaching on Pain and Divine Justice*. Leiden and Boston: Brill, 2000.

Hick, John. *Evil and the God of Love*. New York: Harper & Row, 1966.

Hick, John. "Soul-Making and Suffering." In *The Problem of Evil*, edited by Marilyn McCord Adams and Robert Merrihew Adams, 168–187. Oxford: Oxford University Press, 1990.

Hick, John. "An Irenaean Theodicy." In *Encountering Evil: Live Options in Theodicy*, edited by Stephen T. Davis, 38–52. Louisville: Westminster John Knox Press, 2001.

Hick, John. "Soul-Making Theodicy." In *God and the Problem of Evil*, edited by William L. Rowe, 265–281. Malden: Blackwell, 2001.

Inati, Shams C. *The Problem of Evil: Ibn Sina's Theodicy*. Albany: SUNY Press, 2000.

Jackson, Sherman A. *Islam and the Problem of Black Suffering*. New York: Oxford University Press, 2009.

Khalil, Atif. "Contentment, Satisfaction and Good-Pleasure: *Riḍāʾ* in Early Sufi Moral Psychology." *Studies in Religion* 43, no. 3 (2014): 371–389.

Khalil, Atif. "On Cultivating Gratitude in Sufi Virtue Ethics." *Journal of Sufi Studies* 4, no. 1–2 (2015): 1–26.

Khalil, Atif. "The Embodiment of Gratitude (*shukr*) in Sufi Virtue Ethics." *Studia Islamica* 111, no. 2 (2016): 159–178.

Khalil, Mohammad Hassan. *Islam and the Fate of Others: The Salvation Question*. New York: Oxford University Press, 2012.

Khalil, Mohammad Hassan (ed.). *Between Heaven and Hell: Islam, Salvation, and the Fate of Others*. New York: Oxford University Press, 2013.

MacDonald, Charles (ed.). *Being and Goodness: The Concept of the Good in Metaphysics and Philosophical Theology*. Ithaca: Cornell University Press, 1991.

McCord Adams, Marilyn. "A Modest Proposal? Caveat Emptor! Moral Theory and the Problems of Evil." In *Ethics and the Problem of Evil*, edited by James P. Sterba, 9–26. Bloomington: Indiana University Press, 2015.

Ogden, Stephen R. "Problems in al-Ghazālī's Perfect World: Objections and Counter-Objections to His Best Possible World Thesis." In *Islam and Rationality: The Impact of al-Ghazali*, Edited by Georges Tamer, vol. 2, 54–88. Leiden and Boston: Brill, 2015.

Ormsby, Eric L. *Theodicy in Islamic Thought: The Dispute Over al-Ghazālī's "Best of All Possible Worlds"*. Princeton: Princeton University, 1984.

Ormsby, Eric L. *Ghazali: The Revival of Islam*. Oxford: Oneworld, 2008.

Rashed, Marwan. "Théodicée et Approximation: Avicenne." *Arabic Sciences and Philosophy* 10 (2000): 223–257.

Rustom, Mohammed. *The Triumph of Mercy: Philosophy and Scripture in Mullā Ṣadrā*. Albany: SUNY Press, 2012.

Rustom, Mohammed. "Devil's Advocate: ʿAyn al-Quḍāt's Defence of Iblis in Context." *Studia Islamica* 115, no. 1 (2020): 65–100.
Shihadeh, Ayman. "Avicenna's Theodicy and al-Rāzī's Anti-Theodicy." *Intellectual History of the Islamicate World* 7, no. 1 (2019): 61–84.
Steel, Carlos. "Avicenna and Thomas Aquinas on Evil." In *Avicenna and His Heritage*, edited by Jules Janssens and Daniel De Smet, 171–196. Leuven: Leuven University Press, 2002.
Van den Bergh, Simon. "Ghazālī on 'Gratitude Towards God' and Its Greek Sources." *Studia Islamica* 7 (1957): 77–98.
Zilio Grandi, Ida. "The Gratitude of Man and the Gratitude of God: Notes on *Šukr* in Traditional Islamic Thought." *Islamochristiana* 38 (2012): 45–62.

11 The Student and the Sage

Mohammed Rustom

Plagued by the problem of evil, a student of philosophy and religion finds himself in great despair, with many more annoying questions than satisfying answers. The student passes by a certain ḥakīm, *or sage, as he takes his usual route to his early morning philosophy of religion seminar. Drawn towards the sage's luminous presence, the student attempts to approach the old man.*

Student: *Salām ʿalaykum.*
Sage: *ʿAlaykum salām.*
Student: Sir, are you new to the neighborhood?
Sage: No, no. I have been walking through this pathway every morning at 8 a.m. for the past 20 years. And I normally take refuge on that bench over there, which I call the "Ark of Noah."
Student: That's weird. I've been walking by here almost every morning at 8 a.m. also, at least for the past several years. How is it that I have never seen you?
Sage: Well, I have always been here, and have always seen you pass by.
Student: And you never said *salām*?
Sage: It would have been of no use.
Student: Uh, can I ask why?
Sage: Because you were not ready to see me.
Student: Please explain.

The sage looks up to the sun, then turns his gaze to the student.

Sage: Does a blind man see the sun?
Student: No, of course not.
Sage: Even though it is actually there?
Student: Yes, naturally.
Sage: But if the blind man could all of a sudden see, would he then see the sun?
Student: Yes!
Sage: So too is it the case with you. You were blind before, but now you can see, which is why we are talking to one another.

DOI: 10.4324/9781003371670-12

Student: So I can see now because I'm ready?

Sage: Yes.[1]

Student: Ready for what, exactly, dear Sir? I still do not understand.

Sage: One of my brothers once said, "The arrival of Divine aid accords with readiness."[2]

Student: So I am now ready to receive God's help?

Sage: As ready as you can be at this current point along the curve of your life.

Student: I like the way you speak Sir, and I see that you have some special kind of knowledge.

Sage: I tend to think of it as the lack of a common kind of ignorance.

Student: Sure, whatever. I mean, you clearly know things that I don't, and I'd bet you know much more than most people.

Sage: That is because "people are asleep."[3] The one who is not asleep is awake, and thus is more aware than those who are asleep.

Student: I see. So, what you have is an awareness, a wakefulness; it is a lack of sleep, and sleep corresponds to ignorance.

Sage: Whatever I have has been given to me as a gift from His Presence.[4]

Student: Sorry, but what did you do to gain this knowledge?

The sage shakes his head from left to right as he knocks at an invisible door.

Sage: All that one can ever do is knock with sincerity, fervor, and persistence. As the Master of the first and the last said, "If you keep knocking at the door, it is likely to be opened."[5]

Student: So sincerity is the key?

Sage: Yes, sincerity is like a key that can open the door to this knowledge. Fervor and persistence are like the act of opening that door.

Student: I must at least be a little ready for this knowledge that you have, right? I mean, you did say I am ready for "Divine aid."

Sage: Your sincerity is there. But you lack something that will impede you from progressing further.

Student: What is that? Sorry for asking . . .

Sage: Aspiration.

1 The preceding example derives from Suhrawardī's *The Reverberation of Gabriel's Wing*, for which, see Mohammed Rustom, "Storytelling as Philosophical Pedagogy: The Case of Suhrawardī," in *Knowledge and Education in Classical Islam: Religious Learning Between Continuity and Change*, ed. Sebastian Günther (Leiden: Brill, 2020), 1:404–416.

2 The brother in question is Ibn ʿAṭāʾ Allāh. See Ibn ʿAjība, *Īqāẓ al-himam fī sharḥ al-Ḥikam* (Beirut: Dār al-Kutub al-ʿIlmiyya, 1996), # 113.

3 Part of the Prophetic saying, "People are asleep; when they die, they awaken." See ʿAyn al-Quḍāt, *The Essence of Reality: A Defense of Philosophical Sufism*, ed. and trans. Mohammed Rustom (New York: New York University Press, 2022), 99.

4 An allusion to Q 18:65.

5 See ʿAyn al-Quḍāt, *Essence of Reality*, 177.

Student: But I do have aspiration. I often spend all night studying, reading, and reflecting. In fact, I am currently writing an essay which I hope to publish in an important peer-reviewed journal on the concept of grit in the religious life.

Sage: You indeed do have aspiration. But the arrow of your aspiration is set towards the wrong target. So, you always miss the mark.

Student: How do you know that?

Sage: Because it is a common phenomenon—I see it in many students of philosophy and religion. They have intelligence and sincerity of purpose for the most part. And they have a lot of desire and aspiration, but for the wrong thing.

Student: So, what is the right thing towards which I should aspire?

Sage: First you must tell me what it is that you want.

Student: I want to know God and the ways of God.

Sage: Well, if you sincerely seek to know God, you should aspire towards that.

Student: But I thought I do.

Sage: You do, in theory. But in practice it is something else.

Student: How can one practice to know God other than pray the daily prayers, perform litanies, read the Quran, follow the blessed Prophet, etc.?

Sage: That is how one should practice to come to know God. But it is more about the level of intensity of these actions. Have you not heard the noble verse? "Those who believe are more intense in their love for God."[6]

Student: Aah, intensity in action. So, if I am more intense in my practices, I will come to know God, who is the object of my aspiration?

Sage: Perhaps.

Student: But if I just focus on action, will not my intelligence diminish?

Sage: That is what many think. If a person devotes himself to action, he becomes more intelligent, not less intelligent.

Student: I see. Conversely, if one devotes himself just to cultivating his intelligence without the corresponding action, he will be . . .

Sage: Less intelligent.

Student: Strange. I know some pretty smart guys who only write and think.

Sage: They cultivate what is known as "partial intelligence." But the real intelligence of which I speak is more like intelligence with a capital "I"; that is, *Intelligence.*

With a puzzled look on his face, the student throws his hands to the sky.

Student: You distinguish between kinds of intelligence?

Sage: I do. Partial intelligence is good for all kinds of rational operations, and much of our world runs on it. But it is partial, which means it cannot see the big picture.

Student: And intelligence with a capital I?

6 Q 2:165.

Sage: It is like a light that shines from up above and illuminates the entirety of a dark room. Partial intelligence can only shed light on particular corners of that room, leaving many objects in it in obscurity.

Student: Why do people focus on partial intelligence instead of Intelligence?

Sage: The answer is simple. It is as Mawlana says:

"The partial intellect has given the Intellect a bad name.
Desire for the world has made man desire-less for God."[7]

Student: Astounding! I think I understand what you are saying. I see a lot of intellectual know-how and mental acrobatics in my fields of study. And I am sad to say, I often see them in myself.

Sage: Of course. It is natural. The more a person focuses on his partial intelligence and seeks to cultivate it and make it the arbiter of all things, the more will his aspiration suffer.

Student: What then happens?

Sage: What normally happens is that he will aspire for the wrong things. He will, for example, continue to seek God, but not on God's own terms. Rather, it will be on his own terms, in accordance with what his partial intelligence shows him to be real, important, and meaningful.

Student: Can you explain further?

Sage: One time a Friend of God was asked what religion he follows. He replied, "I follow the religion of my Lord."[8]

Student: Interesting.

Sage: Everyone turns towards this direction or that direction. But the sincere ones have turned towards the direction of no direction.

Student: Is this what they also call the "Station of No Station"?[9]

Sage: Yes. Those who have gone to God and subsist in Him never return to any station, and are thus not bound by anything, much less the partial intellect.

Student: That must be a lovely place to be. I mean, one would never be bogged down by any kind of philosophical problem, for example.

The sage folds his arms, smiles, then looks off into the distance.

Sage: Philosophical and theological problems are problems insofar as they are seen from the perspective of the human. But from the perspective of the Divine, there are no problems as such.

Student: I wish they incorporated this vantage point into my philosophy and religion courses.

7 For these lines from Jalāl al-Dīn Rūmī, see Mohammed Rustom, "The Ocean of Nonexistence," *Mawlana Rumi Review* 4 (2013): 193.

8 The reference is to al-Ḥallāj. See Mohammed Rustom, *Inrushes of the Heart: The Sufi Philosophy of ʿAyn al-Quḍāt* (Albany: SUNY Press, 2023), 239.

9 For "the Station of No Station" in Sufism, see William Chittick, *The Sufi Path of Knowledge: Ibn al-ʿArabī's Metaphysics of Imagination* (Albany: SUNY Press, 1989), 375–381.

Sage: That would be a great benefit to human beings. As the Fourth Teacher[10] says, "There is nothing more timely than the Timeless."

Student: You know, Sir, there is a problem I've been having, a philosophical one, concerning what is known in philosophy of religion as the "problem of evil." It would be interesting to see what you have to say about it.

With his right hand on his heart, the sage nods his head.

Sage: At your service.

Student: Thank you. It has kept me up for many nights. I can see very well what you mean about the partial intelligence. It seems that almost every approach to the problem I have seen has been from this perspective. The answers are never fully satisfactory . . .

Sage: How can they be fully satisfactory when they are partial answers? Insofar as a person operates at the level of the partial intelligence, he will be unable to truly address the problem of evil. Only the sages can really answer this question. Indeed, those going to God flee from evil, but those coming from Him move towards it.[11]

Student: What did you mean by these last words?

Sage: This world we are in is the realm of evil, and so it is where evil is a problem. There are those who flee from the world and go towards God, with whom there is no evil. There are those who are with God and come back to the world of evil in order to help those stuck in it. Then there are those who are mired in this world of evil. With their feet firmly planted in the soil of the realm of evil, they try to solve the problem of evil. But a person mired in evil will never solve the problem of evil.

Student: It seems to me that you have already taken me in directions where I never thought this question can or perhaps should go. But explain why this problem of evil is not a problem for you. Is it because you are not "of" this world anymore?

The sage looks down for what seems like an eternity. Then he looks directly at the student with eyes resembling a vast ocean at dawn.

Sage: My place is the placeless, my trace the traceless, and my name the nameless. Going and coming are equal to me, and time and change do not define me.[12]

10 In Islamic philosophy, the First Teacher is Aristotle, the Second Teacher Fārābī, the Third Teacher Mīr Dāmād, and the Fourth Teacher Seyyed Hossein Nasr. See Sayyid Ḥasan Ḥusaynī, "Sayyid Ḥusayn Naṣr: Muʿallim-i chahārum," *Iṭṭilāʿāt-i ḥikmat wa-maʿrifat* 11, no. 11 (2017): 52–55.

11 Several of the sage's following statements are taken from Mohammed Rustom, "Some Aphorisms on God, Evil, and Liberation," *Sacred Web* 48 (2021): 147–149.

12 Cf. Maḥmūd Shabistarī, *Gulshan-i rāz*, ed. Javād Nūrbakhsh (Tehran: Khānaqāh-i Niʿmat Allāhī, 1976), line 9.

Student: So you are beyond the category of evil?

Sage: I would rather say that the sage sees no darkness and evil, for he beholds all things through the light of God.

Student: That is wonderous, and I wish I could someday see things the way you do. But you must surely acknowledge that evil is a real and live feature of the world that we live in. And I don't just mean lesser evils, but also horrendous evils, and what would seem like gratuitous evils.

Sage: Yes, of course: to deny the existence of evil on its own level is to deny the existence of the world on its own level. And on its own level, the world is real.

Student: But why then is there evil in this "real" world?

Sage: It is because of the infinity of God, or what some call His "all-possibility." God's all-possibility entails Self-negation, which entails manifestation, which entails separation, which entails evil.

Student: Oh, I know this argument well: God is all-good, and where He is not, there is evil. Since He is not in the world, evil is in the world.

Sage: Not quite. God is indeed "in" the world, but not by way of essential identification. Thus, the cosmos is not to be identified with God essentially. I once heard it said that God is not in the world per se; rather, the world is mysteriously plunged in Him.

Student: I don't quite get your point, sorry . . .

Sage: You say "sorry" too much. Be real in everything you say and do.

Student: Oh, sorry . . . I mean, thank you?

Sage: Say what is in your heart. "Never move around in the clothing of artificial formality."[13]

Student: Sorry. Agh! I mean, OK. Fine: I don't know what you mean.

Sage: Much better. God is not absent from the world. There is no place wherein God is absent. If that were so, then that place would not be a place. Every place is a place because of the presence of God within it. But there are varying degrees of presence, from the most intense (the Presence of God Himself) to other levels of intensity (ranging from scripture to the heart of the perfected human being), and then lesser levels of intensity (ranging from the cosmos to our world).

Student: But didn't the Proof of Islam[14] say that our world is the best of possible worlds?

Sage: Ours is the best of possible worlds, but it is also the lowest of worlds.

Student: So you mean to say that God is present in the world, but not to the same degree that He is present in higher worlds?

13 These are the words of Khwāja Khurd. See William Chittick, *In Search of the Lost Heart: Explorations in Islamic Thought*, ed. Mohammed Rustom, Atif Khalil, and Kazuyo Murata (Albany: SUNY Press, 2012), 169.

14 A popular title for Abū Ḥāmid al-Ghazālī.

Sage: Precisely. And it is to the degree that He is not "present" in this world that there is evil, which is a privation of good, as you have learned in your philosophy of religion classes.

Student: Yes, privation of good.

Sage: Now, that privation of good comes out of the infinite possibilities that belong to God, hence His infinity. Delimitation is one aspect of God's infinity and perfection, which is why there is evil, since there are levels of delimitation vis-à-vis God's perfection—and these levels are what constitute the cosmic order as we know it.

Student: I understand now. Thank you. Can I pick your brain with some more questions?

Sage: I hope you do not try to pick my brain. That would be painful. You mean, "May I further learn from you?"

Student: Yes. This is what I really meant.

Sage: This strange expression, "pick your brain," presumes that knowledge is *in* the brain, thereby reducing the human act of knowing to a purely physical, even mechanical, process. But the kind of knowledge we are after is something quite different.

Student: Well, where is this knowledge that you have?

Sage: It is not in the brain, that is for certain. At the same time, it has a deep cognitive dimension; that, too, is certain. Yet it is also suprarational—depending on where a person is on the continuum along the upward scale of existence, this knowledge will be more or less deep. But the least of this kind of knowledge already corresponds to a stage beyond the intellect, as that great martyr of Hamadan has explained so well.[15]

Student: Would we call this special knowing faculty the heart?

Sage: Indeed. It is the heart, which is the seat of human consciousness and is in fact a manifestation of God, who is Pure Consciousness.

Student: So the less heart we have, the less awareness we have? And the less we perceive with the heart, the less will we be able to understand the problem of evil?

Sage: Yes.

Student: This really is helpful. You know, dear Sir, I took a course once on the silence of God. It drove me nuts! I always wondered how God could actually be silent. Of course, it is a much deeper problem than that, but it never quite sat well with me.

Sage: How could it? God is never silent since He is the Speaking; but we do not hear Him since we are never silent.

Student: It's amazing how you are able to make such complicated ideas seem so simple.

15 That is, ʿAyn al-Quḍāt. See Rustom, *Inrushes of the Heart*, 149–153.

Sage: It is amazing how you are able to make such simple ideas seem so complicated![16]

The student laughs out loud, with a smile from ear to ear.

Student: And you have a sense of humor! It really is a pleasure to meet you. Can I ask another question?
Sage: Yes.
Student: Why could the world simply not have evil in it?
Sage: Because it would then not be the world.
Student: Huh?
Sage: To ask for a world without evil is to ask for another kind of world. But to ask for another kind of world is to ask for another kind of cosmic configuration which would exclude the presence of freedom, since freedom is unique to our current cosmic configuration.
Student: I get it. Human freedom is the cause of much evil. But what about accidental evils? Why are they present in our world?
Sage: Because they are in the nature of things. After all, fire burns by virtue of the same property that it warms.[17]
Student: Of course! And there is no pure evil in the world, right?
Sage: Yes. Nothing in the cosmos is pure evil, for pure evil is absolute non-existence, just as pure goodness is absolute existence.

The student begins nodding his head in approval and lets out a sigh of grief.

Student: I have to go to my class now. Will I see you again?
Sage: I do not know. God-willing, we will meet again.
Student: You do not know whether you will come here tomorrow, or whether I will come here? I can be here any time you like . . .
Sage: I do not dwell in the past, nor do I look to the future. I live in the Now. The present moment and death are the only guarantees we have.
Student: And don't forget income taxes!

Both men look at each other and laugh audibly.

Student: Well, I hope for the sake of my poor soul that I can see you again. Please give me some parting advice.
Sage: Pull back the veil of evil in order to truly live.
Student: Aha! I knew it would not be that easy. An explanation would be very helpful.

16 The student's observation and the sage's response paraphrase a famous exchange between Ṣadr al-Dīn al-Qūnawī and Rūmī, with the former corresponding to the student and the latter the sage.

17 An allusion to a statement made by Avicenna. See Avicenna, *The Metaphysics of the Healing*, trans. Michael Marmura (Provo: Brigham Young University Press, 2005), IX.6, § 16.

The sage and the student start to walk together, towards the arch at the end of the pathway.

Sage: Well, when we "pull back" the spelling of the word *evil*, that is, reverse it, we get the word *live*. Evil is a *veil* since it veils true life, just as the spelling of the word evil conceals the fact that it contains a veil: through the transposition of the "e" and the "v," we get the word veil, as it is made of the same stuff as the word evil, both substantially and linguistically. On the substantial side of things, we must transcend the veil of evil and see beyond it, which is where true life begins.

Student: Where true life begins. Where true life begins . . .

Lost in his thoughts, the student looks up only to find that the presence of the sage is now replaced by a sweet fragrance that is as strangely familiar as it is otherworldly.

References

Avicenna. *The Metaphysics of the Healing*. Translated by Michael Marmura. Provo: Brigham Young University Press, 2005.

ʿAyn al-Quḍāt. *The Essence of Reality: A Defense of Philosophical Sufism*. Edited and translated by Mohammed Rustom. New York: New York University Press, 2022.

Chittick, William. *The Sufi Path of Knowledge: Ibn al-ʿArabī's Metaphysics of Imagination*. Albany: SUNY Press, 1989.

Chittick, William. *In Search of the Lost Heart: Explorations in Islamic Thought*. Edited by Mohammed Rustom, Atif Khalil, and Kazuyo Murata. Albany: SUNY Press, 2012.

Ḥusaynī, Sayyid Ḥasan. "Sayyid Ḥusayn Naṣr: muʿallim-i chahārum." *Iṭṭilāʿāt-i ḥikmat wa-maʿrifat* 11, no. 11 (2017): 52–55.

Ibn ʿAjība. *Īqāẓ al-himam fī sharḥ al-Ḥikam*. Beirut: Dār al-Kutub al-ʿIlmiyya, 1996.

Maḥmūd Shabistarī. *Gulshan-i rāz*. Edited by Javād Nūrbakhsh. Tehran: Khānaqāh-i Niʿmat Allāhī, 1976.

Rustom, Mohammed. "The Ocean of Nonexistence." *Mawlana Rumi Review* 4 (2013): 188–199.

Rustom, Mohammed. "Storytelling as Philosophical Pedagogy: The Case of Suhrawardī." In *Knowledge and Education in Classical Islam: Religious Learning Between Continuity and Change*, edited by Sebastian Günther, 1:404–416. Leiden: Brill, 2020.

Rustom, Mohammed. "Some Aphorisms on God, Evil, and Liberation." *Sacred Web* 48 (2021): 147–149.

Rustom, Mohammed. *Inrushes of the Heart: The Sufi Philosophy of ʿAyn al-Quḍāt*. Albany: SUNY Press, 2023.

12 Trials as Transformation in Islamic Chaplaincy[1]

Ailya Vajid

Introduction

While suffering causes great pain and distress, it can also inspire deep awakening within us. We can become aware of ourselves, of the world around us, of our purpose in life. Suffering can engender the deepest transformation as we discover and return to our true self, our *fiṭra*.[2] We see this in scripture, in sacred narratives and history, in spiritual poetry and literature. As a chaplain, I have experienced the great blessing of walking alongside college students in their life journeys, being present with them through their joys, their hardships, their grief, their suffering, their spiritual seeking, through figuring out who they are, who they would like to be, and how they seek to contribute to the world. It has been such a gift and privilege to bear witness to their journeys, particularly as they are in such a delicate, transitional stage of their lives, navigating faith, life, and identity, often for the first time away from their homes and families. The role of chaplain is not one that is prescriptive, but rather it holds space for souls as they process and make meaning of the joyous and challenging moments of their lives, search for their purpose, and discover themselves. In this role, I have had the great honor of witnessing the different ways that Muslim students navigate suffering from a God-conscious lens, each walking through it with a unique experience. This chapter will focus on the experiences of those who, after beginning to reach a place of healing and wholeness, recognize their trials and hardship as the root of their greatest growth, strength, and transformation—as a guiding force in their lives that infuses it with deeper purpose. There are countless ways we react and respond to suffering, even from a place of

1 I would like to express my immense gratitude to the editors of this volume for inviting me to partake in such a meaningful project, for their vision and efforts in creating a momentous conference and volume, and for their especially helpful feedback and edits on this chapter. I would also like to thank Wajida Syed and Fuad Naeem for their significant and constructive edits and insights on the first draft of this piece, and Ali Galestan for his close editing of and insights upon the final draft which gave me much greater clarity and understanding, as well as for his insights and wisdom in reflecting on its purpose and what I sought to bring forth.

2 *Fiṭra* is one's primordial disposition as created by the Divine, and by virtue of which one's being is turned towards God.

DOI: 10.4324/9781003371670-13

healing. While for some, their suffering inspires acting compassionately towards others in need and hardship, for others, it also encourages the cultivation of virtues such as empathy, humility, and generosity. For certain people, the experience of suffering is so deeply transformative that it inspires them to embark upon the path of return to their true self—their *fiṭra*, or primordial disposition as turned towards the Divine. It is, in fact, their suffering that often deepens, strengthens, and even accelerates this journey of self-knowledge as they turn away from the world and towards the Divine, connecting to the depths of their true being.[3] This chapter will focus on the last response to suffering that is inspired within hearts, in which students and community members draw inward and begin to discover their true nature by building a loving relationship with the Divine, by engaging in heartfelt worship in their moments of need and pain, by cultivating self-knowledge and knowledge of the Divine, and through it all, shifting away from the ego and realigning with their *fiṭra*, their true self within. Moreover, this chapter will employ the framework of the Islamic theological tradition to interpret students' experiences, which themselves offer meaningful illustrations of how the Islamic theological tradition views suffering in light of life's overarching purpose.

Who Are We and Why Are We Here?

In order to reflect on suffering, let us first establish a foundation in the underlying purpose of life and then approach suffering from this lens. Who are we as humans, why do we exist, and what role do our life experiences play in fulfilling this purpose? While on an individual level there are countless ways to draw meaning from life—fulfilling the human trust to care for the earth and its creatures, struggling for justice, and spreading knowledge, among others—on a metaphysical level, human beings were created to know, worship, and love the Divine. Consider, for instance, the *ḥadīth qudsī*[4] in which God relates, "I was a hidden treasure, and I loved to be known, so I created creation to know Me," and the Quranic verse, "I did not create the *jinn* and humankind except to worship Me."[5]

According to these foundational texts, humans exist to worship, know, and love the Divine. God created human beings because He loved to be known, so the

3 This is not to discount or overlook the deep adversity and distress they experience, nor to say that all those who suffer reach a better place. There are so many ways that each of us walks through suffering, and each experience even in one's own life may be different, let alone the diversity of different human experiences of suffering. Some find themselves in a black hole, unable to emerge, while others discover an inner strength they did not know they have. One always seeks to alleviate the suffering, and while there are so many different ways we experience and react to suffering, this chapter explores one particular response to suffering that is inspired in hearts: that of realigning with the *fiṭra* in the discovery of one's true self.

4 A *ḥadīth qudsī* is a direct revelation from God to the Prophet Muhammad that is extra-Quranic.

5 Q 51:56. All Quranic translations are drawn from: Seyyed Hossein Nasr, Caner Dagli, Maria Dakake, Joseph Lumbard, and Mohammed Rustom (eds.), *The Study Quran: A New Translation and Commentary* (New York: HarperOne, 2015).

purpose of human existence is this very knowledge of the Divine rooted in love. In the Quran, God relates that human beings can know Him through His signs, which He reveals "upon the horizons and within themselves [humans] till it becomes clear to them that it is the truth."[6] Thus, God is known through the cosmos—the celestial bodies, the night and the day, and all the signs of creation referred to throughout the Quran—as well as through the divine names that each creature reflects and manifests. Alongside the macrocosm—the *insān al-kabīr* or "great human being"[7]—God is known through the microcosm, through the human being, who herself is a very reflection of the macrocosm and thus of God's names and qualities. As ʿAlī b. Abī Ṭālib elucidates,

> Your remedy is within you, but you do not sense it. Your sickness is from you, but you do not perceive it. You presume you are a small entity, but within you is enfolded the entire universe [macrocosm]. You are indeed the Evident Book by whose alphabet the hidden becomes manifest. Therefore, you have no need to look beyond yourself. What you seek is within you, if you only reflect.[8]

Thus, humans embody the entirety of existence within themselves. According to the Quran, God breathed of His Spirit into each human being,[9] and in the words of the Prophet Muhammad, human beings were made in the form of God.[10] Thus, human beings carry the very spirit of the Divine within, and are themselves reflections of the Divine Reality. Moreover, the Quran states, "We created man in the most beautiful stature, then We cast him to the lowest of the low, save those who believe and perform righteous deeds,"[11] illuminating the fact that human beings are created in the highest form, their existence in worship and in the embodiment of good works being a preservation of this Divinely gifted eminence. However, placed in the world with free will, human beings have the choice to live according to their *fiṭra*—their self that engages righteous works, embodies virtues reflecting divine qualities, and knows, worships, and loves God—or in forgetfulness of it. This knowledge of, and connection to, the Divine is contained within the human heart, which, according to Seyyed Hossein Nasr, is "the center of our being on all the different levels of our existence," both the "corporeal and emotive" as well as "the intellectual and spiritual."[12] Moreover, "the heart is the *barzakh* or *isthmus*

6 Q 41:53.
7 M. Salim Khan, *An Introduction to Islamic Medicine* (Leicester: Mohsin Health, 2016), 24–33.
8 ʿAlī b. Abī Ṭālib, *Dīwān* (Beirut: Dar al-Kutub al-ʿIlmiyya, 2007), 86.
9 Q 38:72.
10 See William Chittick, *In Search of the Lost Heart: Explorations in Islamic Thought*, ed. Mohammed Rustom, Atif Khalil, and Kazuyo Murata (Albany: SUNY Press, 2012), 11.
11 Q 95:4–6.
12 Seyyed Hossein Nasr, "The Heart of the Faithful Is the Throne of the All-Merciful," in *Paths to the Heart: Sufism and the Christian East*, ed. James Cutsinger (Bloomington: World Wisdom, 2004), 37.

between this world and the next, between the visible and invisible worlds, between the human realm and the realm of the Spirit."[13] It is the place where God penetrates our microcosmic existence—in other words, the locus for the breath of God.[14] This is where the *rūḥ*, or spirit, resides, where God's names are manifested within each human being. In a *ḥadīth qudsī*, God relays that God Himself is encompassed by the human heart: "My Heaven containeth Me not, nor My Earth, but the heart of My faithful servant doth contain Me." Moreover, the Prophet has said that "the heart of the believer is the throne of the All-Merciful." Thus, within the human being resides not only the entire cosmos but the very presence of the Divine. However, according to Sufi tradition, this divine presence, or primordial self that as a soul testified to God's Lordship, is veiled—covered by the rust of the world and human forgetfulness. Given that this is the human condition, the purpose of life is to undertake the journey of coming to know oneself, for as the Prophet says, "He who knows himself knows his Lord."[15] Thus, metaphysically, to live one's true purpose as a human being is to traverse the path of knowing oneself, for this "self-knowledge leads to knowledge of the Divine."[16] The way by which this knowledge is attained is by removing the rust on the mirror of the heart through remembrance of the Divine, for according to the Prophet Muhammad, "For everything there is a polish; and the polish of the heart is the remembrance of God."[17] Nasr discusses how walking the path to God "provides . . . the light necessary to illuminate the dark corners of our soul and the keys to open the doors to the hidden recesses of our being so that we can journey within and know ourselves, this knowledge leading ultimately to the knowledge of God, who resides in our heart/center."[18] Since human beings were created ultimately to know the Divine, every joy, every hardship, every love, every sorrow, every experience, and every moment exists for us to know God.[19] Human suffering then becomes a part of the journey—the journey of awakening, knowing, witnessing, connecting, and being.

Theology of Suffering

Suffering has always been a part of the human condition. Almost every religious tradition speaks of suffering as a central facet of life in the world. In the Islamic tradition, the *dunyā*, or the world, is a temporary abode of distraction and delusional enjoyment,[20] filled with various trials and hardships. The Quran, for instance,

13 Nasr, "The Heart of the Faithful Is the Throne of the All-Merciful," 32.

14 Nasr, "The Heart of the Faithful Is the Throne of the All-Merciful," 32.

15 William Chittick, "On the Cosmology of Dhikr," in *Paths to the Heart: Sufism and the Christian East*, ed. James Cutsinger (Bloomington: World Wisdom, 2004), 59.

16 Seyyed Hossein Nasr, *The Garden of Truth* (New York: HarperOne, 2007), 5.

17 Cited in the commentary upon Q 11:115 in Nasr et al., *Study Quran*, 587.

18 Nasr, *Garden of Truth*, 5.

19 It is our responses to the range of life's experiences that determines how they influence our soul and possible return us to the *fitra* and to knowing God.

20 Q 3:185.

states, "And We will indeed test you with something of fear and hunger, and loss of wealth, souls, and fruits; and give glad tidings to the patient—those who, when affliction befalls them, say, 'Truly we are God's, and unto Him we return.' They are those upon whom come the blessings from their Lord, and compassion, and they are those who are rightly guided."[21] Moreover, as the great Muslim sage, Ibn ʿAṭāʾ Allāh al-Iskāndari, reminds, "So long as you are in this world, be not surprised at the existence of sorrows. For, truly, it manifests nothing but what is in keeping with its character or its inevitable nature."[22] According to the Islamic worldview, the world is an abode of suffering because of its separation from God. Only with the Divine can one be in true peace and contentment. Human beings are not made only for the world, and it is not the ultimate destination; rather, the world is a stop along the way that shapes us, determining the nature of the eternal abode in the hereafter on the basis of our deeds and worship. To the extent that we attach ourselves to the world, we find ourselves unhappy. At the same time, as already mentioned, the world can reflect God's names and qualities and a place for spiritual wayfaring to the Divine, if one walks the path to God, emptying oneself of attachment to the world and instead attaching to the Divine, which could then lead one to witness the Divine in everything in the universe. As human beings, we seek joy, peace, contentment, comfort, and security, but we do not realize that we cannot experience them on the deepest level until we stop seeking them in the world and discover them in the Divine. They are only true and lasting in God. Moreover, it is by dying to our attachments that we experience the greatest freedom and the greatest peace. In emptying ourselves of the world and turning towards the Divine, we realign with our *fiṭra* that witnessed God's Lordship as a primordial soul, and we discover God here and now, before the meeting with Him in the hereafter. This emptying, detachment, and return to God most often takes place through our greatest suffering since it releases us from the torments of the ego. However, the slaying of the lower self is a painful process, and it causes great distress and adversity. While for some, it can bring about a turning away from the Divine, for others, it is exactly what draws them even closer to the Divine, to which we will now turn.

The Prophet Muhammad, known in the Islamic tradition as "the walking Quran" and who serves as the ultimate exemplar for any Muslim, suffered immensely as he spread the message of Islam to the tribes of Arabia. He was tried with great poverty—so much so that his own wife Khadīja passed away from starvation and sickness—as well as with mistreatment, physical violence, and insult as he sought to bring people to God. In addition to being verbally abused and insulted, the Prophet was physically assaulted on several occasions. Most tragically, during his visit to Ṭāʾif, he was pelted with rocks and stones by the children of the town until he and his companion were bruised and bloodied. Moreover, the Prophet faced great

21 Q 2:155–157.
22 Ibn ʿAṭāʾ Allāh, *Sufi Aphorisms*, trans. Victor Danner (Lahore: Suhail Academy, 1999), 27–28.

anguish and grief at the loss of many of his children, as well as the loss of his wife Khadīja and uncle and protector Abū Ṭālib in a single year, which is referred to in the Islamic tradition as the "year of sorrow." All of this demonstrates that the Prophet, the very being who is the most beloved creation of the Divine, was tried with and underwent tremendous suffering. This was not considered a punishment or a way of distancing him from the Divine, but rather this suffering shaped him and allowed him to serve as an example of mercy and goodness—even in the face of affliction and adversity—for Muslims and all humankind.[23] Moreover, it was in fact after the year of sorrow that the Prophet left the terrestrial plane and entered into the Divine Presence during his well-known *mi'rāj* or ascension, reminding human beings that one's greatest ascension can follow upon one's deepest suffering. Thus, it may be in our moments of tragedy, hardship, and grief that we find ourselves closest to the Divine.[24]

Discovering God in Suffering

While human beings always have the opportunity to remember God, it is often through suffering and hardship that souls actually turn towards the Divine. Amidst the fullness of life and the illusion of control, it is easy to become distracted and forget God, and even when we do remember Him in times of ease, it is often in the midst of suffering that our remembrance and surrender is most sincere, opening the way to finding God. While our hardships may lead to breakdowns and even challenge our faith, they may also be the very means to the spiritual breakthroughs that bring us down to our knees, in the deepest of prostrations with the sincerest of tears, bringing us to realize that only God can relieve us of our hardship and our burdens. As Rūmī writes, it is through the wound that the light enters our being;[25] that is, in becoming broken and being humbled, our being is penetrated by the Light of the Divine, for it is through our humanness, our brokenness, *our suffering*, that the transcendence of the Divine is manifested and known.[26]

23 The Prophet is known as "a mercy to the worlds."

24 This is not to say that one should drown in suffering or just suffer one's life away. The example of the Prophet himself was to seek to alleviate one's suffering, and God often responded by sending verses of the Quran that comforted and guided the Prophet through his afflictions. Rather, this is to say that the process of walking through the suffering, striving for relief and healing, turning to the Divine sincerely with renewed trust, and emerging from the trial can engender deep transformation and draw us closer to ourselves and ultimately then to God. But it is important to seek support and help in alleviating the suffering from trusted ones and to ask the Divine for guidance and relief. Ultimately each trial we experience we respond to differently, and some may distance us, while others draw us closer, and all of this is a part of the ongoing living journey of life and building a relationship with ourselves and with God.

25 Rūmī, *Spiritual Verses*, trans. Alan Williams (New York: Penguin Classics, 2006), 292–303.

26 We do indeed seek relief from the trial, while also holding, if we are able, some awareness and perspective that the hardship is Divinely intended with purpose, that it is sent by God to help us ascend in our journeys of knowing ourselves, and thus of knowing God. At some point, we may even come to realize that the trial itself is also a manifestation of God's Mercy, as it comes to transform us into

Without our sickness and suffering, when do we experience the occasion of witnessing God's healing, relief, and mercy with wholesome presence? Like the opposites of night and day, how would one perceive joy without sorrow? How could we know God's qualities without experiencing our own shortcomings, and how do we become aware of our deficiencies and helplessness without becoming humbled through pain and sorrow? It is often through our crumbling that we become transformed,[27] our ego once defiant in arrogance and self-reliance now humbled into realizing its transience, weakness, and even unreality/non-existence. As Ibn ʿAṭāʾ Allah reflects in one of his well-known Sufi aphorisms, "You will perhaps find a benefit in distress which you have not been able to find in fasting nor in prayer."[28] Helpless in moments of hardship, we are humbled as we realize that we can only do what we can do, and despite doing all we can, must then leave things in the hands of God to care for us and to bring us relief.

A number of students have shared experiences of their deepest turning to and discovery of God in such moments of adversity, helplessness, and anguish. Through their struggles, they have come to find God, draw close to Him, and begin to know Him as they experience divine mercy, love, and proximity. The following sections will present their narratives, and through them, we will reflect on an Islamic theology of suffering.

Fatima[29] shared her experience of loss and grief, losing both her mother and cousin within a month of each other, and not being able to attend their funerals and be with loved ones due to a broken bone that prevented her from international travel. She explained that in each hardship, there is a name of God that is present, and God draws one close through this particular name: "One of His names is in that moment, and He is bringing ourselves close to Him by that specific name. His name is the balm that will help us be grateful for the joy we are experiencing or will give us strength to accept and reflect upon a difficulty we are going through." She relayed that divine proximity is realized through all of life's experiences: "He is never far from us. We get closer to Him remembering Him in that moment, be that a happy, a sad, or a tragic one." During this trial, not only was Fatima not able to be with her mother before and after she passed away, but she was also not able to independently care for herself due to her injury. This evoked a sense of helplessness,

---

who we truly are. Typically the reflection, learning, and growth follow the painful period of trial. In the midst of the suffering, one is seeking to survive and find a way through it to the other side so as to ease, comfort, and relief.

27 This is not to say there are no other ways to cultivate this humility. The Divine bestows such mercy and transformation in so many different forms, including through love, and each individual soul has a unique journey. Yet it is often through the journey of suffering that hearts are humbled, awakened, and transformed (even love is accompanied with a dimension of suffering through longing and separation).

28 Cited in al-Darqāwī, *Letters of a Sufi Master*, trans. Titus Burckhardt (Louisville: Fons Vitae, 1998), 57.

29 All names have been altered to protect privacy. Fatima is someone I had the privilege of serving in this moment of grief, though she is a community member, not a college student.

but alongside that weakness also emerged the greatest strength in her surrender to and trust in the Divine:

> Suffering in surrender, surrender in suffering. Trusting that Allah Taʿāla[30] was going to see me through that moment of loss of a beloved one and an accident by which I was restricted [from] mobility. I begged for His mercy after having tasted His power. I reflected on death and how not prepared I was to face it. . .. His mercy healed me as I surrendered to Him. . . . He is the only one who has power over everything, and we must surrender to [the] destiny He designed for us, be patient, and know that death may come at any time.

In her surrender, Fatima discovered resilience. Surrender and trust are qualities that the faithful seek to embody before the Divine, but it is often not until one is tried that one more deeply cultivates and embodies such virtues. Human beings often chart the course of their lives with self-reliant confidence, and it is often not until one endures great suffering or loss that one begins to experience one's lack of control, cultivating qualities such as humility, trust, and surrender before the Divine. It is in this letting go that one experiences the greatest strength and peace because one no longer needs to assert control but can rest in trust and contentment in the divine will, with certitude that God only brings good, even through hardship. Fatima experienced God's mercy through one of life's greatest difficulties, for we can only know mercy if we have experienced harshness, often considered to be God's majesty. Just as we cannot know day without night, joy without sorrow, freshwater without saltwater, we cannot truly witness and appreciate God's names of beauty without also having experienced God's names of majesty. At one point, however, we may realize that there is in fact beauty and mercy in the majesty. For Fatima, God's mercy was experienced both through the grace she felt from all those in her life who came forward to support her and care for her, as well as through the realization that she was not yet prepared for death. She felt this was an opportunity from the Divine to further cultivate her spirituality, emptiness, trust, worship, and connection so that when the moment of death comes, she could be fully surrendered and ready to leave the world. Since humans are created to walk the path of return to God, Fatima's suffering surely deepened her journey and infused truer purpose into her life, making her more aware of God's presence and mercy as she surrendered herself to God's will and trusted more fully in Him.

Khadija is a graduate student who also lost her mother, but in her early 30s. She shared the following poem that flowed into her heart a year after her mother's passing:

525,600 minutes. 525,000 moments without you. 525,000 breaths taken in pain, as if there actually were a physical burden placed on my chest.
525,000 times I knew you weren't on the other end of the phone.

30 This common way of referring to God in Islamic parlance can be translated as "God the Exalted."

One year without you.
Your voice
your truth
your happiness
positivity
smile
I search desperately for you
I resent you for leaving, without even saying goodbye. I resent myself for hurting so much, for not being stronger, not accepting the truth.
How do I fill this hole? It's like I've dug a trench at the beach too close to the waves. Every time I try to build anything it just gets washed away. What do I do now?
Little by little, I try to free myself from your shackles, to try and bring color back into my world of darkness, to lift the clouds.
Whatever I have lost with you, I must now fill, myself.

Khadija walked through years of grief following the passing of her mother, the closest person to her. This was the most difficult, heart-wrenching experience of her life, and, she explained, the most transformative. She expressed the way it deepened her relationship with God: "When you have no one else to turn to, you realize you can only turn to Allah." It was in her moment of great desperation, losing the person to whom she was closest in the world, that she was brought into prostration and tears and turned to God embodying true sincerity, humility, and trust. Losing the person who was everything to her made her realize that there is only God to turn to. This realization and humility have raised her spiritually, and she continues to serve as a role model and guide for so many others walking through life's difficulties and losses. Khadija related that she has never been the same since this loss, and it is what brought her to God, shaping her into who she is today. She can now face life's continued challenges with perspective, humility, strength, groundedness, and trust in God, knowing that she always has somewhere to turn to for support and that God will always bring forth what is best for her.

Hawa embodies a different story. She passed through several great challenges throughout her life and college career, particularly around mental health and identity. As she approached her college graduation, Hawa shared that she discovered great peace and acceptance in who she is while receiving answers to her lifelong struggles, inspired to her by God. Hawa's family was practicing their religion, but they experienced a challenge in their community and found themselves distanced. This affected her life in that she found that the God-conscious language and worldview that was once the underpinning of her home was suddenly lost during her childhood. In the midst of all of this, Hawa endured several mental health challenges that have spanned her life thus far, including anxiety, ADHD,[31] depression,

31 ADHD is an abbreviation for attention deficit hyperactivity disorder.

and PTSD.[32] She was also recently diagnosed with autism. This was not only an incredibly difficult period for her; it was also a profoundly meaningful one, since it turned her towards God even more fervently, deepened her relationship with Him, and helped her come to a place of true self-acceptance and love.

Hawa described some of the pain of her years in school. Every day when she would return home, she shares:

> My stomach was in immense chronic pain, constantly. My heart was always palpitating. I could barely breathe. My chest was so heavy and hurt. . . . I felt like I was on fire every single day of my life for years. It got to a point where my mental health was so extremely bad, I had no choice but to value myself a little bit more than before and decide to get better. But also a lot of the way that initially I was able to convince myself to take care of myself was because of this Audrey Lorde quote, "Caring for myself is not self-indulgence; it is self-preservation, and that is an act of political warfare." So if it is an act of social justice, then I'll take care of myself.

She endured these difficulties for years but finally found strength in valuing and caring for herself in the midst of the physical and emotional pain. "I had no friends. I was super depressed all the time," Hawa shared. As she excelled in certain activities, she began to make friends, who, upon getting to know her and her academic interests—her "nerdy side," as she describes it—abandoned her yet again. She discovered that she had to hide herself (what she now knows as her autistic self) so that she could be protected and liked. She even changed her name in school, assuming her middle name and forcing all of her classmates to refer to her by it, to destroy the part of her that was apparently causing her so much suffering and hardship. She sought to abandon and bury this part of herself and later found herself seeking to do the same with another part of her identity.

As she entered high school and then college, she turned to God for answers and for guidance on how to walk through these challenges. At a certain point, she found herself "*begging*" God to make her like everyone else. She felt God's presence in helping her not only to accept herself but also to love, value, and cherish herself the way God created her. She explained that this was not in such a way to inflate her ego but to accept and find joy in the gifts that she had been given by the Divine, and also to learn to accept others as they are. Through this, she shared, "The way that my spiritual connection to God erupted was in a way that I never thought was possible or experienced in my life."

Hawa explained that it was in her moments of deepest desperation that she turned to God most fully, humbly, and truly, recognizing in the very core of her being that it was only because of God that she exists:

> All of these things in which you are deeply, utterly helpless. I would be like, "God you are literally the reason I breathe, I move, I have emotions. I know

32 PTSD is an abbreviation for post-traumatic stress disorder.

that because You have taken away all of these things and given them back." Humans can understand God in a way other beings can't, and Allah loves to be known—that whole thing you taught—Allah pulls me out of a thing so that I can see it from a completely different angle than before and then puts me back. So, I don't become attached to rules for the sake of rules. I become attached purely to God. That was what He was doing for me. . . . Hardship helps me understand myself. It helps me with my entire life journey. It helps me be true to myself. It helps me trust God very deeply. It's given me a lot of faith. There have been so many situations when I was between a rock and a hard place, and it was only God that would get me out of those situations.

Since human beings exist to know, worship, and love the Divine, Hawa found herself embodying this as she turned to God in utter helplessness and humility, recognizing His Lordship as she drew closer to her primordial state. She began to discover the ways that human beings can turn to and know God, and she found that the best and only attachment was to God. She witnessed that God was taking her through this journey of hardship in order for her to realize all of this, and that she could not have drawn closer to Him without it:

> The test that God is putting me through now is one of the ultimate tests of my trust in Him. A test of my trust also in myself and being able to put those two things together. . . . I would see God as this distant being. Now I can trust myself and trust God.

This journey bore incredible fruit and transformation in college, as she experienced the answers to her prayers and also engaged with mentors who supported her through life's challenges, as well as in making meaning, discovering purpose, and cultivating knowledge of and closeness to God through them:

> All those things I was craving—I couldn't articulate it—we started talking about in Spirituality Series.[33] I was able to come into that group and be myself. We talked about God not from a place of fear and judgement, but of love and mercy. You deepened it in a way I would not be able to do by myself. You helped me learn things. It literally [has] transformed my relationship with God today. Even the way I can understand the signs I am seeing and why I am seeing [them] . . . that laid a foundation for literally all of it.

Hawa describes how her entire way of knowing, recognizing, and connecting to the Divine was transformed through the weekly engagement with her chaplain and

33 This series was a weekly facilitated group centered on coming into one's heart center and on building a relationship with God, knowing God, connecting to God's love and mercy, and deepening trust and worship of the Divine.

other students. This highlights the very role of a chaplain, who walks alongside people as they experience life and who supports them in processing it—in bringing forth what they already know deep within themselves. A chaplain does not necessarily tell someone how to interpret something but provides them the tools to discover those answers within themselves, alongside teaching and reflection circles that uplift meaningful ways of knowing and connecting to the Divine. Hawa's experience also beautifully illustrates how one's greatest hardship and deepest desperation can turn one towards God and help one connect to the Divine in a way that may not have been possible without it: "Allah puts us through everything for something—every difficulty was so I could turn to Allah and see myself in that place and experience God's great forgiveness and mercy."

Divine Intentionality and Cultivating Gratitude

Hawa explained that she experienced God's closeness and mercy through her difficulties. Such an understanding can shift one's worldview so that each trial, hardship, and sorrow becomes a means of spiritual transformation and drawing near to the Divine. There is an Arabic proverb that asserts, "There is good in whatever happens." According to this, there is good in every single occurrence in the world, even those that human beings perceive as negative. The experiences of Fatima, Khadija, and Hawa illustrate this beautifully as these women discovered deep healing, growth, and a returning to their true selves through their suffering.

Recognizing the divine source and intentionality in our suffering can also bring peace and purpose. Ibn ʿAṭāʾ Allāh tells us, "To soften for you the suffering of affliction, He has taught you that He is the One who causes trials to come upon you. For the one who confronts you with His decrees of Fate is the same [one] who has accustomed you to His good choice."[34] To experience trials as infused with divine purpose and for one's own growth and transformation completely reframes one's suffering, imbuing it with meaning. It reformulates suffering not as something to be avoided but, like every other experience bestowed by the Divine, as something to be welcomed or at least accepted because it will become the means to inner growth, to knowing God, and to returning to one's true self, thereby fulfilling one's purpose of existence in the world.

Suffering is often the means for inner wayfaring and cultivation. Hawa's journey with her mental health spanned the entirety of her life. It was only very recently that she was diagnosed with autism and discovered answers to lifelong questions about why she experienced the world in certain ways that she felt no one else could relate to or understand. This is how she reflects on her journey:

> I think each suffering thing I have been through has done a different thing for me in my development. Trauma is, like, rough regardless. But . . . I don't think

34 Ibn ʿAṭāʾ Allāh, *Sufi Aphorisms*, 39.

> I would have learned so much about myself and other people in the way and with the depth I have learned it if it weren't for all the different things I have been through, particularly when it comes to understanding other people, particularly with autism. . . . I don't think I would have learned to advocate for myself, cared for making myself better, if I didn't have to deal with the extreme consequence of not valuing myself. Otherwise, I would have spent my life people pleasing to such a degree that I wouldn't know myself. . . . I know a lot of people who naturally are very open minded and naturally like to be different. I don't think I was actually ever that. I think I just was different, and I just *had* to be open minded because I literally had no choice. In a way it's very different. Two people can get to the same destination, but the journey towards it informs how they relate to that thing.

Hawa testifies here to the ways that each hardship in her life has shaped her as a person, particularly her values and self-knowledge. She further reflects on the ways that she celebrates her autism and the ways that she experiences the world around her as great gifts from the Divine and as a means for connecting more deeply with God:

> I realized that a lot of my gifts when it comes to my spirituality, and the way that I connect with God in general, is very autistic. And it's really cool because it's actually an amazing way for me to celebrate these parts of me and see how meaningful they can be. I'm so grateful it came up now my life. . . . It gives me so many strengths: when there is something I am dedicated to, I can go hard at it. I can analyze well. I learned social cues. . . . The way that I connect with nature. The way I connect with spirituality is through sensory things—[it is] an autistic way of connecting.

We reflected together on a saying of Christ about being in the world like a child and the way that such a lens into the world can actually be a means of returning to our *fiṭra*, and thus that God has given her such a beautiful gift by naturally bestowing upon her this way of experiencing the world. She is most herself when she is in virgin nature.

Conclusion

It is sometimes through life's greatest hardships and suffering that we experience the deepest transformation. Seen thus, suffering can become a means towards seeking our higher self and can be experienced not only as hardship but also as Divine gift and blessing, for it becomes a means of both outward and inward growth, as well as a returning to our *fiṭra* or primordial disposition. The role of a chaplain is to walk alongside people as they encounter, navigate, and make meaning of life's most trying challenges. In cases where suffering overtakes us, a chaplain can be a companion who offers a caring and supportive presence to listen and bear witness to, as well as to hold one's pain on the way to alleviating hardship and attaining healing. In cases where the person is ready to process and learn from the trial, seeking to grow through self-discovery and drawing closer to God, a chaplain can support them in their journey of transformation, providing spiritual insight, as well as awakening appreciation of life's varied experiences, ranging from the joyous to the distressing. Ultimately, a chaplain bears witness to the fullness of the human experience, and in the deepest sense, accompanies souls as they discover their primordial nature, thereby becoming who they truly are.

References

ʿAlī b. Abī Ṭālib. *Dīwān*. Beirut: Dar al-Kutub al-ʿIlmiyya, 2007.
Chittick, William. "On the Cosmology of Dhikr." In *Paths to the Heart: Sufism and the Christian East*, edited by James Cutsinger, 48–63. Bloomington: World Wisdom, 2004.
Chittick, William. *In Search of the Lost Heart: Explorations in Islamic Thought*. Edited by Mohammed Rustom, Atif Khalil, and Kazuyo Murata. Albany: SUNY Press, 2012.
al-Darqāwī. *Letters of a Sufi Master*. Translated by Titus Burckhardt. Louisville: Fons Vitae, 1998.
Ibn ʿAṭāʾ Allāh. *Sufi Aphorisms: Kitāb al-Ḥikam*. Translated by Victor Danner. Lahore: Suhail Academy, 1999.
Khan, M. Salim. *An Introduction to Islamic Medicine*. Leicester: Mohsin Health, 2016.
Nasr, Seyyed Hossein. "The Heart of the Faithful Is the Throne of the All-Merciful." In *Paths to the Heart: Sufism and the Christian East*, edited by James Cutsinger, 32–45. Bloomington: World Wisdom, 2004.
Nasr, Seyyed Hossein. *The Garden of Truth*. New York: HarperOne, 2007.
Nasr, Seyyed Hossein, Caner Dagli, Maria Dakake, Joseph Lumbard, and Mohammed Rustom (eds.). *The Study Quran: A New Translation and Commentary*. New York: HaperOne, 2015.
Rūmī. *Spiritual Verses*. Translated by Alan Williams. New York: Penguin Classics, 2006.

13 Transformative Love Amid Suffering in Hilmi Ziya Ülken

Taraneh Wilkinson

Introduction

It is no easy task to account for suffering without minimizing or ignoring the real suffering of others. Making meaning out of suffering is tricky. The temptation is sometimes to jump quickly to the end—to resurrection, to divine recompense, and triumph. Suffering is not only inevitable but necessary, and countless theodicies have attempted to show that suffering is all for the greater good—a test or an opportunity for moral growth. In some of these accounts it may seem that suffering is a mere means to end, something that lacks reality—in Christian sources this is couched in the Augustinian account of evil as privation, a mere negation of good. Yet, from a first-hand perspective, suffering is not always easily passed over or passed through. Suffering can baffle us and elude our attempts to make sense of it. Beyond trust in the Divine plan or even a mysticism of pain,[1] there are more active and practical ways to address suffering. Ottoman-Turkish philosopher and scholar of religion Hilmi Ziya Ülken[2] offers a perspective on suffering that recognizes both the loneliness and potential moral degradation of the human condition as well as the human potential to transcend such tragedies.

In his iconic *Ethics of Love* (published 1931, 1958, and 1971), Hilmi Ziya proposes that transformative love is both a response to the human condition of suffering and an intentional route to address the suffering and human isolation caused by human injustice and mutual alienation.[3] Specifically, he proposes a

1 See, for example, Kazoh Kitamori, *The Theology of the Pain of God* (Eugene, OR: Wipf & Stock Publishers, 1965).

2 Hilmi Ziya acquired the surname Ülken in 1928 in accordance with new Turkish law. His name appears only as "Hilmi Ziya" on the first publication of his *Ethics of Love* (1931). Here I will refer to him by the earlier version of his name, Hilmi Ziya.

3 Here credit is due to Prof. Recep Alpyağıl at Istanbul University for giving me my first copy of Hilmi Ziya's *Aşk Ahlakı* (3rd edition) during my visit to the theology faculty there in 2019. Prof. Paul Fiddes generously allowed me to give my first analysis of suffering in *Aşk Ahlakı* at an interdisciplinary colloquium at Regent's Park College, Oxford in 2020. Prof. Oliver Leaman at the University of Kentucky also generously reviewed and provided feedback on my earlier attempts at making sense of Hilmi Ziya's thought. Furthermore, Prof. Aydın Topaloğlu helped me access further material on

DOI: 10.4324/9781003371670-14

humanizing love that transcends individual interests yet still affirms individual vitality and uniqueness. In what follows, I lay out his views on transformative love and further show how they are shaped by his commitment to his "monopluralism," or affirming the multiplicity in creation by affirming God's unity (*tawḥīd*). To do this, first I address Hilmi Ziya's "monopluralism" as a vision of unity amid human multiplicity. Then I take up Hilmi Ziya's account of human suffering as an experience of injustice and profound alienation. Finally, I lay out Hilmi Ziya's account of self-sacrifice as transformative love.

Hilmi Ziya and *Aşk Ahlakı*

Hilmi Ziya Ülken (1901–1974), also referred to as Hilmi Ziya, was a late Ottoman intellectual who became a recognized Turkish scholar in the fields of philosophy, psychology, sociology, and religion. Hilmi Ziya was born in Istanbul to Mehmet Ziya, a chemist who had studied in England, where the latter had kept company with Young Turks.[4] Hilmi Ziya's mother's family hailed from the Crimean peninsula, migrating to Istanbul to avoid Russian conscription during the Crimean war in 1856.[5] Hilmi Ziya's childhood and youth bore witness to the last decades of the Ottoman Empire, including the announcement of the Second Constitutional Government in 1908, the fall of sultan Abdulhamid II in 1909, and World War I, during which time he attended a private elementary school and, following that, the Sultani school in Istanbul for his secondary education.[6] After graduating from the Ottoman school for civil service in 1921, Hilmi Ziya obtained a degree in history of philosophy and sociology of ethics from the Darülfünun in 1924 (now known as the University of Istanbul). In 1933 he was appointed at the new Istanbul University and sent by the Department of Education to Berlin for about one year.[7] Upon his return he became a lecturer in Turkish thought. At the university, he worked on the history of Turkish thought, logic, ethical theory, Islamic philosophy, sociology, and systematic moral philosophy, receiving professorial appointments at the university in the Departments of Philosophy and Sociology in 1940 and 1941 respectively (which in the Turkish system fall under the Faculty of Literature). Proficient in many subjects and passionate about education, he also gave lessons at Istanbul Technical University and the Istanbul Higher Institute of Islam (*İstanbul Yüksek İslam Enstitüsü*), as well as reaching out to secondary schools through his

---

Hilmi Ziya's life and thought at the *İSAM* library in Istanbul during my visit there in the summer of 2022.

4 Ayhan Vergili, "Hilmi Ziya Ülken (1901–1974)," in *Türkiye'de Sosyoloji I*, ed. M. Çağatay Özdemir (Ankara: Phoenix, 2008), 587.

5 Hilmi Ziya, "Kendi Dilinden Hilmi Ziya Ülken," *Toplumbilim* 2 (1993): 85.

6 Muhsin Aktaş, "Ülken, Hilmi Ziya (1901–1974)," in *The Biographical Encyclopedia of Islamic Philosophy*, ed. Oliver Leaman (London: Bloomsbury Academic, 2006), 486.

7 Aktaş notes that many credit his success in the early 1930s due to Atatürk's appreciation of Hilmi Ziya's work in sociology. Aktaş, "Ülken, Hilmi Ziya," 486.

affiliation with the Department of Education.[8] In 1954 he transferred to the newly created Ankara University Divinity Faculty, opened in 1949, where he taught logic and systematic philosophy until his retirement, simultaneously maintaining ties to the University of Istanbul until 1960. Upon his death in June of 1974, his colleagues and friends mourned his passing, one of whom exclaimed in grief that Hilmi Ziya was both an "ideal human being" and an "idealist" in one.[9]

First published in 1931, *Aşk Ahlâkı: Halka rağmen halk için Kitap* (in English: *Ethics of Love: A Book for the People in Spite of the People*) is a keystone of Hilmi Ziya's oeuvre. It has also proven formative in some Sunni Turkish intellectual communities, namely those active in or around Turkey's state-funded theology (*ilahiyat*) faculties. Hilmi Ziya republished the work in two substantial subsequent editions during his lifetime (1958, 1971) and continues to enjoy reprintings to this today. In this work, Hilmi Ziya expounds upon an ethics based on love. In its day, critics hailed the book as an ethical and exhortatory treatise that provocatively synthesized Nietzsche's will to power and Jesus as a figure of sacrifice for all of humanity. As Hilmi Ziya explains:

> My thesis is to reconcile Jesus with Nietzsche. The two masters show the extreme poles in ethics. One is mystical, and the other rational and their viewpoints cannot be harmonized. Yet I have endeavored to reconcile them, that is, to reconcile Idealism with Realism, the individual with society, man with humanity. That is the central point in this book.[10]

Monopluralism: Unity Amid Human Multiplicity

Hand in hand with Hilmi Ziya's attempt to reconcile idealism and realism, we see Hilmi Ziya's vision of a world that combines the unity implied in idealism with the plurality of realism. He terms this "monopluralism." This monopluralism is not only a response to European philosophical discussions of philosophical idealism and realism from the previous century, but it also draws explicitly on traditional philosophical discourse of *vahdetcilik*, or Unity of Being—a philosophical rendering of God's oneness as a monism transcending all apparent duality. He states that "*vahdetcilik*" or unity of being is the "most appropriate name" for the philosophy

8 Harun Anay, "Hilmi Ziya Ülken'in Bilinmeyen İki Öz Geçmiş Metni," *Kutadgubilig Felsefe-Bilim Araştırmaları Dergisi* 18 (2010): 196. For other biographical details about Hilmi Ziya's life, see Eyyüp Sanay, "Ülken, Hilmi Ziya," in *Türkiye Diyanet Vakfı İslâm Ansiklopedisi*, https://islamansiklopedisi.org.tr/ (last accessed October 17, 2022).

9 The colleague who said this was reportedly Mehmet Karasan. See Muhsin Balakbabalar, "Iki Dost," *Ankara Üniversitesi İlahiyat Fakültesi Dergisi* 20 (1975): 26.

10 Hilmi Ziya Ülken, *Aşk Ahlakı*, 3rd ed. (Ankara: Demirbaş Yayınları, 1971), xvi–xvii. This quote is taken from the English translation published in *The Turkish Press* (1931). Further citations of *Aşk Ahlakı* are from the third edition and are my own translations from the Turkish unless otherwise specified.

of *Aşk Ahlakı*, further clarifying that he does not intend the "narrow monism of the materialists" but rather a "pan-naturalism" where reality bespeaks a unity through a plurality of nature built out of an emergent chain of being.[11]

Hilmi Ziya writes: "To reach unity, one must cross over the bridge of plurality."[12] This plurality in unity affirms the integrity of distinct individuals in a weft of unity. Unity is not a machine, according to Hilmi Ziya. It does not swallow up or assimilate. Unity is the foundation of freedom, and the aim of freedom is not losing oneself in the machinations.[13] Unity is humanizing, because it is not diametrically opposed to plurality. For Hilmi Ziya, it is love that guides plurality to unity, while maintaining distinctions. Unity affirms reality as goodness while denying any absolute reality to evil.[14] Evil and suffering stem from privation and lack—this vision of evil is foundational for Hilmi Ziya's position on moral progress and attainment. Suffering and injustice, as well as human diversity and difference, are partial manifestations of the Whole. Everything evil is lacking fullness of reality, but not all lack is evil.

Closely connected to his vision of unity is that of the infinite (*sonsuzluk*). In an inclusivist approach, Hilmi Ziya heralds faith in the infinite above all other beliefs.[15] For him, having faith in the infinite entails openness to the new. By affirming unity in the infinite, a believer can safely trust that what comes newly into being is already an expression of divine unity. In this sense, faith in the infinite is central to Hilmi Ziya's ethics based on the unity of existence.

Accordingly, on Hilmi Ziya's account of "naturalism," spirit and matter form one reality: they are not opposites.[16] He writes: "Those ignorant of the unity of spirit and body will try in vain to blow life into their idols made of earth; as a result, they will break their lifeless idols in frustration."[17] Further, spirit is not understood as something occult or mysterious; it is dynamical and integral to all life. On this he says:

> Spirit is not a mirror and a reflection. It is not a concept or a dream. It is not a shadow or an appearance. Spirit, just like energy, is an activity and reality just like life. It is one piece of being in the process of infinite becoming (*oluş*). For the one who believes in the truth of spirit this way and who sees spirit plainly like an object, the meaning of the world has changed.[18]

Spirit is thus a reality that emerges out of consciousness and conscious being. And consciousness (*şuur*) itself is for him already an emergent reality. He writes:

11 Hilmi Ziya, *Aşk Ahlâkı*, XLIV.
12 Hilmi Ziya, *Aşk Ahlâkı*, 35.
13 Hilmi Ziya, *Aşk Ahlâkı*, 38.
14 Hilmi Ziya, *Aşk Ahlâkı*, 105.
15 Hilmi Ziya, *Aşk Ahlâkı*, 106.
16 Hilmi Ziya, *Aşk Ahlâkı*, 12.
17 Hilmi Ziya, *Aşk Ahlâkı*, 27.
18 Hilmi Ziya, *Aşk Ahlâkı*, 66.

"Consciousness is never an eternal being, it is a new reality birthed from the clash of life and society, two distinct natural forces."[19]

In short, for Hilmi Ziya, spirit is reflexive consciousness.[20] In this sense, abstract things like evil and spirit are real, just as matter is real. While some might consider him too naturalistic not to be a materialist, he criticizes materialism just as much as he criticizes what he considers irrational mystical views of reality. For him, materialism stems from an overfocus on material realities, an oversimplification of our experience of the world. The spiritual world, in his view, emerges after and out of the social one.[21] Spiritual and material realities together generate personhood.[22] Personhood, like humanity, is not a given; it is an end.

Hilmi Ziya holds that cultivating love in a non-dualistic manner is key for seeing clearly.[23] For him, cultivating love means a cultivation of non-preferential love for humanity as well as actively pursuing loving company with other human beings who seek to perfect the world in love's name. Both of these goals involve a surpassing of the duality between nature and spirit, and to some extent between self and other. With an orator's rhetorical flourish, Hilmi Ziya calls for his reader to discard all duality and seek only unity.

Human Suffering: Alienation

One of the strengths of Hilmi Ziya's *Ethics of Love* is its attentiveness to different psychological dimensions of human suffering. Although he holds an ideal vision of a humanity perfected in love and sacrifice, Hilmi Ziya is also acutely aware of the brokenness and limitedness of humanity in process, i.e., all our imperfect and circuitous becomings. Further, he is aware of the reality of isolation and loneliness that accompanies our imperfections and brokenness. Rather than judging this broken reality with condemnation, he addresses it with compassion and psychological insight. He does not divide people into hermetically sealed categories of the breakers and the broken but instead recognizes that human beings break out of our brokenness. And thus, he asks where the fault lies when the broken break—if the broken have not been shown the light, i.e., good ethical models of action, others are also partially at fault for not modeling the good for them (31). In this moving

19 Hilmi Ziya, *Aşk Ahlâkı*, 184.
20 Hilmi Ziya, *Aşk Ahlâkı*, 68.
21 Hilmi Ziya, *Aşk Ahlâkı*, 1.
22 Hilmi Ziya, *Aşk Ahlâkı*, 14.
23 For instance, he states we must unite *âşık*, *maşuk* and *aşk* to keep common sense (45), another indication of the underlying unity underpinning his system. As Mehmet Vural notes, Hilmi Ziya stressed that the transcendent must be understood alongside the fully immanent, calling this the "transcendent dyad"—a concept that contains opposing concepts like object and subject in its infinity, and, for Hilmi Ziya, remains a matter of faith. See Mehmet Vural, "Hilmi Ziya Ülken Ontolojisinde Aşkın Varlık Problemi," *İslâmî Araştırmalar Dergisi* 16, no. 2 (2003): 212–216.

passage, he paints a harrowing picture of the human experience of alienation and its accompanying cycles of violence:

> There are china sets standing between souls. . . . Which of you has received an answer from the heart you addressed? When you cried out from your deepest wound know that your closest friend was listening to other melodies. The voice of the one seeking consolation was scattered on the rocks. The one seeking to open her spirit found damnation. The one who hoped fell into frustration. You live in a blind battle. The one who falls into frustration will stay curled up in herself like a mole, either her fire will be smothered or she will pump poison into her teeth like reptiles do to stay alive.
>
> Oh abandoned and broken souls! You sought tenderness, but received suffering's resentment. You waited for friendship and you received the punishment of betrayal. Your spirits are closed to each other across abysses and sets of china. You have long forgotten how to forgive and love. Only despair and revenge remain to you. You are the crushed and the crushers. The accursed and the ones who curse others. Since you experienced injustice you are among those who do injustice. Because you were broken you seek to break.
>
> Have pity on those who feel the torment of loneliness. For those truly merit pity. Amid the noise of urban infernos, surrounded by thoughts, people and things, they live feeling torture and loneliness like residents of a solitary desert. In the midst of community, they are far from community. They have no friend with whom to share their pain. They have no hopes. They have no loves. They do not even have a hand to offer them water in their last breath. Closing inwards upon themselves, they are wrapped in the evening's melancholy as if in a lover's arms. Dark places, streets and coffee benches are the shadow of their souls. Those who feel the torment of loneliness seek to warm themselves in the crowd but remain untouched by the heat. They seek to escape; they cannot endure the horror of aloneness. They are neither with it nor separate from it. In this vast world they suppose themselves abandoned. They carry a whole world within themselves. Surrounded by herds they remain an individual; they are the ones who create communities at the foot of mountains. With all your strength and effort seek these people! Have pity on those tormented by loneliness![24]

From this passage, we can see that the suffering of isolation and alienation has two fruits for Hilmi Ziya. On the one hand, those with crushed spirits are more likely to crush others, and thus continue the cycle of human injustices. On the other hand, loneliness is a crucible that prepares the spirit for leadership, greater insight, and a deeper sense of self and community. That is, if those who feel alienated from humanity ban together in a sense of higher purpose and deeper moral vision,

24 Hilmi Ziya, *Aşk Ahlâkı*, 62–63.

the pains of isolation and alienation become a forge for a community shaped by transformative love. Or, in other words, the way out of the cycle of injustice and suffering is to join together and out of a shared experience of loneliness and suffering to build a community of love. As we shall see, this love is both selfless in its self-sacrificial nature and self-affirming.

Ultimately, Hilmi Ziya's answer to the problem of human brokenness and disconnect lies in the hands of an ethical elite who have attained the highest moral formation and, from this place of love-based ethics, harness their vitality and creativity in the service of creating a more human humanity. Who comprises this ethical elite? These are the ones who have risen above the lower levels of ethical development to an ethics based on altruistic love and unity. Hilmi Ziya's ethics thus involve a four-tier progression in ethical development: (1) fear (*korku*), (2) hope (*ümid*), (3) pride (*gurur*), and (4) love (*aşk*). The first three levels of ethical development are based on lack, whereas the final level is based on a vision of unity. Those levels of ethical functioning which have not yet attained to a vision of unity are still valuable as parts of the whole, but they are themselves not the whole of reality nor the culmination of ethical development, and those who function at these lower levels enjoy a precarious ethical existence. The first level is fear-based ethics. Those scraping by and making do may behave ethically out of fear, but this is not a reliable foundation for ethics. The second level encompasses those hoping to better themselves. Those aspiring to a higher-class status and greater luxury may act ethically out of hope for a better future, but, again, the moment this hope is frustrated, all sound ethical grounding is in peril. The third level of moral development is founded on a sense of pride. For instance, military leaders and great patriots of the ruling class may themselves act ethically out of a sense of pride. The precariousness of their ethics becomes apparent when such men, when stripped of their honor and context of service to the state, behave as monsters. Despite the injustice and suffering caused by those who go ethically awry at the lower levels, Hilmi Ziya, asserts that there is little point in reacting with frustration to lower levels of ethical development. The best approach, he avers, is to treat people according to their level of development. The fourth and final level of moral development is an ethics founded on love. To rise to this level, one must transcend both self and preferential love. Yet, at the fourth level there is also a return to the self—"To be a human being means experiencing a revolution in the spirit. It is a turning to faith (*iman*) after unbelief (*küfür*). It is attaining to a sincere transformation of the spirit. It is a returning to one's self after giving up oneself."[25] Those at this level form a special fellowship—that of friendship (*dostluk*) and companionship (*sohbet*).

At this highest level of moral development, one attained by sacrifice and self-transcendence, Hilmi Ziya acknowledges a range of individuals—from prophets to artists—serving the greater good. Hilmi Ziya lumps prophets, saints, intellectuals, artists, and other creative types into one common category. These are his model

25 Hilmi Ziya, *Aşk Ahlâkı*, 138.

human beings. What they have in common is a willingness to sacrifice preferential love and their own happiness for love of humanity. However, not all human beings are fully mature. In line with his view of moral immaturity as lack of the good rather than as absolute evil, Hilmi Ziya recognizes that some people are not to be trusted or imagined to be better than they are, while at the same time acknowledging that even imperfect people can still be vehicles of truth.

Finally, Hilmi Ziya levels the risk of falling into moral elitism by claiming that all human beings, including prophets, must move up through the levels of moral development. In his view, no one is born with passion for the One. No one is born a prophet, they become one.[26] In this manner he calls out to his reader to take up the mantle of individual responsibility, portraying the ideal human being as an active co creator in her own destiny and calling for active human beings, not passive ones.[27] In this sense, suffering is not a passive experience, rather in love it is an active and transformative venture.

Transformative Love: Self-Sacrifice

Hilmi Ziya claims that the world is perfected in the state of love (*aşk*).[28] This world-perfecting love is founded on strictly non-preferential love. Humanity, in its ideal state, is the universalization of non-preferential love.[29] To this end, he notes how love martyrs like the Buddha, Socrates, Jesus, Ali, or Hussein have helped to bring this perfection into reality bit by bit:

> These great martyrs are ones who give up loving one human being in order to love all of humankind. They are the ones who do not hesitate to destroy one person's happiness in order to provide happiness to all of humanity. They are not afraid of breaking one heart in order to win all hearts.[30]

Hilmi Ziya remains exuberant and confident in the value and efficacy of non-preferential love. For him, love is not a mental illness or primarily about romance, it is the driving force of all humanity.[31] He writes:

> It is a pity those cynics deny love; they see it as an illness and a delusion. Love is the whole spirit. It is all of life. It is thirsting for nature and the

26 Hilmi Ziya, *Aşk Ahlâkı*, 131.
27 Hilmi Ziya, *Aşk Ahlâkı*, 28.
28 Hilmi Ziya, *Aşk Ahlâkı*, 36.
29 Hilmi Ziya, *Aşk Ahlâkı*, 32.
30 Hilmi Ziya, *Aşk Ahlâkı*, 34.
31 Hilmi Ziya's *Love Ethics* also contains an accompanying civilizational theory. Notably, in the case of both civilizations and individual human beings, progress is not assumed or guaranteed. At the same time, just as humans transcend and grow from the sacrifices and contributions of others, civilizations too cannot be viewed in isolation and are linked together in shared historical trajectories.

> infinite. If it did not exist, there would be nothing left of civilization. Knowledge is its work; art is its work. Thought and truth are its doing.[32]

Non-preferential love also comes with elements of distance, lack, and separation—indeed, these are hallmarks of suffering. For him, love is separation, a not-yetness. He pairs a willingness to love devoid of unity with an imperative to cultivate love internally, even in absence and isolation, instructing his reader to see love in herself. For seeing love in oneself is also necessary for seeing the world clearly and for attaining spiritual knowledge (*irfan*): "For love is maturity of spirit; it is both the spirit's weakness and its power, its grace (*lûtfü*) and its violence. A human being tastes hell and wears the crown of suffering with it, she hopes for purity out of suffering (*cefadan safa umar*) and finds life in death."[33] He includes various references to the loving suffering of figures like Hallāj and Jesus, all the while tempering this vision of self-sacrificial love with sobering insights into the self-serving and sometimes brutishly incomplete reality of everyday human beings.

Hilmi Ziya's non-preferential love is not a bloodless Kantian duty. Contra Kant, he affirms universal or eternal ethics to be an ethics of passion.[34] However, this passion must be directed at the right object to properly inform an ethics of love. He writes, "Passion does not seek a finite end, it is satisfied in its seeking and lack of satisfaction."[35] Such passion hinges on an idealism grounded in the infinite, a reference to God, and it is paired with the age-old practical recognition that all things finite eventually disappoint:

> The one who desires infinitely, verily, inevitably and always will achieve something; the one who desires finitely will become frustrated, taken aback, and undergo crisis amid unexpected torment, and when they one day have attained their small, short-term goals, they will succumb to disappointment, thinking, "Was this what I waited for?" Love of effect (*tesir aşkı*) is the unifying motion of spirit and world.[36]

Truly ethical behavior does not seek satisfaction,[37] for when an ethical individual fails to achieve satisfaction, she might lose her ethical motivation. However, as can be seen in the previous quote, truly ethical behavior does seek to shape the world.

For Hilmi Ziya, the basic relationship of self to self-transcendence is as follows: the self must be transcended, but the spiritual power of that self cannot and should

---

On this last point concerning civilizations, see Ömer Mahir Alper, "Hilmi Ziya Ülken'in İslâm Felsefesini Yorumu," *İstanbul Üniversitesi İlahiyat Fakültesi Dergisi* 14 (2006): 131.

32 Hilmi Ziya, *Aşk Ahlâkı*, 56.
33 Hilmi Ziya, *Aşk Ahlâkı*, 70.
34 Hilmi Ziya, *Aşk Ahlâkı*, 73.
35 Hilmi Ziya, *Aşk Ahlâkı*, 31.
36 Hilmi Ziya, *Aşk Ahlâkı*, 102.
37 Hilmi Ziya, *Aşk Ahlâkı*, 73.

not be quelled. Put another way, he wishes to maintain the imperative of self-transcendence while affirming the integrity and spiritual vitality of the individual, in all her finite distinction. Unlike the ascetic, this self is not perfected in isolation from the world; instead the self is transcended in the efforts taken to transform the world. He writes: "It is not enough to correct yourself first, the desire to fix the world is how you correct yourself."[38] Yet, despite this priority of world over self, he insists that he is not speaking of "duty." Life is not simply fulfilling a duty or carrying out an order;[39] self-transcendence must remain an authentic and living self-expression.

While still cultivating passion and maintaining the creative vibrancy of the spirit, the true love martyr is one who has renounced her rights as a self, specifically her right to preferential love: "Those who love all of humanity are the ones who do not say 'This is my right,' who give up the greatest right, the right to love another person, and it is they who attain to the highest [form of] love."[40] In this same vein, love for humanity (*insanlık sevgisi*) transcends national hatred and class hatred.

Importantly, Hilmi Ziya does not advocate for self-transcendence to the point of dissolving the self altogether. In a very practical sense, he asserts that humans need time to relax and rest, to have fun, and to work in a regular fashion. He even offers a formula for happiness by balancing those three activities in a regulated way,[41] while still affirming the vitality and individual specificity of passion. Neither does he believe embracing non-preferential love entails addressing all individuals in the same manner. There is room for discernment amid the continual process of self-examination, which involves identifying false passions based on addictions and preferential loves.[42] Rather than killing the self, the matter is that of weeding egotism from the garden of self (*benliği kaldırmak*),[43] cultivating a self that is free of egotism.

In sum, transcending the self is the path towards seeing reality as it is, a unity that transcends all duality. Transcending the self is also the way to move past traps of self-deception; a way, through love, to realize the unity of self with nature. And while he does occasionally use a turn of phrase like "abolish oneself" (*kendini yok etmek*),[44] he is not interested in quelling the creative forces of the self but rather in harnessing them by eradicating morally unsound egotism. His love-based ethics is not self-punishment, but a seizing of the infinite.[45]

Just as sacrifice and love-based ethics is oriented towards the infinite, it is also active with regards to both agent and world. Hilmi Ziya underscores the active,

38 Hilmi Ziya, *Aşk Ahlâkı*, 15.
39 Hilmi Ziya, *Aşk Ahlâkı*, 57.
40 Hilmi Ziya, *Aşk Ahlâkı*, 35.
41 Hilmi Ziya, *Aşk Ahlâkı*, 40.
42 Hilmi Ziya, *Aşk Ahlâkı*, 49.
43 Hilmi Ziya, *Aşk Ahlâkı*, 45. Hilmi Ziya gives a range of expressions denoting self-transcendence. For another set of terms, see pp. 104–105.
44 Hilmi Ziya, *Aşk Ahlâkı*, 34.
45 Hilmi Ziya, *Aşk Ahlâkı*, 25.

rather than passive, side of suffering and sacrifice with imagery of the cross. He expounds:

> Love of effect for humanity's sake is a love possessed of human beings who accept providential misfortune and sacrifice themselves. A great human being is not only someone who sees the truth and endures the suffering of the journey [to that truth]. A great human being is someone who battles for truth, who puts truth into action, and who takes joy in throwing herself into the fire and being stretched out on the cross for humanity's sake.[46]

The most central sacrifice he has in mind is the sacrifice of preferential love to love for humanity. Once more, the sacrifice of the right to preferential love does not negate actions of personal discernment. An individual should and must know how to read people and choose her friends wisely.[47] Again, he distinguishes his love-based ethics from asceticism. He does not call for extreme bodily privation; he is calling for mature human beings who can see the world clearly, with eyes unfogged by addictive thoughts and habits. Patience is not about setting one's sights on small rewards or expecting little of the world; rather, patience (*sabır*) is desiring the infinite rather than finite things in themselves.[48] All the same, desiring the infinite is a giving of the self that entails a renunciation of one's individual will.[49] Rather than a restriction, he views this self-giving as the road to true freedom, even using the term "Nirvana" to characterize it.[50]

For Hilmi Ziya, sacrifice is not merely an individual affair; it is central to the birth of humanity as such. In other words, sacrifice is the generative force that drives humanity (*insanlık*). Passion means forgetting oneself in actions that contribute to a more human humanity. For Hilmi Ziya, creative, selfless, and sacrificial actions all contribute to the development of humanity in the world. The person who is actively and purposely selfless, driven by both passion and dispassionate love for all, helps create and shape humanity with her sacrifice.[51]

Conclusion

What does a more human humanity look like in the face of suffering? What is an appropriate response to loneliness and disappointment in the midst of our actual and imperfect reality? First, according to Hilmi Ziya, someone interested in attaining an ethics based on love ought to seek unity amid multiplicity, grounding oneself in the infinite. Only with such a foundation can someone build an ethics on

46 Hilmi Ziya, *Aşk Ahlâkı*, 103.
47 Hilmi Ziya, *Aşk Ahlâkı*, 46.
48 Hilmi Ziya, *Aşk Ahlâkı*, 46.
49 Hilmi Ziya, *Aşk Ahlâkı*, 66.
50 Hilmi Ziya, *Aşk Ahlâkı*, 66.
51 Hilmi Ziya, *Aşk Ahlâkı*, 104.

non-preferential love for all humanity. At the same time, this will not be a love without suffering or without potential frustration. Since our world is only in motion towards perfection and not yet perfect, this love is born from and will at times produce suffering. And for those who choose an active love for humanity even amidst imperfection and disappointment, Hilmi Ziya reserves a special guild of friendship. The friendship (*dostluk*) or companionship (*sohbet*) of those who seek to live by the ethics of love transcends creed and country. This companionship combats the faulty ethics that arise from constructing society based on things like material gain, fame, crushing others, etc. Friendship thus serves as a way to cultivate spiritual power at large, between and among individuals. Friendship transforms isolating individualism into humanizing personhood.[52]

With personhood comes responsibility. According to Hilmi Ziya the human spirit, love, and immaterial things such as virtues are as real as matter—they have only emerged recently in the universe through the advent of humanity. In short, humanity itself is a process that is still coming into being. As part of this coming into being, human beings must take responsibility for their reality (which is comprised of both spirit and matter). And it is the love of the infinite here and now amid and through suffering that motivates us as human beings to take responsibility in becoming human together.

With this in mind, how can we summarize Hilmi Ziya's treatment of suffering in a practical sense? What, if any, guidance might Hilmi Ziya's approach to human suffering provide someone looking for solace for themselves or someone they love?

To start, Hilmi Ziya focuses on the kinds of suffering we as human beings pass on to one another in our dysfunction, astutely tracing the trickle-down effect of trauma and deprivation and the way human brokenness often begets more brokenness in others. Second, Hilmi Ziya emphasizes the importance of immanence alongside transcendence. One upshot of this is that by stressing immanence and multiplicity, Hilmi Ziya's position encourages us not to rush past suffering to some higher end, but to stay long enough in awareness of suffering to name it, to acknowledge it. With evil defined as privation, simply a lack of the good, it is easy enough to rush through suffering to the grand finale of some transcending insight, or even the more modest but still idealist goal of graduating to an ethical foundation of love. Yet, Hilmi Ziya's emphasis on immanence and individual passion, on finding the self even in selflessness, allows us to stay longer in the immanent, not jumping to the infinite, where evil is merely privation, giving us more grace to name and hold space for suffering. Further, Hilmi Ziya's message gives us hope amid the imperfect state of reaching towards the infinite, a hope of holding together in and through our experiences of alienation. Even for souls engaged and active in the sufferings of this world, Hilmi Ziya points to a new sense of connection that is founded on a transcendent dimension, i.e., his dream of friendship. Importantly, however, Hilmi

52 Hilmi Ziya, *Aşk Ahlâkı*, 138.

Ziya is not offering a one-size-fits-all answer to the problem of suffering. His vision of an ethical system does not accommodate a once-and-for-all solution to the problem of suffering, because humans are always in process, always becoming, always changing, and always able to grow and perfect themselves in new ways.

In sum, the practical wisdom around suffering we might take from Hilmi Ziya's *Ethics of Love* includes: (1) naming the suffering and being comfortable in multiplicity, i.e., trusting multiplicity's connection to divine unity, (2) responding to suffering with compassion along with understanding and discernment, and (3) striving for greater human connection as part of the fourth level of moral development (love). For Hilmi Ziya, whether we have reached the stage of love-based ethics or not, we may still respond to our own suffering and the suffering of others with compassion and personal responsibility. Doing so brings us closer to the transcendent circle of friendship and self-sacrificing and self-affirming love of those whose moral foundation is love. In the face of suffering, we have the opportunity to connect with each other through compassion and love. His message: you are not alone.

References

Akbaş, Muhsin. "Ülken, Hilmi Ziya (1901–1974)." In *The Biographical Encyclopedia of Islamic Philosophy*, edited by Oliver Leaman, 486–490. London: Bloomsbury, 2006.

Alper, Ömer Mahir. "Hilmi Ziya Ülken'in İslâm Felsefesini Yorumu: İslâm Felsefesi Tarihyazımına bir Örnek." *İstanbul Üniversitesi İlahiyat Fakültesi Dergisi* 14 (2006): 123–146.

Anay, Harun. "Hilmi Ziya Ülken'in Bilinmeyen İki Öz Geçmiş Metni." *Kutadgubilig Felsefe-Bilim Araştırmaları Dergisi* 18 (2010): 195–213.

Balakbabalar, Muhsin. "İki Dost." *Ankara Üniversitesi İlahiyat Fakültesi Dergisi* 20 (1975): 26–27.

Kitamori, Kazoh. *The Theology of the Pain of God*. Eugene, OR: Wipf & Stock Publishers, 1965.

Özberki, Ayşe R. "Hilmi Ziya's Life and Thought from 1928 to 1960, in Relation to the Political and Religious Developments in the Republic of Turkey." M.A. Thesis in Social Sciences, Boğaziçi University, Istanbul, 1986.

Sanay, Eyyüp. "Ülken, Hilmi Ziya." *Türkiye Diyanet Vakfı İslâm Ansiklopedisi*. https://islamansiklopedisi.org.tr/ (last accessed October 17, 2022).

Ülken, Hilmi Ziya. *Aşk Ahlâkı: Halka Rağmen Halk İçin Kitap*, 3rd edition. Ankara: Demirbaş Yayınları, 1971.

Ülken, Hilmi Ziya. "Kendi Dilinden Hilmi Ziya Ülken." *Toplumbilim* 2 (1993): 85–92.

Vergili, Ayhan. "Hilmi Ziya Ülken (1901–1974)." In *Türkiye'de Sosyoloji I*, edited by M. Çağatay Özdemir, 597–628. Ankara: Phoenix, 2008.

Vural, Mehmet. "Hilmi Ziya Ülken Ontolojisinde Aşkın Varlık Problemi." *İslâmî Araştırmalar Dergisi* 16, no. 2 (2003): 212–216.

14 Suffering as Metaphysical Narrative

Exploring an Islamic Theodicy of Authorship

Cyrus Ali Zargar

Introduction

Not long ago I was at the home of relatives who had lost their 23-year-old son to leukemia. While they had their moments of calmness and even joviality, for the most part, as one would expect, they were distraught and inconsolable. Their son was in many ways a pillar of their family, a bodybuilder and an entrepreneur, a person of great charm who had married only months before his sudden diagnosis precipitated quickly. The young man's grandmother was at this gathering. In a room crowded with those who had come to express condolences, the grandmother looked directly at me, during a rare moment of silence. She asked me loudly, so that all could hear, "What can you say to Reza's mother and father to comfort them? You're a professor of religion. Please say something to ease their pain."[1]

I had nothing to say. There was no response that I could give them that did not feel either forced or somehow emotionally manipulative, as though I wanted to coax them out of a grief that was more than warranted. At moments like these, I never know what to say. I usually stand or sit silently and do my best to mutter something about my sympathies, while feeling inside a dual sense of respect and empathy, tinged with feelings of guilt and gratitude that I am not in their place.

Here, though, in this chapter, I would like to give those parents the best response I can. What follows is not so much a philosophical argument, as it is a reframing—a shift in perspective that has helped me in such times. In other words, I offer nothing more than my own humble means of perseverance. It begins with the conviction that life has some meaning to it. Moreover, human life specifically results from acts of creation. I do not mean in any way to disavow scientific claims about the universe or the evolution of species, theories with which I am perfectly comfortable, even as they remain unrelated to the topic at hand. Rather, I want to call on a sense of intuition that I have and share with others: a conviction that there is

1 Incidentally, the suffering and death of innocents—including a case of leukemia—is the topic of Stanley Hauerwas, *Naming the Silences: God, Medicine, and the Problem of Suffering* (New York: T&T Clark International, 1990).

DOI: 10.4324/9781003371670-15

some purpose behind my life and the lives of those around me. In fact, I will go beyond merely a sense of purpose and say that, if viewed as part of a composition or an act of authorship, my life has an author. Informing my view of human life as authored are the ethical and literary perspectives of two great thinkers, one classical, the other more contemporary; the first is the 13th-century Spanish Sufi theorist, Ibn ʿArabī (d. 1240), and the second is 20th-century Russian literary critic Mikhail Bakhtin (d. 1975).

From Ibn ʿArabī, I draw the idea that creation exists for me as a rich and multi-layered experience of imagination. There is, first, my own imagination that allows me to perceive things and know things in a human way, constructed using my own sensory input, the sensory input that I have received from my infancy until today. My sense of imagination has constructed a world that makes sense to me. Yet it is no fantasy. The world that makes sense to me is a world of forms that communicate supersensory meanings. Beyond all of this, beyond my own perception and my own imagination, lies what you might call the imagination of God. Everything I know and see is maintained by this transcendent knower of everything. Were God to divert His attention from anything, including myself, for even an instant, I would cease to be. In this way, God is a constant author and viewer of my reality.

I call on Bakhtin because I live in a modernity that has given me arguably contemporary literature's greatest endowment to human cultures, namely, the novel. The novel has *changed* the way we perceive our world. Relatedly, the novel has also *resulted* from changes in the language that we use to understand the world. For Bakhtin, the novel comes to be in a setting wherein the rigidity of language, language as supported by power structures, begins to break down, succumbing to diverse voices, genres, worldviews, and dialects, a breakdown in the world outside the novel reflected within the novel.[2] One might think of the epic poem, structured both as verse and as a single authorial voice, as contrasting with the novel. This shift in literature describes, quite well, the transition that many communities made from feudal agrarian life to that centered around the city, or what we might call the onset of modernity. This is a shift in emphasis, with emphasis placed on the inwardness of the self. One should not mistakenly assume, however, that such inwardness is a uniquely modern experience.[3]

2 See Mikhail M. Bakhtin, *The Dialogic Imagination*, ed. Michael Holquist; trans. Caryl Emerson and Michael Holquist (Austin: University of Texas Press, 1981), 371. What distinguishes Bakhtin's approach to the narrated self—in comparison with MacIntyre's "narrative unity of a life" and Ricœur's "emplotment"—is his insistence on the essential and dialogical relationship between the I-for-myself and the I-for-the-other. See Daphna Erdinast-Vulcan, "The I That Tells Itself: A Bakhtinian Perspective on Narrative Identity," *Narrative* 16, no. 1 (2008): 3–4.

3 As Muhammad Faruque has shown in his response to Charles Taylor, inwardness is neither "modern" nor "Western." Rather, conceptions of inwardness that emphasize creativity and the infinite potential of the self can be found in classical Sufi and Islamic philosophical writings. See Faruque, "Charles Taylor and the Invention of Modern Inwardness: A Sufi, Constructive Response," *Religions* 13, no. 674 (2022): 17–18.

Bakhtin and the Authorship of Life

For Bakhtin, the novel presents a pluralism of all perspectives contained in it. Each voice in the novel brings its own orientation and even philosophy. There is an author, of course, in the novel, but the author exists only as a careful curator of various perspectives, so much so that he or she has all but disappeared in many novels, or at least those that have the quality that Bakhtin called "heteroglossia."[4] In its fullest effect, heteroglossia leads to dialogism, which is a modality of knowledge in which the convergence of multiple dialogues creates meaning. Bakhtin reflects on the novel, on literature, and the relationship between author and hero in ways that are sometimes surprisingly relevant to readers of Ibn ʿArabī. For example, he tells us about the relationship in classical literature between fate and the hero. Classical literature, such as that of the Greeks, as well as Persian heroic poetry, presents us with a hero who should feel doomed. It accomplishes that by giving us an author who avoids offering any moral frame of reference or perspective.[5]

Imagining an author other than the self for one's life has a twofold quality that becomes clear through Bakhtin's literary theory. First, it creates a sense of predetermined fate, or doom. Yet, second, it also liberates the hero from being the author. Thus, the author's determination of the course of the hero's life bestows upon the hero both meaning and beauty:

> A determined life, a life freed from the claws of what-is-yet-to-be, of the future, of purpose and meaning—such a life becomes emotionally measurable, musically expressive, and self-sufficient (sufficient to itself as totally present-on-hand); its being already determined becomes a valuable determinateness. Meaning is not born, nor does it die; the meaning-governed sequence or progression of one's life, that is, the cognitive-ethical tension of a lived life from within itself, can be neither started nor consummated. Death cannot be the consummation of this meaning-governed progression.[6]

By freeing the hero from having to create his or her own meaning, the author has located a superseding sense of meaning beyond the hero's particular frame of reference: the hero exists within a context of meaning, and that meaning neither comes to be with the hero nor dies with the death of the hero. The hero's narrative becomes an opportunity to witness the lasting beauty of a transitory window into meaning, one window among many. This sense of an author other than oneself for the role one plays in the story of life, I am arguing, can liberate us from having to be the authors of our own individual stories. Suffering, too, then becomes framed within a larger context of meaning that contains each of us.

4 Bakhtin, *Dialogic Imagination*, 400.

5 Mikhail M. Bakhtin, "Author and Hero in Aesthetic Activity," in *Art and Answerability: Early Philosophical Essays*, ed. Michael Holquist and Vadim Liapunov; trans. Vadim Liapunov (Austin: The University of Texas Press, 1990), 176–177.

6 Bakhtin, "Author and Hero," 108.

For Bakhtin, the soul is the self in dialogue. The soul is that part of the self that comes to be within the context of its interactions and experiences among others. The spirit, on the other hand, is the culmination of meanings acquired in that dialogue with others—acquired in life, one might say:

> I experience the inner life of another as his soul; within myself, I live in the spirit. The soul is an image of the totality of everything that has been actually experienced—of everything that is present-on-hand in the soul in the dimension of time; the spirit is the totality of everything that has the validity of meaning—a totality of all the forms of my life's directedness from within itself, of all my acts of proceeding from within myself.[7]

The spirit is far beyond anything that can be described in story, because, for Bakhtin, the spirit remains constantly receptive. It does not give back. The author—for Bakhtin—creates representationally that soul-spirit dynamic in the novel by giving the characters souls, which then lends the novel itself a spirit. The author, in other words, recreates in the novel the world that we all know as life, the life in which we interact with others.

Thinking about Bakhtin's theory, I can begin to see my own life and the events within it not as centered around me, but as part of a larger story that contains me. My story is not really a story at all: it is a role in which I interact with others, creating one dialogue, one conversation among multiple conversations that form the story of our collective novel, the story of reality. This story has an author whom one would call "God." Importantly, I am not that story's hero, because it is not my story; it is, instead, the story of humanity. Thinking about Ibn ʿArabī's description of the Quran, we might say that while I am a soul within that story, the spirit of that story is the Quran. Ibn ʿArabī tells us that the Quran "unveils all the knowledges sent down in the scriptures and contains that which is not contained by them" because "Muhammad was given the 'all-comprehensive words' (*jawāmiʿ al-kalim*)," which means that "the sciences of the prophets, the angels, and every known tongue are comprised" in the Quran.[8] That is, the meaningful dimension of our existence has been summarized in the Quran, and the Quran itself declares that it contains "the most beautiful of stories" (Q 12:3).

Malaise of the Self-Authored Story

Placing one's life within the context of a story often means something different from what I have described. Usually, in modern contexts, we are encouraged to focus on our own unique story—with oneself as author. This, however, seems to create more discontent and disappointment, when life presents a person with events

7 Bakhtin, "Author and Hero," 110.
8 William Chittick, *The Sufi Path of Knowledge: Ibn al-ʿArabī's Metaphysics of Imagination* (Albany: SUNY Press, 1989), 239.

and circumstances that do not fit the narratives we think we choose or create. So argues the American theologian Stanley Hauerwas. Hauerwas is interested in the way that Americans, particularly those who live within a framework of what might be called "modernity," see themselves as the author of their own story. The extent to which I might choose my occupation, select a mate, time the births of my children, and generally determine my own identity—all this is indicative of a modern and American outlook to Hauerwas:

> America exemplifies what I call the project of modernity—the attempt to produce a people who believe that they should have no story except the story that they chose when they had no story. That is what Americans mean by freedom. The institutions that constitute the disciplinary forms of that project are liberal democracy and capitalism. Americans presume that they have exercised their freedom when they get to choose between a Sony or Panasonic television. The same presumption works for choosing a president, and once you have made your choice you have to learn to live with it. So, freedom requires a kind of resignation. . . . It is assumed that you should only be held accountable when you acted *freely*. And to act freely, you had to know what you were doing. One of the difficulties with such an account of responsibility, for example, is that it makes marriage unintelligible.[9]

The problem, he argues, derives from the fact that those ways of defining myself—those ways of writing my own story—almost always lead to disappointment. The person I married 20 years ago will not be the same person I am married to today. Therefore, I can never say that I chose to be married to this person. Moreover, the children that I have will invariably grow up to be individuals entirely outside of my domain of influence. I cannot choose my children, for, in terms of their identities, they just happen to intersect with in my life. This way of thinking of my story as my own story—and me as the author of my own story—leads to frustrations as well as futile attempt after futile attempt to reassert myself, trying to rewrite things, revise matters so that I might be that author I imagine. At best, I fool myself into thinking that I am the author of my own story as well as its hero. At worst, I suffer a crisis of identity, one that brings me to reject any meaningful theory of life. When that story, the story of the self that is both modern and American, does happen to work out, I see my successes as part of my story. I sense that I have earned those successes. Conversely, I begin to see all trials as matters that I should rightly be able to control. A person might say for example, upon getting sick, that I must rise to the occasion to be at war with my sickness. In reality, there is often very little that I can do to predict my own longevity, other than staying in the best health that I can.

9 Stanley Hauerwas, *War and the American Difference: Theological Reflections on Violence and National Identity* (Grand Rapids: BakerAcademic, 2011), 17.

The Quranic Grand Narrative: Another Author's Story

Once I begin to see the author of my story as someone else, and once I begin to see myself not as the hero, but as one voice or one soul within that story, my perspective shifts considerably. I would argue that this difference in perspective appears in the Quran as well. Take the case of Abraham. When Abraham wants to describe God, he describes Him in terms of the interventions God has made within his life:

> "The One who created me, then He guided me; and the One who fed me and gave me drink; the One who, when I was sick, healed me; the one who will bring me death, then return me to life; and the One whom I hope will forgive me of my faults on the Day of the Criterion." (Q 26:78–82)[10]

The way that Abraham knows God is through these major events that he shares with other people. His knowledge of God is as an author, or as a causal factor, in the important times of his life, as well as the more quotidian parts of his life. Recognizing God's activity orients him towards God, but I would add—at least for the purposes of this chapter—that it orients him away from concern for his own ability to act. Such a perspective orients Abraham away from blaming himself for what he cannot control and from taking credit for what he did not control. Instead, he maintains hope in what is completely beyond any human being's control. He begins to see his life as one life among many, a life that makes sense. This yields gratitude as well as a sort of trusting resignation. When he was sick, it was up to God to heal him. If God had decided not to heal him, then he would have remained sick or, worse, perished. Had either of those things happened, not only would Abraham have been affected, but all of those who loved him would be affected as well. Within this scriptural context, those who love him include generations of saintly men and women. It includes both the Children of Israel and the tribes of the Arabs. It includes all monotheists within the Western religions, in fact, because his role in this larger story is that of a grand soul. The dialogue that he has had with others, the voice that he shared with those around him, was a major theme in the novel of existence.

Another case in the Quran of particular significance is that of a dialogue between God and Moses. When Moses comes before God, he fears appearing alone at the court of the Pharaoh. He asks God to make his brother, Aaron, his partner in this act of prophetic bravery. God grants his request, but then reminds Moses of the favors He has done for him throughout his life:

> He said, "We have granted your request, O Moses! And We favored you another time before, when We revealed to your mother what We revealed: 'Put him in the chest and the chest on the open water, so that the water will

10 All translations are my own, unless otherwise indicated.

> bring him to the bank. An enemy to Me and to him will take him.' And I bequeathed a love upon you from Myself so that you would be brought up before My eyes. Recall when your sister was walking, so she said, 'Shall I lead you to one who can care for him?' So, We returned you to your mother, to bring tranquility to her eyes and so she would not grieve. And you killed a person, and so We rescued you from sorrow and tested you in many ways. Thus you passed years among the people of Midian. Then you came to Me at the arranged time, O Moses!" (Q 20:36–40)

Fascinating here is that the events in Moses's life become reframed, each as acts of grace, and the entirety of his life becomes described as God's abiding presence. At every turn, God was there, making sure things went the way they were supposed to go. Moreover, that story is not entirely about Moses—just as Moses's life is not entirely about Moses. The passage also concerns his mother and his sister. It is also about his enemies and his friends. Each of them has some effect upon the other, and each of their lives is changed because of Moses. Again, as with Abraham, we have another major voice in this grand story. Moses, like Abraham, recognizes God's role in his life. We know this because he asks God to change the story, supplicating for God to alter things, which is within the realm of possibility for God and only God. While we remain powerless to change our role, we can direct our attention to its author, asking Him to alter it. The story, after all, is being written, even if it has also been written before. Within that larger story of existence, Moses is a powerful example of someone who is heroic, but even he cannot be called the hero of the story.

We might say, moreover, that the narrative we are a part of is a narrative beyond what we can understand. Because it lies beyond what we can understand, it becomes difficult for us to locate benevolence at all times. We cannot see the story in its entirety, for we can only see our own role in it. Even then, we stand imperceptive to the story's conclusion because we do not know what happens after death to us. This sense of resignation within the context of a grand story appears in the Quran. When one looks for it, one finds it everywhere in that text. For example, those who face calamity according to the Quran are instructed to declare, "Indeed we belong to God, and to Him we return" (Q 2:156). One might say, for our purposes here, "Indeed, we are from God, and to Him we return." This is the barest structure of the grand story. Notice, first of all, the use of the first-person plural. It is not, "I am from God, and to Him I return." Rather, we, humanity, who are from God, return. While we might return upon our deaths at different times and then after death again together, the point is that humanity comes from God and goes to God; it implies that everything in between those two points is unknown to us. Our comfort lies in knowing how the narrative began and how the narrative ends. Our solace is in knowing that there is a narrative and that the narrative is beyond our control. That the author is, as described in the Quran, merciful and loving.

The perspective prescribed to the Quran's followers is one of indefatigable hope. This is because the superseding narrative—containing each believer's role—has been established as a meaningful and even beautiful one. So declared the Prophet Muhammad in a well-known narration, "How wondrous is the affair of the believer! The believer's affair is entirely good, and this is something that applies to no one but the believer." The belief of the believer yields an "affair" (*al-amr*), or, one might say a role in life's narrative, that is good (*khayr*) regardless of the particular circumstances of that life. Knowing this, "When stricken by prosperity, the believer is grateful. When stricken by hardship, the believer is steadfast. This is good for the believer."[11] Many believers die in abject poverty, after decades of strife or ill health. Some of those who embrace this narrative, those who are "believers" in it, suffer constantly, at least externally—even if in some cases their cores remain unshaken. Their belief lies in an understanding of the goodness of their affair; that is, they know the outline of the larger beautiful story.

On one hand, the Quran and Hadith promise a recompense for such suffering, as another narration clarifies:

> God the Almighty will apologize to His servants who were needy in this world just as a brother apologizes to his brother, and say, "I swear by My Honor that I did not make you poor to humiliate you. Now push the curtain aside and see what I have given you instead." When the curtain is pushed aside and he sees what God has rewarded him with instead of this world, he says, "Oh God! There was no harm for me due to what You took away from me (in this world) considering what you have given me instead (now in the Hereafter)."[12]

This is the prevailing sentiment in Islamic scriptures regarding human suffering. Nevertheless, we might read such narrations slightly differently than the surface reading—this time focusing less on recompense than on a sense of belonging. The grand narrative contains all of us, and our experience of prosperity or hardship reflects only our place within that narrative. If at any particular moment the author of that story does not seem benevolent, we have been guaranteed that at the end, He will.

What About Human Will?

To relegate life's authorship to another raises a question, an age-old inquiry common to monotheistic religions. Who is ultimately responsible for human actions and the course of human life? This is a theological matter well outside what literary theory can tell us—and well beyond the boundaries of this chapter. Nevertheless, the question itself creates an opportunity to consider the narrative dimensions

11 Muslim, *Ṣaḥīḥ* (Riyadh: Dār al-Mughnī, 1998), 1598 (no. 2999).

12 al-Ḥasan b. Faḍl al-Ṭabarsī, *The Lamp Niche for the Best Traditions*, trans. Lisa Zaynab Morgan and Ali Peiravi (Qum: Ansariyan, 2002), 712 (no. 1697). Translation modified here, using the original Arabic text provided in the volume.

of "the Decree" (*al-qaḍā'*) and "the Apportionment" (*al-qadar*). Here, again, Ibn ʿArabī's system of philosophical Sufi theory illuminates the discussion—through the lens of a later interpreter. The Twelver Shiʿi Quran commentator, Hadith scholar, and philosopher Mullā Fayḍ al-Kāshānī (d. 1679) places the relationship between God's decree and human autonomy within the terminological framework of Ibn ʿArabī's language:

On the Decree and the Apportionment

"As for each thing, We have created it by apportionment"

(Q 54:49).

This chapter is a word concerning the meaning of the Decree and the Apportionment, and the secret behind the Apportionment.

The Decree is an expression for the divine ruling upon the existent entities, according to the passing states they occupy from eternity-without-beginning to eternity-without-end. The Apportionment is the elaboration of that ruling by bringing [the states] into existence in their appropriate moments and times, as determined by the occurrence of the things in it, as per their particular preparedness. Thus "Apportionment" can be explained as the phenomenon in which every state from the entities' states becomes attached to a designated time and designated cause.

The secret of the Apportionment is that it is not possible for an entity from among the created entities to make manifest in existence an essence, attribute, or action but by the apportioning that corresponds to the particularity of its capability and essential preparedness, which does not accept alteration, substitution, addition, or subtraction.

This is because created things are known to God, the Exalted. He is the one who knows them as they are in themselves. Knowledge leaves no trace in the known that there might appear something that was not already there within the known. Rather knowledge is subject to the known, and any ruling that pertains to the known is subject to the known.

Thus the knower has no ruling for the known but in accordance with the known and what the known's essence determines in accordance with its preparedness, both universal and particular.[13]

The two terms "decree" and "apportionment" correspond to a phrase used to describe God's determination of the course of creation, as debated by theologians. The prevailing Sunni opinions—as expressed by the Ashʿarī, Māturīdī, and Ahl al-Ḥadīth approaches—favored the prerogative of God's will. This contrasted with

13 Fayḍ al-Kāshānī, *Qurrat al-ʿuyūn fī aʿazz al-funūn*, ed. Ḥasan al-Qāsimī (Tehran: Madrasa-yi ʿĀlī-yi Shahīd Muṭahharī, 2008), 76–77.

a longer-standing theological school, the Muʿtazila, who favored the prerogative of human choice, which they saw as necessary to maintain God's justice. That is, one side (the prevailing Sunni opinion) argued that whatever God willed was just. God's will is just by nature and hence defines justice in a way that we humans need not necessarily be able to discern. The other side (the Muʿtazila) argued that God and His will could be expected to abide by a discernable standard of justice.

Fayḍ, the writer of the passage, belonged to the Imāmī school of theology, which borrowed heavily from the Muʿtazila, while also endeavoring to find a middle ground between the prerogative of God's will and that of human choice. Some of that attempt at balancing God's will and human choice can be seen in the passage. More directly, however, he analyzes the issue not as an Imāmī, but rather as a spiritually informed philosopher. It is this that pertains to our discussion.

Put in simplest terms, Fayḍ explains how our will, the story of our decisions, might be contained within God's will, the story of creation. This is because every existing "thing" corresponds to a series of states of being—the states of being that each thing will occupy for all of eternity. God knows these eternally, even before gifting that thing with existence. Based on all the states that each thing will experience, God places each of those states within its appropriate place, a place that suits the well-being of that thing, or, in our case, the well-being of each person. Metaphorically speaking, each note in the symphony of one's existence must be struck at the appropriate time: God has arranged them appropriately. That placement is no accident. It defines each of us, configuring us as an individual composition.

More interestingly, God does not determine the states of our existence based on anything outside of ourselves. Our unique existence dictates all of those states. God knows that existence and all of those states. He knows us, and we are thus known by Him, and Fayḍ reminds us that a knower's knowledge does not shape the known. Quite to the contrary, every known thing determines what the knower knows. This means that we, as compositions, are not written at the whim of a composer. Instead, we come to fruition in a way that the composer knows to be perfect for each of us. The parameters of our being dictate the composition of our existence. The parameters of our being dictate the manner, placement, and timing of states (or events) in our life.

In terms of authorship, the metaphor of the "character" might help clarify this. The author is certainly free to determine whatever He wishes for the character, but any author will tell you that the character determines her own story. Her arc must suit her traits. Her decisions, victories, and mistakes come from a self-contained logic that inheres in the character. Yet the author created the character. The author's imagination gave birth to the particular blend of attributes that is this unique character. The author, also, brings the character's progress and end to realization and completion based on the origins of the character—origins that He created.

Lastly, every character is an extension of the author. The author's knowledge of each character is absolute because the characters are extensions of the author's knowledge, indeed, extensions of the author Himself. The author brings His character into words—into realized existence—from the hidden depths of His own knowledge, which determines all the states and events pertaining to that character.

The hack writer forces his vision and voice on each character. The master novelist disappears into the background, so that each character exists in seeming independence, seeming independence of voice and action. The reality is that the character both is and is not independent. By nature of her being, she makes decisions and reacts to the events in her life. But by nature of her being an extension of the author and the author's knowledge, those decisions and reactions always remain contained within the plan that would allow that character to come to be and would complete that character's arc.

Conclusion

This metaphor of author and divine creator, of course, has its limitations. Among other things, what makes God unlike other authors is the perfection and universality of His knowledge, the detail, breadth, and infinity of the composition. Here we speak not of the controlled setting of the novel—even the most expansive novels. Rather, there are infinite possibilities for an almost infinite number of entities. At times, this complexity might bring us to wonder whether or not there is a plan or composition at all. Isolation, deprivation, or things in disorder bring us to see strings of events with no meaningful ties between them. Thus, the sense of an authored narrative escapes us most in moments of deep suffering, when states of being seem to have no design or relationship to one another. (Famously, the Great Lisbon Earthquake of 1755 was a turning point in Enlightenment thought, because it seemed to undermine existing theodicies.)

Another habit of thinking can keep me from seeing the "grand story" in which I play a small role: my imagined sense of my life being "my story," in which I play the starring role. My importance and centrality contradict the pains of my life—especially when they do not fit with the logic of the story of selfhood I had been constructing for myself. It is either my story or no story—or stories become modified and changed, highlighting these stories as products of whim, rather than expressions of meaning.

Conversely, the sense of an authored narrative grips us most when we can see the interconnectedness between us and others, when our individual character arcs and unique contributions to the universal story interact. When we need each other, love each other, and know each other through-and-through, it is as if everything falls into place. We then see interconnectedness in dialogue with one another. Our lives become more like roles suited to us than disparate and often desperate attempts to attain our own unique forms of happiness.

Practically speaking, we might think of ways to limit our roles and focus on the "other" author: keeping me from overemphasizing the importance of my own personal narrative might mean thinking more clearly about how I live with others, emphasizing controlled interactions with people whose narratives I know. Conjecturing on what this might mean, perhaps smaller, more closely knit communities mitigate the larger sense of meaningless and disconnectedness which we associate with individual instances of suffering. By this I mean communities in which people serve one another, care for one another, and—importantly—know quite a bit about one another. Belonging to a community in which I know my purpose might yield a sense of a narrative beyond my control in which I have a place.

In fact, to some extent, this imagined community corresponds to traditional life, a life contrary to the trend of living in isolation, especially in urban settings, a life facilitated by virtual interactions that have replaced natural multi-dimensional interactions. Here again, while all this is only fodder for future reflection, one might argue that virtual engagement strips me of realizing the limits of my embodiment and displaying the uniqueness of my being in the world. Online, these become replaced by an idealized, synthetic, self-constructed (or at least self-curated) persona, one who interacts with a world that can never know the real, lived, three-dimensional, living me. Through all this, any sense of a grander, real-life story disappears behind a plastic suit of isolation, a façade (or rather multiple layers of façade) that does its best to represent me, but it must do so in ways that can be transmitted in digital code.

With this in mind, let me return to my relatives who lost their son in the prime of his life. Their role in this grand narrative continues, as on some level does their son's. My role has intersected with theirs at this very moment. We can together find solace in the fact that we share this narrative, because the narrative has brought us together. It has bound us by love, a love we would not have known without the history and family ties that made it possible, namely, the intersecting roles we have. This certainly might not serve as any consolation, nor does it seem to function as a full-fledged response to the problem of suffering. At the very least, however, it reminds us that our suffering exists within the context of meaning and purpose. It places our lives within a framework of meaning that towers above us and outlives us. Finally, it brings our intersecting, dialogical roles together, relegating the encumbrance of answerability to another author, an author other than ourselves.

References

al-Ṭabarsī, al-Ḥasan b. Faḍl. *The Lamp Niche for the Best Traditions*. Translated into English by Lisa Zaynab Morgan and Ali Peiravi. Qum: Ansariyan, 2002.

Bakhtin, Mikhail M. *The Dialogic Imagination*. Edited by Michael Holquist; translated by Caryl Emerson and Michael Holquist. Austin: University of Texas Press, 1981.

Bakhtin, Mikhail M. "Author and Hero in Aesthetic Activity." In *Art and Answerability: Early Philosophical Essays*, edited by Michael Holquist and Vadim Liapunov; translated by Vadim Liapunov, 4–256. Austin: The University of Texas Press, 1990.

Chittick, William. *The Sufi Path of Knowledge: Ibn al-'Arabī's Metaphysics of Imagination*. Albany: SUNY Press, 1989.

Erdinast-Vulcan, Daphna. "The I That Tells Itself: A Bakhtinian Perspective on Narrative Identity." *Narrative* 16, no. 1 (2008): 1–15.

Faruque, Muhammad U. "Charles Taylor and the Invention of Modern Inwardness: A Sufi, Constructive Response." *Religions* 13, no. 674 (2022): 1 21.
Hauerwas, Stanley. *Naming the Silences: God, Medicine, and the Problem of Suffering*. New York: T&T Clark International, 1990.
Hauerwas, Stanley. *War and the American Difference: Theological Reflections on Violence and National Identity*. Grand Rapids: BakerAcademic, 2011.
al-Kāshānī, Fayḍ. *Qurrat al-ʿuyūn fī aʿazz al-funūn*. Edited by Ḥasan al-Qāsimī. Tehran: Madrasa-yi ʿĀlī-yi Shahīd Muṭahharī, 2008.
Muslim. *Ṣaḥīḥ*. Riyadh: Dār al-Mughnī, 1998.
al-Ṭabarsī, al-Ḥasan b. Faḍl. *The Lamp Niche for the Best Traditions*. Translated into English by Lisa Zaynab Morgan and Ali Peiravi. Qum: Ansariyan, 2002.

Index

Abel 158–162
Absolute, the 8; relatively, the 9
abstention 30, 37
action 3, 4, 5, 10, 14, 17, 18, 28, 30, 31, 34, 35, 41, 46, 49, 50, 51, 52, 59, 60, 63, 70, 78, 92, 93, 94, 96, 98, 99, 108, 109, 111, 118, 124, 125, 126, 128, 130, 131, 132, 138, 142, 148, 151, 152, 153, 154, 159, 160, 167, 168–169, 174, 176, 180, 190, 205, 209, 211, 217, 221–222, 224–225; of God 10, 11, 12, 13; human 5, 6, 7
Adam 37, 41–42, 77, 86, 90, 104, 113–124, 116–117, 135, 137, 145–146, 149, 158–161
Adams, Marilyn 3, 90
adultery 21
afterlife 25, 126, 139, 145–146, 165, 170–173; *see also* hereafter
Aga Khan III 47, 49, 50, 62–63, 65
Aga Khan IV 47
agricultural practices 14
Ahl al-Ḥadīth 222
Ahriman 7
Ahura Mazda 7
air pollution 14
Alexander of Aphrodisias 19–21
ʿAlī b. Abī Ṭālib 29, 31, 34, 37, 38, 39, 41, 189, 208
alienation 76, 106, 206–207
Allah 37, 64, 104, 114, 127–128, 194–195, 197–198
American 44, 86, 88, 90, 110, 123, 147, 154, 167, 175, 218, 226
animal habitats 14
anthropogenic 21
appetitive power 22–26
apportionment 222
Aquinas 69n11, 86
Aristotle 69n11, 86n106, 135, 182n10
ascension 119, 122–123, 192
al-Ashʿarī 45, 167, 176
aspiration 179–180, 181
atheist 3, 68, 86, 89, 90, 94, 98–108, 110
attention deficit disorder 95
autonomous will and power 3, 93
Avicenna: theory of evil acts 21–22; *see also* Ibn Sīnā
ʿAyn al-Quḍāt 5, 6, 8, 12, 165, 177, 179, 181, 184, 186

Bakhtin, Mikhail 215
baqāʾ 36
baṣīra 38
Bayle, Pierre 86, 90
beauty 7, 9–10, 36, 39–40, 41, 73, 75, 85, 105, 114, 119, 124, 129, 140, 141, 173, 194, 216
Bernstein, Aaron 14
Biden, Joe 17
Blaschko, Paul 89, 110
blessings 4, 12, 31, 40, 106, 119, 125, 127–129, 137, 139, 147, 168–175, 191
Boxing Day Tsunami 3, 90
brain 184
Buddha 10, 208
Buddhism 10, 115

Cain x, 158–163
carbon dioxide emissions 15–16, 22
cardinal sin 9, 123
cataclysmic changes 15
cause 25
celestial power 32
Center for Climate, Health, and the Global Environment at Harvard University 14
chaplain x, 187–189, 191, 193, 195, 197–200
China 155, 204, 206

Chittick, William 24, 26, 34, 42, 79, 85, 87–88, 106, 110, 118, 123, 125, 139–141, 146, 149, 157, 159, 163, 181, 183, 186, 189–190, 200, 217, 225
Chowdhury, Safaruk 4, 123, 131
Christ 9, 10, 12, 82–83, 199
Christakis, Nicholas 1
Christchurch 93
Christian theology 7
church 9, 93, 143, 164
climate change ii, iii, ix, 14–19, 21–28, 155–157
climate emergency 15, 18, 23
co-eternal 25
cognition 4, 46, 54, 61, 86, 123, 128–129, 135–136, 146, 152, 156, 161, 209
collective suicide 17, 28
Command, the 53
consciousness 54, 69, 88, 106, 126, 144, 153, 159, 184, 204–205
constriction 40
consumption 14, 18, 22–23
contemplate 29, 34, 50
cosmology 25, 46, 56, 80–81, 115, 134, 190, 200
COVID-19 i, ii, iii, 1, 2, 6, 14, 15, 27, 89, 95, 97, 111, 141, 142, 154, 155
creation of the world 59, 73, 94

Dante 8
dark 8, 34–35, 63, 82, 181, 183, 190, 195, 206
Dawūd al-Qayṣarī 32
day of judgement 77, 137, 168, 173; *see also* hereafter
death 40, 77, 82, 91, 99, 100–101, 112, 117, 120–121, 123, 125, 138, 139, 140, 141, 145–146, 148–149, 158–159, 160, 168–173, 185, 194, 200, 203, 209, 214, 216, 219
decree 4, 40, 60, 94, 135, 147, 149, 168, 174, 198, 222
determinism 22–23
dhikr 34, 118
Dhū'l-Nūn 152
dialogism 216
dianoia 68
disbelief 108, 170
disciple ix, 29, 31, 33, 35–41, 43, 89, 99, 109, 156
discipline i, ii, iii, iv, 30–31, 39, 42, 69, 172
disobedience 62, 158, 175
Divine: attributes iii, 2, 6, 36, 40, 45, 47, 48, 71–72, 106, 116, 124, 125; decree 4, 94, 147, 149; gift 5, 113, 124, 128, 199; order 40; Principles 8; reality 9, 73, 111, 116, 122, 124, 131, 189; signs 29–31, 112; teacher 41; trial ix, 29, 31, 33, 35–41, 43; Trustee 148; unity 118, 138, 144, 172, 204, 213; voluntarism 4, 94
Ḍiyāʾ al-Dīn Nakhshabī 114
Douglas-Klotz, Neil 126
Draper, Paul 90
dualism 7, 115, 212
dying 5, 82–83, 113, 127, 129, 136–141, 162, 180, 191, 195, 197

Ebola 1
economic suffering 10
embodiment iii, 5, 77, 86, 113, 119, 128, 139–140, 169, 176, 189, 225
emotion x, 52, 97, 100, 106, 120, 164, 168, 173, 175, 196, 214, 216
eternal happiness 23
ethical realism 4, 94
evil i, iii, iv, v, ix, x, 1–15, 18–27, 31, 34, 35, 44–47, 49, 51–55, 57–71, 73–75, 77, 79–81, 83–95, 97–104, 106–110, 123, 131, 135–136, 140, 144, 146, 156–157, 158–159, 161–171, 173–178, 182–186, 201, 204, 205, 208, 212; absolute 4, 57, 208; accidental 166; acts 8, 21, 22, 23; evidential problem of 3, 90, 98, 102, 109, 110; horrendous 3, 6, 90, 107, 109, 183; Humean 67, 89, 92, 94, 96–97, 100, 104; logical problem of 3, 90; necessitated ix, 44, 45, 47, 49, 51, 53, 55, 57, 59, 61, 63; and suffering i, iii, ix, 1–6, 10, 35, 46, 57, 70, 71, 75, 86, 89, 90, 92, 94, 98, 100–101, 106–107, 109–110, 165–167, 176, 186, 204–205; systemic x, 99, 158–159, 161–163
evolution 50, 65, 69, 99, 158, 162–164, 207, 214
existence iv, 3–5, 7–8, 11–12, 15, 17–23, 25, 29, 32, 36, 40, 42, 45, 46, 47, 49, 50–61, 63–68, 73–75, 80–84, 89, 90, 97–104, 111–118, 120, 121, 123, 144, 145, 148, 160, 163, 166, 181, 183, 184, 185–186, 189–191, 193, 198, 204, 207, 217, 219–220, 222, 223
existential threat ix, 14, 15, 17, 18, 19, 21–27
extinction 15, 17, 21, 23–27, 72

Islamic Chaplain x, 187, 189, 191, 193, 195, 197, 199
Ismaili ix, 44–47, 49, 50, 52, 54–57, 62–66
Istanbul Higher Institute of Islam 202
Istanbul Technical University 202

Jabal ʿArafāt 146
Jackson, Sherman 4n9, 45
Jaʿfar al-Ṣādiq 38, 145
jawāmiʿ al-kalim 217
Jesus 30, 38, 40–41, 161n9, 203, 208–209
jihād 31
Joseph 8, 13, 75, 88, 145, 150, 157, 159, 161, 163, 188, 200
Junayd 150
justice iv, 3–5, 20–22, 26, 37, 63, 79, 85, 93–95, 105–106, 144, 152, 160, 167–168, 172, 173, 175–176, 188, 196, 201–202, 204, 206–207, 223; ontological 20

Kaʿba 42, 174
Kant iv, 69, 71, 87, 209
kasb 3, 93
Khalil, Atif 174
Khidr 108
Khwāja Khurd 183n13
Kugle, Scott 114, 117

Lewis, C.S. 143–144, 151, 156, 157
libertarian 51–52
love iii, x, 2, 5, 9, 14, 24–26, 33, 35, 40, 75, 77–79, 94, 96–97, 102, 105, 109, 111, 129, 133, 136–139, 148–150, 156, 164–165, 168–176, 180–181, 188–190, 192–194, 196–197, 201–213, 219–220, 224–225

MacKenzie, Debora 1, 6
macrocosm 77, 82, 115, 120, 189
al-Makkī 31
maʿrifa 29, 71, 88, 126, 182, 186
Mary 150, 161n9
Mattson, Ingrid 115, 118, 139
Māturīdī 4, 222
Mawlana 181; *see also* Rūmī
meditation 118, 122, 140, 153
Michelangelo 10
microcosm 46, 61, 77, 82, 115, 122, 124, 189, 190
Mīr Dāmād 46, 182n10
misfortune 61–62, 96, 106, 168–172, 211
modernism 7, 9
modernization 67, 162
monopluralism 202, 203
Moses 41, 75, 91–92, 108, 219, 220
Mother of the Book 172
Mullā Fayḍ al-Kāshānī 222
Mullā Ṣadrā 5, 6, 46, 97, 100–101, 103, 110, 146, 157, 165, 176
muqarrabīn 35
music 118, 216
Muʿtazilī 3–4, 45
mystery ix, 111–112, 138, 143, 157, 175

Nagasawa, Yujin 99
Naṣīr al-Dīn al-Ṭūsī 46
Nāṣir-i Khusraw 46
Nasr, Seyyed Hossein ix, xii, 7, 8, 10, 12, 67–69, 71, 73, 75–88, 113, 116, 145, 159, 164, 176n10, 189, 190
natural: environment 155; world 14, 94
Necessary Existent 165
necessitarianism 19
Neoplatonic ix, 4, 19, 44–50, 55–56, 64–65, 86–88, 104, 165; *see also* Plotinus
New Zealand 93
Nguyen, Viet 161n7, 163
Nietzsche 203
Nirvana 211

omnibenevolence 19, 44, 45
omnipotent 2, 44, 93, 193
omniscience 4, 44, 45, 144, 148
ontological justice 20
ontology 5, 80, 100, 108
Order of the Good 15, 19–26
Ormsby, Eric 171
Ottoman 201–202

pandemic i, ii, iv, v, ix, 1, 2, 6, 7, 9, 11, 12, 13, 14, 15, 27, 89, 97, 111, 142, 154–157
patience 5, 61, 62, 107, 120, 122–130, 147, 150, 152, 157, 168–170, 174–175, 211
perseverance 95, 214
Persian 11, 66, 127, 138, 216
personhood 2, 3, 161, 205, 212
pestilence 10
Pharaoh 105, 158, 162–163, 219
phenomena 78, 82, 102
physical pain 10
pious, the 35
plants 14, 47, 60, 96, 115, 118
Plato 68, 72

Plotinus 69
pluralism 48, 164, 176, 202–203, 216
postcolonial thought 67, 87
prayer ix, 9, 36–37, 47, 96, 111, 113, 115, 117, 118–189, 120–123, 125, 127, 129, 131, 133, 135, 137, 139, 141, 148, 150, 151–154, 180, 193
predestination 71, 75, 80, 84–85, 144, 175
privation of health 21
protection 14
providence 4–6, 15, 19, 20, 22–23, 26–27, 96, 101, 103, 105, 110, 146
Pseudo-Dionysius 69n11
psychological pain 10, 120

qubḥ 7
qalb 12, 29, 127, 153
Quran i, 8–9, 13, 29–31, 33–36, 38–42, 48, 50, 75, 79, 82–83, 86, 88, 92, 101, 106, 108, 112–113, 116–167, 119, 122, 125, 127, 129, 132, 138–139, 144–150, 153, 157–159, 161, 163, 180, 188–192, 200, 217, 219, 220–222
al-Qūnawī 85, 87
al-Qushayrī 31, 153
quṭb 36

Rashed, Marwan 165
reason 3, 4, 15, 19, 21, 32, 36, 38, 55, 56, 58, 60, 61, 64, 67–69, 79, 83, 86, 87, 90, 93, 94, 96, 98, 100, 102, 103, 108, 126, 135, 143–144, 146–147, 150–152, 161, 165, 170, 171–175, 196
resignation 218–220
resilience iii, 2, 107, 173, 194
resources 2, 5, 7, 22–23, 97, 107, 108, 123
responsibility 10, 132, 208, 212–213, 218
reverent 128, 158–159
Rowe, William 90, 91, 98, 110, 165, 176
Rūmī 8, 100, 101, 105, 109, 110, 122–124, 128, 137–138, 142, 160, 163, 181, 185, 192, 200

sa'āda 145, 148
sage x, 1, 9, 11, 25, 37, 38, 41–42, 77–79, 81, 83, 85, 86, 96, 98, 101, 105, 109, 114, 121, 127–128, 148, 153, 155, 161, 173, 178–186, 191, 206, 212, 213, 223
St. Irenaeus 164
saints 25, 31, 78, 112, 113, 114, 117, 119, 141, 156–157, 207
salām 178
salvation 17, 23, 62, 78, 149, 165, 176
SARS 1
Schuon, Frithjof 9, 68, 88, 111–112
scientia sacra 69
self: -disclosure 24–26; -knowledge ix, 29–31, 33, 35, 37, 39, 41; selfhood 5, 40, 224; -sufficient 36, 47, 58, 216
separation from God 8–10, 73, 83, 191
servitude 120
shadow 8, 12, 160, 204, 206
shahawāt 37
shaqāwa 145–146
sharī'a 36
Shariati, Ali 158, 162–163
Shihadeh, Ayman 3, 5, 93, 165
al-Sijistānī 46
Socrates 72, 208
Solzhenitsyn, Aleksandr 161
soul 10, 21–26, 29–42, 45–47, 54–55, 57–66, 71, 76, 78, 85, 95, 115, 119, 137, 139, 140, 145–147, 149–151, 161, 164–165, 169, 174, 176, 185, 187, 190, 191, 192, 193, 200, 206, 212, 217, 219; animal 32, 34; commanding 34; inspired 35; perfected 36; pleasing 36; rational 21, 23, 24, 26, 32, 33, 165; tranquil 36; Universal 45–47, 54–61, 63–65; vegetal 32
species 14–16, 18, 20–24, 26, 95–96, 99, 117, 146, 214
spirit 29, 148
spiritual: anthropology 111; authority 36; guardianship 36; master 35; resources 7, 107
suffering i, ii, iii, iv, v, ix, x, 1–3, 4–6, 7, 9, 10–11, 13, 15, 21, 23, 40, 45, 61–63, 65–66, 69, 70, 75, 76, 77, 78, 79, 86, 89, 90–112, 119–126, 128–131, 135, 137, 138, 140, 142–151, 153–154, 155, 157, 162, 164, 165, 168, 172–176, 181, 187, 188, 190, 191–194, 196, 198, 199, 201–221, 223–226
Sufism iii, iv, xii, 2, 5, 8, 12, 13, 71, 78, 85, 88, 114, 116–119, 121, 141, 179, 181, 186, 189, 190, 200
Suhrawardī 103, 179, 186
Sullivan, Meghan 89
Sulmasy, Daniel 111
supersensory 215
sustainability 18, 27

taklīf 93
taqwā 158–159

tawakkul 5, 12, 64, 127, 147–148, 157
tawḥīd 38, 42, 47, 202
Taylor, Charles 215n3
Taylor, Steven 1, 2
theism: open 4, 102; skeptical 4
theodicy ix, x, 3–6, 19, 44–47, 55–57, 60, 62–67, 69–73, 75, 77–81, 83–87, 90–91, 93, 97–98, 101, 109–110, 146, 157, 164–167, 171–173, 175–177, 214; Soul-Making 62, 165, 176
theophany 30, 77
therapy 136
threat ix, 2, 14–19, 21–28, 69, 102, 154
Thunberg, Greta 17
totality 5, 60, 67, 78, 83–84, 87–88, 100, 104, 108, 114–115, 117, 217
transcendent 5, 71, 113, 127, 131, 166, 205, 212–213
transformation x, 5, 37, 39–40, 119, 135, 141, 187, 189, 191–193, 195, 197–200, 207
transformative love x, 201–205, 207–209, 211, 213
trauma ii, 5, 146, 196, 198, 212
trial i, ix, x, 5, 15–16, 21–24, 27, 29, 31, 33, 35, 37–41, 43, 62, 75, 89, 91, 93, 95, 97, 99, 101, 103, 105–109, 120, 125, 129, 144, 146, 148–155, 157, 162, 165, 168, 170–175, 187, 189, 190–193, 195, 197–200, 218
tribulation ii, 39–40, 62, 65, 120, 122, 127–128, 146–147, 150, 153–154, 158, 164, 169, 171–175
triumphalism 12
Twelver 46, 222

ugly 9, 10, 75
unintelligible 218
universe 19, 21, 24, 50, 84, 93, 95–96, 103, 105, 107, 115, 117, 151, 171, 189, 191, 212, 214
unseen 33, 35, 41, 156, 172
ʿUrwa b. al-Zubayr 128

Velazquez 10
virtue(s) 2, 5, 35, 55, 112, 119, 120, 124, 127–128, 130–131, 140, 143, 145, 147, 149, 151–153, 155, 157, 172, 188–189, 192, 212; ethics ii, iii, 5, 157, 169, 176
virus 1–2, 154, 156
voluntarism 4, 94
voluntary death 40
vulnerability iii, 2, 5, 115, 121, 122, 135, 136

wars 10
wayfaring 30, 33, 191, 198
well-being 174
will 53
world 106, 144, 145, 146, 149, 190
worship 30, 33, 36, 93, 100, 118, 121, 122, 138, 140, 188, 189, 191, 194, 197

xenophobia 2

Zayn al-ʿĀbidīn 34, 38, 42, 125, 129, 141
Zika 1
Ziya Ülken, Hilmi x, 201–205, 207, 209, 211, 213
Zoroastrianism 8, 208